A WOMAN'S WAR

Southern Women, Civil War, and the Confederate Legacy

INFAMOUS!

VIDE LORD PALMERSTON'S SPEECH.

HEAD-QUARTERS, DEP'T OF THE GULF,
NEW ORLEANS: *May* 15, 1862.

As the OFFICERS and SOLDIERS of the UNITED STATES have been subjected to REPEATED INSULTS from the WOMEN, calling themselves 'LADIES,' of NEW ORLEANS, in return for the most scrupulous NON-INTERFERENCE and COURTESY on our part, it is ordered that hereafter when any female shall by word, gesture, or movement, insult or show contempt for any OFFICER or PRIVATE of the UNITED STATES she shall be regarded and held liable to be TREATED as

A WOMAN OF THE TOWN
PLYING HER VOCATION.

By command of
Maj.-Gen. BUTLER

A WOMAN'S WAR

Southern Women, Civil War, and the Confederate Legacy

To accompany an exhibition organized by
The Museum of the Confederacy on the
occasion of its centennial

Edited by
Edward D. C. Campbell, Jr., and Kym S. Rice

Essays by
Joan E. Cashin
John M. Coski
Drew Gilpin Faust
Amy R. Feely
Thavolia Glymph
George C. Rable
Marjorie Spruill Wheeler

With a Foreword by
Suzanne Lebsock

The Museum of the Confederacy, Richmond,
and the University Press of Virginia, Charlottesville

COVER:
Women and Children of Sharpsburg Taking Refuge in the Cellar of the Kretzer Mansion in that town, During the Battle of Antietam. *(Engraving, by F. H. Schell,* Frank Leslie's Illustrated Newspaper, *25 October 1862.)*
Eleanor S.Brockenbrough Library, The Museum of the Confederacy

FRONTISPIECE:
General Order No. 28. *Bitterly resentful of the Union occupation of New Orleans in the spring of 1862, many Southern women vigorously protested the presence of Federal soldiers in the Crescent City. Some simply walked away whenever they encountered the invaders; some sang patriotic Southern tunes as they passed by; others even spat on soldiers' uniforms. To combat the growing problem, Major General Benjamin F. Butler on 15 May 1862 issued his soon-infamous "Woman's Order," cleverly worded as to be self-enforcing. Considered an affront to Southern womanhood, the proclamation raised a storm of protest throughout the South and in Europe. Nevertheless, with a few notable exceptions, incidents ceased. (Broadside, London, 1862.)*
Historic New Orleans Collection

First edition

Library of Congress
Cataloging-in-Publication Data
A woman's war: southern women, civil war, and the Confederate legacy / edited by Edward D. C. Campbell, Jr., and Kym S. Rice; essays by Joan E. Cashin . . . [et al.]; with a Foreword by Suzanne Lebsock.—1st ed.
p. cm.
"To accompany an exhibition organized by the Museum of the Confederacy on the occasion of its centennial."
Includes bibliographical references and index.
ISBN 0-8139-1739-5 (paper)
1. United States—History—Civil War, 1861–1865—Women—Exhibitions. 2. Women—Confederate States of America—Exhibitions. 3. Women—Southern States—History—19th century—Exhibitions. 4. Confederate States of America—History—Exhibitions. 5. Museum of the Confederacy (Richmond, Va.)—Exhibitions.
I. Campbell, Edward D. C., 1946– . II. Rice, Kym S. III. Cashin, Joan E. IV. Museum of the Confederacy (Richmond, Va.)
E628.W9 1996 96-29648
973.7'082'074755451—dc21 CIP

Designer: Douglas W. Price
Goochland, Virginia

Production Manager: Tucker H. Hill, *Director of Interpretation,* The Museum of the Confederacy

Principal Photographer: Katherine Wetzel
Richmond, Virginia

Printer: Carter Printing Company
Richmond, Virginia

This book was published on the occasion of the centennial of The Museum of the Confederacy and to accompany the exhibition ***A Woman's War: Southern Women, Civil War, and the Confederate Legacy***, organized by Kym S. Rice, guest curator, and the staff of the museum. The exhibition was on view at The Museum of the Confederacy, Richmond, Virginia, from 22 November 1996 to September 1997.

This book and the exhibition were made possible by generous grants from the National Endowment for the Humanities, Washington, D.C.

CONTENTS

A Centennial Note

Northwest view of the White House of the Confederacy, Richmond, Virginia. *(Stereograph, published by Anderson and Ennis, Richmond, Virginia, ca. 1866.)*
Eleanor S. Brockenbrough Library, The Museum of the Confederacy

The institution known today as The Museum of the Confederacy opened its doors as the Confederate Museum in 1896. Its founders were women who, in their youth, experienced the trials of the Civil War and who nurtured memories of the conflict. That the museum was the work of women has always been an important part of the institution's identity and, recently, a subject of interpretive exhibits and books. With this tradition in mind, it seems appropriate that the museum's centennial celebration focus on the wartime experiences of Southern women.

As the essays, photographs, documentary excerpts, and guides in this book demonstrate, the museum's own object and manuscript collections reveal a broad range of Southern women's experiences during the war. The collections testify to strong and unflagging loyalty to the Confederate cause, to suffering, sacrifice, and even participation in combat, but also to divided loyalties and war-weariness.

We believe that the exhibition and the book embody the modern museum's commitment to the objective study of its subject. In the century since it opened, the museum has evolved from partisanship to nonpartisanship—changing its name in 1969 from the Confederate Museum to The Museum of the Confederacy—but maintaining its commitment to caring for and exhibiting one of the world's outstanding collections of Confederate artifacts and documents. *A Woman's War* showcases an often overlooked and underappreciated part of that collection, and sheds light on the museum's founders and their generation. The museum is pleased to make available to students of history a valuable body of research materials that allow a deeper understanding of our past.

Robin Edward Reed
Executive Director

FOREWORD

Ann Carter Bryan.
(Ambrotype, ca. 1861–1863.)
The Museum of the Confederacy

In the decades after Appomattox, all the battles of the war were fought again, once, twice, fifty times, on paper. With pens slashing like sabers, a corps of former Confederates argued about the conduct of men at war. They argued especially about their commanders: whose tactics had been brilliant, whose plodding? Who demonstrated the most courage, whose courage shaded into the foolhardy? Who was responsible for a particular victory, who for a specific defeat? Among the generals who fell, whose loss was most devastating to the cause? In the war of words, reputations were exalted or sullied with every scratch of the pen.

About the conduct of women, there was no argument. The image of the Confederate woman was fixed as early as 1862, and although it grew in pathos as the war claimed more lives, it was not subject to change or debate. Confederate women made willing sacrifice of husbands and sons; they rose early and retired late, dispatching food and medicine, clothing and bandages—the work of their own hands—to the troops; they made do on an increasingly desolate home front; they nursed the wounded and comforted the dying. Above all, they believed in the cause. "They stood like heroines," said Virginia's Governor Charles T. O'Ferrall when the Confederate Museum opened in 1896, "firm, steadfast, and constant."

We should perhaps be grateful for the image: in the written history of this country, and indeed of most countries, women's wartime contributions have ordinarily been trivialized or ignored—a manifestation of a larger tendency to place great historical value on the deeds of men while disregarding those of women. Better to be glorified, as in the case of the Confederate woman, than neglected altogether.

But better still to attempt a comprehensive history of Southern women in wartime. *A Woman's War* is a down payment on this comprehensive history. We are in the process of opening the stage to a wider cast of players, with a greater range of personal aspirations and political aims. We wish to put complex, struggling human beings in place of noble icons. At the same time, we need to recognize the historical (and continuing) importance of the icons, and to explore their meaning and power. We need a history capacious enough to stir controversy and encourage ongoing debate.

Thirty years ago, it would not have been possible to bring into being either this exhibition or the essays in this book. Now, on the one hundredth anniversary of the Confederate Museum, both exhibition and book are made thinkable by two recent developments within the historical profession. Most important is the rise of the history of women. Emerging in tandem with the women's movement in about 1970, women's history has grown at a phenomenal pace, and, since the mid-1980s, considerable light has been beamed on the women of the South. A second and even more recent development among historians is a new curiosity about social memory.

Laura and Neecie.
At the time the artist sketched the two daughters of an African-American soldier killed during the Civil War, the sisters were residents of the Memphis Colored Orphan Asylum. (Pencil sketch, by Alfred R. Waud, ca. 1870.)
Historic New Orleans Collection, 1965.90.238

Historians have taken to studying how a given society remembers and memorializes its past, and what its custom-made past may have to do with its creators' quest for power in the present. This sort of inquiry suggests new questions about the women who founded the Confederate Museum—what was at stake in their claims to guardianship of the Southern past?—even as it heightens the cultural and political significance of their endeavor.

Although the study of Southern women is a youthful enterprise, it has already achieved significant depth, a depth on clear display in *A Woman's War*. The modern investigation of the Southern woman's past dates from 1970 with the appearance of Anne Firor Scott's *The Southern Lady: From Pedestal to Politics, 1830–1930*. Mindful of the litany of all that women did for the Confederacy, Scott turned the question on its head, and asked what the war did for women—or more precisely, for the upper-class women who were the subjects of her pioneering inquiry. Having found a good deal of discontent among elite women in the antebellum years, Scott concluded that for them the war was a watershed. The war, she argued, "speeded social change and opened Pandora's box," creating a more complex social order that gave women new opportunities in education, work, and politics.[1]

Anne Scott's book, with its single notable chapter on the war, stood virtually alone for more than a decade. Then in the mid-1980s, one scholar and then another began to weigh in on the war's significance for Southern women.[2] Collectively, their work has differed from Scott's in two major respects. First, the new work has explored a wider range of social groups, venturing beyond the approximately 20 percent of white women who belonged to slaveholding families. And second, while interpretations vary, no one sees the war as a fundamentally progressive force in the lives of white women; even for slave women, for whom the war ultimately meant freedom, the tone of the new work is decidedly somber.

There is as yet no book that concentrates on the experience of slave women in the war, but Thavolia Glymph's essay in this volume gives us a glimpse of the radical shift in perspective that may be in store. A hundred years ago, the ideal Confederate woman was sometimes portrayed with a black female companion, the faithful slave who hid the silver from the Yankees and stuck by her mistress through thick and thin. We may wish to debate how often slave behavior approximated this white ideal, but it is more illuminating to focus on a different drama. The single most important transformation wrought by the war—whatever the stated intentions of the belligerents—was the demise of chattel slavery. The central contributions of black women, then, were those that hastened the coming of freedom. Were we still living in an age that needed a single iconic figure to represent the war's elemental significance for women, an appropriate choice would be a female slave in the act of escape.

And what of white women? As the introductory essay by Drew Faust, Thavolia Glymph, and George Rable makes clear, the human experience of war varied with one's social position; white women of the middling and poorer classes lived hard lives to begin with, and the war drove them to true desperation. But even the most privileged had difficulty living up to the lofty standards of Confederate lore. In describing the experience of refugeeing, Joan Cashin puts it this way: "There was little that was noble about it, and much that was sordid, horrifying, and sad." For generations, Americans have been arguing with one another about what to call the war. The testimony of women suggests that the soldiers had it right in the first place: the soldiers called it "this cruel war."

The essays in this book further suggest that the war exerted a continuing drag on the aspirations of women. During the war itself, everything about the Southern social order was thrown into question and ripe for change. In the postwar period, however, white women tended to react to chaos and grief and poverty and defeat by retreating to the home and, as much as possible, clinging to old ideas about the proper place of women and men. This hypothesis is one of many in need of testing. As Anne Scott recognized when she proposed quite a different thesis, the war's long-term impact on the South's women is an immense topic, and a persuasive assessment will not be possible until historians have amassed a good deal more evidence about the decades before the war and the decades after. We have our work cut out for us.

In the meantime, Marjorie Spruill Wheeler explores one intriguing dimension of the war's legacy in her essay on the woman-suffrage controversy in the South. Fifty years after the close of the war, the continuing power of the heroic tradition was made manifest in the debates over votes for women, as spokeswomen for both sides tried to rob the Confederate armory for ammunition. The anti-suffragists ultimately carried the day, in part because in their appeals to the white male politicians who would decide the question they succeeded in hitching the memory of war to a complex of other loyalties—to states' rights, to white supremacy, and to the notion that for woman, the only proper mode of influence was indirect, and not in the corrupt world of electoral politics. After fighting many losing battles, some suffragists at length cut themselves loose from tradition, reluctantly concluding that the South, in Wheeler's words, was "wallowing in the past and smothered by its memories."

The Confederate Memorial Literary Society, of course, had more than a little to do with the articulation of those memories. In their essay on the founders of the Confederate Museum, John Coski and Amy Feely show how a group of capable and determined women imagined, established, and sustained a cultural institution of major significance. While this is an important, and little known, chapter in the creation of Confederate memory, it is also an intriguing episode in the larger history of women's voluntarism. The period from 1890 to 1920, we have known for some time, was a great age of public activism among American women, but only recently have historians paid serious attention to the wave of patriotic associations organized by women in the 1890s. The challenge to historians of women is to rewrite the history of voluntarism to encompass groups like the Confederate Memorial Literary Society fully.

The CMLS, as Coski and Feely demonstrate, bore considerable responsibility for its own comparative obscurity. The leaders were rock-ribbed in insisting that the museum was a memorial to the soldiers, not to themselves, and so nary a founder's portrait was permitted to hang in the refurbished Confederate White House. Perhaps after a hundred years, they would think it permissible for us to chronicle their endeavors as well as those of the women who suffered through the war.

The founders would doubtless be less sympathetic to the historical interpretation put forth in these pages and in this exhibition, departing as we do from the orthodoxies they worked so hard to make eternal. And yet because they collected and preserved artifacts and texts—the raw materials of history—they did much to afford each new generation the chance to come to its own conclusions. In one of the final sections in this book, John J. Ahladas, John Coski, and Eric Johnson survey the rich, and to date underutilized, collections held by The Museum of the Confederacy's Eleanor S. Brockenbrough Library, making special note of materials pertinent to the history of women.

There is work for many hands. Join us as we attempt to discover everything that made the American Civil War—the cruel war—a woman's war.

SUZANNE LEBSOCK

PREFACE

Like other Southerners, William Faulkner grew up on stories of the Civil War, many of which influenced his writings. In spite of Faulkner's famous claim that the war turned Southern women into ghosts, his most memorable characters include women who survived the war, although hardly unscathed. Cousin Drusilla, with her hair cut short like a boy's and clad in men's clothes, cuts a memorable figure in *The Unvanquished*. "Living used to be dull, you see. . . . You don't have to worry about getting children to bathe and feed and change, because the young men can ride away and get killed in fine battles; and you don't even have to sleep alone, you don't even have to sleep at all; and so, all you have to do is show the stick to the dog now and then say, 'Thank God for nothing.'" Drusilla, who eventually joins the Confederate army in disguise, echoes the sentiments expressed by the real women described within this volume.

In 1994, The Museum of the Confederacy began planning a celebration of its centennial year that recognized the institution's long stewardship by women. A fortuitous meeting that March with Professor Drew Gilpin Faust helped to shape *A Woman's War: Southern Women, Civil War, and the Confederate Legacy*. Through Dr. Faust's generous assistance, the museum began to conceive of ways it might share some of the most recent research now under way in Southern women's history. This project continues The Museum of the Confederacy's commitment not only to the latest Civil War scholarship, but also to the dissemination of Southern history in the broadest sense. This book, and the exhibition that accompanies it, also follow earlier significant museum projects, most notably *Before Freedom Came: African-American Life in the Antebellum South*.

Aided by National Endowment for the Humanities planning and implementation grants that began in January 1995, the museum engaged a team of academic consultants led by Dr. Faust to join its project. Besides contributing material for this volume, each historian also contributed significantly to the development of the exhibition themes and overall interpretation. Early in the process, the consultants recommended that the project extend its parameters and evaluate, through this publication, the Civil War's long-term effect on women in the South. As a result, the final two essays by John Coski, Amy Feely, and Marjorie Spruill Wheeler discuss the ways in which the war shaped subsequent generations of white women, particularly the members of the Confederate Memorial Literary Society who founded the museum, as well as those women who participated in the South's struggle over woman's suffrage. Additionally, the book's editors created chapter four, a rich assortment of primary source matter—most of it published for the first time—that portrays the wartime experiences of many different Southern women.

During the planning phase, the project team also searched for relevant objects and

Unidentified North Carolina women.
(Tintype, ca. 1861–1865.)
Eleanor S. Brockenbrough Library, The Museum of the Confederacy

information in the holdings of museums and historical organizations across the country. This preliminary survey revealed that The Museum of the Confederacy's own collections, which combine objects and documentary items related to Southern women's wartime history, probably rank as the country's most extensive. The museum's collections are especially rich in objects that reflect everyday life, whether they be handmade children's toys or wartime clothing. These artifacts, textiles, photographs, paintings and prints, rare newspapers, and books—each laden with iconographic meanings—form the core illustrations selected for this volume and the accompanying exhibition. Although weighted toward possessions that reflect elite or middle-class white life, the collections also include artifacts made, worn, or used by enslaved African Americans and poor white women. The museum's important photography collection encompasses numerous portraits of women, from individual images, some carried in soldiers' pockets and recovered from battlefields, to postwar group scenes. Over the course of the project, museum staff members also unearthed a remarkable cache of uncatalogued documents in the museum's Eleanor S. Brockenbrough Library, as discussed in the section "Suggestions for Further Research." A number of these items, plus many more not previously on view, were selected for display in the museum's exhibition, *A Woman's War*.

A Woman's War asks readers to use a new perspective to see the Confederate South through the eyes of all its women—black and white, rich, middle class, or poor. Not surprisingly, the museum's founders originally collected many of the objects selected for this project in the early years of the institution's history, often from the individual most closely associated with the item. They interpreted these artifacts as tangible proof of Confederate loyalty, sometimes gathering details or personal narratives to accompany them, usually entering the information in their cataloguing system. One hundred years later, *A Woman's War* revisits these same objects but places them in a broader context. Taken as a group, together with images and documents, they offer yet another layer of historical evidence to support the story of "a woman's war."

KYM S. RICE
Guest Curator

CHAPTER ONE

A WOMAN'S WAR
Southern Women in the Civil War

DREW GILPIN FAUST, THAVOLIA GLYMPH, AND GEORGE C. RABLE

Southern Women Hounding Their Men to Rebellion. *It was an article of faith among Northern soldiers and pundits that Southern women were more belligerent and wrathful than Southern men. Indeed, early in the war, Southern women actively encouraged men to fight. "A man did not deserve the name if he did not fight for his country," remembered Kate Stone, of Louisiana. In Richmond, Union spy Elizabeth Van Lew observed that "the women became [secession's] strongest advocates, unknowing and unreflecting. 'Ah, ladies, when you see your husbands, brothers, and fathers brought home dead, you'll think of this. . . .'" As Southern women showed signs of war-weariness, Northerners took gleeful notice. The scene is from a two-panel illustration entitled* Sowing and Reaping. *The "reaping" is represented by the famous depiction of the April 1863 Richmond bread riot* (page 22). *(Engraving,* Frank Leslie's Illustrated Newspaper, *23 May 1863.)*
Eleanor S. Brockenbrough Library, The Museum of the Confederacy

The outbreak of Civil War and invasion by Union armies meant that the lives of Southern women, black and white, rich and poor, would never be the same again. A war that freed the slave, reduced the wealthy's living standards, impoverished the yeomanry, and separated thousands of families for four long years required women of all classes and races to reassess their place within the social order. Even though men did the fighting, women faced new challenges, dangers, and deprivations. All across the South, Union offensives turned the home front into a complex battleground of its own. The war's scale and the demands made on the Southern economy required unprecedented mobilization of civilian resources. The departure of three out of four white men of military age for the army altered the structures of Southern society behind the lines as well, burdening white women with unaccustomed responsibilities and offering slave women new hardships and new opportunities.

The shattering experiences of war varied by age, geographic location, and marital status, but, most significantly, by class and race. Although the war had a certain leveling effect and sometimes created a democracy of common suffering, women in slaveholding families faced problems and hardships quite different from those of less privileged whites. The conflict reduced the social and economic distinctions between slaveholding women and their less affluent sisters even as the once comfortable fought to retain their accustomed power in homes and neighborhoods. Amid the upheaval in white society, slave women not only confronted distinctive hardships and losses but also experienced a promise of freedom that served as a beacon of hope.

For white slaveholding women, the Civil War reduced both their privilege and affluence, in effect transforming their social identity. The costs and disruptions of the war itself undermined their accustomed prosperity, but it was the war's assault on slavery that eroded the foundation of their wealth. And as planters and overseers departed for the front, women assumed unprecedented responsibility for the South's plantation economy and slave society. Men might try to wield their accustomed authority through letters filled with instruction and advice, but the longer they were absent, the more frequently women had to make decisions on their own. Their new obligations proved daunting, as plantation mistresses struggled to manage crops and control bondspeople who grew increasingly recalcitrant as Union armies and emancipation drew near. Women across the South grappled with such unfamiliar problems as crop yields and stock breeding and taxes.[1]

Despite their own doubts, many women managed their plantations competently and with growing efficiency. Others longed for the return of their menfolk and the restoration of their old life, but the most urgent problem was the breakdown of slavery itself. Left to direct sixty slaves, a Mississippi planter's wife

***Pincushion, "God bless our Soldiers."** Confederate politicians saw white women as integral to their efforts to create a Southern national identity. Many women expressed their support through traditional craft skills such as needlework. A Miss Smith made the patriotic keepsake for Confederate general Simon Bolivar Buckner. (Velvet, silk, and cord pincushion, ca. 1861.)*
The Museum of the Confederacy

wrote to the governor, "Do you think that this woman's hand can keep them in check?" A Georgian declared that a woman was simply not "a fit and proper person to supervise slaves." Virginian Ellen Moore complained that in her husband's absence, her slaves "all think that I am a kind of usurper & have no authority over them." Indeed, a Federal officer reported that slaves who fled to Union lines shared these sentiments: "They said there was nobody on the plantations but women and they were not afraid of them."[2]

In petitions to state and Confederate governments, plantation mistresses objected to being left defenseless, surrounded by slaves. "I feel unprotected and afraid," "unable to protect myself," they wrote. As a Mississippi woman bluntly explained, "I fear the blacks more than I do the Yankees."[3] On isolated farms and plantations, the war unnerved women whose paternalistic pretensions could no longer bind together black and white and whose supposed expertise about the character of their slaves proved sadly deficient. Plantation mistresses clung to the familiar relationships of the old order only to find their world turned upside down.

The isolation and the demands of war ironically made white women even more dependent on their slaves. The "faithful servant" stories of Confederate legend had their foundation in wartime experience: there were slaves who buried the master's silver to hide it from the enemy; there were slaves, like one described by North Carolinian Catherine Edmondston, who drew knives to defend mistresses against Union troops; there were slaves like Jeff, who acted as farm manager and agricultural advisor to South Carolina's Kate McClure, or Susanna, who offered protection and emotional support to Georgian Leila Callaway while her husband Morgan served as a chaplain in the Army of Northern Virginia. We will never know Susanna's view of this relationship, but Leila was devastated when her "warmest, best friend" died of smallpox in 1863.[4]

In the course of the war, however, many white women would have their illusions about the benevolence of slavery and the contentment of the slaves shattered as their bondspeople fled to Union lines. Even those slaves who remained acted increasingly like free rather than bound laborers. Lizzie Neblett, of Texas, wrote in exasperation to her husband Will in 1863 that "the negros are doing nothing. But ours are not doing that job alone[,] nearly all the negros around here are at it, some of them are getting so high in anticipation of their glorious freedom by the Yankees . . . that they resist a whipping." Some women abandoned any notion of getting much work out of their slaves. As another Texan put it, "I will try to feel thankful if they let me alone." Struggling with their own feelings of betrayal, mistresses began thinking that the peculiar institution was more trouble than it was worth. Sarah Kennedy, of Tennessee, declared in 1863 that she "would rather do all the work than be worried with a house full of servants that do what, how and when they please."[5] These uncertainties seldom arose from moral doubts about slavery so much as from difficulties and inconveniences encountered in efforts to act as masters. Even as slavery collapsed, slaveholding women held to their racial and social assumptions while expressing deep feelings of betrayal as their once-faithful "servants" deserted them. If anything, the erosion of slavery intensified racism and gave it a sharper edge.

Surgical dressing. *Working as individuals or together in groups, women manufactured essential items for the army. Two Washington, D.C., women—M. F. McCalla and Julia Bain, Confederate sympathizers within a Unionist family—worked "secretly at night in their attic by candle light." There they reportedly made this lint for dressing wounds by using material from their shredded underwear. (Cotton-lint dressing, ca. 1861–1865.)*
The Museum of the Confederacy

In part, release from the drudgery of basic household labor had been the foundation of the Southern lady's sense of status. Slavery's demise combined with the war's economic hardships forced even elite women to tackle unfamiliar domestic chores. Women who suddenly found themselves without slave nursemaids had never before realized the trouble of raising children; young ladies regretted having been taught to play the piano instead of to cook; women expert at embroidery and fancywork attempted more practical dressmaking for the first time; females who had purchased clothing or depended on slave weavers and spinners hauled out wheels and looms from attics and tried to learn new skills. Especially in the early part of the war, these efforts seemed like contributions that women could offer to the cause. But as the death toll mounted and victory proved elusive, many women considered such sacrifices unreasonable.[6]

Though more inclined than men to weigh the costs of war on families, most women of the South's master class were at first avid Confederates. Thronging the balconies at state secession conventions, sewing flags, raising money for gunboats, and organizing hospital and relief associations allayed their fears. By helping send their men off to battle, they could avoid being, as they so often worried,

J. E. Taylor 1898

***"Saucy minx."** The war challenged notions of Southern womanhood. Many women acquired a reputation for fierce patriotism, provoked, in part, by their frequently aggressive demeanor towards Federal soldiers in the occupied South. Sarah Morgan, of Baton Rouge, Louisiana, who disliked the Union troops' "rude, ill mannered behavior," concluded, "I would not like to live in a country governed by such tongues." (Watercolor, by James E. Taylor, 1898.)*
Western Reserve Historical Society

"useless" and prove that the war was "certainly ours as well as that of the men." Perhaps as many as four hundred women, North and South, disguised themselves as men and served as soldiers during the war, and women such as Belle Boyd used their femininity to mask their work as Confederate spies. Others armed themselves for self-defense and even took target practice. Far more typical, however, were women who simply longed to be men, yet settled for more traditional contributions of service and sacrifice.[7]

War work became an obsession. In Charlottesville, Virginia, in 1861, ladies assembled each morning to sew garments for departing soldiers. "Our needles are now our weapons," Lucy Wood explained, "and we have a part to perform as well as the rest." Organized in churches and other public buildings, sewing societies reflected a deep commitment to the cause, and their contribution to the often poorly clad Confederate soldiers was both highly practical and richly symbolic. With only minimal help from state and local governments, women held bazaars, raffles, concerts, and plays to raise money to buy the increasingly expensive cloth, thread, and needles. To the poor and the pious, the more lavish entertainments seemed decadent and inappropriate in a time of general austerity. Aristocratic ladies, moreover, might limit their benevolence to officers. By 1862, then, the enthusiasm for charitable work among all classes was waning.[8]

As war's human misery mounted, women attended to the wounded, brought delicacies to the sick and dying, and offered to comfort and console. In the fall of 1862, the Confederate Congress authorized women to serve officially in Confederate hospitals because the wards managed by females reported significantly lower mortality rates. Yet only a few respectable middle- and upper-class women served as matrons and nurses. While nursing was consistent with traditional nurturing roles, caring for men's bodies seemed demeaning and indelicate; women such as Mary Chesnut and Sara Pryor could barely face the horrors of the hospitals. Casual visitors offered some assistance in the wards but could also become nuisances. Phoebe Pember, Kate Cumming, Ella Newsom, Sally Tompkins, Juliet Opie Hopkins, and the other elite women who devoted themselves to hospital work day after day were exceptional, and even they were a step or two removed from direct patient care.[9] They supervised and managed the wards while slaves or poor white women bandaged, bathed, and fed the soldiers. Some nurses barely concealed their contempt for women who performed these menial chores and kept their social distance. As a young Mississippi wife reassured her husband, "ladies have none of the drudgery of nursing, there are convalescents detailed to do that, besides servants." Kate Cumming raged at her reluctant and overly delicate Southern sisters: "Are the women of the South going into the hospitals? I am afraid candor will compel me to say they are not."[10]

For those who overcame their hauteur and squeamishness, however, the experience was unforgettable. Growing accustomed to the noises, sights, and smells of the wards, nurses closed the eyes of dead patients and, as Phoebe Pember remarked, wondered if they had "any feeling and sensibility left."[11] Even the strongest nurses occasionally broke under the strain of winning acceptance from skeptical doctors while dealing with so much suffering with so few resources.

Wealthy women occasionally attended sewing circles or worked in the hospitals, but the exigencies of war forced some to seek remunerative work outside the home for the first time in their lives. Although teaching seemed respectable and closely related to women's traditional maternal obligations, some young women from more affluent backgrounds dreaded the prospect of offering music lessons or facing a room full of unruly children. Northern women had flocked to the classrooms in the antebellum era, but no similar development had taken place in the

Minutes of the Ladies' Aid and Defense Association. *In 1862, elite women across the South entered "into an activity regarded as the proper province of men"—the organization of societies to raise funds for the manufacture of gunboats to protect coastal waters and rivers. Some Southerners clearly believed that the women threatened traditional gender relations. In questioning the soundness of the Augusta Gunboat Society, for example, one Southerner remarked that "if this is allowed, the next call, of course, will be for women to man them. Have we no men left, that this thing should be tolerated?" (Manuscript, Richmond, Virginia, ca. 1862–1863.)* Eleanor S. Brockenbrough Library, The Museum of the Confederacy

Resolved 1st That this be called "The Ladies Aid and Defence Society."

2nd That we, as the weaker sex, being unable actively to join in the defence of our country, will encourage the hearts, and strengthen the hands of our husbands, brothers, fathers and friends by all means within our power.

3rd As our sisters of the capitol have undertaken to build a gun boat for the defence of James' River, we will by making and soliciting contributions, aid them in their laudable and most necessary work.

4th That the work and contributions may be more peculiarly ours as women, we will give such ornaments of gold, and articles of silver, as are our private personal property. For should it be our sad fate to become slaves, ornaments would ill become our state of bondage; while if God in his infinite mercy shall crown our efforts with success, we will be content to wear the laurel leaves of victory, and point our children to our civil and religious liberty so gloriously achieved and say "These be thy jewels."

Ann, Walter, and Dora Bryan. *The Bryan sisters' brother Walter, a Confederate private, was killed on 15 January 1865. The death of a family member in the war was a loss experienced by countless Southern women. Virginian Lucy Breckinridge's beloved brother John died during the battle of Seven Pines, fought on the outskirts of Richmond, 31 May–1 June 1862. Throughout the remainder of the war, she visited his grave frequently and thought about him constantly. "This is my precious Johnny's birthday," she wrote on 14 July 1863. "He would have been nineteen today. I try to imagine how he would have looked as a man, but it is very sweet to think of him as a bright, happy boy—will always have one little brother." (Ambrotype, 1861.)*
Eleanor S. Brockenbrough Library, The Museum of the Confederacy

South. In North Carolina in 1860, for example, only 7 percent of the teachers were women. By the end of the war, however, there were as many female teachers as male in the classroom.[12]

These new teachers could barely eke out a living on modest salaries in an era of hyperinflation. Teaching itself offered little but frustration. On a plantation near Camden, South Carolina, Emma Holmes admitted that she did not like working with children of "rather common parents."[13] Discipline problems and the exasperation caused by poorly prepared and unmotivated students quickly discouraged novice teachers.

Some educated women from prominent families worked for the government, particularly in the Treasury Department. There ladies with elegant penmanship signed the thousands of Confederates bills needed to finance the war. Many pathetic pleas for work poured into the cabinet departments, but vacancies were few. These jobs often required political connections, and the general salary—at least six times that of an army private—suggests that such posts became sinecures for women of the master class who had fallen upon hard times.[14]

Lower-class white women also sought government work to support their families, but neither their salaries nor their circumstances matched those of the "Treasury Girls." Class distinctions mattered a great deal in public employment. For example, thousands of seamstresses toiled in the Confederate Clothing Bureau in Richmond, usually doing piecework for paltry sums—for example, thirty cents for making an entire shirt. In Augusta, Georgia, five hundred women employed by the Georgia Soldiers' Bureau earned a mere six dollars a week. Arsenal workers in the same city prepared cartridges for a dollar a day. More than forty of Richmond's female ordnance workers were killed in a March 1863 explosion; fifteen died in a similar accident in Jackson, Mississippi. By the last years of the war, ordnance workers in Richmond had become so dissatisfied and desperate that they struck for higher wages.[15]

Beginning in 1863, protests by white women against wartime deprivation erupted in bread riots. Want and near starvation threatened families: "i ame a pore woman with a pasel of little children and i wil have to starve or go naked," one North Carolina woman informed Governor Zebulon Vance.[16] Women married to Confederate soldiers, or to factory workers, or to artisans, railed against the indifference of the wealthy and against inadequate public relief. Substantial increases in state and Confederate welfare spending could never keep pace with inflation or the overwhelming needs of suffering families. In High Point, North Carolina, and Milledgeville, Georgia; in Savannah and Mobile; in Petersburg and in Richmond itself, crowds of women seized bread and other provisions they believed were their due. Across western North Carolina, in sections of rural Alabama, "women riots" and "female raids" were reported, as hungry women seized wheat and corn gathered for sale or impressed for army use. The overwhelmingly lower-class rioters and their actions horrified the Southern elite. Yet bread riots also represented a rejection of female suffering and sacrifice that paralleled upper-class women's growing disenchantment with the war's costs. Women at all levels of white society came to question how a war that brought so much misery and killed their husbands, brothers, and sons could be in their interest.[17]

The option of "refugeeing"—of fleeing from advancing Union armies, often with movable property, including valuable slaves, in tow—was not available to families without resources and social connections. For refugees, one of the most difficult questions was timing: to avoid leaving at the first alarm but not staying put until it was too late. Those traveling the roads and railroads often found poor accommodations along the way and complained of having to eat or even sleep with people they usually scorned as social inferiors. Once-comfortable families who helped more than double the populations of Confederate towns and cities were not always

Presentation of a Flag to the Thirteenth Connecticut Regiment by Loyal Ladies of New Orleans. *Support for the Union persisted in the South throughout the war. Angela Snyder and Lucena Courcelle, two New Orleans Unionists, presented a plain, blue-silk battle flag of their handiwork, decorated with silver stars, fringe, and the word, "Union," to a Connecticut regiment. The women reportedly came forward even though "thousands of men were afraid to speak to a Union officer." (Engraving,* Harper's Weekly, *2 August 1862.)* Historic New Orleans Collection

welcome arrivals. Elite women refugees, who spent the war at various Southern resorts, in temporary households, or in the homes of friends or kin, often bemoaned the loneliness and disruption that these relocations introduced into their lives. Tensions between refugees and natives flared into nasty quarrels.[18]

Poorer Southerners regarded refugees as privileged deserters who had used their wealth to escape war's hardships while others had to stay and endure. When the more prosperous left, their less fortunate neighbors eagerly begged castoff clothing; others ransacked abandoned houses scavenging for the remains of plantation finery. In the course of the conflict, and especially in its last months, many less-well-to-do Southerners were driven from their homes as well, but these individuals did not consider themselves "refugees," with that word's connotations of free choice and of unjust advantage. These families lived in tents, abandoned boxcars, or even caves; food was scarce and often spoiled or repulsive.[19]

Living closer to the margins of survival, white women of the nonslaveholding South were also more likely to take on hard physical labor—labor that had previously been done by men. Left on subsistence farms by husbands departed for war, wives had to assume exclusive responsibility for field labor. Driving oxen and mules, they found that their exertions too often produced meager harvests. A North Carolina woman wrote Governor Vance in 1863 to beg "mearcy from your hands" and food for her family's table. "I have plowed & hoed & worked in the field like a negro I have . . . no relations near me that is able to help me now."[20] Meat disappeared from many tables; families lived on monotonous diets of greens, field peas, fatty cakes, or just tomatoes. State and local government created rudimentary welfare programs to help the most desperate citizens, but thousands of temporarily or permanently fatherless families felt the pangs of hunger. "Deaths from Starvation," a group of residents in Randolph County, Alabama, informed Jefferson Davis in 1864, "have absolutely occurred; notwithstanding the utmost efforts that we have been able to make; & now many of the women and children are seeking & feeding upon the bran from the mills."[21]

The distribution of food was haphazard at best and subject to the vicissitudes of local politics. Private groups opened up "free markets" that quickly ran low on provisions. Evoking paternalistic traditions, the rural poor expected their more comfortable neighbors to tide them over but were too often disappointed. "They [the wealthy] would sooner throw what they have to spare to their dogs than give it to a starving child," a Virginia woman complained to Jefferson Davis.[22] Social resentment festered as women struggling to feed their families came to believe that their more prosperous neighbors were somehow escaping wartime deprivations. The frustrated and starving lashed out at speculators, Jews, foreigners, politicians, or anyone else who could be blamed for their suffering.

In areas where slaveholding had not been widespread, disenchantment with the war appeared early on, often growing out of antisecessionist sentiment. From the beginning, some women had only reluctantly sent their men off to fight and soon thereafter flooded the Confederate War Department and state governments with requests for exemptions and furloughs. These petitions contained moving accounts of hunger, poor health, and family troubles, but public officials became increasingly hardened to such pleas as the war's demand for manpower grew insatiable. Resentment grew against a "rich man's war and a poor man's fight"—especially over provisions in the conscription laws for hiring substitutes and exempting overseers. The most frustrated and angry actively encouraged desertion and helped shield their men from Confederate patrols who in turn sometimes abused their authority and terrorized Southern families. As Nancy Mangum explained to North Carolina's Governor Vance, "we wimen will write for our husbands to come home and

help us we cant stand it."[23]

Civilian morale was always a delicate matter. Some women, especially those far removed from the fighting, were perennial optimists regardless of how the war was going. Wild rumors and fantasies about carrying the war to the Northerners persisted despite bad news. By 1864 and 1865, however, many women began to question their own patriotism and their society's priorities. "Oh what a falling off is there," wrote a lady to the *Montgomery Daily Advertiser* in July 1864. "The Aid societies have died away; they are name and nothing more. . . . Never were the theatres and the places of public amusement so resorted to . . . the extravagance and folly are all the greater for the brief abstinence which has been observed." Searching a battlefield for her wounded cousin, Constance Cary found men "in every stage of mutilation"

Confederate ersatz. *Most ersatz items, or substitutes, proved to be poor surrogates for the genuine article. Cordelia Peake McDonald reminisced after the war about reading or sewing by the light of her "Confederate" candle: "I often wonder now how my eyes stood the ordeal. . . . Every minute it had to be snuffed and drawn farther through the loop, as it wasted away. Not much of anything could be done by its light as constant attention had to be paid to the candle."* Left to right: *raccoon-skin shoe, biscuits made during the 1863 siege of Vicksburg, persimmon-seed buttons, "Confederate" soap and candle.* The Museum of the Confederacy

and declared herself "permanently convinced that nothing is worth war!"[24]

Women of all classes described the emotional toll. "I fear," Virginia French wrote, "that I am giving way under this long, long pressure of anxiety and tension upon the nerves." By 1865, Mary Lee, of Virginia, felt "completely unhinged." Annie Upshur, of Lynchburg, declared herself "almost upon the borders of craziness." What in the twentieth century has been termed "traumatic stress" afflicted soldiers and civilians alike in the invaded South. The suffering and destruction appeared increasingly pointless, "precious blood poured like water," declared one South Carolina refugee.[25]

Throughout the war, white women searched for religious consolation, trusting that they could, as South Carolinian Emma Holmes affirmed, "place entire confidence in the God of Battles."[26] Women attended regular prayer groups in communities across the region and even tried to organize national days of prayer. When churches were forced to abandon regular services in areas threatened by the armies, women made worship at home part of their domestic routine.

But the comfort of divine protection often proved elusive. Death and defeats made Confederates wonder if they, like Job, were having their faith tested for some larger but unknown purpose. Clinging to the Lord's promises, it was nevertheless hard to dispel doubts as the war dragged on and the pain of bereavement mounted beyond endurance. Susan Caldwell, of Warrenton, Virginia, regretted her inability to "gain power over my own rebellious heart to say *God's will be done*. Oh! how hard to be submissive." The combined effects of war and the ever-present evangelical guilt only heightened the pain and despair. Alice Ready, of Tennessee, confessed, "I would not [wish to] rebel against His decree, but my faith has never been so weak as tonight." Most women resolved what Grace Elmore called her "Hard thoughts against my God" and regained their faith. But they would inevitably come to see God differently, as a less personal, a less predictable, a more distant force, one not necessarily concerned with every sparrow's fall.[27]

With war's end, white women of the South confronted the overthrow of a social system that had offered the prerogatives of freedom without the perquisites of masculinity. Their brief, wartime experiences with male responsibilities, however, left many white women convinced that any revolution in gender roles would bring more burden than benefit. Most white women rallied in the postwar years to support the restoration of as much of the prewar social arrangements as could be salvaged. The advantages of whiteness and the protection of femininity remained too precious to abandon.

Black emancipation, however, represented for many white women a loss of wealth and labor that deeply affected their households and the South's economy. And for white women of the middling and lower orders, the postwar years brought new hardships and for many a grinding poverty. The death of so many men could not leave white society unchanged. Women of all classes entered the work force in larger numbers, in roles that ranged from textile workers to school teachers to owners of small businesses. Middle- and upper-class women discovered new opportunities for education and for organizational activism outside the home. War's hardships had made many white Southern females determined, like Scarlett O'Hara, never to go hungry again.[28]

For African-American women, the promise and realization of freedom made war a strikingly different experience. Yet the black woman's war also differed from that of her husband, brothers, or sons. The slaves who first fled to Union lines after the outbreak of the conflict were overwhelmingly males, less encumbered by ties to young children and kin. It was nevertheless not long before Union commanders were confronted with "entire families" of fugitive "men and women and

"Your men bin stealing my hogs." *When two soldiers snatched her chickens, an elderly Virginia woman chased them around her farmyard with a clothesline pole. Her grandson reported that "it came down with a resounding whack on the head of one of the fleeing Yanks," while Federal troops cheered, "'Hit him again, old lady! Soak him!'" (Pencil sketch, by Alfred R. Waud, Aldie, Virginia, 17 June 1863.)*
The Library of Congress

FACING PAGE:
"Manufacturing Corn Meal." *Slaveholding mistresses quickly discovered the extent to which their comfort relied on enslaved domestic labor. "I'm housekeeper, nurse, housemaid, dishwasher," Portia Baldwin Baker complained in 1863, and admitted, "We did not appreciate or esteem our comforts and blessings in peace." (Detail of an engraving,* The Effect of the Rebellion on the Homes of Virginia, *by William Waud,* Harper's Weekly, *24 December 1864.)*
Eleanor S. Brockenbrough Library, The Museum of the Confederacy

MANUFACTURING CORN MEAL

their children." In Virginia, by July 1861, some nine hundred men, women, and children had claimed their freedom at Fort Monroe. Farther north in Virginia, several self-described Unionist slaveholders in the spring of 1862 petitioned the commander of a Federal flotilla for assistance in recovering a number of fugitive slaves. One of the Lancaster County slave owners, Louisa Dunton, describing herself as "a widow in small circumstances," pleaded for the return of her only female slave, thirty-five-year-old Mary. Thirty-two slaves, Mary included, escaped to the Union vessel *Young Rover*.[29]

Some were not so fortunate. At Port Royal, South Carolina, in the fall of 1861, thousands of slave families from nearby islands and the mainland made their way to Union lines. With the roads and waterways under heavy guard and subject to random Confederate attack, many did not make it. A January 1862 Confederate expedition to Edisto Island captured eighty slaves, including "Paul . . . Penny, his wife, and Victoria, his child." The men, some of whom confessed to attacking Confederate pickets, were arrested to be tried "for their lives, and in case of acquittal . . . removed from this district." The women and children were sent to a Charleston workhouse. The raid caused the deaths of at least three slaves, including two women, who "ran into the water, and, refusing or failing to come out, were fired upon and disappeared beneath the water." In other places, Confederate authorities hanged recaptured slave women along with their husbands.[30]

Yet many black women took the risk. Rather than await rescue by Federal raiding parties (which often included their soldier husbands, fathers, or sons), they ran away alone, or with their children or other women. Dressed in men's clothing, one woman journeyed two hundred miles alone through Confederate territory before reaching the safety of Fort Monroe in 1863. Reports of Virginia and Maryland slave "women and children . . . walking, as if for dear life, to reach Washington" were common. Dangers nevertheless remained. A mother and daughter arrested as fugitives in the Federal capital were returned to their owners in Maryland. Both were beaten and jailed.[31]

Slaves thus became increasingly aware of the different dangers female fugitives faced and of Union officers' spotty record of compliance with evolving Federal policies. The result was a growing reluctance to flee as families, even when males were present. In a significant departure from strategies adopted at the beginning of the war, slave men went ahead of their families to scout Federal camps, to see for themselves whether particular commanders abided by the laws of Congress. In the words of one group of slave men, they needed to "see how it was." At Fort Monroe, the superintendent of contrabands encountered "hundreds who had left their wives and families behind" in North Carolina, Richmond, and elsewhere but who intended to return for them. "I am going back after my wife," said one. "I am going for my family," declared another. Even after the conflict had become more openly a war for freedom, fugitive slaves recognized that much still depended on the attitudes and beliefs of individual Union officers and soldiers. Flight in family units became less an option.[32]

Black women left behind on farms and plantations or at independently established contraband communities often found themselves, as had their white counterparts, living in a world of women. Traditional gender divisions of agricultural labor broke down, and slave women took on more men's work—besides their usual hoeing, more women were soon plowing and taking on the most physically demanding jobs. There were other tasks as well. Nancy Johnson remembered how her mistress's "mighty mean" treatment left her "nearly frostbitten" and exhausted from weaving clothes for Confederate soldiers until midnight. Yet even as the work requirements increased, food shortages appeared. Raids by both Union and Confederate armies worsened

"Treasury Girl." In response to wartime labor shortages, Southern white women worked for wages in increasing numbers. As a "Treasury Girl," Nannie Semple held one of the choicest positions open to a woman, one in which her monthly pay exceeded that of the average soldier. One of her colleagues, Malvina Gist, derived great satisfaction from her work signing Confederate currency. "Mr. Tellifiere says I am a treasury girl worth having," she confided in a letter, with evident pleasure, "and I did a big day's work and a good day's work." (Cabinet card, Johannah "Nannie" McKenzie Semple, Richmond, Virginia.) Eleanor S. Brockenbrough Library, The Museum of the Confederacy

"Rules for governing the Matrons of Jackson Hospital," Richmond, Virginia. *Confederate officials recruited white women "not so much as nurses, [but rather] to superintend the different departments," one woman noted in her diary, "to read to them & in fact to supply all the charms of home to soothe the sick beds of our noble soldiers." (Manuscript, 1864.)*
Eleanor S. Brockenbrough Library, The Museum of the Confederacy

Rules for governing the Matrons of "Jackson" Hospital

The Chief Matron of the Culinary Department will see that the provisions are received from the Stewards, and placed in the hands of her assistants to be properly cooked and equally distributed among the patients as may be required. She will have the entire control over the cook and nurse rooms subject alone to the orders of the Surgeons; give personal attention to the cleanliness of the departments; she will also give what directions may be necessary for the proper preparation of the nourishment prescribed on the diet book and see that it goes into the hands of the Ward Matrons or ward Master of the particular ward designated. She will also frequently pass thro' the wards and see whether the patients receive their food properly and well prepared.

The Chief Matron of the Linen Department will visit the linen room daily; see if it is kept properly ventilated; the clothes properly arranged and counted. She will often pass thro' the wards to see if the beds are kept clean; will have the pieces counted and properly marked when sent to the Laundry, and properly arranged when returned.

The Asst. Matrons will aid and assist the Chief Matrons of their respective departments, in carrying out these orders, and will be subject to their instructions.

The Ward Matrons will devote their time to their respective Wards, administering the Medicines, Food when necessary, and giving their undivided attention to the cleanliness and comfort of the patients of their Wards, in every respect.

(Signed) F. W. Hancock
Surg. in Chge

Hd. Qrs. Jackson Hospital.

Copy for
Miss Lizzie Rowland

Nursing paraphernalia. *Regardless of their work, all hospital personnel directly witnessed the horrible injuries and suffering inflicted by the war. "I sometimes wonder if I am the same person who was afraid to look at a dead person for I have no timidity and hardly any sensibility left," Chimborazo Hospital matron Phoebe Pember wrote her sister in 1863. "After the Battle of Fredericksburg I stood by and saw men's fingers and arms cut off and held the brandy to their lips, washing the wounds myself." African American Susie King Taylor echoed, "It seems strange how our aversion to seeing suffering is overcome in war,—how we are able to see the most sickening sights, such as men with their limbs blown off and mangled by the deadly shells, without a shudder; and instead of turning away, how we hurry to assist in alleviating their pain."* Left to right: *porcelain hospital bowl, used in Frederick, Maryland, ca. 1863; Jackson Hospital brass bell with wooden handle, ca. 1862–1865; ceramic feeding-cup used at Emory Hospital, ca. 1862–1864.*
The Museum of the Confederacy

the situation, leaving slaves, as they remembered after the war, "all hungry many a time."[33]

Expanding Union efforts to recruit black soldiers in the South brought freedom to some slave women. To others it brought more hunger, more work, and unprecedented threats to their lives. Some plantation owners punished the wives and children who remained behind. Patsey Leach reported that when her master learned of her husband's enlistment, "from that time he treated me more cruelly than ever, whipping me frequently without any cause and insulting me on every occasion." Ann Valentine informed her soldier husband: "They are treating me worse and worse every day." Captain A. J. Hubbard, serving in a black Missouri regiment, sought guidance from his superior officer after he learned that the wives of two of his men were repeatedly beaten by their master and denied letters from their husbands. Angry masters in many instances drove the wives and children of black soldiers from their homes. Running away from her master's threat to kill her "by piecemeal," Patsey Leach succeeded in taking her youngest child with her but was forced to leave four others behind.[34]

Fear of such treatment combined with the sense of freedom's inevitability prompted women to flee in ever greater numbers. Union raids and campaigns liberated others. And as the Confederacy shrank and morale plummeted, the roads to freedom multiplied. Most female slaves, however, chose to spend the entire war on their home ground. Left behind or located far from the military fronts, they moved to take their freedom where they stood. And slaveholders, looking defeat in the eye more each day, were prepared to bargain.

With tens of thousands of husbands, fathers, brothers, and sons, black and white, dead or wounded or with one of the armies, it was often female slaves who negotiated the first wartime free-labor arrangements with slave owners. Leveraging the promise of freedom and their increasing ability to escape a labor-short market, slave women bargained with shattered masters and visibly shaken mistresses. Some demanded wages for their labor. Some, claiming the protection and authority of the United States government, refused to perform any labor that did not meet their own independently determined needs. In numerous cases, slave women openly invaded their owners' smokehouses and larders. And given the opportunity to earn a fair return from their sweat, some women labored harder than ever before. One planter reported of "one old woman who has taken six tasks of cotton and last year she would do nothing."[35]

A shadowy existence somewhere between slavery and freedom would not suffice, and flight still often seemed a better alternative. As Federal troops marched deeper into the heart of the Confederacy, thousands more women saw their chance. Since the beginning of the war, slaves—in the face of all manner of contrary evidence—had come to rely on the Union armies to help them. Slave women, as much as slave men, had become adept at forging this partnership. In 1862 when the Union army threatened Memphis, for example, Lydia Penney saw her chance, took refuge in the city, and awaited her liberators. Nancy Johnson, although she lived "way back in the country," also waited and "became free when the army came." With her daughter held hostage in another county, Johnson and her husband probably waited longer than they might have otherwise. She had, after all, already sent her fourteen-year-old son out of slavery, allowing him to leave with Union troops rather than be killed by her master who suspected him of collaborating with the Federal army. She never saw her son again. Maggie Dixon remembered that when "the Union cavalry came past our plantation, told us to quit work and follow them, we were all too glad to do so."[36]

What African-American women found behind Union lines, however, was often further hardship and oppression. With their newfound freedom often came hunger. They also

Sally L. Tompkins's commission as a Confederate army captain, issued by Secretary of War Leroy P. Walker in 1861. *Tompkins received the commission in recognition for establishing the private Robertson Hospital in Richmond. In accepting the honor, however, Tompkins noted that she "would not allow my name to be placed upon the payroll of the army." (Manuscript, 9 September 1861.)*
Eleanor S. Brockenbrough Library, The Museum of the Confederacy

Confederate States of America,
WAR DEPARTMENT.
Richmond Sept 9th 1861.

Sir:

You are hereby informed that the President has appointed you

Captain

IN THE ARMY OF THE CONFEDERATE STATES. You are requested to signify your acceptance or non-acceptance of said appointment: and should you accept you will sign before a magistrate, the oath of office herewith, and forward the same with your letter of acceptance to this Department.

L. P. Walker
Secretary of War.

Captn Sally Tompkins
Richmond
Va

I accepted the above Commission as Captain in the C.S.A, When it was issued. But I would not allow my name to be placed upon the pay roll of the army
Sally L. Tompkins

Southern Women Feeling the Effects of Rebellion, and Creating Bread Riots. *Rioting constituted the most notable act of female subversion against the Confederacy. To protest government food-distribution methods and the prevalence of price-gouging, nonelite women rioted in many Southern cities, including Richmond, in April 1863. One Savannah rioter passed out cards at her trial that stated, "Necessity has no law & poverty is the mother of invention. These shall be the principles on which we will stand. If fair words will not do, we will try to see what virtue there is in stones." (Engraving,* Frank Leslie's Illustrated Newspaper, *23 May 1863.)*
Eleanor S. Brockenbrough Library, The Museum of the Confederacy

faced the constant threat of brutal beatings and rape at the hands of unsympathetic Union soldiers or the prospect of recapture and death at the hands of Confederate soldiers and guerrillas. A contingent of the Federal force occupying Port Royal, South Carolina, in November 1861 raped a female slave child. In Virginia, a white Union soldier recoiled from the sight of slave women being abused by men from his Connecticut regiment. The soldiers turned two of the women "upon their heads, & put tobacco, chips, sticks, lighted cigars & sand into their behinds."[37]

Although wives often remained near their soldier husbands for both companionship and protection, it was not enough. Complaints from black men that "white men were trying to seduce their wives" did, however, help call attention to the problems. In the Department of the South, the Reverend Abram Mercherson requested that the commander deny white soldiers and sailors nighttime passes to the black settlement at Mitchelville, South Carolina. Drunken Union soldiers, he complained, used passes obtained on the pretext of recruiting black soldiers to enter black settlements where they committed atrocities against slave women, including the rape of one man's wife. "We have been trubled very often by these officers & Sailers & i think a stop aught to [be] Put to it"—"for thay will not," he added, "Behave them Selves as men." A group of Union chaplains and surgeons also complained to their commanding officer that slave women were being "molested by white soldiers to gratify their licentious lust."[38]

Slave women who made it to Union-occupied territory were hard pressed to find employment, food, or shelter. Some joined regiments as washerwomen, cooks, and hospital workers. Susie King Taylor explained her duties: "I was on hand to assist whenever needed. I was enrolled a company laundress, but I did very little of it." Instead, she prepared food, nursed the sick, and taught unlettered black soldiers to read. In occupied cities and towns, black women tried to make a living at sewing, cooking, and marketing foodstuffs to civilian and military populations. Some resorted to prostitution.[39]

Some Union commanders regarded the presence of black women—including the wives of their soldiers—as a nuisance and dangerous to troop discipline and sought to remove women and children from military encampments. Late in 1864, for instance, the Union commander at Camp Nelson, Kentucky, ordered the temporary huts erected for black soldiers' families to be torn down. The army then placed the women and children in government wagons and drove them behind the lines with no provision made for their safety, shelter, or food. The problem of female refugees was never satisfactorily addressed, and black women found themselves shuffled from camp to camp, kidnapped back into slavery, or put to work growing cotton or sugar on plantations in Union-held areas. Sometimes, mothers saw their older children—at twelve or thirteen years of age—taken from them and assigned to work elsewhere.[40]

Whether clinging to freedom in wretched contraband and army camps, or in abandoned or barely functioning plantations, or in devastated areas repeatedly swept by both armies, slave women became active participants in slavery's disintegration. The fugitive slave Lydia Penny volunteered as a nurse, she explained, because it allowed her to be with her soldier husband and because of "the love which she had for her country—the cause which nerved the soldiers to pour out their life-blood was her cause, and that of her race." Nancy Johnson risked her own life and that of her children by hiding escaped Union prisoners. She also hid Southern soldiers who—"opposed to the war & didn't own slaves & said they would rather die than fight"—had deserted the Confederate cause. Soldiering, as Johnson understood, was not the only way to be "a good Union man during the war." Her husband, for example, did not wear the soldier's uniform but "liked to

List of laundresses, Winder Hospital, Richmond, Virginia. *Cleaning, cooking, and other menial nursing jobs fell largely to African-American hospital workers. On evening rounds in the Charlottesville, Virginia, hospital where she worked, white nurse Ada W. Bacot observed that many patients were troubled by foot blisters, "I told the girl who waits on them, to dress the blisters." At Richmond's Winder Hospital, African-American women made up the entire laundry staff. (Manuscript, 1864.)* Kate Rowland Mason Collection, Eleanor S. Brockenbrough Library, The Museum of the Confederacy

A list of Laundresses in 1st Division Winder Hospital from 1st January 1864 to 31st Dec 64

Names	Masters	Time	amt	
Ann	Mrs. Furgarson	Jany 1st 64	25$	
Emily	Free	" 1-64	20$	
Bettie	S. Wheeler	" 6 "		Discharged 26 July
Letisia	Dr Watkins	" 6 "		
Lucy Ann	J. Alsop	" 1 "	15$	
Mariah	" "	" " "	12$	
Eliza Lilly	Free	May 23 "	20$	
Caroline	"	" 23 "	20$	
Martha Bradley	"	" 23 "	20$	Discharged
Susan	"	" 30 "	20$	discharged
Mary	Mrs Smoot	" 22 "	20$	Discharged
Mary Francis	Free	June 6 "	20$	Discharged
Eliza	S. H. Ayres	" 6 "	20$	
Keziah	Wm Allen	" 10 "	20	
Beckie	" "	" 10 "	20	
Elizabeth	" "	" 10 "	20	
Milly	" "	July 8 "	20	
Adaline				
Nancy Martin	Free	June 29 "	20	
Louisa White	Free	" 29	20	

have lost his life by standing up for the Union party." His "heart was right" and "so was mine," she stated.[41]

Black women who were indifferent to the needs of their owners or refused to obey a master's or mistress's command helped to cripple slavery as much as those who became fugitives or went to the front to help nurse, cook, clean, teach, and care for black soldiers. And, on captured plantations operated by Northern lessees or under the auspices of the Federal government, black women's labor put cotton bales in Union hands and the receipts into the Federal treasury.

When the war was over, the nation counted its dead soldier husbands, fathers, sons, and brothers. Southern black women, like white women, rejoiced that some men still lived. Black women also celebrated their freedom. As one former slave proclaimed, "I yet live and I am free, and I thank God." Another woman, who had seen her oldest son hanged by the Confederacy as a spy and watched as another left for the Virginia front, celebrated the surrender of Charleston with the news that a third son, sold away into slavery, was still alive. Slave mothers greeted sons, husbands, and brothers who had left home as

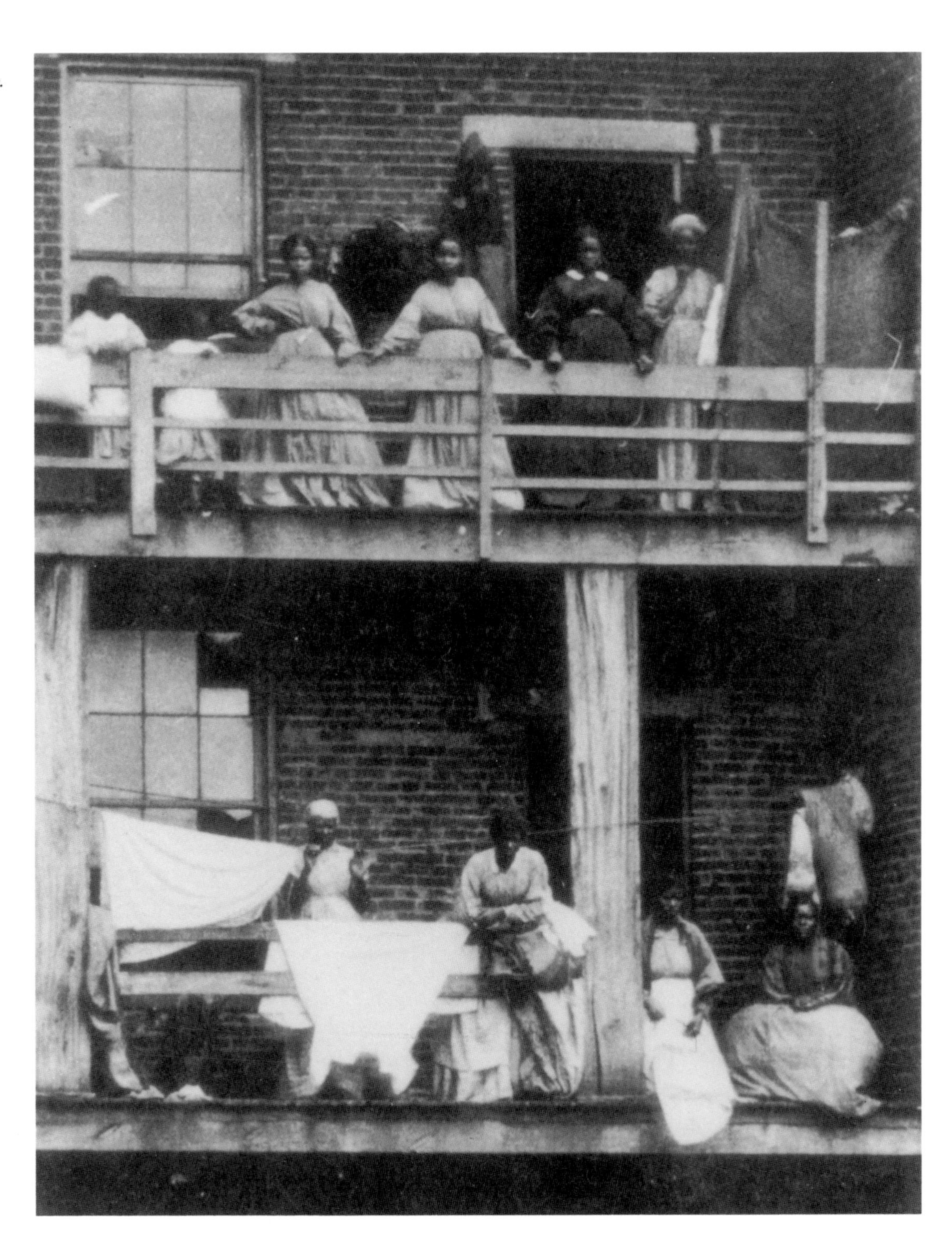

Laundry staff, Hospital No. 3, Nashville, Tennessee. *(Detail of an albumen print, 1863.)*
National Archives

Female contraband, Yorktown, Virginia. *If a contraband managed to find work, it was often varied and always hard. For example, although officially enrolled as a laundress with the Thirty-third United States Colored Troops on the Sea Islands off South Carolina, Susie King Taylor "did very little of it, because I was always busy doing other things through camp." Her work included nursing, cooking, and packing military equipment. (Stereograph, 1863.)*
The Library of Congress

slaves "but had returned in the garb of a Union soldier, free, a man." As important, they greeted them as free women who had played a role in their own liberation.[42]

Like white women throughout the South, African-American women wrote or dictated letters to male relatives spelling out the pain and hardships they suffered, seeking money to relieve hunger and homelessness, and detailing the heartache caused when the affections of separated husbands or lovers shifted. The differing objectives of Southern black and white women were, however, always clear. In a letter to her soldier husband, a slave woman recounted the increasingly harsh treatment she and their daughter suffered. But though she and the child were "almost naked," she encouraged her husband and underscored her understanding of freedom: "do the best you can and do not fret too much for me for it wont be long before I will be free and then all we make shall be ours."[43]

In the postwar South and well into the twentieth century, whites used many devices to brace themselves against the rising tide of black freedom, the battle over woman's proper role, and the demand for extending the vote, whether to African-American men or

white women. Two perceptions that proved particularly seductive in reinforcing the past and forestalling change were the notions of the loyal black female servant and her benevolently protective mistress. Over time, the two icons became so strong they stubbornly supplanted the historical reality of Southern women, black and white, in the war. It was a trap Catherine Edmondston would have understood. So would Leila Callaway. So, too, would the slave women who served them. Even Lizzie Gibbs, who served as her mistress's "bodyguard all during the war" and assisted her mistress in establishing a sewing circle to benefit Confederate soldiers, would have perceived the danger.[44] The war did not simplify the place of gender in the South. Instead, it complicated the issue in ways never imagined. The war sometimes forced, sometimes aided change, bringing with it new perspectives and a new debate over the contributions and potential of black and white women.

CHAPTER TWO

INTO THE TRACKLESS WILDERNESS

The Refugee Experience in the Civil War

JOAN E. CASHIN

***Detail from* Southern Exiles on Their Way North.** *(Engraving, by Thomas Nast,* Harper's Weekly, *19 September 1863.)* Eleanor S. Brockenbrough Library, The Museum of the Confederacy

Two years after the Civil War ended, Sarah Anne Dorsey published a thinly disguised account of her wartime saga in a novel, *Lucia Dare*. The title character flees from Louisiana in 1863 with her friend, Louise Branger, Louise's two small children, and a number of the Branger slaves. The party takes a caravan of wagons toward Texas but halts after the children contract measles. Mrs. Branger makes up a pallet for her son and daughter as they toss about in delirium. After much suffering, they both die. Since no coffins could be procured in what the narrator calls "this trackless wilderness," the mother wraps their bodies in a sheet and makes a funeral shroud from some of the household goods she brought with her—a skirt, a shawl, and a blanket. As the children are lowered into a roadside grave, she collapses with grief. The bondsmen shovel dirt over the bodies, and the party moves on, leaving the unmarked grave behind.[1]

As the story suggests, the refugee experience for Southern women during the war was filled with danger, illness, and catastrophic loss. This has been the case for many refugees since the word entered the English language in 1685 to describe the Huguenots who left France after the revocation of the Edict of Nantes. Students of refugees in the modern era have recently begun to explore the distinctive ways that women experience flight and exile, but the literature on the American Civil War contains little on the subject. Yet, as we shall see, most white Southern women were especially ill-prepared for the refugee experience. Many of them led parochial lives before 1861, focused almost entirely on family and household. After 1861, they faced an altogether different existence. With the war came the breakup of innumerable households, a simultaneous rupture in the antebellum bargain between men and women, and unprecedented challenges to white women's assumptions about class, ethnicity, race, and gender.[2] These particular women were literate white Protestants from the Confederate states as well as the border states of Maryland, Kentucky, and Missouri. Their fathers or husbands were members of the slave-owning class (planters, affluent farmers, commercial elites, or professionals), and most of them supported the Confederacy with varying degrees of enthusiasm.[3]

As many scholars have noted, Americans have long celebrated the experience of being in motion across geographic space. In one writer's pithy summary, it has been hard for us to sit still, and even today most believe that anyone should be free to pick up and go. But this was not true for all Americans in the past. White women in the early-nineteenth century usually traveled with male escorts, and this custom seems to have lasted longest and been upheld with the greatest fervor in the Old South. As Eliza F. Andrews, of Georgia, recalled, a "'male protector'" was "indispensable" for any respectable white woman who wished to travel. This was true

The Women and Children of Louisville, Kentucky, Leaving the City.
In the face of approaching armies, many Southern women became refugees. The Confederate attempt to capture Kentucky in the fall of 1862 panicked Louisville residents. A visitor commented in a letter to his daughters that the hotels were crowded with refugees and "the city in great confusion." (Engraving, by Henri Lovie, Frank Leslie's Illustrated Newspaper, *18 October 1862.)*
Eleanor S. Brockenbrough Library, The Museum of the Confederacy

for middle-aged matrons as well as schoolgirls, Andrews stated, for journeys of several miles or two hundred miles. When a woman left home, her father, husband, brother, cousin, or some other kinsman made the arrangements and accompanied her throughout the trip, whether she was going to church, visiting relatives, or traveling to one of the fashionable spas. If she was traveling by carriage, he sat next to her or rode on horseback nearby. If she was traveling by horseback, he rode beside her. If she was traveling by train, he bought the tickets (since women from the slaveholder class rarely carried money), took her to the station, carried her luggage, sat with her during the trip, and at its end accompanied her until she was safely in the hands of some other kinsman in the bower of another household. In carriages and on trains, women did not engage in conversation with strangers if it could be avoided. Many women wore veils when they traveled, the better to discourage conversation and conceal their faces from prying strangers.[4]

Women experienced other restrictions on their geographic mobility in their daily lives. Whenever a white woman stepped beyond her front yard, custom dictated that she needed a companion. Girls from slave-owning families did not take walks alone on the streets of New Orleans or Charleston, and young women did not make social calls by themselves. As absurd as it might seem today, an unmarried woman did not even cross a ballroom floor alone lest she appear to be too forward. During courtship, the same restrictions applied. A maiden took a carriage ride with a man only if an adult chaperone accompanied her, and some families even thought it was inappropriate ("rather fast," as one matron recalled) for a girl to go horseback riding with her fiancé before the nuptials. Nor could adult women easily escape prevailing customs. They did not go to the post office or attend a camp meeting without an escort; they dared not venture from home on election day when crowds of men and boys filled the streets.[5] Poor white women had more latitude—it cannot really be called freedom—to go wherever they wished. Because they lived outside the ambit of so-called respectable society, no one seemed concerned if they routinely traveled alone. One of the many ironies of Southern women's history is that the more affluent a white woman was, the less likely it was that she could travel where and when she wished.[6]

Why did Southerners make such a fuss about white women traveling with a male companion? Why did it matter so much? These arrangements were based on what might be called the antebellum bargain between the sexes, that women gave up autonomy in exchange for male protection, an assumption that underlay the entire social order. This idea had special implications for travel customs. White men did not believe that white women were strong or sensible enough to cope with the hazards of travel alone. If a woman fell ill, got lost, or was robbed during a journey, a man should be there to protect her from harm. Moreover, white men in the antebellum South placed the highest premium on the sexual purity of white women. They feared that women could be assaulted during a journey by other men, including other whites, slaves, or free blacks. So a male escort was deemed a practical necessity, a matter of respectability, and an ideological obligation. Therefore a white woman who disregarded these beliefs and traveled alone might be suspected as inviting sexual activity. She was at the very least what one teenage girl from Tennessee called less than a "proper lady," and she might be a prostitute. Decent women traveled under a man's protection, while only "public women" went out alone.[7]

Some white women bristled at these constraints on their mobility, but most acquiesced to the customs of the time. Their mothers raised them to travel only with male escorts and to trust these men to guide them through harm. They agreed that the world beyond the household could be a dangerous place, so the antebellum bargain, to forsake autonomy for protection, made sense to them. For most white women, it seemed natural that a man should be at their elbow whenever they went away from home for any length of time. Nor did they wish to sully the family's reputation by traveling alone or risk their own marriage prospects by "fast" behavior, and they had no desire to be mistaken for prostitutes. Most never attempted to travel alone, and many felt distinctly uncomfortable if for some reason they were left to themselves for more than a few moments during a journey, say while waiting for an escort at a railroad depot.[8]

Women's lives were centered almost exclusively on the household, which was the workplace as well as the dwelling place. The typical slave owner's home most likely consisted of four to eight rooms in a clapboard house with a chimney and a front porch, rather than the white-pillared mansions of lore. Lacking every modern convenience, these buildings were often uncomfortable, hard to heat in the winter, and hard to keep clean throughout the year. Most white women labored in the house, sewing, cooking, or cleaning, and they sometimes worked alongside slave women. Housework kept white women close to home for long stretches of time, and contrary to popular legend, they did not enjoy much leisure. Letitia Dabney recalled that her mother, mistress of six slaves, made clothes for everyone on the farm and added, "I never saw her idle, day or night, except on Sunday." If the work was tedious or distasteful, it was nevertheless a woman's duty to get it done.[9]

The household was also the center of emotional gravity, the hearth in every sense, the place where most women gave birth to their children, welcomed visits from kinfolk and friends, and attended the deathbeds of their relatives. Here much of their daily labor bore fruit, in the meals on the table, the clothes their children wore, and the quilts that covered the family at night. Here women kept their wedding gifts, daguerreotypes, and mementos of the dead. Although some women longed for a more stimulating existence, most were profoundly attached to the household as a physical place and as a symbol of all they held dear. As Virginian Judith McGuire once remarked, "Home and its surroundings must ever be our chief joy." "While shut out from it and its many objects of interest," she observed, "there will be a feeling of desolation."[10]

This home-centered life inevitably bred a certain provincialism among white Southern women. Even the wealthiest women had no education beyond the academy (roughly equivalent to a modern high school), for almost all of the South's universities were closed to female students. The great majority of women had never traveled outside of the United States, most had never journeyed beyond the South, and many had not traveled extensively within their native region. Before the Civil War, many women had never even been on board a train. One slave owner's son recalled that his mother rarely traveled beyond the immediate neighborhood, while his father and other male relatives were "frequently out with their market and merchant wagons." Most women of the slaveholder class were profoundly domestic in their outlook. Recalling the small horizons of many white women, Emma Tyler Blalock wrote in 1891 that "we had no advantages of travel as our daughters have." Devoted to their families, loyal to their friends, most of whom were from similar social backgrounds, these women knew little of the greater world.[11]

The larger world began to reach into their households in April 1861, of course, as thousands of men went off to war. Many departing soldiers wondered how women would manage alone, the men's apprehension not quite concealed by all the bravado that the fighting would be over in a few weeks. Some men remained at home, however, such as those planters and businessmen exempted from military service, men who purchased substitutes to fight for them, or men who were too old for the draft. So the familiar customs persisted into the early years of the war, for long and short trips. Many women still expected, and received, male escorts, and many still traveled wearing veils over their faces. Most women wanted the old practices to continue for as long as possible. One matron was afraid to leave Charlottesville for Richmond to meet her son because "I don't know how to get there, it rains incessantly & your Father is not here." Another dreaded traveling alone from Richmond after her husband, her "protector," died in an explosion in the city in 1862.[12]

As the battlefield and the hospital killed off thousands of other white men, more Southern women had no choice but to travel on their own. In early 1862, Fannie Hume, of Orange County, Virginia, could still count on a few of her relatives being available for escorts, but by the end of the summer all of them were gone, either in the Confederate army, dead, or fleeing the Union forces, so that she began to travel by herself. Another "lady" had to drive her carriage some thirty miles across central Kentucky to pick up a

The Inhabitants of Louisville, Principally Women and Children, Driven from the City . . . Camping on the Banks of the Ohio.
While wealthier citizens could afford to escape on steamboats or stagecoaches, poorer residents—like these women camped outside the city along the river—traveled on foot. (Engraving, by Henri Lovie, Frank Leslie's Illustrated Newspaper, *18 October 1862.)*
Eleanor S. Brockenbrough Library, The Museum of the Confederacy

paroled Confederate officer. A few women seem to have adjusted to the new practices easily, such as the Virginia matron who traveled alone with as much aplomb 'as she would have exhibited with an escort of a "score of gentlemen," but most viewed it as an unfortunate necessity.[13]

To become a refugee, to leave the household, perhaps forever, was another matter altogether. Some women, in no immediate danger, had time to prepare carefully for their departures. They put their households in good order, gathered ample provisions and plenty of money, and traveled along meticulously plotted routes to the homes of relatives. Julia Gardiner Tyler, widow of President John Tyler, devoted several months to putting her plantation in order before leaving Virginia for Bermuda in 1863. More typically, women had to leave suddenly as the Federal army bore down on their communities. Some had postponed flight until the last minute, and others were surprised into flight. Cornelia Black and her spouse removed from New Orleans on a day's notice, packing all night before escaping to the Ouachita River. These departures happened in various sections of the South at different times, of course. Many women who resided in northern Virginia had to set off quickly after hostilities commenced in 1861. Others who lived in relatively quiet places did not have to quit their homes until the last months of the conflict. In the spring of 1865, Parthenia Hague, of Alabama, prepared to flee and then kept a nighttime vigil listening for the "tramp of the mighty Northern host."[14]

Regardless of when they became refugees, most women found it hard to leave their beloved homes. Years later, one Virginian remembered the anguished cries of women evacuating Fredericksburg, wailing, *"My things! Oh, my things!,"* meaning the familiar objects they were leaving behind. What one scholar has called the "small-scale" material culture of home meant a great deal to white women. As she packed to go, Elvira Scott recalled ten years of effort to "improve, ornament, and beautify" her house; every tree and bush in the yard was "dear to me." After she took flight, Judith McGuire's mind often returned to the Bible, books, and pictures she had to leave behind, "things which seemed a part of ourselves."[15]

When women left home, many departed amid scenes of pure bedlam. In May 1861, Anne Frobel met a crowd of her neighbors at a railroad depot with "wagons, carts, drays, wheelbarrows all packed mountain high with baggage," women crying, and everyone looking "as forlorn and wretched as if going to [an] execution." The impending arrival of the armies in Mississippi in 1862 incited what Roxanna Cole called an "indescribable" atmosphere of "terror and confusion." With her children and several slaves, she hurriedly threw some belongings into a wagon and took to the road, some of her companions riding, others walking, many of them weeping. Eliza Ripley, of New Orleans, provided an unforgettable depiction of the throng of women, elderly men, and children pouring out of the city in August 1862,

> tired, exhausted, broken-down, sick, frightened, terrified human beings—all roused from their beds by firing and fighting in the very streets; rushing half-clad from houses being riddled with shot and shell; rushing through streets filled with men fighting hand to hand; wildly running they scarce knew whither, being separated from children and wives and mothers in the midst of the roar of battle, and no time to look for them; no turning back. . . .[16]

In the midst of such chaos, white women understandably felt they needed their male protectors more than ever. Some white women took slave men to work as drivers, but they much preferred their own kinfolk or, if they were not available, a white man who was a family friend. When Margaret McCalla vacated her Tennessee home in 1863, one Mr.

Witt accompanied her, her children, her mother, and some slaves as they traveled by wagon across the Smoky Mountains to South Carolina. Another matron in flight from Germantown, Tennessee, to Tippah, Mississippi, persuaded a family friend to drive her carriage because "I did not like to travel [in] such fearful times with only a servant." White men shared the expectation that they would escort their womenfolk, but the war's exigencies prevented many people from adhering to the old customs. After Mrs. Henry Lay moved to Huntsville, Alabama, her husband hoped to join her from Arkansas, where he served with the Confederacy. He promised her, "I will come and take care of you somehow or somewhere," but he could not do so.[17]

Naturally most refugees found it difficult to learn to travel alone. One young woman was almost overcome with panic when she had to travel through Kentucky. Her husband was in the Confederate service, her father was in Mississippi, and she did not even know which road to take, crying, "Oh Sister what is to become of me." When Frances W. Wallace, her cousin, and their children had to travel from Vicksburg to Jackson, Wallace was "very disconsolate" and thought it "quite hard" to go forth alone, but go forth they did. Sarah Morgan, the sheltered daughter of a judge, had to find lodging for herself and several relatives near Mandeville, Louisiana, in 1863. Feeling "timid" and hating to be what she called a "pioneer," she managed to secure a place for them to stay. Other women had to learn travel skills for the first time, handling money, hiring wagons, negotiating with innkeepers, most of them disliking it intensely but impelled by practical necessity and the will to survive.[18]

Many refugees covered a considerable geographic distance in their wartime journeys. A few dashed to the nearest safe place, twenty, thirty, or forty miles from home, and lingered there, hoping they could return home quickly.[19] Many, though, traveled hundreds of miles before their odysseys were done. Louise Clack left New Orleans for LaGrange, Georgia, and then fled to Columbia, South Carolina, and back to Georgia, residing in Augusta, Milledgeville, and finally in Warm Springs, while the LeGrand sisters, also of New Orleans, lived in Jackson, Mississippi, then Newnan, Georgia, and later Thomasville, Georgia, before they fetched up in eastern Texas. Some women exited the Confederacy altogether and lived quietly in the North, while others went into exile in Canada, Cuba, or western Europe.[20]

Most refugees remained within the South, however, and most left home with some destination in mind. Some headed for the cities, while others moved to the countryside, but almost all of them sought out the home of a relative—a sister, a cousin, a grandfather, a niece—drawing upon the large kinship networks so prevalent among the white Southern population. They were hoping for shelter with someone they could trust, an adequate supply of food, and physical safety.[21] Up until the last year or so of the war, the South contained enclaves where the conflict had scarcely made a mark. When Frances Wallace withdrew to Tuskegee in 1864 to live with relatives, their larders were still bursting with food. Residing with kinfolk, even for a short time, could do much to reduce the discomfort of being a refugee. When Eugenia Bitting stopped with an aunt and uncle at their Georgia plantation, she not only ate well but learned essential household skills. Her aunt, who realized that slavery would probably end with the war, taught the newlywed Bitting how to cook.[22]

Daily life as a refugee was nevertheless marked by extremes. In some instances refugees, paradoxically, experienced a good deal of boredom. In others, anxieties dominated daily life. Fearing theft, some women wore money belts containing cash, gold, or silver beneath their clothes, and others sewed their valuables into their underclothes or the hems of their dresses. Many refugees worried continually about finding a place to stay. The affluent lodged in hotels along the way, but others sometimes had to ask strangers to take them in, and during the early phases of the war many white Southerners were willing to do so.[23] Meanwhile, refugees spent much of their time waiting to hear about the outcome of a battle, the progress of an army, or the migration of relatives, so that they might determine their next move. Some women passed the time by sewing or reading, while others entertained themselves by playing chess, putting on tableaux, or making social calls.[24]

Women from the most privileged echelons of planter society could even enjoy their

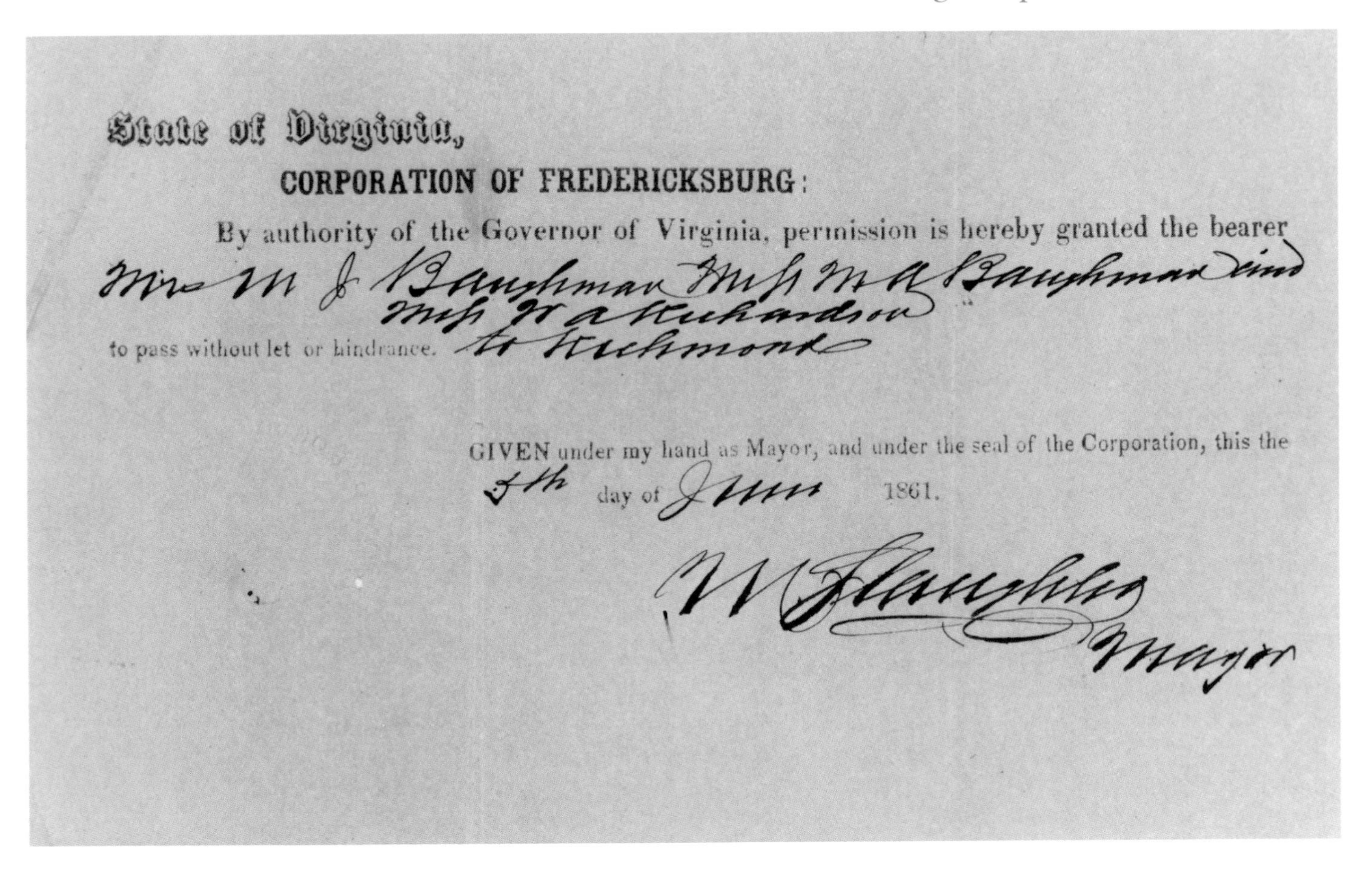

State of Virginia,

CORPORATION OF FREDERICKSBURG:

By authority of the Governor of Virginia, permission is hereby granted the bearer Mrs M J Baughman Miss M A Baughman and Miss W A Richardson to pass without let or hindrance. to Richmond

GIVEN under my hand as Mayor, and under the seal of the Corporation, this the 5th day of June 1861.

M Slaughter
Mayor

Pass issued to Mrs. M. J. Baughman, Miss M. A. Baughman, and Miss W. A. Richardson. *To regulate civilian movements, each army required passes for travel through military lines or into occupied territory. When a Confederate sentry outside Strasburg, Virginia, requested one woman's pass, she gave him a tongue-lashing: "Passes! Passes for white folks! I never heard of such a thing. I ain't got no pass. . . . This is a free country, and I'se agwine to Strasburg this night; so you might as well take your lantern out of my face." To the amusement of her fellow travelers, the woman proceeded unscathed. (Manuscript, 5 June 1861.)*
Eleanor S. Brockenbrough Library, The Museum of the Confederacy

migratory existence. In 1861, Virginia Clay, wife of the Confederate senator and emissary Clement C. Clay, was rich, well-traveled, childless, and a member of a large family. She began traveling the region the next year and boarded with relatives in Georgia, North Carolina, Alabama, Virginia, Tennessee, and South Carolina. Initially she sought out Georgia because many considered it to be the safest and wealthiest Confederate state; she returned in 1864 expecting a "care-free" summer. In November 1864 she told her husband in Canada to buy some silk dresses, a sable fur, and a coral necklace, among other items, all of which he dutifully purchased. (The booty disappeared in Columbia, South Carolina, when Union troops occupied the city in 1865.) She occasionally traveled with a military guard, and wherever she resided Clay managed to find enough food. Her social and political status buffered her from the worst of the refugee experience.[25]

Others, much less fortunate, traveled simply to dodge the armies, with no destination in mind. They relied on hearsay, newspapers, or the occasional hand-delivered letter for information about where to go. Mrs. M. P. Stringer departed New Orleans in 1863 and landed in Pascagoula, Mississippi, with "the world before us—or rather the Confederacy, without any particular point of destination." This kind of aimless wandering was probably harder than leaving for a specific place, for these women had to train their energies on survival every day and live entirely in the present. As Kate Stone confided to her diary, "We cannot bear to think of the past and so dread the future."[26] Some women moved almost continuously, ricocheting from one place to another. Rebecca Latimer Felton moved with her family through a series of towns in 1864 and 1865, plunging from central Georgia down to the Florida border. Esther Cheesborough shuttled between Chester, Laurens, and Columbia, South Carolina, during the last two years of the war, cut off from her home in Charleston. Sometimes refugees miscalculated when choosing a destination, such as the plantation mistress who traveled to Alabama only to run headlong into the Union army.[27]

Few accounts show a more chaotic pattern of mobility than Judith McGuire's diary, published in 1867. The middle-aged wife of a

Southern Exiles on Their Way North.
Headed to Texas from Lousiana, Kate Stone noticed "thronging everywhere were refugees—men, women, and children—everybody and everything trying to get on the cars, all fleeing from the Yankees or worse still, the Negroes." This chaotic scene of Southerners "thrown upon the world," the artist noted, could be "witnessed almost daily on any highway in Tennessee, Kentucky, and Missouri." (Engraving, by Thomas Nast, Harper's Weekly, *19 September 1863.)*
Eleanor S.Brockenbrough Library, The Museum of the Confederacy

schoolteacher, she and her elderly husband had to leave their home near Alexandria, Virginia, in May 1861. She moved thirty-four times before the war concluded, crossing the state in a zig-zag pattern to avoid the armies and remain within Confederate lines. She and her husband stayed for days, weeks, or months at a time at various locations, sometimes joined by their adult daughters. One night McGuire was separated from her husband at a railroad station amidst a "shouting, hallooing, hurrahing" crowd of soldiers. Mrs. McGuire quailed at the thought of going on alone, but a minister offered "his purse and his protection" and accompanied her to the next stop. Two days later her husband arrived on a later train, and they continued their journey. Typically the McGuires sought out relatives or good friends for lodging, boarding free of charge, but they also rented rooms whenever necessary. In January 1864 Judith McGuire began working for the Confederate government in Richmond, where she resided on seven separate occasions during the conflict. She became a clerk in the Commissary Department with numerous other "ladies," many of them refugees. Glad to have a source of income, she was still living in the capital when the war ended.[28]

Refugees who were forced to travel without male escorts expressed a good deal of embarrassment. Sarah Morgan was distinctly uncomfortable when she and her sister turned out to be the "only ladies" on a train in Louisiana in 1862, and she felt "abashed" when she realized that a full regiment of Confederate soldiers in Port Hudson was looking at them as they rode by in a carriage. Pauline Heyward found herself "very uneasy" at the gallery of strange faces at a railroad station in Augusta. She had never been "in a crowd of men without a protector before." Many refugees felt exposed in a deeply personal way. Mary Chesnut, who was already depressed about leaving home, wrote that her "spirit was further broken" when she lost her veil in transit from Lincolnton, North Carolina. After Kate Stone slept outdoors in a makeshift camp, the mattresses divided only by a curtain, she wanted to blush and added, "I never felt so out of place." *Out of place,* indeed. A woman's solitude in public carried connotations that are elusive to most modern readers, for a woman alone in a crowd of men might well be there to ply a trade in flesh.[29]

Women traveling alone were vulnerable to many improprieties, such as verbal harassment from men, that escorts had once deflected by their presence. Confederate troops could be "rude" to displaced families, trying

Trunk. *Frances Elizabeth Taylor used this trunk for smuggling supplies and other goods during her travels between Norfolk and Baltimore. Taylor reportedly also carried packages of quinine pinned inside her hoop skirts. (Leather-covered-frame and brass-reinforced trunk, ca. 1861–1865.)* The Museum of the Confederacy

Crinoline and Quinine—A Delicate Investigation. *Young women were especially attracted to the usually masculine enterprise of smuggling. With the help of several friends, Belle Edmondson "pin'd the Hats to the inside of my hoops—tied the boots with a strong list . . . all my letters, brass buttons, money, &c. in my bosom." Federal soldiers stopped Virginian Alicia Buckner—whom they dubbed the "Fair Apothocary"—with 127 ounces of quinine concealed under her skirts. (Engraving,* **Frank Leslie's Illustrated Newspaper,** *22 November 1862.)* Eleanor S. Brockenbrough Library, The Museum of the Confederacy

to keep refugees off a train in Louisiana, but many women reported that Federal soldiers ridiculed them more frequently and with more venom. Some Union troops waged informal psychological warfare against civilians throughout much of the war, which may have been intensified by their resentment of the slave-owning class. In any case, Northern troops mocked refugees for their losses, the loss of men, of community, of the home itself. When Roxanna Cole wept as a litter of dead Confederates was carried to a graveyard in Mississippi, she was "laughed at" by soldiers in blue watching nearby. According to Catherine Cochran, men in the Federal army routinely "insulted" refugees; when she protested the arrest of a man sick with consumption, a soldier shouted, "If he dies we'll have him decently buried." After Union troops burned Anna Guignard's house in South Carolina, forcing her to become a refugee, they jeered as she shivered in the woods nearby, calling out, "We have made it hot for you."[30]

One way to ward off shame, prove respectability, and make refugee life more bearable was to preserve the household's material culture as much as possible. Women tried to bring along the practical items necessary to support their families. Frances F. Moore, for example, departed home with the bare essentials, a kettle and a shovel tied over a horse. Most women took as many housewares as they could, loading kitchenware, wardrobes, sewing machines, and furniture into wagons, carriages, or railroad cars. They struggled to keep their belongings, however humble, with them as they kept moving. For instance, the Dabney family hauled their "scanty" furniture with them as they refugeed through Mississippi. Refugees purchased cloth, carpets, furniture, or other items as they could afford them, and many endeavored to make their new residences as "home-like" as possible, even if that meant only acquiring a rug to cover a bare floor.[31]

Many women also took their keepsakes to preserve some sense of the family's history. Most refugees brought something—a daguerreotype, a wedding present, a scrapbook—to provide a tangible connection with home, and those objects took on even greater emotional significance on the road. Many women brought their favorite dresses, too, although most of them soon had to put aside their finery for more practical homespun. Some refugees went to considerable lengths to take a piano, that longtime symbol of gentility and femininity. Most had to discard the bulky instrument along the way, but a few women managed to have it transported to their new lodgings. In 1864 Sara Pryor arranged to have her piano as well as books and a costly painting shipped from Petersburg to her new domicile, a rented house near Richmond.[32]

Most of these efforts to preserve either practical household tools or precious souvenirs of home were doomed, however, to fail. Amid the upheavals of the war, it proved to be almost impossible to hold on to their possessions as refugees moved from place to place. Women's belongings were lost, damaged, or stolen on the road, sometimes by civilians, including other refugees, sometimes by Confederate troops, Federal soldiers, or other military personnel. After Elizabeth Rennolds and her family abandoned their Virginia home, they chanced upon some of their belongings in a nearby town, where a Union officer was preparing to mail a box of their books, including the family Bible, to his mother in the North. Other women were shaken to discover that Southern troops, what one Louisianan called "our own people," stole from refugees. Federal nurses broke into Fanny Tinsley's baggage and took her dresses, but then "our men," as she indignantly recalled, stole the wedding gifts she had carefully packed away.[33]

Managing a refugee household could be much easier if a white woman had slaves working for her, especially female slaves. Elizabeth Lacy's half-dozen slaves made it "comparatively easy" for her to keep house when she moved from Fredericksburg to southwestern Virginia. (After they ran off, her work duties increased markedly.) Kate Stone's mother managed to keep some house slaves with her for two years after family members departed their plantation in March 1863; these slaves did the laundry and in general tended to the white family's needs. But sooner or later most slaves ran away, and most whites had to do the work that black women had once performed, washing their own clothes and chopping their own firewood, according to one refugee. Mary Chesnut reluctantly began to do some cooking and cleaning in her place of lodging in North Carolina after she moved in with a single slave in early 1865.[34]

Some refugees had to begin working for a wage to support themselves and their families. Women labored as nurses, tutors, or government employees, and one South Carolinian, Esther Cheesborough, even wrote for the newspapers. Some women from the slave-owning class began doing work that had traditionally been performed by men. After her husband, father, and brother died in the war, Frances Moore traveled alone on horseback through Missouri selling hogs and sawing wood for pay. Others survived by cannibalizing what remained of the household's material base. One woman returned from Georgia to her Mississippi home to auction off the family's remaining possessions, selling everything for cash. Even "ladies" began trading their belongings—clothing, books, jewelry, a ball of yarn—for food.[35]

To be sure, most refugees had to cope with food shortages across the Confederacy. Those residing in the cities probably felt the shortages first, followed by those in the countryside, where plantations continued to operate in the first years of the war. But the Union blockade eventually had its effect, and many farms fell into disuse or were trampled by the armies. By 1863 food had become scarce almost everywhere, even in the countryside. Josephine Hooke walked seven miles in rural Georgia to purchase "anything we could find to eat" and came home with nothing but a chicken and a dozen eggs. Whenever refugees managed to have a fine meal, they recounted it in gorgeous detail. What had once been ordinary items, such as a glass of fresh milk, became luxuries, and a cup of good coffee, the great *desideratum*, was cause for rejoicing. By the last year of the war, many refugees subsisted on two meals a day.

Like many undernourished people, women became obsessed with food. The sight of a basket of bread transfixed one group of South Carolinians with "joy."[36]

As the war ground on, refugees found it ever more difficult to preserve their cleanliness and privacy, and therefore their dignity. From the beginning, shoes were hard to acquire—one woman called it "our greatest trouble"—and many had to make ersatz out of animal skins, saddles, or pieces of wood. Maintaining a presentable wardrobe was almost as challenging. Living in a refugee camp outside Atlanta, Josephine Hooke could not keep her dresses clean. Sarah Morgan felt "ashamed" of her dirty clothes after she fled on foot from Baton Rouge in 1862, and when Frances Moore asked for shelter at a house in rural Missouri, she was so embarrassed by her wet, muddy attire that she asked to sleep on the floor. As the Southern economy disintegrated, once-common household implements became highly prized indeed. The dwindling supply of bed-linens made for many an awkward moment as well as considerable bodily discomfort. The everyday objects necessary for running a household, such as brooms, or items essential for personal hygiene, such as toothbrushes and combs, became irreplaceable. By 1865, cooking utensils became so scarce in some parts of the South that they were rented out for use.[37]

Physical shelter, one of the prerequisites for survival, became harder and harder to secure. Bolder refugees claimed the homes emptied by other civilians—sometimes immediately after the owners fled—while more desperate women stayed in filthy, rat-infested, derelict buildings, in tents, wagons, or makeshift shelters under the open sky, or, in the case of Eugenia Bitting, in a private home that the Federal army had used as a field hospital in Georgia in 1864. After inspecting several other buildings nearby that had "blood splashed clear to [the] ceiling," Bitting chose a house that had only one stain, the bloody outline of a man's body on the floor. Her husband hired two slaves to scrub it away, but the stain would not come off, so she covered it with a carpet. The odor in the house was almost unendurable, but Bitting and her husband were relieved to have a roof over their heads after three years of the gypsy life.[38]

As refugee women traveled through the Confederacy, many found that the earth had indeed turned red with blood. Given the region's high mortality rates before 1861, Southerners were more intimately acquainted with death than most modern Americans. Many women had witnessed the deaths of family members, either their offspring felled by childhood diseases, other women who expired in childbirth, or the elderly who died of old age. But the killing-machine of war was so terrible, the carnage so overwhelming, that refugees had to confront the horrors of death in an entirely new way. The armies could not bury all of the dead properly, and thousands of bodies were piled into hastily dug mass graves that opened up after a hard rain or exploded with gas formed by decaying bodies. Bands of deserters and guerrilla fighters sometimes had to abandon their dead where they fell, so that portions of the landscape were littered with human remains. When Fanny Tinsley traveled to Richmond in 1862, "the dead were strewed on every side" of the highway, and "the most horrible sights" met the eye. As Frances Wallace journeyed through Mississippi in 1864, the roads were lined with dead horses, and the stench was overpowering. Indeed, the armies abandoned thousands of dead livestock wherever they went, for burying animals was not a priority when so many men had to go without the dignity of a proper burial. Throughout the Confederacy, refugees witnessed familiar, beloved landscapes transformed by the grotesque. Before Elizabeth Neely bid goodbye to her Tennessee home, she watched the building being turned into a Union army hospital. As her yard filled up with amputated limbs, she turned away feeling "crazed."[39]

Disease soon became a serious problem in such an environment. Before the war, the South was already an unhealthy place, subject to some unusually virulent infectious diseases. The wartime mobility of several million soldiers and civilians, poor sanitation methods, the end of the usual methods of preparing, serving, and preserving food, the ignorance of germ theory—all of this added up to illness on a scale not seen since the Revolutionary War, as epidemics of the measles, smallpox, scarlet fever, typhoid fever, and other diseases swept the region. Women who became refugees were thrown into contact with many people in rapid succession and thus exposed

Refugee family. *"Refugeeing" in the Valley of Virginia in July 1863, Cordelia Peake McDonald and her family traveled roads crowded with soldiers and fleeing civilians. "We were constantly in sight of, and often jostled by moving crowds of people and vehicles," McDonald remembered, "... fugitives of every grade and degree of misery were toiling on, on foot, or in any kind of broken-down vehicle. Sick men, hungry men, and women with crowds of children, all hurrying on." (Albumen print, 1863.)* The Library of Congress

to many illnesses. After Mrs. Charles Smith and her children ducked into a house in Virginia, she realized that the hostess's child was covered with running sores. Fatigued and malnourished, refugees were therefore more susceptible to illness. Fanny Tinsley, for example, ran through a battlefield and then past a field hospital, sustaining cuts and bruises in the process, and then washed at a pump alongside some wounded soldiers. Perhaps it was no coincidence that she began to feel "very sick" a few days later.[40]

Members of other refugee parties succumbed to serious illnesses, as women lost children or adult relatives to sicknesses they contracted on the run. Mary Robarts feared

dying far from kinfolk who would give her a decent burial, and Arabella Nash died just such an ignoble death. The pampered favorite of her parents, she expired in a boxcar in Augusta, Georgia, surrounded by strangers, one of whom buried her nearby and marked her resting place with a flimsy wooden tablet. When her relatives tried to adopt her children, they could locate only four of her five offspring. Some refugees died even more horrible deaths. In 1864 a Union soldier chanced upon a gruesome scene in a house in Tennessee. The building was crowded with women and children, all of them refugees from Georgia and South Carolina and all infected with the measles. In one room he discovered the corpse of a woman and her young son, and in the next room another woman who had just given birth to a child, both of whom had little chance of survival in that house.[41]

Many women feared not only disease but also violence, and violence shadowed the refugee experience from the first moments of flight. So many civilians rushed to the railroad depot in Nashville in 1862 that those already on board the cars beat back the crowd (both men and women) with clubs. On a few occasions refugees met violence at the hands of the military. As women and children evacuated Fredericksburg, the Federal army fired by mistake at a train of refugees.[42] Refugees faced danger from civilians, too, as impoverished communities, unable to provide for their own indigent population, began to express open hostility toward refugees. Along the Louisiana-Texas border, local people refused to shelter homeless families, and residents of private homes in Virginia began to turn away lone women. One Tennessean reported that there was so much ill will toward refugees that she feared she might be murdered on the southbound road from Memphis. Refugees could inflict violence on each other, as women sometimes engaged in fist fights over food or over seats on passenger trains. Some even took part in mob actions. When a crowd gathered in front of one refugee household in North Carolina, determined to rob its inmates, the mob included women as well as men, many of them armed with hoes, rakes, and axes.[43]

Female refugees also had to contend with harassment from soldiers that had a distinctly sexual undertone to it. In most modern wars, soldiers have learned to see women as con-

Citizens of Charleston, South Carolina, Taking the Oath of Allegiance. *Federal commanders frequently compelled Southerners, in exchange for particular privileges, to take loyalty oaths to the Union. Trying to reach New Orleans, refugee Sarah Morgan took the oath only because she was threatened. "Half crying I covered my face . . . and prayed breathlessly for the boys and the Confederacy, so that I heard not a word he was saying until the question 'So help you God?' struck my ear. I shuddered and prayed harder. There came an awful pause in which not a lip was moved. Each felt as though in a nightmare until throwing down his blank book, the officer pronounced it 'All right!'" (Engraving,* **Frank Leslie's Illustrated Newspaper,** *15 April 1865.)* Eleanor S. Brockenbrough Library, The Museum of the Confederacy

temptible for their physical weakness and supposed cowardice, and American men in the Civil War seem to have been no exception. White women complained much more about Union troops, but Southern men, as well as deserters from both armies, also accosted refugees. In Mississippi, jayhawkers tore the jewelry off women's dresses and the earrings out of their ears, and Federal troops in Louisiana pulled the rings off women's fingers. Sometimes troops engaged in more direct physical intimidation. When Northern troops searched the house where Kate Stone was staying in Louisiana, a soldier carrying a cocked pistol walked up to her, stepped onto the hem of her dress and "looked me slowly over," before laughing and turning away. Other troops went further. Men in uniform occasionally searched the "persons" of white women suspected of concealing money, and individual soldiers sometimes threatened to strip-search refugees. Most Southern women shrank from uninvited physical contact with soldiers, especially, of course, with Northerners. When a Federal soldier kissed teenager Letitia Dabney, saying that she reminded him of his daughter, her cousin exclaimed that she had been "polluted."[44]

Refugee women recorded several instances of what they believed to be attempted sexual assaults by men in both armies. A Northern soldier tried to enter Roxanna Cole's residence, but when she screamed, and the slave women in the house screamed, he ran away. Cole added that she would have been less frightened if "mere robbery was all I had to fear." Meanwhile, two of her female neighbors decided to hide in the woods nearby, "fearing for their lives and their honor." Refugees complained most often and most bitterly about Union troops, but Confederates could on occasion be just as menacing. After Cornelia Black rented a house in rural Louisiana, two drunken Confederate deserters staggered into the house in an "ugly, threatening mood." They refused to leave, so a slave woman pushed them out the door. Many refugees understandably came to distrust men outside the family. When Kate Stone, her mother, and siblings rented a place near Oak Ridge, Louisiana, she was relieved that there were no "gentlemen in the house to molest [us] or make us afraid."[45]

The worst of all violations was rape, and being a refugee made a woman more vulnerable to this crime. The scholarship thus far has yet to uncover evidence of the widespread rape of civilians, or rape as official or unofficial policy, such as what happened to women in the Asian and European theaters during World War II. Very few soldiers were executed for the crime in the American Civil War, but the number of executions almost certainly does not reflect the actual occurrence of the crime, if indeed it ever has. For example, a recent study by the United Nations High Commissioner for Refugees reaffirms that rape has remained unrelentingly commonplace during armed conflicts, in large part because perpetrators are often motivated by a "desire for power and domination."[46]

During the Civil War, many white Southern women certainly believed that Northern troops were capable of committing sexual assaults. The story of Kate Nichols, who died in an insane asylum after allegedly being raped by Federal troops in Georgia in 1864, spread quickly through the ranks of refugees. Many refugees feared rapes whenever Union troops arrived nearby. Mary Jones stayed awake one night in 1864 praying aloud with her daughter after Sue, a slave woman, warned them that troops with "the most dreadful intent" had asked her if there were "any young women" in the family. They all prayed to be spared what Jones called "a fate worse than death," imploring the Almighty to keep the enemy away from "our persons." Although the region contained what one veteran called "vicious, unprincipled, and unmitigated scoundrels" from both armies, accounts of rape of white Southerners by Confederates are rare, perhaps because these troops were loath to assault other white Southerners or because civilians were reluctant to report it.[47]

All of these experiences help explain why many refugee women gave such ready credence to the atrocity stories that circulated through the refugee population. Whether these were vague rumors, such as allegations that Federal troops offended "*public decency*" during campaigns in Virginia and Alabama, or specific charges against individual soldiers, most women were ready to believe the worst. The stories seemed to get more lurid in the last year of the conflict. In 1864, a wayfarer in Georgia heard that William T. Sherman's troops promised to "starve out even the women, this year, and if that would not conquer us, KILL us the next." Flora Bryne, a refugee in Alabama, told her sister that Union soldiers beat white women with horse whips, and she relayed a scarifying tale from Natchez, where troops allegedly threw an infant into a burning house in front of the mother's eyes. Bryne accepted the story as true and called the soldiers "demons" who were bent on destroying the civilian population.[48]

These refugee experiences, in all their variations and hardships, challenged many of the prevailing assumptions about social relations in the antebellum South. As they traveled through the Confederacy, slave-owning women came into contact with whites from all social classes. People from widely divergent backgrounds met on trains, wagons, and carriages, and sometimes they ended up living together in impromptu households. For instance, a menage near Nashville included several working-class and yeomen women plus one whom a Northern soldier described as a woman of "refinement." As the formerly prosperous mingled with women who had never been rich, it became harder to tell them apart. While it is risky to generalize about so many transient meetings under such duress, it seems clear that the war did not erase all social distinctions among refugees. The once-affluent felt contempt and pity, sometimes mixed together, for women who had absolutely nothing as their households fell apart. When a poor woman appeared at Mary Mallard's door in Atlanta on a cold, wet night, Mallard, herself a refugee, gave her shelter but could not resist calling the woman's blunt-spoken children "regular little crackers."[49]

Conversely, refugees who had once been prosperous began to envy those who had managed to keep their households intact and their comforts at hand. Judith McGuire came to Richmond in 1862 and asked a wealthy acquaintance if she and her husband could board in the woman's home. The lady of the house refused, looking "cold and lofty," and "meant me to *feel* that she was far too rich for that." As McGuire moved on, she mused on the strange turns that the "wheel of fortune" could take over a lifetime. Two years later she was less philosophical as she walked the streets again in search of a room. In 1864 she keenly resented the families whose cozy, well-lighted homes were still adorned with "showy" furniture and wondered why they did not share their wealth with the less fortunate. Other refugees such as Frances Wallace envied the privileged they met on the road; she was awed by the Mississippians who still enjoyed a sumptuous diet and extravagant clothes in 1864. Mary Chesnut, a high and mighty lady if ever there was one, burned at the arrogance of a woman she met in Chester, South Carolina, "high and mighty with money and a large house." The fortunes of war had indeed turned the tables in unexpected ways.[50]

Repeated hardship, want, and fear usually do not bring out the best in human nature, but a few refugees broke the crust of stereotype and saw working-class white women anew, almost as if they were seeing them for the first time. Kate Stone scorned what she called the unrefined natives she met in Texas, but her arrogance softened after two years' residence in the state, and she became friends with some of them. After Louise Clack departed New Orleans in 1862 with her two young daughters, her Irish nurse, Kate Shannon, and several slave women, Clack's circumstances became increasingly desolate. Her house was looted, her husband died in battle, and she had to leave her aunt's home in South Carolina where she had taken refuge. The mistress quickly came to admire Kate Shannon's resourcefulness—Shannon once secured their passage on a boat by pretending that Clack was pregnant—and to rely on it, especially after the slave nurses disappeared. During the war, something resembling a friendship, albeit one born of extremity, developed between the two white women. When Federal troops fired on their train in Georgia in 1865, they held hands and prayed together, tears streaming down their faces. An

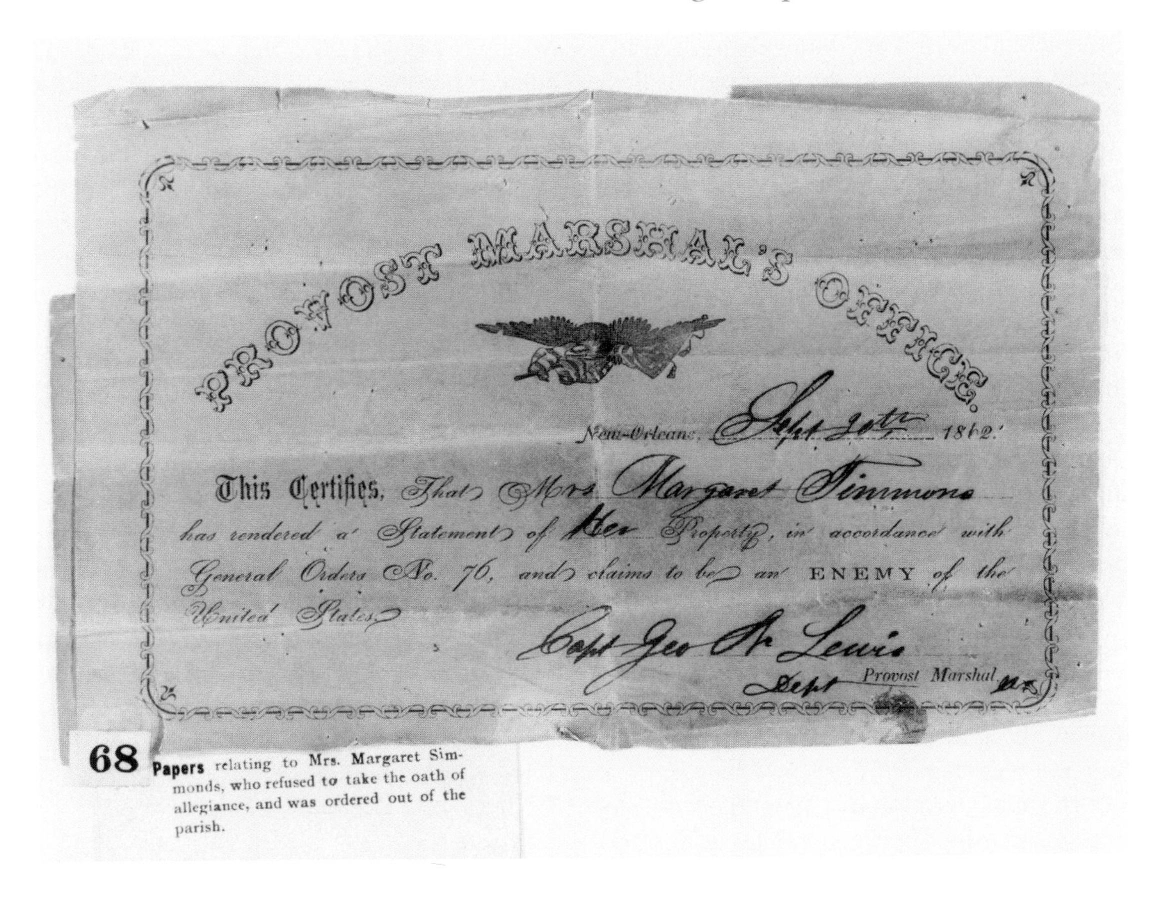

PROVOST MARSHAL'S OFFICE.

New-Orleans, Sept 30th 1862.

This Certifies, That Mrs Margaret Simmons has rendered a Statement of Her Property, in accordance with General Orders No. 76, and claims to be an ENEMY of the United States

Capt Geo W Lewis
Dept Provost Marshal

68 Papers relating to Mrs. Margaret Simmonds, who refused to take the oath of allegiance, and was ordered out of the parish.

Enemy oath. *Margaret Simmons's refusal to take a loyalty oath resulted in her expulsion from occupied New Orleans. (Manuscript, 30 September 1862.)* Eleanor S. Brockenbrough Library, The Museum of the Confederacy

even more interesting encounter took place between one affluent matron known only as "Agnes" and a dressmaker's apprentice in Richmond. They met in the milling crowd just before the city's famous bread riot of 1863 and had a brief conversation. The younger woman asserted her right to take enough food to survive; moved by the woman's thin appearance, Agnes exclaimed, "I devoutly hope you'll get it." This exchange might be dismissed as nothing more than a friendly word on the street, but it evidently inspired some genuine soul-searching on Agnes's part. A few months later she told a friend that this stray encounter haunted her and added that such women were paying a high price for the bombastic pro-slavery rhetoric of Southern politicians before 1861. It was extremely unusual, however, for a woman to draw such pointed conclusions about the causes of the war or its impact on civilians.[51]

In fact, most refugees found it hard to jettison their assumptions about ethnicity or race, despite the war's many blows to the antebellum social order. Poorly educated, many women were highly susceptible to anti-Semitic stereotypes about Jewish businessmen, whom they blamed in part for the wartime collapse of the household. Some Protestant refugees attributed the shortages of food, housewares, and furniture, and the high prices of these goods, to the greed of Jewish merchants. Catherine Cochran persuaded herself that "crafty Jews" were enriching themselves rather than serving the South. The irrational nature of these attitudes is revealed in women's own writings. Another refugee made scathing remarks about the avarice of Jewish businessmen, even though her memoir shows that men of all ethnic backgrounds practiced usury during the war. The same inconsistency was evident in women's individual encounters with Jewish Southerners. One refugee, for example, disdained a tradesman she met in San Antonio even though he graciously gave her several items free of charge. A few women, however, admitted that the Jews they met did not fit bigoted stereotypes. During Eugenia Bitting's journey from Georgia to North Carolina, a wealthy family shared some food with her, to her lasting gratitude. Years later she declared, "I will never go back on the Jews." Bitting's remarks imply nonetheless that few gentiles shared her outlook.[52]

Furthermore, most refugees continued to relate to black women primarily as workers who should assist them during their trials, and rarely as human beings with families of their own. Many white women told themselves that slaves preferred to travel with them rather than join their own relatives, and they felt bewildered when those same slaves ran away. Kate Sholars convinced herself that a slave woman left only because her husband made her to go against her will. The close proximity that the refugee experience often forced on the races did little to bring blacks alive to whites as individuals. After Frances Moore settled at her mother's farm, she worked in the fields with her sister, her nephew, and a teenaged slave. "We all worked faithful," she recalled, but neglected ever to mention the slave girl's name. With a sharp jolt, some white women realized that they did not know slaves well after all. One refugee was astounded to overhear some bondswomen calling the mistress "that Woman" and deriding the white family.[53]

The war introduced a new element into the relationship between white and black women, however, and that was the possibility of sexual assault from troops in both armies. If we may judge by the size of the region's mulatto population in the antebellum era—at least 10 percent of the South's four million slaves—many white men had forced sexual relations on slave women. But during the war thousands of white women were themselves vulnerable to assault in a new way. Nor could many whites ignore the fact that soldiers from both armies raped or tried to rape black women, probably more often than they assaulted white women. Rebecca Latimer Felton recalled that slave women asked mistresses for "protection" from "bad men" in the Union army as the soldiers approached. Some white women felt horrified by these assaults. Mary Jones was enraged at the "infamous" Federal soldiers who pawed at slave women in the quarters, sometimes pulling them out of their husbands' arms, and especially at the soldier who grabbed the slave woman Sue by the collar and started to drag her into a bedroom—the same woman who had warned the mistress earlier of their evil intentions. The threat of rape sometimes evoked compassion from white women. Elizabeth Neely asked her aged cook, Mimey, to sleep in her bedroom rather than outdoors because the slave woman was afraid of Northern soldiers. But the two women still abided by the antebellum hierarchies, for Mimey slept on a pallet on the floor while the mistress slept in the bed; Mimey's husband slept in his clothes in another room. Relations between white and black women, far from simple before the war, were further complicated by the issue of sexual assault even as slavery was unravelling around them.[54]

Yet the refugee experience during the war seems to confirm what most historians suspect, that there was no interracial women's culture in the mid-nineteenth-century South. White refugees could strike up friendships with other white women they encountered on the road, especially if those women came from the slaveholder class. After Mrs. Charles Smith met a "lady" during her flight from Richmond in 1864, the trip became almost enjoyable, as the two women talked together and shared lodgings whenever possible. White women wanted female companionship

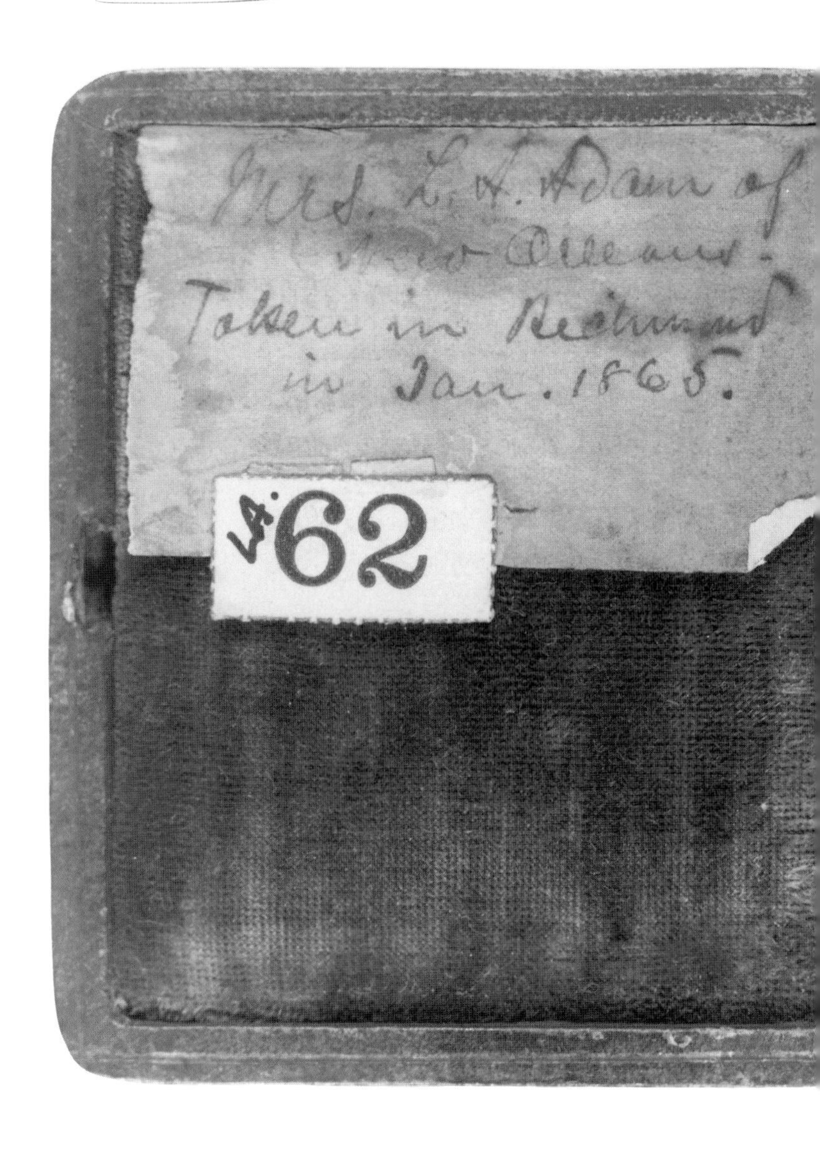

to provide the protection that was no longer given by their menfolk. When Emma T. Blalock exclaimed in her memoir, "Only a woman could understand a woman!," she referred to the sexual perils that women faced during the conflict. She recalled that young women walked arm-in-arm through the streets because "we were our own defenders," but she meant white women, for she did not link arms, literally or symbolically, with black women. On occasion a lonely refugee might reluctantly accept some companionship from a black woman if there were no whites available, but it proved almost impossible for these white women to relate to blacks as their equals. When Sara Pryor lived near a small Virginia town, a black woman named Charity was her "only female companion," and, as she again tells the reader, "my only female friend and companion." But Pryor depicts her as someone with no family of her own, no history, and no identity other than as a hired servant. Although the two women spent some eight months together in a small house in 1863, Charity never comes into focus as an individual, and she disappears from Pryor's memoir after the white woman moved on to Petersburg to live with relatives.[55]

Mrs. L. A. Adam, of New Orleans. *Even well-to-do Southern women found refugee life unsettling. "We cannot look into the future of this world at all," Betty Herndon Maury reflected. "We cannot form an idea as to where or in what condition we will be one month hence."* ***(Daguerreotype, Richmond, Virginia, January 1865.)*** Eleanor S. Brockenbrough Library, The Museum of the Confederacy

Childbirth might be the one event that could overcome class and racial barriers among Southern women, but the record here is mixed at best. A few refugees strongly identified with other white mothers, regardless of their apparent class backgrounds. Eliza Ripley gave baby clothes to homeless white women and shared food with women she met on trains or by the roadside. (The death of one of Ripley's children while she was a refugee probably strengthened her feelings of identification.) Her generosity seemed to invite kindness from strangers. After Ripley gave birth to another child in Matamoros in 1864, a white woman she met on the road visited her every day for a week. But the barriers between women of different races proved to be much higher, usually insuperable. Elizabeth Meriwether, a pregnant refugee living in Mississippi, sent for a doctor when she felt the first contractions of childbirth coming on. No physician was available, so a black woman whom Meriwether called simply "the granny" assisted her until the child was born. She paid five dollars to the anonymous woman, who then disappeared into the night, as Meriwether wanted her to do.[56]

In the last phases of the war, many refugees grasped the hard truth that the conflict could overwhelm the white men they turned to for protection. Mary Robarts, a young woman in charge of her invalid mother, begged a kinsman for advice on where to go as the Federal army approached Marietta, Georgia, in 1864. She was flabbergasted when he admitted that he was "at sea himself" and did not know what to do. Other women began to realize that men could exhibit poor judgment, even cowardice. Sara Pryor persuaded a Confederate general to send an escort to accompany her as she departed Richmond, but the driver was two days late, then took her to an empty house in the countryside, let her out at nine o'clock at night, and rode away. Margaret Beckwith's father arranged for a white man to guard their house in North Carolina while he was absent. A Union soldier then began to search the house, and as he became "insolent," Margaret Beckwith seized a pistol and threatened to shoot him. The soldier ran away, whereupon she discovered that her guard had disappeared, on purpose, she believed, to avoid a fight.[57]

Many refugee women were stunned that men in uniform could put military duty before their duty to white women. One wealthy Georgian asked a Confederate officer to give her an escort through the countryside one winter night in 1864, telling him that she was a widow and had to reach her daughter right away. The captain refused; she remonstrated; finally, he shunted her aside with the comment, "I cannot help you," to her utter astonishment. Refugees were just as shocked when white male civilians would not assist them. As one elderly woman undertook to cross the Tallahatchie River, she asked the ferryman if he would assist her party. He responded abruptly, "No, I won't," and agreed only when she offered to pay him liberally for his help. When Frances Wallace and her cousin stopped their wagon at a private home near Morton, Mississippi, they asked the white man of the house for shelter for the night. As they pleaded their case, saying that they were tired and their children asleep, one of the mules collapsed from exhaustion. Still the man refused. When they protested that they were trying to join their husbands, his stinging reply—"A great time to go to your husbands"—infuriated them so much that they jumped into their wagon, flogged the mule back to life, and drove off.[58]

Even more painful, white men whom they knew personally sometimes abandoned them. As Sarah Morgan and her sister left Baton Rouge in 1862, they trudged down a country road only to be passed by a party of "gentlemen" in a carriage. These men called out to "Judge Morgan's daughters," but, as Morgan added, they did not offer any assistance. When stragglers from Ulysses S. Grant's army arrived at a home in Mississippi, Letitia Dabney's uncle, the head of that refugee household, happened to be away on business. The soldiers arrested the family's overseer, tied him to a tree, and threatened to shoot him for espionage. When Dabney and her five female cousins threw their arms around the overseer, crying as loudly as they could, the racket intimidated the soldiers so much that they cut him loose. The overseer then leaped on a horse and rode off, leaving the Dabney girls "at the mercy of those wretches." Hardest of all to bear must have been a husband's infirmity. Federal troops stopped one refugee family in a carriage in rural Alabama and confiscated the horses on the spot, taking them right out of the harness. The wife upbraided them with so much fury that one soldier threatened to shoot her. Her husband, a disabled Confederate veteran, was forced to sit by and do nothing. If, as historian Clarence Mohr suggests, the refugee experience destroyed the myth of "planter invincibility," it also exposed the invincibility of white Southern men as a myth.[59]

In the last months of the war, the refugee experience was nothing short of harrowing for some women. Large sections of the Confederacy had in fact degenerated into a wilderness. Many roads were impassable, the trains jammed with people—if the trains were running at all—and wagons, horses, and mules were increasingly scarce. By the spring of 1865, Southern cities were congested with refugees who wandered through the streets, begging for food and looking for shelter. Women and children roamed the countryside, most of them homeless, many camped in the outdoors. Some were so famished that they took to scavenging the battlefields for scraps of food. Although private charities sheltered the homeless and distributed food to the hungry, as did the Confederate authorities and the Northern army, these efforts were not sufficient to deal with a distraught, needy population. A Confederate officer met an impoverished refugee on a riverbank in South Carolina in the spring of 1865, her possessions bundled up in a canvas bag. The woman's daughter had drowned while attempting to cross the water, and she was waiting to claim the body when it floated downstream. Whether or not Federal policymakers intended to wage a "total war," many such displaced women had descended into the "total crisis" that has characterized the experience for most refugees in the modern era.[60]

After Robert E. Lee surrendered to U. S. Grant in Virginia in April 1865, the refugee population began to flow back toward home. Women made the journey greatly relieved that the conflict was over, grieving for the dead, but hoping to rebuild the household. Some refugees came back to a pile of cinders, their houses torched by the armies, while others returned to find their homes defaced, plundered, and rundown, but still standing. Mary Chesnut reached Mulberry plantation in South Carolina in May 1865 to discover the furniture smashed, all of the doors and many of the windows broken, and the family's books, papers, and letters blown about the road for miles. When Sara Pryor came home, "millions of flies" were swarming over the traces of food, human waste, tin cans, and debris scattered all over the house. Other women saw their homes despoiled in an especially ghastly way. A Virginian found a dead Union soldier sprawled at her front door, so she paid a Confederate soldier to bury the body. He insisted on digging the grave right in front of the door, no doubt to humiliate the dead, but it also had the effect of desecrating the home for those who wanted to live in it. Whether or not they intended it, soldiers in both armies sometimes undermined the household.[61]

After the war ended, however, most refugees could not admit as much, not even to themselves. They had lived through a disastrous breakdown in the bargain between the sexes regarding female dependency and male protection, but most women dealt with it by denial. They overlooked or excused the rupture in gender relations, anything rather than face the fact that white Southern men had not protected the household from the war's onslaught. Instead they began to lionize Confederate troops and demonize the Union army, even though their own experiences did not match those stereotypes, and the self-deception continued in much of their postwar writing. Although it probably would not have comforted them much to know it, these white women did not experience the mass executions, wholesale physical abuse, or forced labor that refugees suffered through during the world wars of the twentieth century. Nor did the numbers of refugees in the South ever approach the five to six million refugees in World War I or the estimated sixty million in World War II. Nor did many have to endure the direct attacks on civilians that a few Union officers contemplated during the American Civil War. But they nevertheless felt the deep alienation that most modern refugees have carried home with them, expressed in the sulfuric bitterness toward the North that many white Southern women expressed in the postbellum era.[62]

Their reactions were perhaps understandable after so much hardship, for surviving the refugee experience was something of an accomplishment. There was little that was noble about it, and much that was sordid, horrifying, and sad. Yet white women still had to concentrate on survival after they returned home, trying to feed and clothe their families despite the region's blasted economy and ruined landscape. The continuation of this elemental struggle, undertaken when many people had already forfeited so much, helps explain why most white Southern women retreated to the household when the war ended. Rather than launching reform movements or entering politics, as other women have done at the conclusion of other modern wars, many focused on reconstructing the household, where they had been anchored before 1861. In the South after Appomattox, that effort would consume much of their energies.[63]

CHAPTER THREE

"THIS SPECIES OF PROPERTY"

Female Slave Contrabands in the Civil War

THAVOLIA GLYMPH

Woman, Drayton's Plantation, Hilton Head, South Carolina. *For some African Americans, the war crystalized their feelings towards whites. An enslaved cook—hired out to a hotel against her will by her mistress—commented with bitterness when she saw her owner and other white women weeping as their sons marched off to war, "Now white ladies knows how niggers feel when their children is taken away and hired out and sold." (Detail of an albumen print, by Henry P. Moore, 1863.)*
The New Hampshire Historical Society

Arriving in the summer of 1863, James Bryan—newly appointed medical inspector for black troops stationed along an eighty-mile stretch of the Mississippi River—reported "about ten thousand women and children . . . roving about without adequate support or protection."[1] In southern Louisiana the previous October, Union general Godfrey Weitzel reported that he had more fugitive slave men, women, and children than soldiers in his camp. While male fugitive slaves were able to find employment in the camp, the women and children, he wrote, were "compelled to pillage for their subsistence."[2] Elsewhere, a Northern journalist wrote confidentially to Massachusetts governor John Andrew: "I am sorry to say that the Massachusetts 24th has been acting outrageously here—robbing, burning houses . . . ravishing negro women—beating their husbands who attempted protection." After narrating such stories, historian Allan Nevins concluded twenty-five years ago that "the story of the freedmen in wartime is one of gross mismanagement and neglect."[3] Countless such incidents, spread across time and the geographical canvas of the Civil War South, increasingly typified the experience of black women—women who fled the South's plantations and farms and, in their own parlance, "entered the army." They were women who understood the conflict just as Frederick Douglass did: it was, he wrote, "a war for and against slavery." And like their fathers, husbands, brothers, and sons, slave women "were engaged in a war with only one object: to secure their freedom."[4] In fleeing slavery, they contributed to the disintegration and final destruction of slavery in the American South.

From the beginning of the Civil War to its conclusion, fugitive slave women commanded the attention of Richmond and Washington, slaveholders and nonslaveholders, and Southern and Northern commanders and soldiers in the field. Like slave men, slave women fully realized that freedom lay on the side of the battle line held by their masters' enemy. And like slave men, they, too, came to be officially designated as "contrabands of war." Forsaking caution and risking their lives and those of their children, female slaves proved just as likely to run away as males. And in doing so, they defied Southerners' assumptions about their loyalty and Northerners' contempt for their ability to construct their own ideas about freedom.

Acting on their own understanding of the situation, fugitive women provoked cries of outrage from both sides: Southern planters and their wives were quick to bemoan the loss of valued labor while Northern policymakers and military officers vigorously protested the arrival of unwanted contraband women. Yet in much of the public and scholarly imagination since, the term "contraband of war" has most frequently evoked descriptions and narratives of fugitive slave men. Although contraband women have not been

Contrabands Building a Levee on the Mississippi Below Baton Rouge. *Young Martha Forrest, enslaved in Tennessee, took advantage of the war's chaos to escape to occupied Nashville. After Union soldiers took her father to work on the fortifications and her "mother also went," she became "determined to follow my parents." One Sunday when she attended church with her owners, she was able to get away undetected from her seat in the slave gallery and begin a two-day walk to the city. (Engraving, by F. H. Schell,* **Frank Leslie's Illustrated Newspaper,** *9 May 1863.)* Historic New Orleans Collection

entirely ignored within the scholarship on the Civil War, they have nevertheless too often seemed like passive participants in the fight for freedom.[5]

The experience of female fugitives differed in important ways from that of male fugitives—just as it did from that of slave women who did not or could not flee. Like male contrabands, African-American women endured the dangers of flight along with the uncertainty of how they would be received by the Federal army. But, as women, they came to know a more hostile reception. Increasingly, they found themselves living in a world that could be as dangerous and dehumanizing as the one they had left behind. The demands of Northerners could be equally as painful and exacting. Union soldiers, for example, despised their presence and often demanded that they leave. And even when they could find a relatively safe haven, female fugitive slaves soon discovered that Northern white female missionaries expected black cooks and black household help no less than had their former Southern mistresses. But as the slave mother who carried her dead child, "shot by her pursuing master," into a Union army camp "to be buried, as she said, *free*" understood so well: within the Federal lines there was at least the promise of freedom.[6] That promise, of course, was not universally recognized. Even less recognized was the belief among slave men and women that slave women, too, had a stake and a standing in the conflict.

Although the crisis of the Civil War provided the opportunity for tens of thousands of slave women to smuggle themselves to freedom, in the first year of the conflict President Abraham Lincoln worked feverishly to keep the Federal war effort focused solely on restoring the Union. Lincoln knew that to tamper with slavery so soon would only heighten the fears of slaveholders in the loyal border states and discourage any lingering hope of unionism within the Confederacy. In 1862, for example, George B. McClellan urged a field commander set to take New Bern, North Carolina, to "say as little as possible about politics or the negro," to "merely state that the true issue for which we are fighting is the preservation of the Union and upholding the laws of the General Government." Some commanders required no prompting whatsoever. Receiving fugitives, Major General John A. Dix commented, would subject the North "to the imputation of intermeddling with a matter entirely foreign to the great questions of political right and duty involved in the civil strife," and thus "taint" the "holy" cause of Union.[7] But if the first fugitives who made their way to Union lines compromised the Federal government's official position, the thousands who followed rendered it utterly untenable. In fleeing, slaves declared the unholiness of a war fought only to reunite the nation. Moreover, a growing number of commanders and their soldiers—facing the prospect of death from Confederate breastworks built with slave labor, Confederate soldiers fed by slave-grown produce, and Confederate armies supplied by the profits of slave labor—became less and less patient with the notion of coddling their enemy by ensuring that slavery must somehow be unaffected by the war.

In 1861 at Fort Monroe, Virginia, Union general Benjamin F. Butler had taken the first step toward dealing with the question of what to do with fugitive slaves. Registering his opposition to the unofficial and confusing Federal policy of non-interference on the question of slavery, Butler opened his lines to fugitive slaves who had escaped from masters believed to be disloyal to the Union. Since many of the slaves had been forced by their owners and the Confederate government to work on Confederate fortifications, Butler further declared that the African Americans were indeed contraband of war—a form of property, Butler wrote, "that was designed, adapted, and about to be used against the United States." The slaves "in this neighborhood," he added, "are now being employed in the erection of batteries and other works by the

FACING PAGE:
Negroes Driven South by the Rebel Officers. *Some Southern slaveholders moved their slaves to safer locales to prevent their liberation by Federal soldiers. With one hundred or so others, Adeline Henderson walked from Lynchburg, Virginia, to Missouri over some three months. "We didn't know what it was all about but we had to do what we were told." Another woman recalled, "us all walk barefeets and our feets break and run they so sore and blister for months. It cold and hot sometime and rain and us got no house or no tent." (Engraving,* Harper's Weekly, *8 November 1862.)* Eleanor S. Brockenbrough Library, The Museum of the Confederacy

rebels, which it would be nearly or quite impossible to construct on their own."[8] Besides, such fugitive slaves, Butler believed, could just as easily and advantageously be folded into the Federal military force as laborers, depriving the enemy of much-needed help while aiding the Union army. But even the usually politically nimble Butler found himself at a loss when it came to the question of fugitive women and children. The "contrabands of war" policy, as Butler had to admit within days of promulgating it, was not designed to encompass female slaves and children. "I am in the utmost doubt," he wrote, "what to do with this species of property."[9] Moreover, as Union commanders and President Lincoln came to understand all too well, however belatedly and reluctantly, human prizes of war, unlike cargos of smuggled cotton or guns, had wills of their own. Indeed, smuggling their own persons out of enemy lines, fugitive slaves more accurately might be termed *contrabandists*, active participants in the war and in their own fate, rather than as *contraband*, passive prizes of war. And as more and more women made their way to freedom, the term *contraband* became by the end of the war virtually synonymous not with black men but with black women and children who were, as several Northern missionaries remarked in June 1865, largely "the families of soldiers."[10]

The establishment of Union bases along the coasts of South Carolina, North Carolina, and Virginia in the early months of the war provided the first opportunities for slaves to test the Federal boundaries of freedom. Thousands of slaves became contrabands by virtue of their residence in areas that came under the control of Union forces. Thousands more fled to these areas or, rescued by Federal forces, were brought to them. In makeshift camps and shanty towns they attached themselves to Union areas of occupation and began their journey to freedom. Union-occupied communities such as New Bern, North Carolina, were quickly "overrun with fugitives from the surrounding towns and plantations," two of whom had "been in the swamps for five years." "It would be utterly impossible, if we were so disposed, to keep them outside of our lines, as they find their way to us through woods and swamps from every side," one Union officer admitted.[11] Ultimately, the unexpected crush of fugitive slaves on Union lines forced Northern policymakers and field commanders to follow Butler's lead in opening his camps, but fugitive slaves, and fugitive women in particular, never ceased to draw the ire of some commanders. Midway through the war, a Union general besieged with "whole families of them . . . stampeding and leaving their masters," described them as an "evil."[12]

By mid-summer 1861 the number of contrabands at Fort Monroe had grown from only several to nearly a thousand. By 1863, more than twenty-six thousand were under the protection of Union forces in the Virginia tidewater region.[13] There and elsewhere as the conflict escalated, women and children made up a growing proportion of contraband populations. Just as the war's promise of freedom continued to encourage flight, other factors also played a significant part: the increased brutalization exacted by extra work, the growing anger of masters and mistresses, and the greatly accelerated disintegration of black families and communities all provided additional motivation. Until the end of the war, however, flight remained a risky, dangerous, and often deadly enterprise for slave women and their children.

As the effort to separate the cause of Union from the cause of freedom floundered, the United States Congress passed several measures that conceded the wisdom of Northern generals, soldiers, and civilians who—whatever their views on emancipation—were increasingly and vigorously opposed to allowing the South to brace its military power with slave labor. The

Confiscation Act of 1861, followed the next year by another Confiscation Act, the Militia Act, and the Emancipation Proclamation, were all important in helping to expand the boundaries of freedom and the opportunities for black women to secure protection within Federal lines. None of these measures, however, succeeded in dispelling the prevailing sentiment that black women had no place within Union lines and no right to the respect or privileges accorded white women.[14]

If Southern black women's racially imbedded status as slaves did not pose enough of a problem, their gender seemed to seal their fate. In contrast, white women—although excluded from the public debate over national sovereignty, citizenship, slavery, and freedom—were nevertheless still considered to have a stake in the Civil War and an important supporting role. "Manning" the home fires in the South and in the North, white women took on the tasks of managing and sometimes working farms and plantations, raising children alone, nursing the wounded, and keeping up morale amid death and growing hunger and despair. But together, race and gender established a rigid line of demarcation that seemed to rule out any public or quasi-

public supporting roles for black women.[15]

For black men, however, policymakers and armies on the march on both sides of the conflict had quickly realized the value of employing them in building fortifications, digging ditches, cutting roads and canals through swamps, cooking, and cleaning. It was the South, though, that first drafted female slaves to nurse, cook, and clean in Confederate hospitals.[16] Still, neither side believed that slave women had any real part to play in the conflict or even imagined that black women themselves might come to a different view. These beliefs persisted even after the unexpected scope and cost of the war shifted opinion and policy in the North to allow the enrollment of African-American men as soldiers. That decision, of course, would have a major impact on the public perceptions of black "manliness" and help engineer the transformation of the war into a larger struggle, a struggle for emancipation. Most conspicuously, it thrust black men into the masculine role of soldiering for union and freedom. No corollary role emerged for black women.[17]

Theoretically—with no hearths of their own to protect and without lawfully recognized spouses, fathers, or sons to nurse, cheer on in battle, worry about, or grieve for—female slaves in the eyes of whites did not merit even the unofficial, temporary standing accorded Northern and Southern white

General Sherman's Rear-Guard. *With the sound of Federal guns echoing in the distance, Sarah Debro's owner began to cry. Concerned, the young slave ran to an elderly cook who told her, "She ain't cryin' kaze de Yankees killin' de mens. She's doin' all dat cryin kaze she skeered we's goin' to be sot free." In search of freedom, thousands of slaves—men, women, and children—fled their plantations to follow Sherman's army. (Engraving,* Harper's Weekly, *2 April 1864.)* Eleanor S. Brockenbrough Library, The Museum of the Confederacy

women in the war. In appeals to Confederate and Union authorities for support, charity, and compassion, white women successfully coupled their rights and interests to patriotic duty. As Confederate Mary C. Moore, of North Carolina, succinctly put it: "We are all Soldiers' Wives or Mothers."[18]

Standing for freedom and the Union and as the wives, mothers, daughters, and sisters of black soldiers, black women found their efforts rebuked and Federal guarantees of protection rarely honored. Yet they continued to push for a reformulation of the war's objectives and for a definition of freedom that would encompass their lives and hopes. On plantations and farms and in urban areas they hastened freedom's arrival by refusing any longer to defer to mistresses or masters, or they deferred in ways that signalled they understood that the world of slavery was crumbling. Many women became more *contrabandists* than *contrabands*: they smuggled themselves and their family members out of Virginia into Washington, D.C.; out of the interior of North Carolina, South Carolina, Georgia, Louisiana, and Mississippi into Union-held areas along coastlines and riverways; and out of Missouri into Kansas.[19]

Running from slavery and against the tide of Northern and Southern white opinion, slave women increasingly found themselves running alone or in the company of other women and children. As tens of thousands of black men enlisted in the Union forces and thousands more were impressed as laborers by both armies, the number of slave women left to cope alone soared as the routes to freedom grew simultaneously more restricted and more open. On the one hand, black enlistment and the penetration of Union forces into the Confederate interior enhanced the possibilities for self-liberation and for military-assisted "rescues." On the other, Union raids could result in the impressment of able-bodied men who had no choice but to leave their families behind. In general, the opportunities for the particular kind of family and community flight that had characterized the first two years of war diminished.[20]

In Georgia, the pattern of slave flight at the beginning of the war revealed a clear preference for collective escapes in family and community units.[21] The escape of Susie King Taylor in the company of her uncle, his family, and other relatives typified the early pattern. "Two days after the taking of Fort Pulaski," Taylor wrote, "my uncle took his family of seven and myself to St. Catherine Island. We landed under the protection of the Union fleet, and remained there two weeks, when about thirty of us were taken aboard the gunboat . . . to be transferred to St. Simon's Island; and at last, to my unbounded joy, I saw the 'Yankee.'" When Robert Smalls hijacked the Confederate steamer *Planter* and delivered it to Union forces, several women, including his wife, the wife and sister of another man on board, and two women described as "unprotected women in the party" (presumably because no ties of kin bound them to any of the men in the group), made it to freedom with him.[22] Whenever Union gunboats appeared along coastal waters, there were similar patterns of flight—but there were also occasional instances of tragedy. In 1862, one such flight by three South Carolina women and their husbands ended in disaster. The party was captured by Confederate authorities—and every one of them was hanged.[23] By the end of 1862, the pattern of slave flight had changed, with women, not men, increasingly leading children and elderly relatives out of slavery.

Leaving slavery was one thing; finding a new home and a source of livelihood within Union lines was another matter altogether. The ever-growing and increasingly female-centered contraband population challenged the resources of commanders in the field. Even where commanders were able to implement some facsimile of Butler's approach—putting as many of the women to work as possible—they could not always find employment for all of the women who wanted or

needed work. Even sympathetic commanders could do little when military exigencies demanded reallocations of manpower that forced the complete evacuation of an area or the removal of all but a token military force, leaving female contrabands without a source of income and without protection from Confederate raids.

For some, the task of finding a place within Federal lines was further complicated by the determination of some Union officers and soldiers to return fugitive slaves to their masters in defiance of congressional acts and military orders. On the Mississippi River in the summer of 1862, David Dixon Porter, commanding a Union flotilla off Vicksburg, protested the action of a fellow officer who delivered up a group of forty-seven slaves, including twenty women and children, who had entered the lines seeking sanctuary, "to persons claiming to be their masters." One of the individuals claiming ownership of the slaves was, Porter wrote, "the wife of a notorious rebel."[24]

View of the Darlington Court-House and the Sycamore Tree where Amy Spain, the Negro Slave, was Hung. *Some white Southerners reacted savagely to slaves who welcomed Federal soldiers. Most of Darlington, South Carolina, turned out to witness the execution of Amy Spain in 1864. Spain was hanged for reportedly hollering, "Bless the Lord the Yankees have come!" when William T. Sherman's soldiers passed through the town. Elsewhere in South Carolina, young Margaret Hughes watched while her master hanged a young female slave who revealed his hiding places to Union troops. (Engraving, by N. N. Edwards,* Frank Leslie's Illustrated Newspaper, *30 September 1865.)*
Eleanor S. Brockenbrough Library, The Museum of the Confederacy

Fugitive slaves learned early that nothing could be taken for granted. Sanctuary within stable Union lines was never guaranteed. In June 1862, for example, Edward Stanly, a Unionist appointed as the Federal military governor of North Carolina, sought assurances from Washington "that this is a war of restoration and not of abolition and destruction." In the meantime, he granted masters who took an oath of allegiance to the Union permission to retrieve their slaves from Federal camps. He also ordered a school that had been established for blacks at New Bern closed; educating black children, Stanly argued, did not comport with his instructions to "restore the old order of things."[25]

As word of abuse at the hands of the Federal officials filtered back to the slaves still on plantations and farms, many decided to stay where they were or to establish independent communities in close proximity to, but not within, Federal lines. Such was the case early in the war in tidewater Virginia as well as along the coasts of North Carolina, South Carolina, and Georgia after the arrival of Union forces and the flight of slaveholders. Fugitives in these settlements struggled to evade unsympathetic Union soldiers or raids by Confederate partisans, but many of the new communities were short-lived. At Edisto Island, South Carolina, a Confederate raid in January 1862 captured a large group of fugitive slaves that "had assembled here from all points."[26] By mid-summer that year, Union forces had to evacuate the still-threatened survivors at Edisto, forcing out of employment some two thousand blacks who had been cultivating the land. At nearby Botany Bay, between one thousand and fifteen hundred contrabands tried to avoid capture by Confederate forces by destroying the bridges that connected them to Edisto Island.[27] But with Confederate forces intent on destroying the settlement, a Union officer decided to evacuate that community, too. The contrabands, he wrote, had become "a great annoyance to me and also the commander of the Gun Boat as one or the other must be on hand to protect them or they are run off by the rebels."[28]

Some independently established communities held together for the duration of the war, but their existence remained fragile and dependent on the presence of Union forces, sympathetic commanders, and often the assistance of Northern aid societies. Yet, despite the potential and real dangers independent settlements faced, they allowed slaves to hold families and communities together or to reconstitute them. Whether at Botany Bay in South Carolina, or Roanoke Island off the North Carolina coast, or at Hampton, Virginia, female contrabands could for a time count on the support of the husbands, fathers, and brothers with whom they had fled slavery. At Craney Island near Norfolk, Virginia, for example, female fugitive slaves were able to re-establish family life with their male kin and also find work as seamstresses and cooks.[29] When alone, the risks were great. Knowing that, male contrabands at Edisto Island in March 1862, recruited to go to Key West as military laborers, were willing to leave only if they could be assured that their wives and children would be cared for.[30] It was of no small consequence that as the war spread into the Confederate interior, as lines of battle and positions shifted, and as armies were more often on the move, the independence of contraband communities of all types was threatened. A settlement behind Union lines could in the matter of an hour find itself back within Confederate lines.

Contrabands at Craney Island, the majority of whom were refugees from Suffolk, Virginia, faced such a situation at the end of 1864 when Craney Island was declared outside Federal lines. The Craney Islanders were still more fortunate than many evacuees. They were removed to the mainland where several hundred were resettled on government farms. Others found housing in a newly established contraband village where they were provided with one-acre plots for growing vegetables.[31]

FACING PAGE: ***African-American community, J. J. Smith plantation.*** *The Federal occupation of the Sea Islands turned the South Carolina low country into a haven for thousands of escaped slaves. One group resettled on the former plantation of J. J. Smith outside Beaufort. There, on 1 January 1863, government officials, soldiers, and former slaves celebrated the first Emancipation Day. (Albumen print, by Timothy O'Sullivan, 1863.)* Getty Museum of Art

But even in the best of circumstances, hunger and insecurity threatened their efforts to construct new lives as free people. At Craney Island, a Northern missionary reported, rats had become part of the contrabands' diet.[32] And the continued threat of Southern military action forced yet another move for some of the Craney Island farmers.[33] But just as threatened military lines and shifting commands could create havoc in the lives of the contrabands, so also could demographic changes in contraband populations—resulting in inadequate food, shelter, and clothing. Any or all of these factors could dictate evacuation and resettlement.

Unlike the Craney Islanders—who despite several relocations were able to remain within the general vicinity of their old homes, friends, and family in the Hampton Roads area—the fortunes of war more often than not carried thousands of female slaves far from their homes and male kin. Slave women freed during Union raids in Florida, for instance, found themselves evacuated to Hilton Head, South Carolina. "Poor creatures! They are the most wo-be-gone set—no shoes, hats or clothing," one observer wrote.[34] Federal raids into the interior of South Carolina, in turn, sent thousands of contrabands to the coastal town of Georgetown.[35] Each new arrival of contrabands stretched the resources of the army and often created tensions between the new arrivals and the established contrabands.

The women who left Florida for Hilton Head or inland South Carolina for the coast with their Union escorts more and more typified the gendered pattern of slave flight. Especially after 1863, it became less and less likely that fathers, older sons, or husbands would accompany female kin to freedom. More women took the chance on their own, sometimes spurred by encouragement sent back by absent husbands but as often as not with nothing more than the promise of freedom to urge them on.

Burdened with added work and family duties in the absence of their fathers and husbands, confronted by mistresses who believed only they could grieve for dead or absent husbands and sons, faced with the wrath of slaveholders and other whites eager to wage war on slave women whose male kin enlisted in the Union army, thousands of slave women secured their own freedom and that of their children. Yet the notion that female contrabands were more vagabonds than refugees, more nuisances than helpers, more "whining and complaining beggars" than suffering wives, daughters, and mothers, persisted and continued to influence the character and implementation of wartime policies affecting them.[36] As slave women increasingly walked out of slavery either alone or with their children, Union commanders, exhausted by the business of waging war or simply crippled by racism, were ill-disposed to accommodate them.

The flight of slave women prompted a storm of criticism and complaint, particularly when their goal was to be near their soldier husbands. As one Union officer in the Mississippi Valley complained: "the innumerable huts of contrabands in the vicinity of the camps and fortifications are a nuisance besides being an expense to the Government." Particularly galling was how the female contrabands and their children were "obtaining Rations and clothing from the Soldiers, notwithstanding the strict watchfulness of officers and the heavy penalty inflicted upon offenders." Like so many Union officers elsewhere, Colonel Herman Lieb recommended removing the women to a point somewhere outside the main Union lines where they could be made to support themselves.[37] Colonel John Eaton, Jr., a chaplain and General Superintendent of Freedmen for the Department of the Tennessee and State of Arkansas, objected to such "indiscriminate expulsion of the people" and protested that some commanders issued passes to "lewd women and others" to wander about the black regiments' camps while at the same time they "*opposed* efforts to secure the legal marriage of their soldiers."[38] The white com-

Woman with a laundry tub, Hopkinson plantation, Edisto Island, South Carolina. *African-American women experienced cruel treatment, including rape, at the hands of both Federal and Confederate soldiers. During an 1862 visit to Somerset Place on Lake Phelps, North Carolina, the overseer reported, "Capt. W. did his best, I am sure, to prevent any disorder among his men, yet one of them went into our Cook House, & shamefully ravished a bit Lovey, threatening her that She should be shot, if she resisted or made any noise, he also drove away some servants who went to her assistance, by threats." Other women reported beatings and whippings. (Detail of an albumen print, by Henry P. Moore, 1863.)* The New Hampshire Historical Society

mander of a black Missouri regiment issued an edict against marriages between the men in his regiment and the "Common place women of the town."[39]

Northern white perceptions stood in striking contrast to those of black soldiers who defied orders not to feed and clothe their families. Even without blood ties to contraband women, the generosity of black troops stood. After rescuing 450 slaves, the men of the Twenty-fifth United States Colored Infantry Regiment proudly "gave them our tents, and . . . put them up in our old camping place."[40] Slave women, generally unable to write or receive mail from their male kin, often had no choice but to travel to see them when possible. In Alabama, problems arose when a group of wives who had travelled more than one hundred miles from Tennessee to visit their husbands were refused both admission to the camp and visits with their spouses. To prevent their going out of camp to visit the women, husbands were handcuffed. Defending his position, the commander maintained that the policy was the only way to "prevent the camp . . . from becoming a brothel on a gigantic scale." He had previously, he wrote, been forced to deny entry to "large herds of colored prostitutes" who "flocked" to his camp following payday. When his men protested that the women were their wives, not prostitutes, the commander wrote: "it is

Contraband camp, Hilton Head, South Carolina. *Although frequently crowded and dirty, contraband camps offered newly freed African Americans makeshift homes as well as food, fuel, and clothing rations. Women who were not formally employed by the army made a living selling food, cooking for the soldiers, and doing odd jobs. (Albumen print, by Samuel A. Cooley, 1864.)* National Archives

just within the bounds of possibility that some virtuous wives may have been amongst the number so excluded from camp, but I gravely doubt it."[41]

Contraband women at Camp Nelson, Kentucky, faced similar treatment at the hands of Union officials. Fleeing abusive masters and seeking the protection and support of their spouses, hundreds of "women and children of colored soldiers," as a Northern missionary described them, took up residence at the camp, some earning a livelihood cooking and washing for the soldiers. In November 1864 the huts and cabins of the soldiers' families were ordered torn down and the residents driven outside Union lines with no time to prepare. Many had no food, or shoes and clothing to protect them from the cold. All had nowhere to go.[42] The following January, contraband women living in temporary huts near Memphis were similarly humiliated. They have, wrote the commander of the black regiment to which they clung, "no visible means of support, and . . . are, for the most part, idle, lazy vagrants . . . exercising a pernicious influence" over the black soldiers who aid them and "claim them as wives." The commander sought permission to remove the several hundred black women to President's Island in the Mississippi River. Again, the effort backfired. As they had the previous year, the women resisted and were supported by their husbands. They "run . . . for protection" to their husbands, the commander complained, and the "husbands swear their families shall not be moved to the Island and in some instances have come out under arms to prevent it."[43] Despite hostile commanders as well as other obstacles, Union camps and Federal lines remained the most logical target of flight. There, contraband women could take comfort in being free, in having their children, soldier husbands or other male relatives, and friends nearby, in the joy that came when families separated through sale were reunited in contraband camps.

While slave women planned escapes with their children in mind, many were forced to leave them behind. For these women, to the general problems of contraband life—disease, death, poor food and housing—were added the pain and anxiety of not knowing where their children were, if they were still alive, or whether they had been sold or otherwise abused by their masters. When her husband enlisted in the U.S. Army, Frances Johnson's master beat her and attempted, she stated, "to make an indecent exposure of my person before those present." She fled, making her way to her sister's home seven miles away in Lexington, Kentucky, where she found lodging for herself and her three children. But when she returned for her children, she was captured with two of them after finding one too ill to travel. Finally, with her master holding one child hostage and with no hope of getting the others safely away, she fled alone to Camp Nelson.[44]

The Civil War ended with no satisfactory solution to the question of contraband women. To the extent that any consensus emerged, it had mainly to do with how best to put black women back to work. For white women North and South, the expediencies of war had blurred the gendered boundaries of the workplace. But for black women, there was no need to explain the phenomenon of their wartime work. Justifying her presence, along with other female family members, in the field doing men's work, a Northern white woman told Mary Livermore: "we're serving the country just as much here in the harvest-field as our boys are on the battle-field—and that sort o' takes the edge off from this business of doing men's work, you know." Sanctioning this interpretation, Livermore observed that "the women in the harvest-field were invested with a new and heroic interest, and each hard-handed . . . woman was a heroine."[45]

No such noble sentiments influenced white perceptions of black women's work. Discussions of what to do with them rarely went beyond how to employ them in army and contraband camps or on Northern-held plantations. Few whites saw African-American women's work as either heroic or temporary. Rather, the goal was to maintain black women as permanent laborers, self-supporting and self-sufficient if possible, and integral to reestablishing the South's plantation economy. That the reconstruction of the plantation would proceed in part on the backs of black women was taken for granted. During the war, female contrabands were increasingly put to work on abandoned and confiscated farms and plantations operated by the Federal government or by Northern lessees. Some of the enterprises were in safe areas; many were not. Confederate guerrilla raids too frequently resulted in the capture of black women, the separation of children from their families, and death.[46] In Louisiana in 1863, a Confederate force shelled a contraband camp at Goodrich's Landing; homes were burned and twelve hundred contrabands were captured after the attackers surrounded the small force of black troops protecting the settlement. Unknown numbers died. When reinforcements arrived, they were shocked at "the sight of the charred remains of human beings." At Lake St. Joseph, guerrillas carried off more than one hundred contrabands after raping the women and separating them from their children.[47]

Throughout the war, black soldiers

Officers of the Fifth Army Corps, James River.
Aided by a Federal commander, one group of Virginia contrabands took revenge on their old master, William Clopton. "I found half a dozen women among our refugees, whom he had often whipped unmercifully," the officer reported. "I laid him bare and putting the whip into the hands of the Women, three of Whom took turns in settling some old scores on their masters back." (Albumen print, 1863.)
National Archives

Freedman's Village, Virginia, scene. *Former slaves prized literacy and the promise the knowledge bestowed. "All these [contraband] negroes want to learn to read and write," a former army provost marshall testified in 1863. An unknown photographer posed residents of the Freedman's Village community, built on the grounds of Robert E. Lee's Arlington estate, gathered together with their books. (Albumen print, 1864.)*
National Archives

protested policies and actions that denied their families fair treatment and the basic civilities accorded white women and children. They protested policies that removed their families and those that sought to force their wives to work. At Memphis, black troops, supported by their officers, sought the exemption of their wives from plantation labor.[48] In fact, complaints regarding the unfair and abusive treatment of contraband women poured into every department of the army throughout the occupied South. Abusive white soldiers and corrupt quartermasters frequently made life for women within the lines as difficult as possible, and oftentimes orders requiring the maintenance of soldiers' wives were routinely ignored.[49]

Contrasting the wartime experience of Southern African-American men and women, the Northern missionary Elizabeth Botume wrote: "I think the men understood what freedom meant much better than the women did. They comprehended that they had rights, and this alone would make heroes out of chattels. The women sang 'We must fight for liberty': The men had already fought for it."[50] Botume's assessment, though contradicted by the behavior of the black women among whom she lived, has unfortunately been little challenged. But thousands of slave women had challenged just such assumptions by braving the unknown as well as the ire of white

Northerners and Southerners by fleeing slavery at the risk of their lives. Thus had they fought for freedom no less than their male counterparts. By 1864 hundreds of refugee and contraband camps had witnessed the arrival of hundreds of thousands of fugitive slaves, a large proportion of whom were women. Keeping pace with William T. Sherman's army in its march across Georgia, black women suffered like all those who had followed other Union armies. In the train of Sherman's army, one Union officer wrote: "Babies tumbled from the backs of mules to which they had been told to cling, and were drowned in the swamps, while mothers stood by the roadside crying for their lost children." It has been estimated that of the approximately twenty-five thousand blacks who joined Sherman's army, fewer than seven thousand made it to the coast.[51]

The question raised by Butler in 1861 haunted Federal policy until the end of the war. Butler's solution, replicated by Union commanders in other areas, put able-bodied women to work along with men and charged the cost of supporting children and the elderly against their wages. Under the force of military exigencies, the crushing weight of slavery's disintegration, inadequate wages, and the prejudice that cast black women as a special "species of property," the policy withered.

In the end, the slaves' understanding of the conflict had triumphed, and the flight of slave women, no less than that of slave men, helped to force a redefinition of the war's goals to include freedom. Freedom indeed came with the end of the war, but the image of black women as somehow not women lingered and took on new life with the reconstruction of the cotton plantation and of white womanhood in the postwar South. A month after the war, for example, authorities issued orders in the former capital of the defeated Confederacy to round up all unemployed black women. Even into the twentieth century, the idea that black women's participation in the Civil War could be deemed heroic or patriotic was slow to emerge. Susie King Taylor, pleading for justice at the turn of the century, wrote:

> There are many people who do not know what some of the colored women did during the war. There were hundreds of them who assisted the Union soldiers by hiding them and helping them to escape. Many were punished for taking food to the prison stockades . . . although they knew the penalty, should they be caught giving them aid. Others assisted in various ways the Union army. These things should be kept in history before the people.[52]

In the American Civil War, female slaves contested gender and racial boundaries and whenever possible—like their husbands, brothers, fathers, and sons—took advantage of and reshaped policies meant to render them mute, uninterested bystanders. In the end, just as enlistment in the Union army had recast black men as active participants in a new struggle, black women throughout the South by their actions, too, had become their own agents for change.

CHAPTER FOUR

VOICES FROM THE TEMPEST

Southern Women's Wartime Experiences

KYM S. RICE AND EDWARD D. C. CAMPBELL, JR.

***Detail from* The Starving People of New Orleans Fed by the United States Military Authorities.**
(Engraving, Harper's Weekly, *14 June 1862.)*
Eleanor S. Brockenbrough Library, The Museum of the Confederacy

What follows are excerpts drawn from the remarkably wide selection of Southern women's diaries, letters, petitions, and other personal testimony available within the collections of the National Archives and the Library of Congress and especially within the holdings of numerous archives, libraries, historical societies, museums, and other cultural institutions scattered throughout the South. Each of the selections says much about the tasks and circumstances of Southern women, black and white, in the Civil War—and much, too, about the hardships and dangers many of them faced in their day-to-day lives.

Whenever possible, the texts are presented as the women wrote them. In a few instances, however, basic punctuation and paragraph indentations are added to assist the reader. In other instances, ellipses designate those passages where text has been abridged or where the handwriting is unclear or obscured by stains, paper damage, or fading; where necessary, reconstructed words or syllables are noted within brackets. In order to retain as much of each writer's style as possible, the excerpts are otherwise presented as they were written.

"I fear our happy days are all gone"—

Sarah Rousseau Espey, from Cherokee County, Alabama, kept a diary throughout the Civil War. Presented here are twenty-nine entries for the period from 19 March 1861, only three and a half weeks before the firing on Fort Sumter, through 31 December. Even that early in the war, Sarah Espey was already struggling to bring in a crop with fewer men about and considering the grim possibility of slave insurrection. She also found herself quickly at work providing clothing for her own and the army's needs while musing over the Confederacy's ability to withstand the superior resources of "the Abolitionists."[1]

Her comments and trepidations are particularly interesting in light of the debate within her own neighborhood over the issue of secession. While there was never any doubt which course Alabama would take, Cherokee County proved to be less headstrong than many localities. Of the four delegates elected from the county to the state secession convention in December 1860, three were regarded as "cooperationists," with only one as a "straight out," or secessionist. However, the margin of victory in each case was slight, ranging from only fifteen to, at most, forty-five votes.[2] Alabama seceded on 11 January 1861; within a month, on 18 February, Southerners raised the first Confederate flag over the provisional capital, Montgomery. On 13 March, Alabama ratified the Confederate Constitution; the excerpts from Sarah Espey's diary begin six days later.

19 March 1861

Thomas has been to Centre to day, and heard bad news concerning our new republic; that the North is determined to coerse the Leeding states; and that Lincoln has ordered 12 war-vessels to Mobile. The volunteer company of this country is ordered there to assist in repelling them. I feel badly, for when the war commences when is it to end and what dire consequences will not fall on us! I fear our happy days are all gone.

23 March

Only one of C's [her son, Columbus] trunks have arrived at Dublin [Alabama], which was brought home this morning; It contained keep-sakes of the clothing of my Father, Brothers, and also some of my husbands; also, my Father's Family Bible and some other books of his. How melancholy was the sight to me! and how I grieve that they are all gone and left my poor children and myself in the wilderness of this world in which I feel there are no strong friends now. May the great and compassionate Being be with us in our desolation and keep us from all evil.

25 March

Pretty day, C. started to Georgia this morning, our folks [the slaves] commenced planting corn; I still feel that strange depression of spirit, and dread of coming evil for which I cannot account; it seems that something dreadful is before us. commenced fringing a counterpane.

16 April

A stormy day and getting cold, I fear a killing [frost] to night;—Thomas [a son] went to Hale's and learned that the Carolinians have taken Fort Sumpter and that our other volunteer company is ordered to Fort-Pickens; so I suppose the war is now opened; may the Lord be with us in our weakness, and grant that we may conquer the strong. Columbus went to see Virginia. Her husband will have to go; and I doubt not C. will too.

3 May

Still clear and cool with a slight front, Columbus is assisting in planting our last corn; the ground has been too wet to do it sooner. Went to Mr Brewers this evening; great preparations are now making for war, by both South, and North, and both parties seem eager for the contest; May Right prevail over Might.

4 May

Warmer,—putting plaster on her corn; I went with B. to Yellow-creek,—A good many persons there, but no preacher, it is said that he has enlisted and if so, he is to day at Centre [Alabama], as this is drill-day. C. has gone there to day, and will probably learn when the company has to leave. He did not come to night but went to Hale's. The rust has made its appearance on our wheat, and I fear will destroy it. It will be a great misfortune, and I feel badly about it. Should it be common, I know not what is to become of the people as it is the main dependence.—rain to night.

22 May

Still cool but clear,—the wheat has improved much in colour since the rains;—it is common in the country, and the crop will be severely injured. heard today that a negro-insurrection is on foot in the country, and old negro man of Mr Dejernette's being taken up, and pretty strong evidence against him

3 June

Warm day, C. helped out wheat this morning at Mr Rudd's; The wheat crop will be heavy generally. Ours though badly injured will I hope make enough for us. It is now believed generally, that a negro-insurrection is on foot in this vicinity. The confederate-guards are going to look into the matter. . . .

6 June

Very warm day. I spent it at Col. Hale's, C. went with me; I made some purchases, and settled back accounts. I have always detested the credit system, and rarely buy anything without paying for it. Goods of all kinds are now going up; and coffee is worth 25 cts per lb.

11 June

Sultry, we have 13 hands reaping our wheat to day; it is better than we thought it [would] be; though badly injured; they will not finish to day; our rye is also ready for the sickle.

12 June

Still sultry.—they finished our wheat, and cut some of the oats;—Mr Rudd says they have made the greatest waste of the grain he ever saw,—this grieves me very much, for we needed it all; besides I expected them to be faithful. I always try to be so myself.

24 June

Still warm, and so dusty, Mr Finley, who is one of the home-guard, came this morning and set us to work making shirts for the soldiers at Fort Pickens, It seems that the Silver-greys [a name adopted by several Southern military units] are to have a hard time of it, what with supporting the families, and clothing the soldiers too. . . .

1 August

An excessively warm day . . . C. is going round collecting brown-jeans, of which their uniform is to be made

6 August

Still cloudy. C. came home this morning; busy sewing for the soldiers. . . .

13 August

Warm, a fine rain to day . . . busy preparing C. for his start to-morrow; I have sent his provision to Hale's (they go by public conveyance but find themselves) and packed his carpet-bag, it may be for the last time. . . .

14 August

Clear and cooler, we went with Columbus to Dublin, at which place a good many of the volunteers took the boat; a large assemblage of people were there to take leave of them; the scene was most impressive for us for we cannot expect to see them all again.

27 August

Showery. knitting woolen socks for the volunteers; every lady in the state is requested by the governor to knit one pair of socks.

23 September

Warmer, drew in our cloth this morning, this evening O [Olivia, her daughter-in-law] went with me down to the tan-yard, to see about getting our winter shoes made. Mr Mackey agreed to make them. . . . I wanted groceries, but he had none. it seems we must learn to do without such things.

26 September

Cloudy. Thomas went with O. down to Shady-grove church, at which place, the ladies are [meeting], and make the uniform, for Capt. Truitte's company, Only a few met, and concluded to divide the work among them and meet there no more. O. brought two suits home with her; one of them fore the Misses Patterson, a good deal of rain to day.

28 September

Clear and quite cool, Mr Truitte called this morning to see about our work, I got him to order two sacks of salt for me; it is now worth 5 dollars per sacks, and is going up; bacon is worth 25 cts per lb in Rome [Georgia], and every thing else in proportion.

14 October

Pretty day, commenced making dresses of domestic gingham; it is getting quite fashionable, since we receive no goods from the north, people are put on their own resource

***Young girl in Varina, Virginia.** (Albumen print, 1863.)*
The Library of Congress

30 October

Cooler and beautiful; finished yesterday, getting in our corn crop; a bountiful one too, for which we should be thankful. The crop generally is abundant. . . . Leak, a servant, who formerly belonged to my father, and with whom I was brought up, came to visit us; turning colder.

13 November

Warm as summer . . . heard of the removal of our boys from Huntsville to Pensacola,—we were going to start Mr Brewer in a few days with a load of clothing to them and other things. the Abolitionists are invading our sea-ports in large numbers, and I much fear will get the advantage of us, for they have so many ships and we, but few, finished the flannel, and cut a pair of pants for him

16 November

Cooler, T[homas] went to a meeting beyond Centre; O[livia] and M. to a corn husking, at Cousin J's, it was a novel affair,—a lady-corn-husking; the absence of the men in the service accounted for it. . . . We learn that our boys are sent to Mobile, instead of Pensacola.

7 December

Pleasant weather, I am knitting a comfort, for C. . . . there is a call for 60 more companies from this state and it is said that all between the ages of 16 and 60 are subject to military duty; if so, Marcellus is subject and I shall miss him more than any other of my children, and will dislike so much for him to be exposed to the evils of camp life. He and O[livia] went to see Virginia this evening. My birth-day.

12 December

Pretty cold morning, we killed 8 hogs to day which weighed out 1777 lbs.

13 December

Ice this morning, we rendered up our lard; had about 19 gals. also ground 27 lbs of sausage meat.

24 December

Christmas day, and very cold; had our customary egg-nog, this morning. . . . I never knew so still a Christmas, but men are scarcer now.

31 December

salt is now worth 20 dollars per sack in Rome. The last day of the old year; may the close of the incoming year, find us better and our country in peace and happiness.

"Young ladies are not wanted"—

On 23 April 1862, a year into the war, "A Lady of Louisiana" wrote from her home, Oak Grove, to Confederate general P. G. T. Beauregard, encamped at Corinth, Mississippi. Seventeen days earlier, on 6 April, a Confederate army commanded by Albert Sidney Johnston had attacked a Union force under Ulysses S. Grant at Shiloh, Tennessee. Johnston had concentrated his forces near Corinth, and at first managed to surprise the Federal army. But in the initial headlong rush through the Federal lines, Johnston had been mortally wounded. Beauregard, the hero of Fort Sumter the year before, took command. On the next day the Union army, by then reinforced, pushed the Confederates back. It had been a bloody draw, with more than twenty thousand dead and wounded. Neither army was prepared for losses on such a scale; the Confederate force alone lost nearly one of every four men over the two-day battle.[3] Despite that, Beauregard on 28 April politely declined the woman's offer to help nurse "the poor wounded soldiers."[4]

Sir

I hope you will pardon the liberty I take in addressing you as the subject on which I write is interesting to all.

I have long been anxious to offer myself as a nurse for the poor wounded soldiers, but as I am a young lady my friends object, and tell me that I can be of no service, that young ladies are not wanted &c. Now I think differently. I think I could go in company with an elderly lady, and be of great service. My heart is in the work and I do not consider any sacrifices I would be called upon to make for our brave soldiers; my heart bleeds for them, and could I not alleviate their sufferings I would deem myself happy. My country is dearer to me than life itself and they are its defenders. I know General that you are the best judge whether I can be of any assistance, and if your opinion coincides with my own you will confer a great favor by informing me of it through the columns of the "Picayune" I am General

Your's respectfully
A Lady of Louisiana

Dear Young Lady—

I should be most happy to grant the above patriotic request to nurse the gallant defenders of our cause & country, who are sick or wounded, if it were possible but your friends are right when they inform you that this is no place for a Young Lady, even under the care of an Elderly one—moreover our sick & wounded are cared for as well as our circumstances will permit—but the families of many at home require even the necessaries of life to these the sympathetic hearts of the fair daughters of [Louisiana] must devote themselves & the blessings of our sick & wounded will ever accompany them—Respy Yours

G. T. Beauregard

"We do sincerely ask of you arms & ammunition"—

Left alone on farms and plantations, many women feared for their lives if the slaves decided to revolt. On 15 September 1862, Miss Lettie Kennedy—"on behalf of the ladies" of Jasper County, Mississippi—wrote from her home, Twistwood, to the Confederate secretary of war, George Wythe Randolph. Fearing violence, she and her neighbors asked for assistance—or for the means to defend themselves that they might "die with honor & innocence unstained."[5] As early as May 1861 the captain of the county Home Guards had agreed that the threat of rebellion was possible and that the fear was palpable: "Rumours are rife that the negroes of the surrounding neighborhoods are making preparations to raise an insurrection . . . as soon as our Volunteers leave."[6] At the same time Kennedy wrote her letter to the Confederate government, an army officer in Mississippi's Jackson County said much the same thing: warning his superior that there were too few white men left at home to control the slaves and that "pernicious influences have already been manifested upon many of these plantations."[7]

Sir

On the twelfth of this month I sent to you a petition signed by the Ladies of the north east seat of Jasper County Miss—subject of said petition being a detail of six men to Guard the neighborhood from the insurection of the negro population in said Seat. Being troubled, and in haste, I neglected to sign said petition, or date it. The object of this, is to inform you that if the said petition meet with your approbation that you inform the P[rovost] M[arshal] at Twistwood.

If you cannot grant the detail of men we do sincerely ask of you arms & ammunition that we defend our desolate homes and firesides from their demoniac invasion. That we die with honor & innocence unstained—You will very much oblige us if you answer this apeal as soon as praticable.

Your most obet.
Miss Lettie Kennedy—
in behalf of the Ladies. . . .

"I'am afraid abbout to get a breath"—

Writing from her Nelson County, Virginia, home on 22 June 1862, Fannie Christian pleaded with the Confederate secretary of war to grant her husband a discharge from the army. Private James B. Christian had enlisted in Company G of the Nineteenth Virginia Infantry only three and a half months earlier. At first, Fannie Christian had written Governor John Letcher. But he could do nothing to help her. He did, though, recommend that she write the War Office. Mrs. Christian once again composed a lengthy letter detailing her predicament: with only "myself and three Children the oldest not six years old" and with her husband's employer confined to his bed, she struggled to maintain a farm and keep the slaves at work. Could the authorities not see, she wondered, how important overseers such as her husband were to the war effort?[8]

Mrs. Christian may well have known that there was at least a slim chance of success. The Confederate government had, in fact, grappled with the question of overseers that April. In particular instances, overseers of twenty or more slaves might win exemption. The demands of war, however, forced several successive revisions to the policy. In Virginia by the end of 1863, for example, only two hundred overseers were exempt from military service—thus leaving women such as Mrs. Christian still very much alone. Private Christian remained in the service. His company was in the thick of many a fight, including Pickett's Charge at Gettysburg on 3 July 1863. At some point during the Pennsylvania campaign and retreat, wounds or disease felled Mrs. Christian's husband. According to regimental records, Fannie Christian was widowed in July or August that year.[9]

Dear Sir

I take my seat to arsk you to do me one favor and that is to give my husband a discharge from the Army. I think if you knew my situation you would. I will explan it to you now. my husband was doing business for Mr Jordan and also for his three sons which is in the Army and has been every since the war began leaveing both without any one on them white but myself and three Children the oldest not six years old and Mr jordan confined to his bed and has been for some time. he is not able when he is well. he is sixty six years old and you know he is unable to attend to his bisness he has a large crop of wheat on hand now very near ripe and no one to attend to saveing it for him and a large crop of tobacco hanging in the house moulding no one to see to packing it down. im just surrounded with a gang of negroes i'am afraid abbout to get a breath. one of my nabors came in to see me the other day when they went to start home. I walk about two hunard yards with them and when I came back one of the negroes had gone in the house and pull off her shoes and stared up [stairs], what to do I can not say. I could not do nothing but tell her to go out her master was to sick to let him know about it. I have no one to correct them when they do [wrong]. I have neather Mother nor father to see to me on neather side. my husband Mother . . . has but the one son when he was at home he would give directions for her to go by but now she cant do nothing in the way of farming for she has noone to instruct her about it. you know the farming must go on to keep up our Army. Mr jordan told me he thought if I would write to you explain . . . his situation you would give my husband a discharge. he said he knew that his labor was worth more to the Confederacy than where he is. his health is very bad—not able for duty half of his time. he said if you can possible let him come home by the time his wheat get ripe if it is possible for you to discharge him. if you should dout what I say Mr jordan will give you a [certificate] stateing it is so and also Flem & James & Jack Jordan will give you a surstifficate stateing he was ther overseer over a large force the farms about three miles apart and Mr Jorden lives about three from one and about six from the

P. P.

The Battle of Manassas,

BY SUSAN ARCHER TALLEY.

Now proudly lift, oh, sunny South,
Your glad, triumphal strains,
From fair Virginia's verdant hills,
To Texas' sandy plains.
Now glory to the Southern band
That swept away their gathered hosts,
And laid their banner low!
Long wave our Southern Standard
O'er hearts that never yield;
Like those who won the victory
On proud Manassas' field!

The Summer sun rose gloriously
That peaceful Sabbath morn,
O'er wooded hill, and verdant vale,
And fields of waving corn.
No solemn bell was tolling out
A welcome to the day—
But there, upon the tented plain,
Our quiet army lay;
When sudden pealed the bugle's blast,
And rolled the stormy drum,
And swiftly ran from man to man,
"The foe! they come! they come!"

Oh, there were quick and stern commands,
And hurried mounting then!
Up rose our gallant officers,
Upsprang our eager men!
Each heart, alike of young and old,
Beat high with martial zeal,
As we caught upon the distant hills
The gleam of Yankee steel.
And, silently and slowly,
Our serried ranks fell back;
While onward, marching to their doom,
They followed in our track.

At length our destined point is won—
The order we obey,
And silently our ranks defile,
And form in war array.
There stands the hoary headed sire
Beside his stalwart son;
And there the youth, elate as though
The victory were won;
While on each manly visage,
In every earnest eye,
Is writ the stern resolve,
To conquer or to die!

It was a great and glorious sight,
That dazzling Summer day,
As face to face those armies stood
In all their proud array!
There stretched their lines of infantry
In rows of glittering steel,
And thundering o'er the echoing plains
Our fiery troopers wheel;
While on each crowded eminence
We marked with eager eyes,
Defended front, and flank, and rear,
Their boasted batteries.

Now comes a brief, expectant pause—
A hush of solemn awe—
When sudden from their cannon pealed
The thunder notes of war!
We stood as stony statues stand,
And scarcely drew a breath,
While thick amid our columns flew
The messengers of death.
We gripped our sheathen sabres,
We reined our chargers hard—
And looked to where brave Johnston stood,
And gallant Beauregard.

Now quick-defiling, right and left,
Their infantry came on—
When sudden, on our distant flank,
Out pealed the signal gun!
And as from out the brooding cloud
The tempest's wrath is poured,
So 'mid the whirling sulphur clouds,
Our cannon flashed and roared.
Rank after rank is swept away,
Yet still their numbers swell—
A thousand rushed in the breach
Where but an hundred fell.

As pour the angry ocean waves
On Nova Scotia's banks,
So downward rushed that Northern horde
Upon our serried ranks.
As stands against the tempest might,
Gibraltar's living rock,
So stood our gallant Southerners
To meet the mighty shock.
The earth beneath us trembled,
And clouds obscured the sun;
He seemed to pause, and gaze aghast,
As once at Ajalon.

Now fast as falling hail-stones—
Their shot around us pour—
With din of clashing bayonets,
And cannon's thundering roar.
And thrice their bristling ranks advance,
And thrice before us yield,
Till foot to foot, and hand to hand,
We grappled on the field.
They slowly closed around us—
They wrapped us in their coil;
And Southern blood is poured like rain
Upon the Southern soil!

Down came their fierce artillery,
Down came their fiery Zouaves!
While two to three, each Southern arm
A path before him carves.
But hark! the signal of retreat!
And stubbornly and slow
Our gallant remnant backward falls,
Still fighting as they go;
Still fighting—some with mangled hands,
And some with glazing eyes:
Not one of all the dying yields,
Or of the living, flies.

Ho! courage, noble comrades!
Not yet the day is lost;
For see, upon the dusty hills,
Yon downward-rushing host!
Two weary leagues, that Summer day,
To the quickly-timing drum,
Through blinding dust, and burning heat,
Unweariedly they come!
Now, "ELZEY TO THE RESCUE!"
No pause of rest they know,
But charged with levelled bayonets
Upon the shrinking foe!

Again in deadly conflict
Our scattered numbers close;
When, high above the battle's din,
A mighty shout arose!
Now grappled foemen loose their hold,
And gaze with eager eye;
Whose was that signal of defeat?
And whose the victory?
"Hurra! hurra!" that mighty shout
The very skies might stun—
"Charge Cavalry! the day is ours!
Their batteries are won!"

With sabres flashing overhead,
With wildly-flowing rein,
A thousand gallant horsemen
Are thundering o'er the plain.
Woe, woe! unto the Northern hordes
In that terrific hour!
They fly, as flee the autumn leaves
Before the tempest's power.
Their foot are swept before them,
And horse and rider reel,
As right and left in Southern hands,
Flashes the Southern steel.

On, on! ye gallant victors,
And press your charges hard;
For yonder leads our President,
And noble Beauregard!
"Hurra! for gallant Davis!"
The dying strain their eyes,
And feebly join the mighty shout,
That rends the very skies.
"Hurra!" the foe is vanquished!
Their scattered numbers yield;
And proudly floats our Southern flag
Above Manassas' field!

Oh, God! it was an awful sight—
That gory battle-plain,
Where horse and rider mingled lay—
The dying and the slain.
There, foeman, gripped in fierce embrace,
Were lying side by side;
And some had crossed their shattered arms,
And, calmly smiling, died;
And hoary heads, all steeped in gore,
Gasped out their latest breath;
And near, the fair and youthful lay,
Still beautiful in death!

Wail, wail! ye Western matrons—
Weep, maidens of the North!
Who, in the foul oppressor's cause,
Have sent your kindred forth
And weep, ye Southern women!
Your hearts shall vainly yearn,
For the manly form and the youthful brow
That never can return.
Yet mourn ye not disconsolate;
Their names be ever bright,
Who perished in the cause
Of freedom and of right!

Yea, glory to our noble dead
As to our living brave!
And o'er them may our Southern flag
Forever proudly wave.
Long live our gallant Davis!
And honored ever be
Our Johnston and our Jackson,
Our Beauregard and Lee!
And glory to the Lord of Hosts,
Who was our strength and shield,
And crushed the tyrant's boasted might,
On stern Manassas' field.

RICHMOND, *Aug.* 3, 1861.

Wartime poetry.
Through the publication of songs, poems, and editorials that appeared for the most part under their own bylines, women helped establish their wider public presence in the Confederacy. (Broadside, The Battle of Manassas, *by Susan Archer Talley, 1861.)*
Eleanor S. Brockenbrough Library, The Museum of the Confederacy

other. my husbands name is James B Christian belong to the 19 Regment Va Volinters Company G, W Boyd Captain. I am willing to spend half of my time in wating on the sick soldiars I feal it to be my duty to do all I can for our Confredracy as mutch so as any lady in the Confredracy and if please give him a discharge for the sake [of] one feeble woman. if you dont, write to me and let me know your reason for not dischargeing him. my post office is at Dillards station Nelson Co Va let me hear as quick as posble if you please I [k]now it is in your power to say yes or no if you please dont say no. dont think because I write to you I think my husband better than any oneelse. no that is not my thought. it is the situation around me. wrote to the Govener last week he said he was not the one to give the volenters discharg. he thought if I would write to you and explane every thing to you I might stand chance to get him off.

yours truly
Fannie Christian

"Their speedy deliverance from bondages . . . renders them very obstinate to female authority"—

Among the thousands of pleas received by the Confederate War Office in Richmond was one written by Mrs. Mary E. Bullock from Borina, Warren County, Mississippi, on 21 September 1862. As "a lone woman who has the assurance to address you in behalf of her only protector," she like so many other Southern women sought "a favorable consideration . . . for my husbands return home." Although her husband had enlisted "with a heart fired with patriotism," Mary Bullock by late September 1862 was fearful for her safety and hoped, with the better turn in Confederate military fortunes, that her husband might come home to resume his duties as the local postmaster. Otherwise, she was alone with her four-year-old son and several servants increasingly "obstinate to female authority."[10]

Dear Sir

I have the boldness to address you; but the peculiarly trying circumstances by which I am surrounded must excuse me for calling your attention to a matter so insignificant when compared to matters of a great nation struggling for independence. When the stars & bars of our beloved South were almost hurled to the dust by the hirelings of the North, and the hope of separate nationality was almost blasted by our many disasters in the early part of the present year, my husband left home with a heart fired with patriotism and entered the ranks as a private soldier, not with blind enthusiasm as many have done, but from the conscientous conviction of the faithful discharge of christian duty in so doing.

He left me and our little boy (four years old), servants, place &c. in charge of a nephew, who has since he left, arrived at the age of eighteen (18) years, which compels him to now leave me alone on the place at the mercy of the servants. The conscripts and militia laws have almost taken the entire male population from the neighborhood and I find it impossible to get any one to take charge of the place, and plainly see my own inability to perform the duties incumbent on me. I live only twelve (12) miles from the Yazoo river where the gunboats of Yankees have once landed, and destroyed some private property and taken some negroes, which seems to have had the effect of impregnating the minds of the negro population of their speedy deliverance from bondages which renders them very obstinate to female authority. If I understand the last law of Congress relative to the matter, it renders it unlawful for a place worked by slaves to be left with a woman alone on it.

—Mr Bullock is besides a government officer having had charge of the post office at Borina Miss as a deputy for five (5) years and for the last three years, post Master by appointment which you can see by referring to the post office book of appointments. I hope this plain simple statement of facts—together with the brightening aspect of our countrys affairs

will lead you to a favorable consideration of my appeal for my husbands return home, and excuse me for my boldness in addressing you. I would be very thankful for a reply if you will condscend to answer a lone woman who has the assurance to address you in behalf of her only protector. My husbands name is William W. Bullock is in Jackson's command, Longstreets division, Featherstons brigade, and a member of Capt Moores company of Vicksburg Volunteers. It has been more than a month since I last heard from him. If you consider my appeal favorably pleast let him know as his presence at home is greatly needed.

My address is Mrs. Mary E. Bullock, Borina, Warren Co Miss

"I hate all the sights and sounds that reach me"—

Throughout the Civil War, young Laura Lee lived with her aunt by marriage, Mary Greenhow Lee, in the Shenandoah Valley town of Winchester, Virginia. Because it was located at the northern end of the Valley, it was a frequent strategic objective for both armies. The community was also the site of three pitched battles: on 25 May 1862, 14–15 June 1863, and 19 September 1864. The Union army first occupied Winchester in March 1862. One woman listened all afternoon and into the night to the sound of the Confederate evacuation, then fell into "violent fits of weeping" and "thought . . . of what might happen." A young girl, hurrying southward, later recalled that "we imagined [that] even women and girls were unsafe."[11] In the end, though, because so many of them were ardent Confederates, Winchester's women proved particularly troublesome to the Federal troops who regularly occupied the town.

Excerpted from Laura Lee's wartime diary are passages for the period from mid-March, during the first Federal occupation, to late September 1862 and a single passage from the spring of 1863. Lee was twenty-five years old at the time she wrote her journal entries.[12]

As it would be throughout the war, Winchester during this period was occupied, liberated, and reoccupied in a seemingly never-ending cycle. Laura Lee, in exasperation, could only remark that perhaps for the community itself it was not worth the Southern soldiers' effort. She, for one, would "dread their coming back, unless they can stay." That was not to be. Winchester would change hands ninety-seven times during the course of the conflict. Moreover, the community by the second week of September was filled with thousands of Confederate casualties: on 9 September, R. E. Lee designated Winchester as the rendezvous point for men disabled on his march into Maryland; less than two weeks later endless lines of wagons arrived with casualties from the 17 September 1862 battle of Sharpsburg, or Antietam, the single bloodiest day of the Civil War.[13]

11 March 1862

From 12 till half past we were busy putting into a place of safety, silver, papers, swords, flags, military clothese, war letters in short, everything contraband, except the servants, who could not conveniently be stored away. I do not think the yankees with all their cunning, will find our hiding place.

12 March

The Yankees marched in at 8 o'clock with flags flying and bands to every regiment playing 'Yankee Doodle,' 'Hail Columbia,' and 'Dixie.' They marched in perfect silence through the streets entirely deserted by the citizens. . . . It looked like a vast funeral, and it felt even more so. . . . On Main street some Union flags were thrown out, and a few handkerchiefs waved by people who have always been known here as disloyal. . . .

13 March

I hate all the sights and sounds that reach me. I feel as if it would have been preferable to have left everything. . . . We do not go out at all, but a good many persons come in to give in their experience. Some of the ladies talk very freely, and rather abusively, to the officers. I think it a very bad plan. . . .

22 March

[A "loyal" servant leaves.] It was a great shock . . . there are few who can withstand the temptation to be free, they do not look forward to the hardships and difficulties of a free negroes life. . . . It is only young men and boys who they entice off.

25 March

About 20 of our wounded were removed today to private houses, and then the surgeons stopped it, and said no more should go, as their nurses were already complaining of the partiality shown the Confederates, and that if they were not at the hospitals the ladies would stop carrying food and delicacies for them. Was there ever such audacity? These hordes of robbers and murderers who come here to destroy all we hold most dear, complaining of partiality to our own men. . . .

14 April

The streets are filled with runaways [slaves] who have flocked to the town from all around the country and who lounge about in everybodys way. The Yankees walking and talking with them in the most familiar way, even Betty has been infected with uppishness. . . .

20 April

Hundreds of negroes now in town, quartered in empty houses and ware-houses.

1 May

We are also in a state of starvation here. No fresh meat for a fortnight and almost impossible to get eggs and butter, and what we do get at fabulous prices. We can scarcely get wood enough to cook with and the country people as well as the merchants are charging an immense discount on Virginia money.

14 May

No one can leave the town without a pass, and a pass can only be obtained by the person's swearing that he or she is a loyal subject of the U.S. and will continue to remain so. Of course no decent person will take such an oath. . . .

15 May

The Provost yesterday arrested Mrs. John Cambell for speaking her mind too freely but she was so outrageously abusive that he was quick to dismiss the charge in order to get rid of her.

16 May

Our sovereign Master Provost Philleborn says that these secesh women shall not wear calico sunbonnets on the street, as they are intended as a disrespect to the soldiers, neither shall they wear white muslin aprons with bodies!

Calico and gingham sunbonnets are worn by all the ladies here and styled secession bonnets. They were adopted for their cheapness and for their defense against staring soldiers, but they resent it and say they are intended as an insult by intimating that we do not care how we dress while they are here.

19 May

It is evident that they are leaving this place.

24 May

[Upon the Federal soldiers' departure,] the Provost announced that if any woman dared to show exultation, she would be shot.

27 May

Thanks be to the Lord we are free!!!!!!!!!!!

A great many of the colored fugitives have been brought back. The slaves to be returned to their owners, and the free people to be held as prisoners of war. Numbers of the free people fled in terror on Sunday and have lost everything. Many children have died from exposure and from being accidentally killed in the terror and confusion of the flight.

31 May

We can scarcely bear to think that our little gleam of liberty is ended. The soldiers all seemed so sorry & grieved to leave us.

2 June

We do not know who we belong to, but the prospects are that we will know before long that we belong to the Yankees.

7 June

The lower class of people and even the free colored people fare no better than the wealthier class. They seize and carry off provisions from all kinds of people, pretending to believe that they were their stores which they left here, which were taken by the citizens. . . . They say they intend to take the starch out of the 'secesh' here.

9 June

I dread their [the Confederates'] coming back, unless they can stay. Our condition has been so much more terrible since we have been left a second time in the hands of these horrible creatures. They make feeble threats all the time that they will destroy the town, if they are driven out again.

7 July

Our men in the hospitals are getting on well. Many are entirely well now. The Yankees are still bringing immense quantities of stores of every kind here. I am so worn out with the incessant sound of the wagons. Last night we scarcely slept at all, from the noise and the heat, combined.

28 July

We mounted a little wagon, and very coolly tried to get through the pickets with a pass Mr Barwell had for two days before, but they turned us back saying we must get one for the day. We knew there was not much hope of that, but went out to the Camp, and after being kept waiting in the sun for nearly an hour, were informed that no citizen of Winchester could get a pass to go any where. It is said that the soldiers are to be brought into the town to day, to be quartered upon the citizens, and that the oath of allegiance is to be administered, according to Pope's new order, requiring all the men to take it, or be sent beyond the Yankee lines.

31 July

It is getting unbearable here. We have had no marketing for a week.

2 August

Orders from Washington not to exact the oath from the citizens of Winchester at present. We think our government has interfered, as notice was sent to Gen Robertson four days ago, of what was intended. It is wonderful what a spirit is shown by all classes, even down to the lowest and poorest, then men are unanimous in refusing, even though the alternative is banishment. . . . Some marketing has been allowed to come in to town to day. We are having some trees in the garden cut down for firewood, some people have been without wood for days, but all make light of these privations. It is wonderful how much less of everything is necessary for comfort than we used to think.

5 August

14 of Mrs Matt. Page's servants came in to day. The soldiers are trying a new story to induce them to go. They tell them that all the coloured people are sent to Mr Jackson's army. Old Aunt Mary went from Mr Barton's yesterday. Some of the prisoners have left Fort Delaware to be exchanged. I sent the new suit of uniform I have had made for Bob out to Mrs Richard Barton, this morning, as she is going up to Staunton, and will communicate with the boys as soon as they are released.

6 August

They say all persons detected in carrying letters will be regarded as spies and traitors, and treated accordingly, but their threats are

Home of a Unionist planter's family, Lookout Mountain, Tennessee.
(Albumen print, 1863.)
Mathew Brady Collection, National Archives

disregarded, and the market people, who are always escorted around by a guard, constantly have letters about them. This afternoon we were arranging with a woman to bring in letters from Newtown, while her guard stood at a little distance, looking on, but of course not hearing. The country people are eager to do anything which will outwit the Yankees. We heard that there was four hundred letters at Newtown for people here.

27 August

We had a very annonying affair this morning with Emily. She took offense at some imaginary grievance, and took up her baby and walked off, saying that as she could not give us satisfaction, she would go somewhere else. I followed her, and told her to go back home and behave herself, and not act in such a silly way. She came back very readily, and went on with her work. But I should not be surprised at any moment to find she has gone off in earnest. A large party of servants from Clark, determined to return to their Masters, saying that they are starving here, went this morning to try to get through the picketts on their way home but they were ordered back to town.

9 September

Orders have come here to day to prepare for the reception of 3,000 sick and wounded from [Loudoun] and Fairfax. They are coming in all the time, and the wagon trains are all on the way here, and an immense Artillery force. This is to be the point of communication with the Army in Maryland. We can hear no certain accounts from there, but all the reports are that we are prospering.

13 September

I have had a most fatiguing day. The Hospital in the morning, the Factory in the afternoon, and company at night. My darling Bob arrived during my ab[sence]. . . . There is a report to night that the Yankees at the Ferry [Harpers Ferry] have surrendered, but it is not confirmed. . . .

19 September

After many wild and alarming rumours, we have just gathered from Mr Boteler something like the truth. He is just from the army, and says that the battle of Wednesday was really the bloodiest of the whole war. McClellan with 100,000 made the attack. After fighting desparately the whole day, he withdrew a short distance, and sent to ask leave to bury his dead, which was granted him yesterday (Thursday). During the day and last night Gen Lee crossed with his whole force, bringing everything his sick and wounded, stores &c to this side of the Potomac. . . .

20 September

This has been the most awful day we have ever spent. Directly after breakfast the lines of ambulances began to come in, and since then it has been an incessant stream. 3,000 wounded men have been brought in. Every place is crowded with them, and it is perfectly heartrending to know how much suffering and misery there is around us. We have been hard at work getting our cooking room established. . . .

21–23 September

Days of incessant and most painful exertion. Every place is crowded with sick and wounded, and the one idea of all is to try to do something to alleviate the suffering. We are kept constantly excited by reports of advances on the part of the enemy. Already many persons are convinced that we shall be left again in the hands of the Yankees. It will be a time of despair if our army does retire from the border, for it will be a proof of weakness, as it intended by the government to hold it if possible.

24–28 September

A repetition of my last entry. Constantly busy at the cooking room, and hospitals. . . . A great many visitors whenever we are at home, and inceseant bustle and excitement every where. The reports this evening are that the Yankees are crossing the river in large force our Army is falling back, that the sick and wounded who can be moved are ordered back from here, and that we are to be left again in the hands of our enemies. This is an awful life we live here on the border. There are now 7000! [sick] and wounded in and around this place.

7 April 1863

The most shameful outrage which has yet occurred here, was perpetrated to day. Mrs. Logan, her three daughters, and her son were sent off to day, after a few hours notice with out any charge against them except a suspicion of having goods concealed. They were permitted to take their clothing, but nothing else, not even a tea spoon, not enough provisions for them to dine on. Mrs. Milroy [wife of Union brigadier general Robert H. Milroy] and her family arrived before the Logan's left, and she laughed very much, and ran into the house saying she believed she was mistress there now. Even the officers who had been conducting the proceedings were shamed, and begged her to desist for a little while. She took possession of Mrs. Logan's keybasket, and ordered a fire to be kindled in the parlour at once. The house is one of the handsomest in the town, and well supplied, with provisions of every kind, and plenty of groceries, all which Mrs Milroy took into immediate use. They hung a Union flag over the door while the family were going out, and then took it down. Mrs. Logan is always very delicate, and Mary has been very sick for a fortnight with crascpallus, and is not fit to leave the house in such weather as this. It will cause her death. Milroy says this is only the beginning of this sort of thing, and there is no telling where it will end. He says he is going to play the D— with these rebel women. . . .

"A Union woman from beginning to end"—

Not every Southern white woman supported the Confederate cause. Delila Day, for one, insisted six years after the war that she had been "a Union woman from beginning to end." Many wartime Unionists had suffered at the hands of the Confederacy. Undaunted, many had also provided Federal troops with whatever material aid they could muster. But after the war, they discovered that the United States government frequently looked the other way, neither distinguishing them from their former-Confederate neighbors nor paying them the money many thought was their due for their sacrifices.

The Southern Claims Commission, formed by Congress in 1871, finally presented an opportunity for redressing such grievances—provided that individuals petitioning the commission furnished sufficient, detailed, and convincing evidence of their wartime loyalty to the Union and just and specific cause for any repayments. For two years the commission accepted applications. However, because it received so many claims—more than twenty-five thousand—the organization was for several years thereafter involved with investigating requests that totaled approximately $60 million. Some came from individuals who had remained steadfastly loyal to the Union throughout the war; others came from belated Unionists, those who had turned against the defeated South and hoped to benefit from their late change of heart. And some came from those intent only on cheating the government and pocketing a profit. Realizing that there was money to be made from all three groups, independent agents charged five dollars to file the necessary papers. In the end, the commission awarded $4.6 million in claims.[14]

Some, though, chose to make their own argument. In a 21 June 1871 petition submitted from Culpeper County, Virginia, Delila Day succinctly stated her case. Whatever the merits of her particular argument, in the midst of so many claims, her petition was disallowed.[15]

My name is Delila Day. . . . Well Sir, I tell you the truth I was a Union woman from beginning to end. I never wanted the Union destroyed it would never have done for the South to gain the day. I see it more and more

Entered according to the Act of Congress in the year 1863, by FRANK LESLIE, in the Clerk's Office of the District Court for the Southern District of New York.

No 395—VOL. XVI.] NEW YORK, APRIL 25, 1863. [PRICE 8 CENTS.

MOURNERS STREWING FLOWERS ON THE GRAVES OF THE SLAIN.

THE cemeteries of New Orleans are very interesting places, for almost every fine day may be seen parties of mourning relatives and friends decking the grave of some loved one, who, by an early death, has been spared the pangs of regret. Since the present war the number of these melancholy groups has been increased, and our Artist was so impressed with one of the little gatherings that he sketched them. They are evidently the widow and daughters of some officer who had fallen in the war, but whether rebel or loyal he could not learn. Our Artist says: "It was a touching sight to see the stately matron, with her blooming daughters, standing in silence before the grave which hid that once familiar form. Battle is terrible, but I think the calm anguish of the bereaved ones raises in my bosom a deeper sorrow than the immediate presence of the dead or dying."

Scatter fresh roses over the grave,
Where slumber for ever the loved and the brave;
The dew of the morn are the tears of the flowers,
Let us mingle them now o'er the green sod with ours.
Scatter the roses, mingle our tears,
For the heart's sweetest fragrance is the love of past years.

THE OPERATIONS AGAINST CHARLESTON, S. C.

ADVICES were received in the city on the 7th April that the 100th New York Vols., Col. G. B. Danby, landed on Cole's Island, at the foot of James Island, nine miles from Charleston, on the morning of the 28th March. This regiment is part of the 18th Army Corps, and may be considered the pioneer of the grand expedition against Charleston.

A reconnoissance of the island disclosed a rebel battery near the end of the causeway that leads from Cole's to James Island, and also evidences of numerous concealed works on Folly and James Islands, where the rebels had gathered a very large force. As everything portends a struggle of fearful interest, we will briefly describe the topography of the present scene of action.

John's Island is to the south-west of James Island, and may be said to include Seabrook and Cole Islands, which are only separated from it by a sort of marshy bayou, which at times is almost emptied of water.

The correspondent of the New York *World* says: "A landing was on Saturday last effected by the large portions of our land forces in the Department of the South on that part of John's Island called Seabrook Island, or Edisto Island, south of the North Edisto river—these points being about 20 miles south-east of Charleston—and at about the same time on Cole's

Women in Mourning. *Following nineteenth-century mourning practices, elite white women donned heavy black dresses, hats, and veils. After a gathering in rural Botetourt County, Virginia, young Lucy Breckinridge commented, "There were so many Ladies there, all dressed in deep mourning, that we felt as if we were at a convent and formed a sisterhood . . . 14 ladies dressed in black." As for poor women, few could afford a proper mourning costume. (Engraving,* **Cemetery in New Orleans—Widow and Daughter in full mourning, Frank Leslie's Illustrated Newspaper,** *25 April 1863.)* Eleanor S. Brockenbrough Library, The Museum of the Confederacy

every day. The Southern people are so overbearing, it would have been worse than it was before the war. Poor people and darkeys would have no chance at all. . . . I tell you I was glad enough that the war ended as it did altho I had two brothers in the army but they came out alright. one was forced in. they were both away from home. . . . I used to cook and wash and sew for the Union soldiers when camped on and around my place and for the officers too. . . . There was a hospital on my place where the sick were taken care of. . . . I took the union side of course. I was a poor woman and my father was a poor man and a union man too. he was very much opposed to secession. . . . The confederate soldiers used to abuse us and call us yankees and would search my house where any union soldiers had been there to see if they had left us anything. they threatened to kill my father. they called father a damned old yankee. The South Carolina troops threw a rock at him and struck him in the face and injured him so he was not entirely recovered yet from the effects of it. The Union soldiers had built a bush fence around our garden and when they left, the South Carolinians came and destroyed it and abused us all. They told my mother they had not killed her damned old yankee husband and they would do it before they got through.

"They were making things good for me"—

Many of those petitioning the Southern Claims Commission enclosed additional testimony to bolster their case. In some instances, claimants called upon their neighbors, business associates, or family members. And in some circumstances claimants called upon the recollections of their former slaves. Who better to prove to the U.S. government the sincerity of the applicant's support for the Union and for Reconstruction? For the former slave, several factors might have been at work. In some cases, the individual may have been somehow obligated to the claimant for shelter, food, and employment. Sometimes threats were made. Occasionally, an individual simply wanted to help somebody else. And in some cases, confusion played a part. In the intricate twist of government programs, many people, black and white, went through whatever was necessary to participate in any application, in hopes that somehow the effort might bring them one step closer to meeting their own needs. On 26 August 1874, Clarise Randall submitted testimony in support of a claim by her former owner, Marcia Carnahan, of Rapides Parish, Louisiana. Randall's account is perhaps carefully crafted: it is a straightforward one, filled with specific details but without any statement in support of, or against, her former owner's wartime allegiance or position as a slaveholder. Like Delia Day's, Marcia Carnahan's claim, too, was disallowed.[16]

My name is Clarise Randall my age 50 years my residence Natchitoches Parish. I formely lived in Rapides Parish, I was the slave of the claimant and am not now in her service do not live on her land and am not in her debt. I have no interest in this claim if allowed. I was living with claimant at the time of the retreat of the US Army from Mansfield. I was her cook, I was present and actually saw some of the articles taken charged in this claim, I saw them take one Horse Cattle Bacon, corn & fodder sugar, & molasses. All these things were taken in the day time and a portion of the corn and fodder taken after night. I do not know of but I did myself complain to the Officers about the taking of this property and I was told that they could not help it that the Army had to be fed, and that they were making things good for me. I know they were officers from their dress and because they had Swords and had no guns like the other soldiers and were giving orders.

The cattle taken were good for Beef cattle, I saw over a dozen taken, they were butchered there on the place, and fed to the soldiers, I do not know their value, I did not hear any officer tell the men to kill these cattle.

The corn was on the ear, there was about 20 or 30 Bushels, as the Army went up to Mansfield they took a great quantity of corn in the shuck and this was what little there was left, and they took it or they went back, I do not know how much fodder there was and I can't give an idea what it was worth. As to quantity quality and price of other articles taken I do not know I just saw them take it, and carry it away, it was all put in waggons and carried off. The Army remained in the neighborhood 24 hours I know of nothing else.

"No one to control them, but helpless females"—

On 19 October 1864, three women—the "Mothers & wives of the detailed men"—wrote Confederate president Jefferson Davis asking for help. Fifteen days before, their sons and husbands had been detailed to assist the army. Susan M. Robinson, Nancy Powers, and Margaret V. Misszener wanted to know whether the men would soon return, or whether "they will be kept in the Field as regular soldiers." By the fall of 1864, the Southern armies needed every man that could be found, no matter how desperately the new conscripts were needed "back home" to protect both crops and families. In exchange for their menfolk, the three women offered Davis their "able bodied negroes"—laborers they were in any case unable to control.[17] For many Southern women, this fear of their slaves was more than unsettling; it was foreign. As Mary Boykin Chesnut, for example, wrote in her dairy in 1861, "hitherto I have never thought of being afraid of negroes. I had never injured any of them. Why should they want to hurt me?"[18] By October 1864, though, few Southern white women could be so confident. The promise of freedom had changed all that, leaving them feeling vulnerable and often afraid.

Mr Davis,

We, The Mothers & wives of the detailed men, who have been sent to the Field, from This part of the county, within the last Fifteen days, wish to know whether they will be kept in the Field as regular soldiers or sent back home to save the [crops?] & fatten & cure the Meat which they have toiled so hard to raise, and for which They have given their Barels to the Government?

If we may be allowed to give our feeble opinions in a matter of so much importance to our Government—now is the time that they are most needed at home. All of them were just preparing to sow large crops of Wheat, which had to be left to servants who care not whether there is anything made for the Confederacy or not—and who will in all probability, steal more than they will sow; for we being delicate females, cannot stay with them in the Fields and see the Wheat sown as it should be. consequently next Spring you will see that there will be a very short crop carried into Market.

Not only will the Wheat crop necessarily be neglected, but the corn, which is now standing in the Fields, will have to be gathered by the Negroes, who haveing been [worked hard?] all the foraging part of the year by their masters (that they might raise and save enough to supply the demands of the Government), will waste . . . the greater portion of what has been produced during the year. . . . Here are not men enough in this neighborhood to keep the negroes in their proper place before the Detailed men were called out, and now that they have been called out, we are very much afraid from the present prospects . . . all of our means of subsistence will be destroyed by servants who have no one to control them, and who seem to feel they are perfectly free. There are not even old grey-headed men and boys enough in this neighborhood for one to be in each family when there are many servants. . . . there are many servants with no one to control them, but helpless females and small children.

President Davis we have heard that you were a good man and a Christian, and now we appeal to you as the Chief Magistrate of our Country to send us protection in the shape of our Sons & Husbands, and we will send you able bodied negroes. . . .

"They fought like demons"—

In north Georgia throughout the spring and early summer of 1864, Joseph E. Johnston and William T. Sherman feinted and probed, trying to size up one another's strength—and one another's willingness to fight. In the maneuvering, numerous small Georgia hamlets, such as Dallas, became battlegrounds. In

Frances Russell Hill.
(Ambrotype, ca. 1865.)
Eleanor S. Brockenbrough Library, The Museum of the Confederacy

Sewing needles used as barter.
Because wartime prices fluctuated so dramatically, women often bartered for food and other supplies. Sarah Espey, an Alabama widow, noted in her diary, "this morning I also exchanged some hats with a trader for needles." A resident of northeastern Georgia, Katherine Stiles used these needles for currency in the war's final year. (Steel needles, used 1864–1865.)
The Museum of the Confederacy

May alone, Sherman lost nearly ninety-three hundred men, Johnston about eighty-five hundred. On 3 June, Robert Ardry—a Union soldier encamped near Dallas and still "in line of battle"—wrote his father about an engagement on 26 May in which "the enemy viciously charged our works." He and his fellows had "poured a hot fire" into a fierce attack that included at least three or four "rebel women soldiers."[19] No one knows how many Southern women fought alongside Confederate regiments. The difficulty of finding first-person accounts such as Robert Ardry's suggests there were extremely few. Whatever the real numbers, though, Ardry's letter home leaves little doubt as to the fighting capacities, and ferocity, of the women soldiers he faced.

Dear Father;

I take pen in hand to let you know that I am well. We are now encamped near Dallas, Georgia where we found the enemy in force on the 26th inst. The 111th was in the front line of breastworks, and we drew a hot fire from the rebs until about 4 o'clock when the enemy viciously charged our works. We poured a hot fire into their ranks and several times their lines broke, but they rallied again and came on with guns blazing and flags waving. They fought like demons and we cut them down like dogs. Many dead and dying Secesh fell prisoner. I saw 3 or 4 dead rebel women soldiers in the heap of bodies. All had been shot down during the final rebel charge upon our works. One Secesh woman charged to within several rods of our works waving the traitor flag and screaming vulgarities at us. She was shot three times but still on she came. She was finally killed by two shots fired almost simultaneously by our boys.

Another She-Devil shot her way to our breastworks with two large revolvers dealing death to all in her path. She was shot several times with no apparent effect. When she ran out of ammunition, she pulled out the largest pig-sticker I ever seen. It must have been 18 inches in blade. When the Corporal tried to shoot her she kicked him in the face smashing it quite severely. Then she stabbed three boys and was about to decapitate a fourth when the Lieutenant killed her. Without doubt this gal inflicted more damage to our line than any other reb. If Gen. Lee were to field a brigade of such fighters, I think that the Union prospects would be very gloomy indeed for it would be hard to equal their ferocity and pluck.

Our regimental losses were about 6 killed and 10 wounded including Lt. Col. Black who was slightly wounded I believe in the thigh. Please give my best regards to all inquiring friends and love to the family.

"We propose to leave our hearthstones"—

On 2 December 1864, a group of ladies wrote from Harrisonburg, Virginia, to James A. Seddon, the Confederacy's fifth secretary of war. What they proposed was "a full regiment of *Ladies*" for "regular service" in the coming Shenandoah Valley campaign, particularly as they had grown increasingly impatient by the "incompetency of the Confederate Army" to protect them. Eleven Valley women signed the letter. Sixteen additional women "& others [too] numerous to mention" agreed to be listed on the letter jacket. What discussion the request generated is unknown. However, in a notation on the outside of the letter, Seddon made a brief comment: "We are not quite ready to call the Ladies to our help in the Field. The Men of the Country it is hoped will suffice. . . ."[20]

In truth, women had already been serving in the Confederate army, although as individuals rather than as members of distinctly female units. In his 1863 account of his journey across the South, the Englishman Fitzgerald Ross recounted how he "discovered a Confederate captain" among his fellow train passengers. The wife of a major, she "had taken an active part in the war and fairly earned her epaulettes." Ross added that "she was no longer in uniform, having lately retired from the service, was young, good-looking, and lady-like, and told her adventures in a pleasant quiet way." Another Englishman, Lieutenant Colonel Arthur J. L. Fremantle, of the Coldstream Guards, spied a woman soldier on a train between Chattanooga and Atlanta. She had "served as a private soldier" at Perryville and Murfreesboro with a Louisiana regiment and "had been turned out a short time since for her bad and immoral conduct."[21] Moreover, the *Lynchburg Virginian* in early October 1864 reported that "a beautiful, dashing lady, in the uniform of a Captain, passed on the Northern train towards Richmond yesterday afternoon." A veteran, too, she "wore a straw cap, set jauntily on her head, adorned with a heavy black ostrich feather, and her jacket was adorned with two rows of miniature gilt buttons."[22] There are enough other instances to confirm that women soldiers, while extremely rare, were not unknown: two women, for example, were found among the Confederate dead at Gettysburg; a woman served in the Eighteenth North Carolina Infantry, another in the Twenty-sixth North Carolina; and in December 1864 an apparently well-disguised Confederate officer imprisoned at Johnson's Island, Ohio, gave birth to

Family of John Stewart. (Cartes-de-visite, ca. 1865.) Eleanor S. Brockenbrough Library, The Museum of the Confederacy

a son. And at war's end, a women's "home guard" unit supposedly confronted a Wisconsin cavalry regiment.[23]

The undersigned true & loyal citoyennes of the Confederate State propose to organize a volunteer segment for purposes of local defence. In as much as the latest conscription bill takes every lord of creation from sixteen to sixty—we suggest that the right to bear arms in defence of our homes be delegated to certain of the fairer portion of this illstaned Confederacy. With the permission of the War department we will raise a full regiment of Ladies between the ages of 16 and 40—armed & equipped to perform regular service in the Army of the Shenandoah Valley. Our homes have been visited time and again by the vandal foe—many of them . . . subjected to every conceivable outrage & suffering and this we believe is owing to the incompetency of the Confederate Army upon which we depend for defence. [T]herefore . . . we propose to leave our hearthstones to endure any sacrifice—any privation—for the ultimate success of Our Holy Case—If you approve of our design please favor us by sending immediately properly authenticated orders for the carrying out of our wishes. All arrangements as the enlisting of troops, selections of field officers etc. have been effected & we now only wait to the approval of the War department.

We have the honor to be from most respectfully—

Annie Samuels	*Irene Bell*
Eliza Strayer	*Annie R. Wartmann*
Alice M. Wanfield	*Mary C. Kyle*
Kelly M. Liggett	*Kitty K. Surley*
Sallie E. Moore	*Annie Bell Liggette*
Alice M. Moore	

"Untill we meet again"—

On 31 March 1865, less than two weeks before the surrender at Appomattox, Ann Rozier wrote her soldier husband. The extreme difficulties of wartime correspondence are evident in her acknowlegment of his last two letters, "dated February and March." Despite the lengthy periods between letters, and the likelihood that many would never survive the journey from writer to recipient, many Southern women stubbornly clung to the only way they had to impart detailed news of home and family—and to involve the missing husband, or father, or other male relative somehow in what was once a settled day-to-day world. In the case of Ann Rozier, she sent news of their new daughter, who "grows very fast," while leaving to him one of the parental joys of a child's arrival: she asked that he "send her a name next time as I have not named her yet."[24]

Dear Husband

I received your very welcome letters dated February and March. I was more than glad to hear from you. we are all as well as common and I hope this may find you well also. you must not expect a long letter as times are very dull and consequently not much news. Pleasants the Sheriff was down at Affs to day but did not get to see him. he also enquired for you. he wants Aff to appear at court the second Monday in April. Wad and John Shumate are still at home but expect to leave for their commands next Monday. Leiddell is at home now come after the men belonging to the 15th Regiment from what I can learn they have nearly all reprorted to him at Carrollton. I hear that John Wootan is dead. I do not know how true it is. Well I reckon you want to know how we are getting on with the crop. we get on slowly the rain has put us back considerbly the fence has been washed down twice it is now put up the second time. I have had a little early corn and Irish Potatoes planted. I would have had a good deal planted this week if it had not been too wet. I will plant next week if it is dry enough. every body is very late about planting it has rained so much. I will now tell you about the stock. the cherry heifer has been missing ever since Tuesday. I have had her looked for but have not found her yet. I will not have milk cows enough to do me. Aff could not get that cow from Leeflores. there was a very large fine cow there with a young calf that he wanted to swap for for you but Frank Hendric had got her and their was no other one their that would suit you. Well I must tell you the news that Patsey and family have moved down to the Oneal Place have been their 3 or 4 weeks I reckon. they will make a fine crop this year. I wish I could write more but have nothing to write about. you must excuse me this time and I will try and do better next time. I have heard no news only that the militia is ordered and I suppose they are to go around conscripting in the place of keeping others out at the business. Well it is getting late and I must close. the children are all tolerably well they send their love to you. the baby is well and grows very fast. send her a name next time as I have not named her yet.

The black people join me in love to you Vera got a letter from Bettie the other day she said Ralyy was a prisoner as they are exchanging prisonors. I hope he will be home soon. they are looking for the . . . boys home soon. Mat Clark is at home now he is not as well as he was when he left home. I believe I have told you all the news. write as soon as you get this as I will be glad to hear from you. I do trust this awful war will soon end and you come home and stay with your family so no more so good bye my dear husband untill we meet again which I hope will not bee long. your affectionate wife. Ann Rozier

"When i come home and look on you[r] hat it felt like my heart would brake"—

Little is known of the letter below except that it was written from a wife to her husband one springtime during the war and that, whatever the writer's difficulty with composition, she imparted an affection of exquisite depth.[25] The letter, however, as with several of the others assembled here, raises the question of educational opportunity for average women in the South. The census of 1850 showed that 8.27 percent of white Southerners, men and women, above the age of twenty were illiterate. While that might at first seem excessively high, in comparison to almost any other part of the world that was a remarkably small proportion in the mid-nineteenth century. In England and Wales, for example, 48.1 percent of the women applying for marriage licences in 1846 were unable to sign their names. Increasingly in the rural South, however, most children by 1860 were exposed to at least a rudimentary education, attending schools (usually funded by subscription) for a five- or six-month term for several years. Moreover, between 1850 and 1860 public school attendance in the South grew by more than 413,000, a 43 percent increase.[26]

Mr J A Walters

This my love is now writing. it is a line some time to me. oh if you was only with me I would ask no mor. Sallie is sleep and I am seating in the door writing all a lone. my Deare you do not know my feeling oh if this War would only end and you could stay with me my life would be a . . . pleasure. I did not know I loved you so well untill you had to leave me but oh I had rather seen all . . . I have left nevr to return then to of parted with you. o oh my Deare that morning when you left . . . it seemed to me that all in the World that I cared for was you. oh when i come home and look on you[r] hat it felt like my heart would brake and eve knight I cry . . . my self to sleep but I lookes to God. I hope he will let us meet again. I am a ever your prayar

To Mr J A Walters my love
Read these lines and think of her who
would give all to see you

Was I possesser of all the Earth
And called the stars my own
Without thy face and thy self
I could be a wretch undon

Let others stretch their armes like seas
And grasp in all the shore
Grant me the visits of thy face
And I will ask no more

I do not be discouraged
For Jesus is your friend
And if you lik for . . .
Knowledge he wont refuse to lend

This blessing is mine through the
faver divin
And oh my Dear the prase shall be thin[e]
In heaven [we'll] meet in harmony sweet
And Glory to God we will then be compleet

my Deare farewell & do you tell
Sence you and I must part
You are gone away but here & say
And still we are joined in heart

Your love to me has been most free
Your conversation sweet
How can I [bear?] to Journey Where
With you I can not meet
Rember me when this you see

I rot this last sunday wile I was so lonely

Plate used in self-defence. *Women tried to protect their personal property from thieves in both armies. Mrs. Emily H. Booton, a resident of Luray, Virginia, reportedly used this plate to fend off a Federal soldier caught stealing some butter. (Stoneware plate, ca. 1862.)* The Museum of the Confederacy

"I was alone,—left in charge"—

The following five excerpts are from a single chapter of a postwar account by Fannie A. Beers, a hospital matron for most of the war.[27] Born in the North, probably Connecticut, circa 1840, Beers married a Yale-educated southerner in 1850 and soon thereafter moved to New Orleans. There she became a staunch supporter of her adopted region. Caught in the North when the war erupted, she made her way to Virginia. She worked first at a private hospital in Richmond, the Soldiers' Rest, then as a matron in the city's hospital for Alabama soldiers. It was in the summer of 1862 that she aided Dr. William T. McAllister in organizing the Buckner Hospital first at Gainesville, Alabama, then in Georgia: at Ringgold, Newnan, and finally Fort Valley. She later requested an assignment closer to the front and during the winter of 1864–1865 served in a primitive tent hospital at Lauderdale Spring, Mississippi. After the war, she and her husband returned to New Orleans where she became active in veterans' activities and worked as an assistant editor for the *Southern Bivouac*. It was in 1888 that she completed her memoir, *Memories: A Record of Personal Experience and Adventure during Four Years of War.*[28]

Although she lost her Civil War diary and other papers during a Federal raid, Fannie Beers in her postwar memoir was able to recollect many of the specific problems that

A plantation mistress and her slave.
To manage their plantations or farms with any real success, Southern women needed the cooperation of their slaves. On the Fulton County, Georgia, plantation where she lived, Pauline Grice recalled that the war brought her mistress "trouble, trouble and more trouble." One day the mistress called her slaves together, telling them, as Grice paraphrased it, "The war am on us. The soldiers done took the rations. I can't sell the cotton. . . . I can't [help] it 'cause retions am short, and I'll do all I can for you. Will you be patient with me?" Grice remembered that "all us stay there and [help] Missy all us could." (Pencil and china-white sketch, by Alfred R. Waud, undated.)
Historic New Orleans Collection, 1965.64.28

plagued the Confederate medical corps throughout the war. The account presented here includes her description of the Union attack on Newnan, Georgia, and of the stark conditions within her crowded hospital there.

Beers was equally concerned with hospital organization and the medical exigencies of war. Her memoirs, for example, are filled with references to inadequate supplies and the inordinate number of patients with horrific wounds for which the medical staffs could do little. Staffing, though, was for Beers—as it was for so many veterans of the hospital system—an equally constant worry. Early in the war, the Confederate Medical Department assigned a chief surgeon to each general hospital, an additional medical officer or contract physician for every seventy or eighty patients, and various hospital stewards. The male stewards, authorized by the Confederate Congress in May 1861, were to possess a knowledge of pharmacy, serve as custodians of the hospital stores, and be "responsible for the cleanliness of the wards and kitchens, patients and attendants, and all articles in use."

It was not long, though, before the Medical Department realized it needed far more help. Thus, on 27 September 1862, a congressional act ratified what had already evolved: new regulations permitted each general hospital two matrons "to exercise a superintendence over the entire domestic economy of the hospital, to take charge of such delicacies as may be provided for the sick, to apportion them out as required, to see that the food or diet is properly prepared" and to complete "all such other duties as may be necessary." There were also to be two assistant matrons, to oversee the laundry, and two ward matrons (for every one hundred patients), responsible for preparing beds, ensuring food was prepared and divided appropriately, and seeing that medications were administered properly. The same act, however, still detailed soldiers to serve as nurses and ward masters. Reality—particularly in the form of manpower shortages in the army and horribly overcrowded hospitals—forced a reappraisal of women's role as nurses.[29] By 1862, when Fannie Beers joined her first hospital, it was already evident that "all such other duties as may be necessary" allowed great scope to women in caring for the wounded and the dying.

Rumors of the approach of the Federal forces under [Major General Alexander M.] McCook had for days disquieted our minds. The little town of Newnan and immediately surrounding country was already full of refugees. Every day brought more. Besides, the presence of hundreds of sick and wounded . . . rendered the prospect of an advance of the enemy by no means a pleasant one. . . .

One night, however, a regiment of [Brigadier General Philip D.] Rodd[ely's Confederate Cavalry quietly rode in, taking possession of the railroad depot at the foot of the hill, and otherwise mysteriously disposing of themselves in the same neighborhood. The following morning opened bright and lovely, bringing to the anxious watchers of the night before that sense of security which always comes with the light. All business was resumed as usual. I had finished my early rounds, fed my special cases, and was just entering the distributing-room to send breakfast to the wards, when a volley of musketry, quickly followed by another and another, startled the morning air. . . . I ran with the rest. "The Yankees! the Yankees!" was the cry. . . . When the smoke cleared away, our own troops could be seen drawn up on the railroad and on the depot platform. The hill on the opposite side seemed to swarm with Yankees. Evidently they had expected to surprise the town but, finding themselves opposed by a force whose numbers they were unable to estimate, they hastily retreated up the hill. . . .

It was evident that the fight was only delayed. An attack might be expected at any moment. An exodus from the town at once began.

. . . Only those unable to bear arms were left in the wards. Convalescents would have resented and probably disobeyed an order to remain. Not only were they actuated by the brave spirit of Southern soldiers, but they preferred anything to remaining to be captured,—better far death than the horrors of a Northern prison. So all quietly presented themselves, and, with assistant-surgeons, druggists, and hospital attendants, were armed, officered, and marched off. . . .

Meantime, I had visited all the wards, for some of the patients were very near death, and all were in a state of great and injurious excitement. I did not for a moment pretend to withstand their entreaties that I would remain with them, having already decided to do so. . . . So I promised, and quietly passed from ward to ward announcing my determination, trying to speak cheerfully. Excitement, so great that it produced outward calm, enabled me to resist the angry remonstrances of the surgeon and the tearful entreaties of Mrs. McAllister [wife of the chief surgeon], who was nearly beside herself with apprehension. At last everybody was gone; intense quiet succeeded the scene of confusion. I was alone,—left in charge. A crushing sense of responsibility fell upon my heart. The alarm had been first given about eight o'clock in the morning. By three the same afternoon, soldiers, citizens, all had disappeared.

Only a few men who, by reason of wounds too recently healed or from other causes, were unable to march or to fight had been left to act as nurses.

In the "wounded wards," and in tents outside where men having gangrene were isolated, horrible sights awaited me,—sights which I trembled to look upon,—fearful wounds which had, so far, been attended to only by the surgeons.

These wounds were now dry, and the men were groaning with pain. Minute directions having been left with me, I must nerve myself to uncover the dreadful places, wash them, and apply fresh cloths. In the cases of gangrene, poultices of yeast and charcoal, or some other preparation left by the surgeons.

Entering Ward No. 3, where there were many badly-wounded men, I began my work upon a boy of perhaps nineteen years, belonging to a North Carolina regiment, who had one-half of his face shot away.

My readers may imagine the dreadful character of the wounds in this ward, when I relate that a day or two after a terrible battle at the front, when dozens of wounded were brought in, so badly were they mangled and so busy were the surgeons, that I was permitted to dress this boy's face unaided. Then it was bad enough, but neither so unsightly nor so painful as now that inflammation had supervened. The poor boy tried not to flinch. His one bright eye looked gratefully up at me. After I had finished, he wrote upon the paper which was always at his hand. "You didn't hurt me like them doctors. Don't let the Yankees get me, I want to have another chance at them when I get well." Having succeeded so well, I "took heart of grace," and felt little trepidation afterward. But—oh! the horror of it. An Arkansas boy lay gasping out his life, a piece of shell having carried away a large portion of his breast, leaving the lungs exposed to view. No hope, save to alleviate his pain by applying cloths wet with cold water. Another, from Tennessee, had lost a part of his thigh,—and so on. The amputations were my greatest dread, lest I might displace bandages and set an artery bleeding. So I dared not move the cloths, but used an instrument invented by one of our surgeons, as may be imagined, of primitive construction, but which, wetting the tender wounds gradually by a sort of spray, gave great relief.

My own sleeping-room was in a house situated at the foot of the hill. I could have gone there and slept securely, but dared not leave my charges. Sinking upon the rough lounge in my office, intending only to rest, I

Annie McManus.
The high prices charged by speculators angered many women. "For everything that we are compelled to buy from the merchants and speculat[ors] we have to pay as much for it as if we were allowed to sell at our own will," a Georgia woman complained to the state's governor in 1863. "If we are still to be brought down from this time on as we have been since the establishment of the Confederate government to this time, I for one hail the day of its overthrow." (Tintype, ca. 1865.)
Eleanor S. Brockenbrough Library, The Museum of the Confederacy

A bill "To regulate the Pay and Allowances of certain Female Employees of the Government."
Late in the war, the Confederate government granted a much-needed measure of supplementary compensation to female workers. The act entitled specific groups of women—such as those who filled ammunition cartridges, laboring at dangerous tasks at low pay—to extra rations and firewood. (Imprint, Confederate States Senate Bill 155, Richmond, Virginia, 5 January 1865.)
Eleanor S. Brockenbrough Library, The Museum of the Confederacy

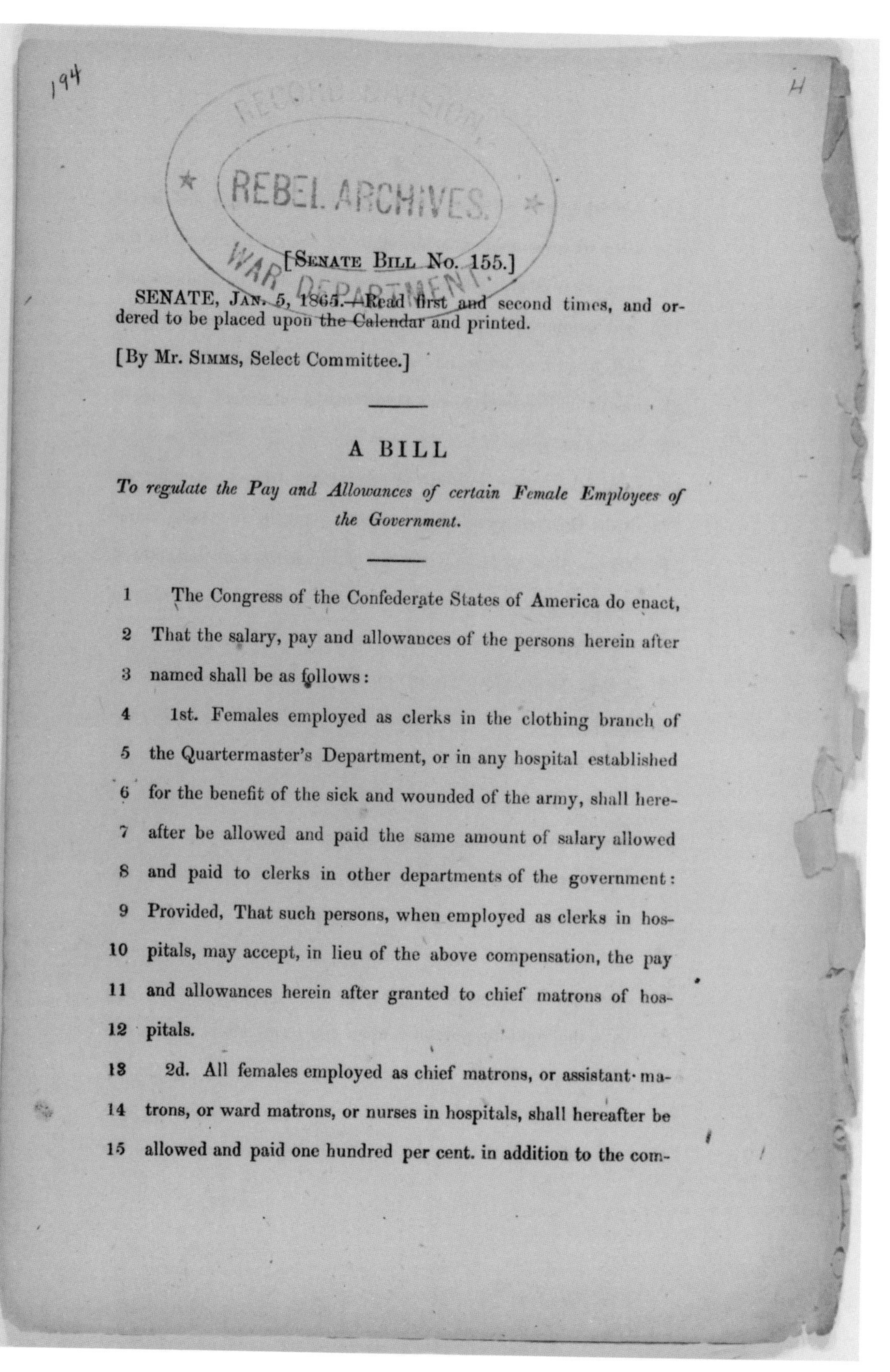
194 4

[SENATE BILL No. 155.]

SENATE, JAN. 5, 1865.—Read first and second times, and ordered to be placed upon the Calendar and printed.

[By Mr. SIMMS, Select Committee.]

A BILL

To regulate the Pay and Allowances of certain Female Employees of the Government.

1 The Congress of the Confederate States of America do enact,
2 That the salary, pay and allowances of the persons herein after
3 named shall be as follows:
4 1st. Females employed as clerks in the clothing branch of
5 the Quartermaster's Department, or in any hospital established
6 for the benefit of the sick and wounded of the army, shall here-
7 after be allowed and paid the same amount of salary allowed
8 and paid to clerks in other departments of the government:
9 Provided, That such persons, when employed as clerks in hos-
10 pitals, may accept, in lieu of the above compensation, the pay
11 and allowances herein after granted to chief matrons of hos-
12 pitals.
13 2d. All females employed as chief matrons, or assistant ma-
14 trons, or ward matrons, or nurses in hospitals, shall hereafter be
15 allowed and paid one hundred per cent. in addition to the com-

fell fast asleep. I was awakened by one of the nurses, who had come to say that I was needed by a patient whom he believed to be dying, and who lay in a ward on the other side of the square.

As we passed out into the street, another beautiful morning was dawning. Upon entering Ward No. 9, we found most of the patients asleep. But in one corner, between two windows which let in the fast-increasing light, lay an elderly man, calmly breathing his life away. The morning breeze stirred the thin gray hair upon his hollow temples, rustling the leaves of the Bible which lay upon his pillow. Stooping over him to feel the fluttering pulse, and to wipe the clammy sweat from brow and hands, I saw that he was indeed dying, a victim of that dreadful scourge of the Confederate armies more surely than many battles,—dysentery,—which, if not cured in the earlier stages, resulted too surely, as now, in consumption of the bowels.

He was a Kentuckian, cut off from home and friends, and dying among strangers. An almost imperceptible glance indicated that he wished me to take up his Bible. The fast-stiffening lips whispered, "Read." I read to him the Fourteenth Chapter of St. John, stopping frequently to note if the faint breathing yet continued. Each time he would move the cold fingers in a way that evidently meant, "go on." After I had finished the reading, he whispered, so faintly that I could just catch the words, "Rock of Ages," and I softly sang the beautiful hymn.

Two years before I could not have done this so calmly. At first every death among my patients seemed to me like a personal bereavement. Trying to read or to sing by the bedsides of the dying, uncontrollable tears and sobs would choke my voice. As I looked my last upon dead faces, I would turn away shuddering and sobbing, for a time unfit for duty. Now, my voice did not once fail or falter. Calmly I watched the dying patient, and saw (as I had seen a hundred times before) the gray shadow of death steal over the shrunken face, to be replaced at the last by a light so beautiful that I could well believe it came shining through "the gates ajar."

"The Rebels said they was going to kill us because we were going to be free"—

Amelia Kimball, a former slave, on 28 June 1873 submitted an application to the Southern Claims Commission from her home in Chatham County, Georgia.[30] Her account of how Confederate soldiers threatened her is certainly not unusual. Nor is her account of how the Union army confiscated animals and foodstuffs. Federal soldiers desperate for food and intent on destroying any aspect of the South's ability to wage war often made few distinctions between white and black property.

Postwar narratives by former slaves are filled with similar accounts of what the victims could only perceive as theft and ill treatment. One black woman noted after Federal soldiers passed through her district that "all us had to thank them for, was a hungry belly, and freedom." With food gone, the slaves then had to "scour de woods for hickory nuts, acorns, cane roots, and artichokes." Soldiers sometimes burned the slaves' houses. They also sometimes physically abused the women. One slave, Bessie Lawson, watched as soldiers whipped her mother. Whatever the dangers, though, the soldiers' arrival often brought the excitement of emancipation. Learning of freedom, one elderly Virginia woman "dropped her hoe an' run all de way to de Thacker's place—seben miles it was—and run to ole Missus an' looker at her real hard. Den she yelled, 'I'se free! Yes, I'se free! Ain't got to work fo' you no mo! You can't put me in yo' pocket now!'"[31]

My name is Amelia Kimball. I was born in Chatham Co. a slave; became free when the Yankee gang came in. I can't tell my age. I think I am over 50. I reside at White Bluff Chatham Co. I resided from the first of April 1861 to the first of June 1865 at White Bluff

Group of women, Hilton Head, South Carolina. *(Detail of an albumen print, by Henry P. Moore, 1863.)*
The New-York Historical Society

Chatham Co Ga. I used to attend market for my master. I used to drive the [horse] & wagon in to the city & attend market here in Savannah. I used sometimes to come in 3 times a week. . . . The rebels caught my fowls & shot my hogs just before they left the city. The Rebels said they was going to kill us because we were going to be free & they wanted to take our things & many a night I have had to hide in the bush for fear of them. . . . I was never molested in any way except they almost starved me by eating up my victuals. . . . I never contributed anything in aid of the United States Government. . . . I cooked & washed & mended for them that is all I did for them. This was after the Army came in. Before this I came in the city & went to the prison where the Union prisoners were & gave them cakes; went on purpose to see them. . . . At the beginning of the war I sympathized with the Union cause. When I heard the war was going on I was sorry for the people injured, but I was glad for the time to come. I continued to feel this way all the time till it came. . . . In conclusion I solemnly declare that from the beginning of hostilities against the United States to the end my feelings were always with that cause, that I never of my own free will did anything to retard that cause and injure its success; & that I was at all times ready & willing to help that cause so far as my power & the circumstances of the case permitted.

I was a slave at the beginning of the war & became free when the Army came here. When

I got my freedom I went to nursing. My husband was of Indian descent & was free all the days of his life. He owned the horses. My husband I think died about a year & a half ago; long since the war. My first master was old Richard H. Williams & my next who was my last master was Benjamin Burroughs. They are both dead. I do not owe either of them or their estates anything. My husband left no children. After the death of my husband this property all belonged to me. My husband bought this property after we were married most of it; he had some before. We were married about 2 years before the war. My husband was a carpenter & he worked & earned it (his property) & I helped him by nursing at the same time I worked in attending market for my master & I was a midwife. I lived at White Bluff when Gen Sherman's Army came here. I never worked in the field in my life. I was a house servant, & worked in the house for my master. After I was married to my 2nd husband I went & lived with him & paid my master wages. I paid him $6.00 a month because I was feeble & sickly. I was not able to make much over that for myself but I helped my husband by keeping house for him & he worked. My husband worked hard but was sickly. We had these two horses a horse & a mare about a Year & a half before the Army came here. My husband first bought the horse & then bought the mare. one of these horses my husband bought at auction in the city & the other of a Mr Wartmare in the country. My husband used to tend the farm & I used to tend the market. He used one on the farm & I used one in going to attend Market. My husband used to have fish & things for other people who wanted hauling done. We raised hogs by buying a pair of pigs, & from these we raised other pigs.

When I came out of the house they were done taken; the horse out of the stable already. My husband was there & asked them what they were going to do. They never said anything. They went right ahead & took the property & never asked of who the property belonged to. My master's house was about 2 miles from me, but he died before the war reached here about a year before the Army come here. . . . These things were taken at my house at White Bluff. My husband rented the land we lived on of Mr. Burrough. There was 10 acres of it. He paid $5.00 an acre for the land. He made a garden of it. It was cleared land. This property was taken when the Union Army came through here about in the Christmas. Can't tell the year. The Union Army Soldiers took this property. There was more than one taking it, there "was too much." They took all of the property in two days. . . . There were officers there when they took the corn. The officers rode back & forth on horse-back & followed the Army wagons & ordered the men to take the things, except the horses. there were no officers there when they were taken. The officers told me to move as quick as I could because they were going to pull the house down to make camps of. The house belonged to my master Mr. Burroughs. . . . They came there soon in the morning & took three horses out of the stable & pitched them in the wagons . . . & drove off with fowls & ducks of mine they had caught. They caught the hogs & what they couldn't catch they shot & they put them into their wagons. . . . I spoke to one of the officers when he came in but he said he couldn't do nothing about it; they would take what they wanted.

"I always prayed for them night & day"—

Jane Holmes, a former slave from Georgia, years later in her petition to the Southern Claims Commission recounted several of her Civil War experiences. From the beginning of the war, "or as soon as I heard of it," she had been "all the time with the Union cause." And "when they called us," she added, "we come."[32] Union soldiers were often impressed that the slaves they encountered in small Southern hamlets, along the roadsides, or on farms and plantations drew upon a remarkably efficient system of communication. For example, sometimes when Federal soldiers encountered African Americans at some back-country crossroad, the slaves appeared to be patiently waiting, having chosen a specific spot ahead of the line of march from a variety of clandestine reports. During Sherman's March to the Sea, one soldier recounted how a young black woman "knew about Burnside, McClellan, and Sherman, also the fall the Atlanta, and even the recent unsuccessful rebel attack there." The soldiers were impressed, too, with the considerable risks a slave might take to help them, an act of defiance all the more daring if the Union troops were only passing through. A Federal officer in December 1864 recounted how a young black woman "came to our regiment an hour after dawn" from her plantation "thirty miles back." She then showed the soldiers where her mistress had hidden her horses and mules, "in return, for which, after the column passed," her owner "took half a rail and like to wore the wench out. Broke her arm and brusied her shamefully." It was, though, worth the dangers: an elderly black woman, freed during the same Georgia campaign, thanked the soldiers: "God bless you, yous come at last. We've been waitin' for you all more'n four years."[33]

My name is Jane Holmes. I was born in Liberty Co Ga, a slave; became free when Sherman's Army cam̃e here. I think I am over 60 years old. I reside at Mr. Legers plantation Reiceboro [Riceboro] Liberty Co. I work in the field. I am the claimant in this case. . . . I cooked for the soldiers after they came in here with the Army & did anything else for them that they wanted me to do. . . .

At the beginning of the war rebellion or as soon as I heard of it my feelings were all the time with the Union cause & when I heard the guns I used to go & pray for them & I always prayed for them night & day.

In conclusion I solemnly declare that my feelings were with the cause of the United States & I am friend to the Yankees till I die. When they called us, we come & we said you come & they said, we is come & we couldn't be rejoiced enough we were so glad. I never done anything against the Yankees, we did pray for them that God would help them.

At the beginning of the rebellion I was a slave & became free when the Union Army came through here. I went right to farming as soon as I became free I came out of Savannah in July & went right at farming & been farming ever since. I labored for this property. I worked by tasks. My master gave us tasks & when we done we worked for ourselves. I raised chickens & hogs & got a cow & by raising & increasing I got my horse. For more than 30 years before the army came here I was working & raising in this way. It is more than 30 years since I bought my first mare, I raised 9 horses from her, I sold one to Peter Harden, I sold one to my borther Dembo Bird, & one to Cato Holmes, & the Reebels stole one from me that makes 4 I forgot to tell that when you asked me if the Reebels took any of my property. I sold the rest to other parties. My master would allow me to buy & sell & raise anything except cotton. he wouldn't allow us to raise cotton. Joe Bacon was my master's name. I am not now in his employment—I hoe on Mr Lyons land now, since the Army came through. I mean I work on his land, but I bought one acre of him to build my house on. I do not owe my master anything. No one but my self has an interest in this claim. I am a widow. my husband died. it will be 4 years in September. . . .

They come up . . . right across the field & the first thing they did they took the Buggy out of the shed, & went under the house & caught the ducks, & went in I got a jug of honey & some butter & they put them in the buggy & they took the horse too the first day. They said they was looking out for a boat, & the boat didn't come & they must live till it come in. They fed their horses off the corn & rice the 2nd day & after that they went in & took something till it was all gone.

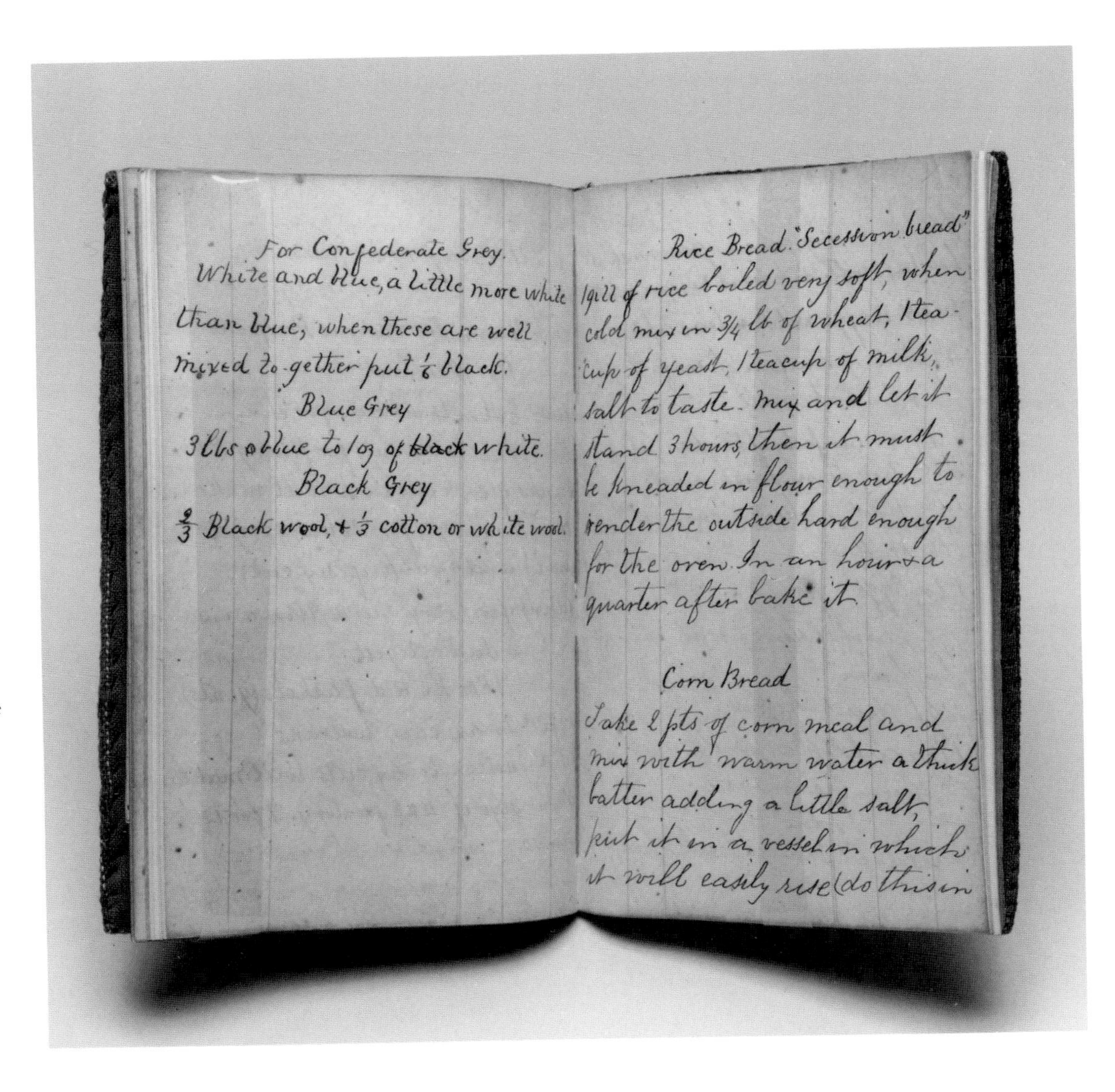

For Confederate Grey.
White and blue, a little more white
than blue, when these are well
mixed to-gether put 1/6 black.
Blue Grey
3 lbs of blue to 1 oz of ~~black~~ white.
Black Grey
2/3 Black wool, + 1/3 cotton or white wool.

Rice Bread. "Secession bread"
1 gill of rice boiled very soft, when
cold mix in 3/4 lb of wheat, 1 teacup of yeast, 1 teacup of milk,
salt to taste. mix and let it
stand 3 hours, then it must
be kneaded in flour enough to
render the outside hard enough
for the oven. In an hour & a
quarter after bake it.

Corn Bread
Take 2 pts of corn meal and
mix with warm water a thick
batter adding a little salt,
put it in a vessel in which
it will easily rise (do this in

Receipt, or recipe, book. *In response to wartime shortages, Southerners tried numerous substitutes for everyday necessities. "After experimenting with parched potatoes, parched pindars, burned meal, roasted acorns," refugee Kate Stone noted in 1863, "all our coffee drinkers decided on okra seed as the best substitute." This recipe book, which has a South Carolina history, includes a recipe for "Secession bread," made largely with rice flour. (Manuscript, by an unknown woman, possibly Martha Gourdin DeSaussure, probably of Charleston, South Carolina, ca. 1861.)* Eleanor S. Brockenbrough Library, The Museum of the Confederacy

"I was . . . employed by General Rosecrans to go into the Enemy's lines"—

Military commanders on both sides employed every means at their disposal to discern enemy troop movements, strength, and especially plans. On many occasions, officers utilized scouts and special patrols; on others, they turned to members of an evolving "secret service" of agents. Commanders also depended on numerous women volunteers. For the South, Rose O'Neal Greenhow, Bettie Duval, and Belle Boyd won considerable fame for their exploits; for the North, Elizabeth Van Lew, Sarah Emma Edmonds, and the double agent Pauline Cushman became equally renowned. Most of the women involved in military espionage, however, became spies by happenstance, usually for a brief time as the armies passed nearby or occupied their communities: military reports, correspondence, and other official records are filled with accounts of women who suddenly appeared at headquarters with vital information.

Occasionally, too, commanders actively recruited women to gather information. Mary Smith was one such individual. A native of Tennessee, she was serving as a laundress for the Eighth Kansas Infantry when she was employed in September 1863 by Union major

The Starving People of New Orleans Fed by the United States Military Authorities.
The war propelled indigent Southern women and children into deeper poverty. Even though each army offered some measure of assistance when possible, the more traditional sources of relief dwindled away. Women scavenged for food in city trash heaps and on abandoned battlefields throughout the countryside. An 1864 petition for aid presented by a group of Alabama citizens to Jefferson Davis acknowledged, "Deaths from Starvation have absolutely occurred." (Engraving, Harper's Weekly, *14 June 1862.)*
Eleanor S. Brockenbrough Library, The Museum of the Confederacy

general William S. Rosecrans, commander of the Army of the Cumberland. The Union army had been badly mauled at Chickamauga, Georgia, on 19–20 September, in large part through Rosecrans's own error. The general had then compounded his failure by allowing the enemy the high ground outside Chattanooga. In short, with his army battered and Chattanooga besieged, he needed whatever information he could find and thus recruited Smith—and probably others—"to go into the Enemy's lines for the purpose of getting information," even, if possible, "to go to Richmond Va." Smith made her way through the lines outside Chattanooga on 29 September. Three weeks later, on 19 October, Rosecrans was relieved of his command.

Mary Smith's account of her adventure is an incredible one. How much of it is true, however, is impossible to tell. On several points, her account seems highly improbable. On other points, though, the details are certainly possible. For example, she reported that while she was in Richmond she came upon several captured Union soldiers. She recognized some of them as members of the Second Tennessee, Fifteenth Wisconsin, and Eighty-first Indiana Regiments. All three units were by November 1862 serving in the Army of the Cumberland, under Rosecrans, and all three—with the Eighth Kansas Regiment she knew so well—had been actively involved in the recent Tennessee campaigns.[34]

She submitted her report in December 1863 to the Department of the Missouri, summarizing her journey from Nashville to Richmond and her return through Knoxville and Murfreesboro, Tennessee.[35] For all the risk, she was unable to provide much of real significance—but she had ably accepted the danger, and survived. As fate would have it, General Rosecrans assumed command of the Department of the Missouri on 28 January 1864. One hopes he had the opportunity to read her report.

I am a native of Tenn Resided in Nashville. When the 8th Kansas came to Nashville I having a son in the Regiment attached myself to it, acted in the capacity of Washerwoman just after the battle of Chickamauga. I was . . . employed by General Rosecrans to go into the Enemy's lines for the purpose of getting information With instructions to go to Richmond Va if possible.

I left Chattanooga about the 29th of Sept in the morning, went to their Pickets opposite of Fort Wood. I was there arrested and taken directly to Genl [Braxton Bragg's] Hd qtrs. I was there asked where I lived. I told him in Huntsville Ala and that I had a Son who was under age and I was in search of him. I told him that I had not been in the Yankee Army, that I had come from Bridgeport, and had not been in the Federal Camps. I then asked for a pass to go through the Army to find my Son and recd a pass to Richmond and any place in the south. I went under the name of Susanah Johnson. I was treated with great kindness and had full permission to visit all the Camps. I staid there one day and went to the Headquarters of Genl Longstreet who gave me all the assistance and information he could. I then walked to Graysville and there got transportation from Genl [John C.] Breckinridge to go to Richmond. reached Richmond on the 3d day of October at daylight. went from the Depot to the Camps of the Army, showed my pass to a Captain who went around with me to look for my Son. Could not find him and the Captain suggested that he might be in the Prison. Went to the Prison where the Federal Soldiers were confined. I recognized Col McLean of the 2nd Tennessee Union Army and several other Officers and Privates of the Federal Army, also 3 Chaplains of Federal Army. One of the 81st Ind and one of the 15th Wisconsin, the other I did not know. Col McLean came towards me to shake hands but I made a sign and he went back. Several Officers and Men nodded to me, and then got together and commenced talking occasionally looking towards me which excited the suspicion of the Officer, we then started

Georgia Bryan Conrad. *In occupied areas of the South, the Federal army prohibited women from wearing miniature Confederate flags on their clothing as a public gesture of defiance. Some women put on black mourning bands in protest. In New Orleans, young Clara Solomon noted—with disapproval—that "some so excited my displeasure by wearing upon their shoulders black crepe bows. How silly! All know that our hearts are in mourning, but why make any outward demonstration. . . . Our* cause *is not* dead, *it is only* sick." *(Daguerreotype, ca. 1861–1865.)*
Eleanor S. Brockenbrough Library, The Museum of the Confederacy

out. I had just got to the Battery when I was arrested and sent to the State House. I was then searched by some woman and after being confined three days, I was released and recd a pass for Charleston S.C. Went from there Richmond to the Head Quarters of Genl Lee, talked with his Adjutant Genl and asked him if he could give me any information in regard to my Son, told me he could not and advised me to go back home, and said if he was found he would be sent to me. I then went back towards Richmond. bought a horse of a [soldier] and started towards Knoxville Tenn . . . got within 25 miles of Knoxville when I ran into a force of Rebel Cavalry, who took my Horse and ordered me to go back. I went about 2 miles and turned to the right, laid only two days and two night and then went to a town on Cumberland River where Federal Cavlry stationed. I was then arrested and taken to Genl [Ambrose E. Burnside's] HeadQuarters at Knoxville. I reached his HdQrs two days after my arrest. Genl Burnside sent me from Knoxville to Murfreesboro. I left Knoxville on the 25th of November. I went direct from Knoxville to Cumberland Gap, saw Rebel scouts at two different places on the road. from Cumberland Gap I went to Alexandria, from there to Liberty and then to Murfreesboro. Did not hear anything in regard to any boats on the Tennessee River.

I asked Genl Burnside if he could give me a pass to Chattanooga. said he could not as Longstreet was coming in 15 miles below on the river

I saw Genl Beauregard in Richmond, heard him say to Jeff Davis that if Charleston was burnt it would be impossible for him to hold the place. Davis said he must do it. Beauregard said the Yankees were bound to take Charleston. Davis said they could not take it, if it was properly defended and then said I will send you 60 Siege Guns. Beauregard said that the fortifications were about battered down and that he must have more men if he (Davis) wanted them fixed up. Davis said they could do nothing on them this wet weather. Davis said that Richmond and Atlanta could not be taken. he also said he did not want the North to send anything to their Prisoners, that he could keep them alive on Bread and Meal and that the Prisoners should not have anything that was sent from the North, that he was not in favor of any such compromise in regard to Prisoners. I counted 780 pieces of Artillery during my trip.

Our prisoners at Richmond was ragged barefooted and dirty and looked as if the[y] had little to eat. I saw the Corn bread that they gave the Prisoners. it did not look as though it was fit to eat. I am a good judge of Corn Bread. I cannot recollect the names of the Towns I passed through.

Secession cockades.
The debate over secession awakened many Southern women's interest in politics. A witness to the Florida legislature's four-day debate on secession in January 1861, fifteen-year-old Susan Bradford, noticed that supporters wore arresting political badges called cockades. "In every direction [there] could be seen Palmetto cockades, fastened with a blue ribbon; there were hundreds of them. . . . Judge Gwynn came in and pinned a cockade on Father and one on me. Oh, I was so proud." (Palm and silk cockades, 1861; silk cockade, Baltimore, Maryland, 1861.)
The Museum of the Confederacy

Printed on Satin
and sold
on the streets of
Baltimore, Md.
on the
19th of April, 1861,
by the donor,
E. J. Herbert.
No 14

Unknown Confederate woman. *More than a few Confederate women expressed an ardent desire to step into the male realm of soldiering. Some wore military caps and sashes and carried weapons. "I wish you could see me now with my hair parted on the side with my black velvet zouave on & pistol by my side & riding my fine colt, Beula," one woman wrote an old school friend. Sarah Morgan similarly confided in her diary "how I longed to give my hoops, corsets, and pretty blue organdie in exchange for their boots and breeches!" Lucy Breckinridge added, "I wish the women could fight. . . . I would gladly shoulder my pistol to shoot some Yankees if it were allowable." (Ambrotype, ca. 1861.)* The South Carolina Relic Room and Museum

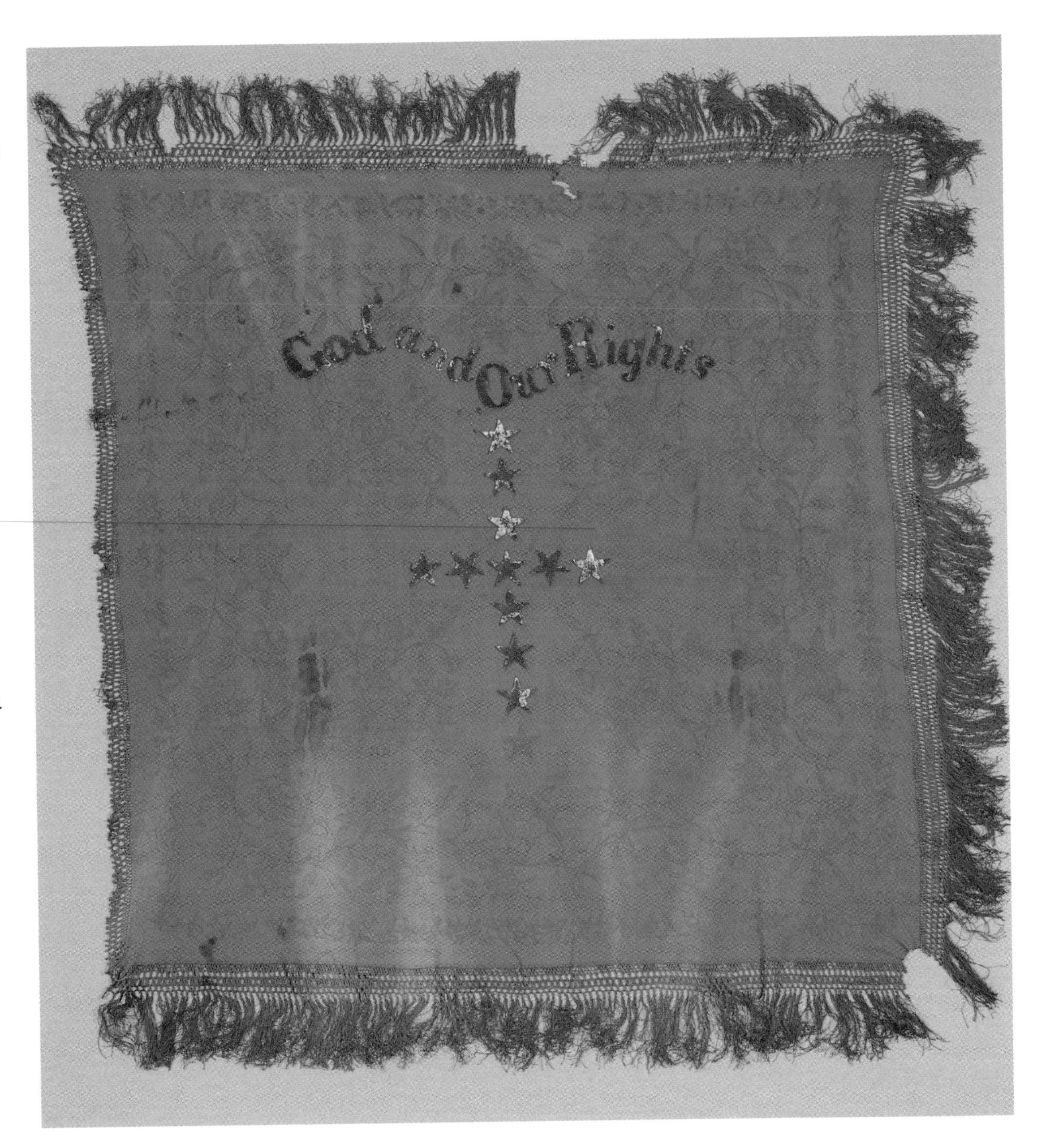

Battle flag, Marion Light Artillery, Florida Battery, made by the Ladies of Orange Lake Soldiers' Association and presented on 8 April 1862 at Camp Langford. *Women spear-headed the movement to create symbols of Confederate identity and unity. With "heart and hand," elite women devoted many hours to sewing intricate battle flags, sometimes incorporating bridal or trousseau costumes into the banner. In the war's early days, an elaborate ceremony—what one historian terms "gendered choreography"—accompanied the presentation of each flag, with the men marching past and the women looking on as cheering spectators. (Silk flag, made from a bridal shawl owned by Mrs. Mary Elizabeth Dickison, 1861.)*
The Museum of the Confederacy

Hair relic made by Jeannetta E. Conrad. *Following directions found in popular women's magazines, Victorian women constructed elaborate creations made out of hair and wire to memorialize their (usually deceased) beloved. Jeannetta Conrad made this "National relic" from the hair of several Confederate generals she contacted through Mrs. Robert E. Lee. (Hair, ink, and satin wreath; Harrisonburg, Virginia, ca. 1862–1863.)* The Museum of the Confederacy

FACING PAGE: ***The Alabama Women's Gunboat Fund quilt.*** *Early in 1862, groups of Alabama women formed gunboat societies similar to those then appearing in other parts of the Confederacy. The* Montgomery Advertiser *appealed to the state's "noble women" to exert an influence beyond making bandages and visiting hospitals. "The women of the south wield an influence in the struggle for her independence, which is impossible to estimate. They should exert it." Reportedly made by Martha Jane Hatter, a widow with two sons in the Confederate army, this quilt was auctioned on four separate occasions to benefit the Alabama Women's Gunboat Fund. As the Union blockade of Southern ports tightened, gunboat societies disbanded and transferred their funds "for the use of sick and wounded." (Silk taffeta quilt, attributed to Martha Jane Hatter, Greensboro, Alabama, before 1862.)* The First White House of the Confederacy, Montgomery, Alabama

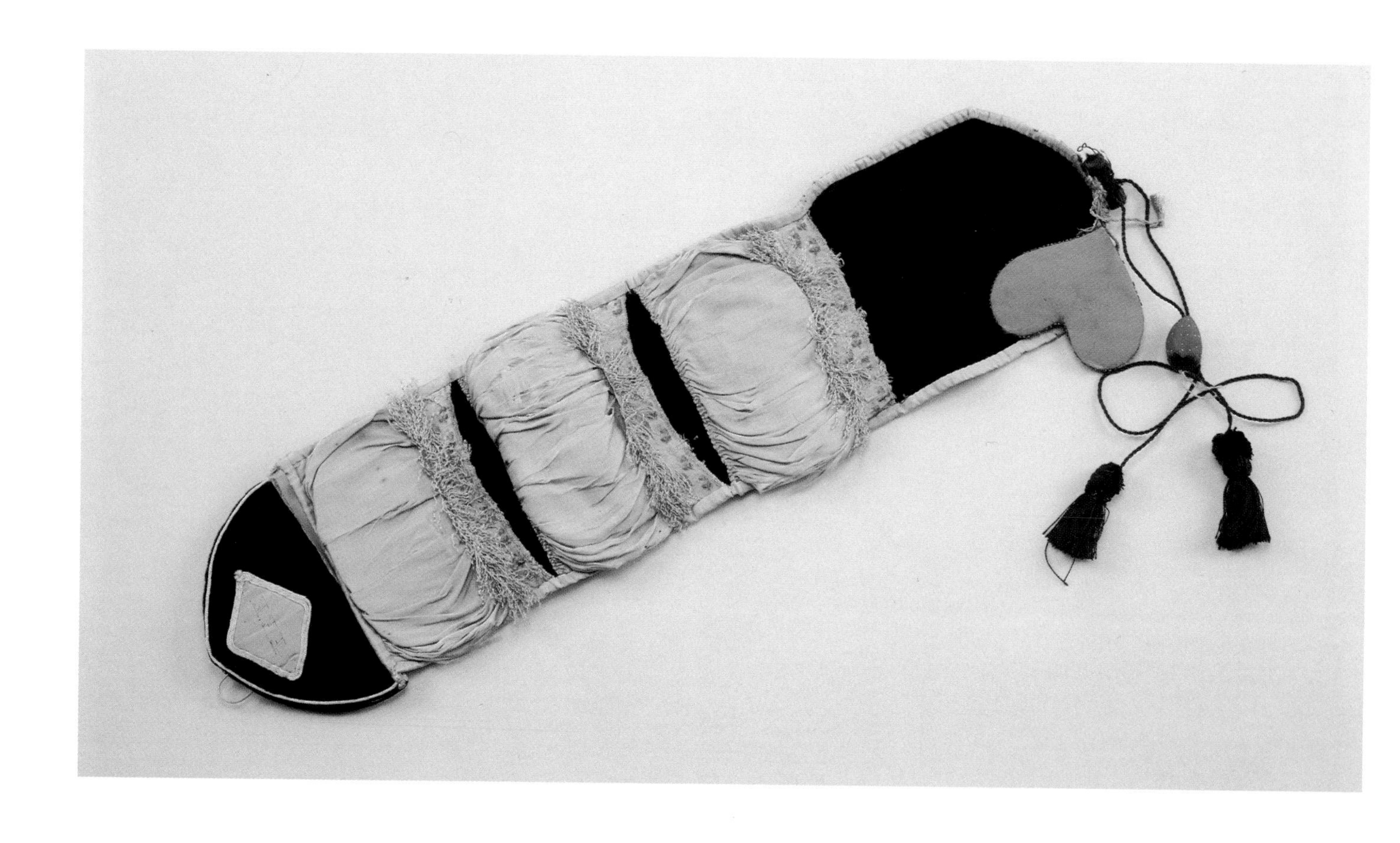

FACING PAGE:
***Housewife.** Both Southern men and women speculated on their new wartime roles. For the first time, soldiers found themselves cleaning, cooking, and sewing. Young Kate Sperry jokingly wondered about a possible permanent effect. "Everything will be new after the war—the 'masculines' will cook, wash and iron and the ladies attend to business—whew! Won't we have fine times—voting, attending to patients—electioneering etc. We'll have a little heaven below—husbands in blue cotton aprons with dishcloths on their arms." Mrs. N. J. Steger made this example of a soldier's sewing kit, called a "housewife," for Lieutenant Edmund Early England. (Silk, silk thread, black velvet, and silk tassle housewife, ca. 1861–1865.)*
The Museum of the Confederacy

***Palmetto hat.** Many women proudly recorded their attempts to stay fashionable, including their efforts at hatmaking. In April 1863, one woman, together with three friends, formed a "regular milliner's shop." "Rosa & aunt Sue being head workers & Lila & I apprentices: she making a corn shuck Garibaldi hat, & I one out of an old dyed cloth talma, ten years old, while aunt Sue was cleaning, whitening and trimming sister Fanny's hat. We certainly strikingly developed 'the native resources, talent, and industry of the South.'" (Palmetto hat, Saint Tammany Parish, Louisiana, ca. 1861–1865.)*
The Museum of the Confederacy

***Everyday dress.** Because of high prices and the scarcity of material, few women could afford imported cloth. Charlestonian Emma Holmes turned to teaching school during the war. In 1864 her nine-month teaching salary was only "enough to buy me a calico, a muslin & a pair of shoes." "Well it is better than nothing," she commented ruefully. (Cotton dress, ca. 1861–1865.)*
The Museum of the Confederacy

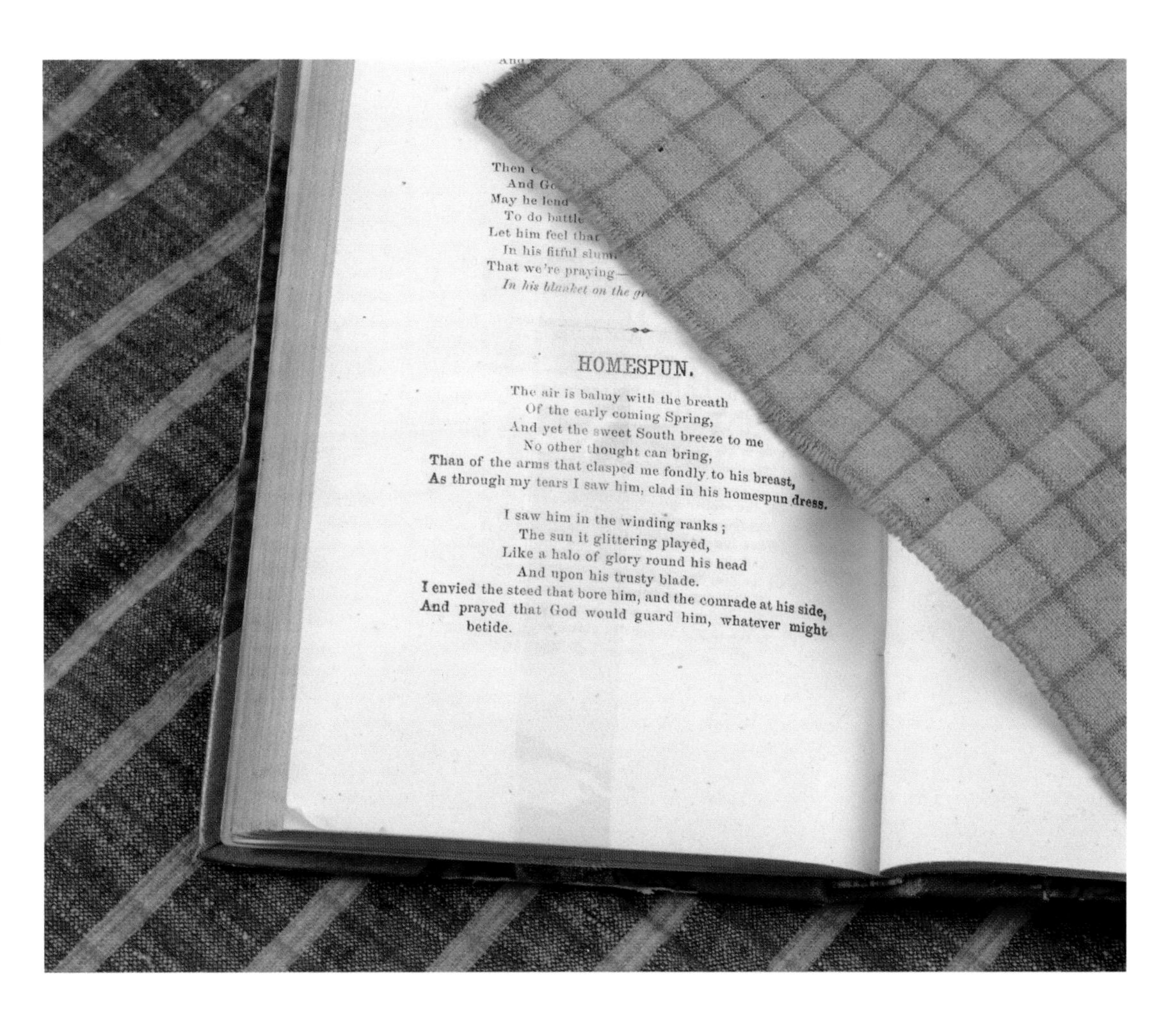

Homespun. *"Nothing but homespun was respectable," Cordelia McDonald explained. For elite women, the wearing of homespun clothes became a Confederate badge of honor. A popular wartime song proclaimed, "My homespun dress is plain, I know/My hat's palmetto, too/But then it shows what Southern girls/For Southern rights will do." In reality, African-American and poor women manufactured the bulk of domestic textiles. (Cotton homespun, by an unidentified African-American woman, South Carolina, ca. 1861–1865.)* The Museum of the Confederacy

FACING PAGE:
Departure from Fredericksburg before the Bombardment. *Women and children stranded in towns near major battles experienced especially harrowing conditions. After the December 1862 battle of Fredericksburg, Jane Howison Beale watched the town's residents attempt to contend with the chaos and confusion all around them. "Crowds of women and children had sought refuge in this sheltered spot and as night grew on they were in great distress, they could not return to the town which was already in possession of the enemy.... Some few had stretched blue yarn counterpanes or pieces of old carpet over sticks, stuck in the ground—and the little ones were huddled together under these tents, the women were weeping the children crying loudly, I saw one walking along with a baby in her arms and another little one not three years old clinging to her dress and crying, 'I want to go home.'" (Oil on canvas, by David English Henderson, 1865.)*
Gettysburg National Historic Park

Lucy Ann. *Dolls offered the perfect means for smuggling, as children—tightly clutching their toys—seldom were searched. The owners of "Lucy Ann" hid quinine in the doll's head cavity. (Papier-mache head; glass, human hair, cotton, and leather doll; cotton, wool, braid, taffeta, coral, felt, and ribbon costume; perhaps European made, ca. 1863.)*
The Museum of the Confederacy

LEFT:
Sylvia Connor.
(Tintype, New Bern, North Carolina, 5 June 1863.)
The Tryon Palace Restoration, New Bern, North Carolina

RIGHT:
Mary Jane Connor.
Well known as a local cook during slavery, Mary Jane Connor operated a restaurant and boarding house in Federal-occupied New Bern. Her sister, Sylvia, previously a domestic slave, secured employment in town as a seamstress. A Union private, Henry Austin Clapp, stationed in New Bern between 1861 and 1863, befriended the women and commissioned photographic portraits of each of them. The sisters posed wearing clothing sent to them by Clapp's mother from Massachusetts. (Tintype, New Bern, North Carolina, 5 June 1863.)
The Tryon Palace Restoration, New Bern, North Carolina

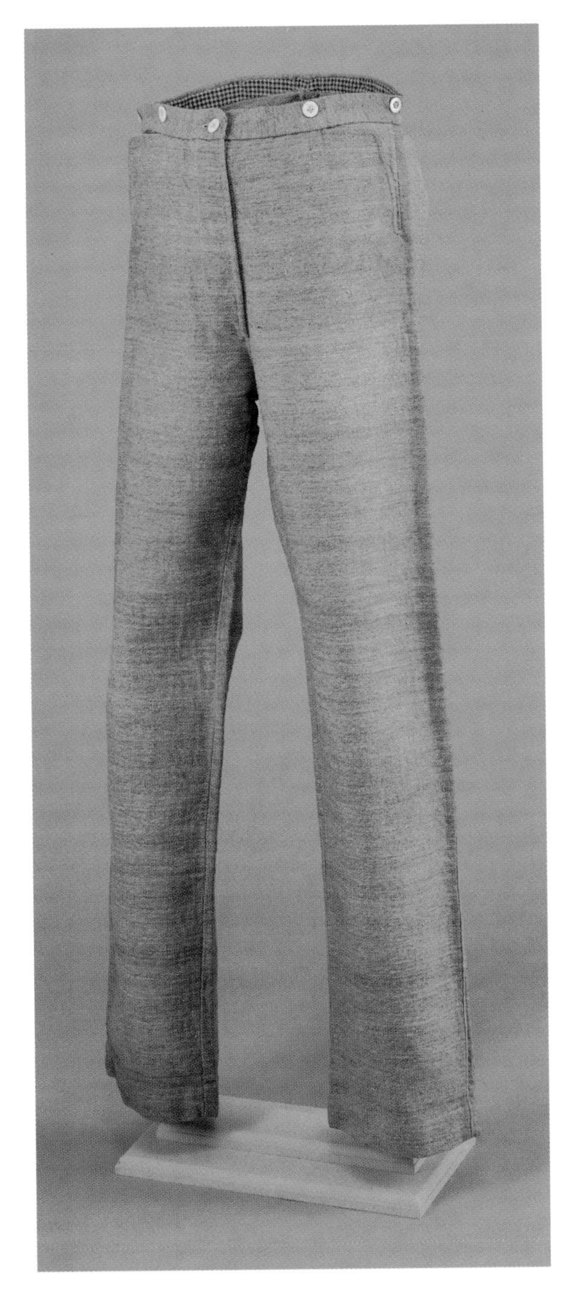

Plantation-made trousers. *Unusual wartime domestic manufactures included a fabric made from cow hair and cotton, which resembled wool. It was satisfactory enough that Mary Collins in 1863 purchased 1,566 pounds of cow hair for the slaves at her Hurry Skurry plantation to weave into cloth. These cow-hair pants were made, probably by slaves, on the plantation of Mrs. Alfred J. Lester near Americus, Georgia. (Cow-hair and cotton trousers, Americus, Georgia, ca. 1861-1865.)*
The Museum of the Confederacy

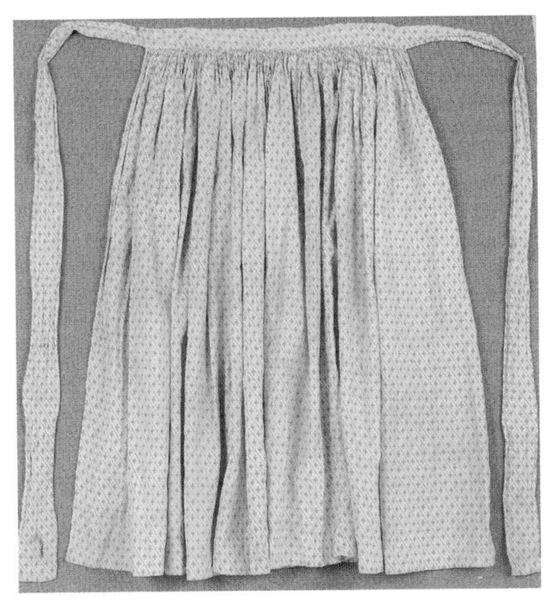

Nurse's apron, Winder Hospital, Richmond, Virginia. *Kate Mason Rowland worked in several Confederate hospitals, including Richmond's Winder Hospital. After hearing many ambulances pass by, Rowland reported for duty one evening in May 1863 carrying a tin bucket and sponge to moisten the soldiers' wounds. "Sounds of misery greeted our ears as we entered—some [men] groaning, others crying like children, & some too weak & suffering to do anything.... Such a sight it was; the men black with dirt & powder—some barefooted; and every form of wound.... Oh it was fearful—I had no words to say to them, only prayers & tears." (Calico apron, ca. 1862-1865.)*
The Museum of the Confederacy

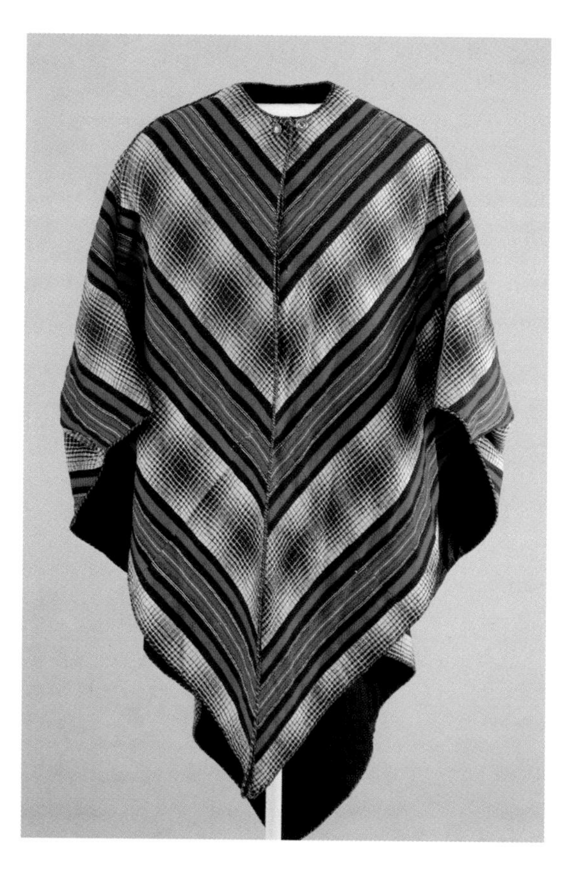

Varina Howell Davis's opera cloak. *Some Southerners distrusted Jefferson Davis's northern-educated wife, Varina. Concerned for his family's safety as a Federal army approached Richmond in May 1862, Davis sent his wife and children to Raleigh, where she was closely scrutinized. "Mrs. Davis is, I hear, a Philadelphia woman! That accounts for her white nurse & her flight from Richmond. I fear she is not worthy of her husband," a North Carolina planter's wife wrote in her diary in 1862, "for I learn that she is neither neat or Ladylike in her dress, travels in old finery with bare arms covered with bracelets. Would that our President, God bless him, had a truehearted Southern woman for a wife." (Plaid flannel, braid, and satin opera clock; Richmond-made?, ca. 1861–1865.)*
The Museum of the Confederacy

Confederate Memorial Bazaar plates. *A large bazaar held in the spring of 1893 by the Confederate Memorial Literary Society raised funds for the restoration of Richmond's former White House of the Confederacy, the site of the proposed "Museum for Confederate Relics." Presented by committee members to Rebecca Alice Starke Hotchkiss, chairwoman for the bazaar, the plates each carried a Confederate state seal. (Porcelain plates with gilding and hand-painted scenes, originally a set of fifteen, of which thirteen remain; France, ca. 1893.)*
The Museum of the Confederacy

LEFT:
***Mourning jewelry.** After her soldier husband's death in 1863, Mary Vaughn, a Mississippi woman, wrote mournfully to her sister, "I don't think I have had one thought apart from Charlie since we married. My every wish has been to try in some small measure to return his devotion and untiring kindness. . . . He must come home yet. It cannot be true he has left me to suffer and endure alone." Among numerous mourning practices, it had long been the custom for widows to wear special jewelry. This necklace contains photographs of Lucy Ellen Nalle Yewell and Lieutenant Joseph Henry Yewell, Company A, First Kentucky Cavalry, who died near Bardstown, Kentucky, in early October 1862. (Gold and hair necklace, ca. 1862.)*
The Museum of the Confederacy

WAR-RELIC

This is the material that Southern Ladies wore,
When the South-land was cursed with battle's deadly roar.
On common cards were made the warps and filling,
The cards can now be bought for something like a shilling.
Then, they cost a hundred dollars perhaps a little more,
And came by wagon-trains from the land of Mexico.
The dyes were crude and dull as you may clearly see,
Which were made from the leaf and bark of the native forest tree.

While our fathers were marching to the gory battle field,
Our mothers were also marching beside the spinning wheel,
And while their hearts were saddened by ever present gloom,
They humbly wove these dresses on the old fashioned loom.

God speed the monument in memory of the slain,
But in doing so, let us not forget mothers' toil and pain;
Think of the sacrifice-the greatness of it all;
Then let us be up and doing-in answer to the call.

***"War-Relic."** The Lost Cause tradition sentimentalized Southern women's wartime activities. Annie Milam's poem urged, "Let us not forget mother's toil and pain/Think of the sacrifice—the greatness of it all/Then let us be up and doing—in answer to the call." (Homespun, cotton, and silk ribbon, ink on paper, made by Annie Milam, ca. 1892.)*
The Museum of the Confederacy

Confederate Monument quilt (detail), made by the ladies of Fayetteville, North Carolina. *The quilt was made in 1865 as a raffle prize to raise funds for a Confederate monument, then presented to Jefferson Davis. (Silk quilt, 1865.)* The Museum of the Confederacy

MOX

CHAPTER FIVE

A MONUMENT TO SOUTHERN WOMANHOOD
The Founding Generation of the Confederate Museum

JOHN M. COSKI AND AMY R. FEELY

The Louisiana table at the Confederate bazaar, Richmond, Virginia, 1903. *Fund-raising bazaars sponsored by Confederate women's organizations blended ideology with exotic decorations and lighthearted entertainment. The "great object" of the 1903 Richmond bazaar, declared the inaugural issue of a specially published newspaper, the* Confederate, *was to fund "the Monument—too long deferred—to the South's [civil] leader, Jefferson Davis, the first and only President of the Confederate States of America, the model gentleman, Christian and patriot." The bazaar included tables, with individual themes and signature souvenirs, representing each of the former Confederate states. The Louisiana table, "Down the Bayou," offered Louisiana-made cups and saucers as keepsakes for the event. "Live alligators are on sale at the Louisiana booth," noted the* Confederate, *"as well as a superb collection of pottery made and sent by the pupils of the Newcomb College in New Orleans." (Photograph, by Huestis P. Cook, Richmond, Virginia, 1903.)*
Eleanor S. Brockenbrough Library, The Museum of the Confederacy

After several days of chill and damp, 22 February—George Washington's birthday—1896 dawned bright and sunny in Richmond, Virginia. It was in happy contrast to a cold and rainy day exactly thirty-four years earlier. On that day in 1862, Jefferson Davis had been formally inaugurated in Richmond's Capitol Square as president of the no-longer-provisional Confederate government. Memories of the late Confederate president were again on everyone's minds: the Richmond house that had served as his official wartime residence was to be dedicated that 1896 day as the new Confederate Museum. At two o'clock in the afternoon, the building opened to thousands of visitors. The museum's officers—all of them women—greeted their guests in what had been the central parlor of the three-story executive mansion. Close by, in the home's former state dining room, ladies served refreshments, including oysters and other delicacies. Like the dining room, each of the rooms had been assigned to one of the southern or border states that had belonged to or supported the Confederacy. Eventually, war "relics" from those states would fill their respective rooms. But on that day, owing to the crush of people, the rooms appeared sparse, decorated only with appropriately colored bunting, festoons, flags, flowers, palm leaves, and occasional portraits on mantels and walls.[1]

The ceremony's keynote address was by former Confederate brigadier general Bradley T. Johnson, of Maryland, who took the opportunity to vindicate the Confederate cause. In high oratorical fever, Johnson recounted the "crimes" perpetrated against the South during and after the war and offered unreconstructed sentiments so strong that reconciliationists in the audience must have squirmed in their seats. The new museum, he remarked, would prove to "all true men and women" that "we were right, immortally right, and that the conqueror was wrong, eternally wrong."[2]

Preceding Johnson's keynote address was a speech by Virginia governor and Confederate veteran Charles T. O'Ferrall, who paid homage to the women who founded and administered the new museum and to their immediate foremothers. "History," O'Ferrall observed, "is replete with bright and beautiful examples of woman's devotion to home and birthland, of her fortitude, trials and sufferings in her country's cause, and the women of the Confederacy added many luminous pages to what had already been most graphically written." "Yes," he added,

> those spartan wives and mothers, with husbands or sons, or both, at the front, directed the farming operations, supporting their families at home and supplying the armies; they sewed, knitted, wove and spun; then in the hospitals they were ministering angels, turning the heated pillow, smoothing the wrinkled cot, cooling the parched lips, stroking the burning brow, staunching

The First Memorial Day, Petersburg, Virginia. *Women led the postwar memorial movement in the South. Their organizations—frequently continuations of wartime groups—maintained cemeteries, created monuments, and established the holiday, Memorial Day. In Petersburg, Virginia, women gathered on 9 June—the day the wartime siege of the city began—to decorate soldiers' graves. (Paper print, ca. 1865.)*
Eleanor S. Brockenbrough Library, The Museum of the Confederacy

> the flowing blood, binding up the gaping wounds, trimming the midnight taper, and sitting in the stillness, only broken by the groans of the sick and wounded, pointing the departing spirit the way to God, closing the sightless eyes and then following the bier to a Hollywood [Richmond's Hollywood Cemetery] or one humbler spot. . . . But amid flame, carnage, death and lamentations, though their land was reddening with blood, and their loved ones were falling like leaves in autumn, they stood like heroines—firm, steadfast and constant.

"And now, why is it we are here?" O'Ferrall asked the people gathered about the rooms of the former Confederate executive mansion.

> The answer is ready upon every tongue, Southern women's love for the memories of a generation ago; Southern women's devotion to the cause which, though enveloped in a cloud of defeat, yet is circled in a blaze of glory, has called us from our firesides and businesses to this spot. The daughters and granddaughters of the women who did so much to make this sunny clime of ours so classic and rich in traditions of that period by dedicating this structure as a depository of Confederate cards and relics.[3]

Neither the ceremony nor the rhetoric were unusual. Both, in fact, were typical of the dedications and memorials that occurred frequently throughout the South at the turn of the century. Equally typical at these events were women—specifically middle- and upper-class white women—playing important roles. Women tended and decorated the soldiers' graves in the cemeteries where the first monuments were placed. Moreover, they were often the most successful fund-raisers for those monuments. As in the 1896 ceremony dedicating the former "Confederate White House" as a new museum, the leadership of women in memorializing the Confederacy was considered proof of their undying devotion to what southerners then called the "Lost Cause." It was on those occasions that organizations such as the Confederate Museum and the United Daughters of the Confederacy developed and disseminated the orthodox southern interpretation of the Civil War and the role of southern women in the conflict.

Organizations of self-styled "Confederate women" warrant and are now receiving attention for their role in shaping the twentieth-century southern perception of the Civil War.[4] The Confederate Museum and its parent organization, the Confederate Memorial Literary Society, offer a particularly revealing case study of such turn-of-the-century southern women's organizations. Studies of Confederate women and of the Confederate memorial period have, however, traditionally ignored the museum.[5] And yet, four years older than the UDC, the Confederate Memorial Literary Society created the most important institutional embodiment of Lost Cause sentiment.

The Confederate Museum, like so many southern memorial organizations of the time, was founded by women who had lived in the Confederate States of America. They were the wives, daughters, and sisters of men who fought for and governed the Confederacy. Their museum gave three-dimensional expression to the collective memory of the war—to the home front as well as the battles. Its founders conceived of the museum as a complement to the written histories, the periodic rituals, and the monuments and markers that seemed to occur everywhere in the South at the turn of the century. Moreover, the institution's founding generation—those women who had personal memories of the Confederacy—lived well into the 1930s, thereby providing a continuity that maintained the museum's original concept long into the

FACING PAGE:
Elizabeth Rutherford Ellis. *A Columbus, Georgia, women's group is generally credited with the establishment of the South's Memorial Day in 1866. Their leader, Elizabeth Rutherford Ellis, is identified on this photograph as "the first to propose & keep Memorial day by placing flowers on soldiers graves April 25th 1866." (Paper print, ca. 1866.)*
Eleanor S. Brockenbrough Library, The Museum of the Confederacy

twentieth century. Their work, therefore, provides a window into how southern women remembered and commemorated the Confederacy, the war, and their own wartime experiences.

The Confederate Museum traces its organizational roots to one of the many women's memorial associations created immediately after the Civil War. After several discussions throughout the winter of 1865–1866, a group of prominent women on 3 May 1866 met at Saint Paul's Episcopal Church and formed the Hollywood Memorial Association of the Ladies of Richmond. According to a resolution adopted that day, the association's purpose was "to collect funds to be applied in Enclosing, arranging, returning & otherwise placing in order the graves of Confederate dead, interred in Hollywood Cemetery, so that the tombs of our fallen Soldiers may be permanently preserved from oblivion & their last resting places saved from the slightest appearances of neglect or want of care." The association met six more times in preparation for its first Memorial Day services at Hollywood Cemetery.[6]

On 31 May, only four weeks after that first formal meeting, an estimated twenty thousand people turned out for the memorial services. Shopkeepers even closed their stores so Richmonders could attend. The association's members gathered at a Main Street church to prepare the flowers and wreaths brought to the city from surrounding counties and towns, and transportation companies offered their omnibuses for carrying the flowers to the cemetery. Although the women had planned and coordinated the event and decorated the graves, it was the veterans of Richmond's various Confederate military units who played the major public role. They marched in a parade from downtown into the cemetery, then visited the graves of their fallen comrades and leaders. Subsequent Memorial Day services were more elaborate and featured formal speeches by politicians and other dignitaries, but the role of the women remained the same. Even though they continued to organize the annual event, the officers of the Hollywood Memorial Association typically waited in carriages a few blocks from the cemetery, then discretely fell in at the rear of the parade as it neared the cemetery gates. While at least the wives of dignitaries joined their husbands on the platform, no woman spoke at the earliest Memorial Day ceremonies.[7]

Although orchestrating the annual ceremony was its primary business, the association was one of the most ambitious in the South. The organization raised money through membership dues, with direct appeals to individuals and groups throughout the South, and by events traditionally associated with women's organizations, such as theatrical tableaux and bazaars. In the spring of 1867, for example, the Hollywood Memorial Association held a fund-raising bazaar, selling and auctioning various crafts and "war relics." The event netted more than $18,000. The association used the funds to improve the grounds of the cemetery's soldiers' section and to erect there one of the earliest Confederate monuments: a ninety-foot-high granite pyramid, dedicated on 9 November 1869. With partial financial assistance from the Virginia General Assembly, the association was also able to exhume the bodies of nearly three thousand Confederate soldiers from the Gettysburg battlefield and move them to Hollywood for reburial. By 1873 the grim project of repatriation was complete, but the debt incurred in coordinating the huge effort hampered the association for decades afterward.[8]

The Hollywood Memorial Association was not unique in the South. It was not even the first women's memorial organization in the city of Richmond. Two weeks before the association's own initial gathering, another meeting had occurred at Saint John's Episcopal Church to arrange for the care of another cluster of Confederate soldiers' graves, this one at

Mrs Elizabeth Rutherford Ellis
"The Soldier's Friend" Columbus
Georgia
The first to propose, & keep Memorial
day by placing flowers on Soldiers graves April 26th
1866.

To the Ladies of the South. *The Lee Memorial Association's William Nelson Pendleton directed his fund-raising appeal to southern women. Their involvement, Pendleton acknowledged, was "the surest and readiest way of" raising the necessary funds. Although Pendleton left the "particular means... to the discretion of the Ladies," he recommended each group hold fund-raising "fairs, suppers, concerts or lectures" on the anniversary of Lee's birth. (Broadside, Lexington, Virginia, November 1872.)* Eleanor S. Brockenbrough Library, The Museum of the Confederacy

Lexington, Virginia, November, 1872.

To the Ladies of the South:

The Lee Memorial Association, incorporated by the Legislature of Virginia, was organized for the purpose of placing a suitable memorial of Gen. R. E. Lee over his remains, which rest beneath the Chapel of Washington and Lee University, at Lexington, Va. At the suggestion of Mrs. Lee, the Association selected as the design of the memorial a sarcophagus with a full sized, recumbent figure of Gen. Lee to be cut from the purest marble. A contract has been made with Mr. Valentine, the distinguished sculptor, for the preparation and erection of this memorial, and the cast of the work in plaster has been already completed. In its very impressive likeness to our beloved Commander the figure is admirable, and the entire work, as a specimen of Art is in every way worthy of its great subject. Means are now needed to enable Valentine to go forward and put his beautiful conception into marble.

The total cost of the work undertaken by the Association will be $20,000. Of this amount $5,000 have been already contributed by those anxious to do honor to the great and good Robert E. Lee. *Fifteen thousand dollars* are yet required to complete the memorial.

At a recent meeting of the survivors of the Army of Northern Virginia, the soldiers who had followed Lee on so many fields, heartily approving the objects of this Association, determined to make an earnest effort to complete without delay the statue now in the hands of Valentine. As the surest and readiest way of effecting this they have appealed to the Ladies of the South to join in celebrating the coming 20th of January, 1873, and in taking such steps on that day as will secure the moderate sum needed to finish the work. The resolutions unanimously adopted by the soldiers of the Army of Northern Virginia, on motion of Lt. Gen. Jubal A. Early, are as follows:

Resolved, By the officers and soldiers of the Army of Northern Virginia, That it is a duty of perpetual obligation to cherish and honor the memory of our great leader, Robert E. Lee.

Resolved, That our sympathies are most heartily with all efforts on the part of others to perpetuate his name and fame, and to do reverence to his exalted character and virtues.

Resolved, That the sarcophagus now in course of preparation by our Virginia artist, Valentine, to be placed over the tomb of Lee, at Lexington, commends itself to special favor as promising, from the beauty of the design and the skill of the sculptor, to be a worthy memorial of our departed chief.

Resolved, That for the purpose of assuring and expediting the completion of this noble work of art, to be placed as a fitting token of a whole people's love and homage above the ashes of their dead hero, we commend to the ladies of the South to hold memorial meetings on the next anniversary of the birth of General R. E. Lee (Monday, 20th January, 1873), and to take such measures as shall to them seem best for collecting money on that day to be especially appropriated to the decoration of his tomb by the erection of the sarcophagus.

We believe the completion of this work to be dear to the whole people of the South; that there is not a man or woman in our land who will not esteem it a privilege to aid in erecting this simple, yet beautiful testimonial of a people's love and gratitude over the grave of our lamented Chief. May we not then confidently appeal to the women of the South who so nobly bore their share in the trials of the war to come to our assistance in this effort to cherish its holy memories, and to honor the dust of one who has conferred such imperishable honor upon our cause and people!

We would suggest that an *organized* effort be made upon the day named, to raise the money needed by private contributions, fairs, suppers, concerts or lectures. The particular means to be resorted to in each locality we desire to leave to the discretion of the Ladies.

Funds should be remitted to C. M. Figgat, Esq., Cashier of the Bank of Lexington, Lexington, Va., who is Treasurer of the Association.

W. N. PENDLETON,
Chairman Ex. Com. Lee Memorial Association.

Oakwood Cemetery on Richmond's north side. Apparently without any centralized coordination, groups met all over the South to honor the Confederate war dead. Before the end of 1866, Memorial Day traditions had been established in eight former Confederate states. "We cannot raise monumental shafts and inscribe thereon their many deeds of heroism, but we can keep alive the memory of the debt we owe them by dedicating, at least one day in each year, to embellishing their humble graves with flowers," wrote the secretary of the Columbus, Georgia, memorial association—the group later recognized as the founder of Confederate Memorial Day. "Let the soldiers' graves, for that day at least," she continued in an open letter in March 1866, "be the Southern Mecca to whose shrine her sorrowing women, like pilgrims, may annually bring their grateful hearts and floral offerings."[9]

The ladies' memorial associations were able to spring up so quickly after 1865 because in both form and substance they were extensions of women's wartime activities. Mourning the dead had long been a traditional province for women, but the scale of death during the Civil War had greatly magnified their role. Organizing for mourning was, in fact, a natural extension of organizing on behalf of the war effort itself. Many of the ladies' memorial associations thus grew directly from the wartime soldiers' aid societies. Associations in Fredericksburg and Winchester, Virginia, for example—both of which challenged Columbus, Georgia, for the honor of founding Confederate Memorial Day—were former Confederate aid societies redefined for new roles.[10]

These and other Confederate memorial activities evolved in the half-century between 1865 and 1915. The immediate postwar associations were products of what has been called the "bereavement" phase of the southern memorial movement. While the associations hoped to vindicate the Confederate cause, their primary emphasis was initially directed to caring for soldiers' graves and erecting monuments in Confederate cemeteries. By the time a younger generation of Richmond women resurrected a by-then-moribund Hollywood Memorial Association in 1886, Confederate memorial activities had entered a second, or "celebration," phase. By that time, memorials to Confederate soldiers more commonly took the form of granite or marble monuments on courthouse lawns, each one dedicated with festive ceremonies celebrating the rightness and righteousness of the Confederate cause, lost though it was. Celebrations of the Confederacy flourished beginning in the mid-1880s, reached their apogee in the first decade of the twentieth century, then waned with the passing of the conflict's veterans in the years after World War I. While they eventually dwindled in frequency, scale, and importance, the celebrations even then never completely disappeared from the social landscape of white southerners. It was during the height of the celebration period that southern memorial groups erected and dedicated the most ambitious and famous Confederate monuments, including those among the national battlefield parks and along Richmond's Monument Avenue.[11]

The expansion of memorial activities in the 1880s brought a new kind of women's memorial organization: the local auxiliary dedicated to supporting veterans' organizations. The groups' purpose was to raise funds and coordinate social activities for the various veterans' "camps," or local chapters, and for the soldiers' homes that began to proliferate in the late 1870s. For example, the ladies' auxiliary for Richmond's prestigious Robert E. Lee Camp, No. 1, United Confederate Veterans, held a bazaar in 1884 to raise the initial funds for the Lee Camp soldiers' home. Different from the older memorial associations, the auxiliaries dedicated themselves not to the memory of the dead, but to the welfare of the "living monuments" among them.[12]

From such auxiliaries grew perhaps the most famous southern women's organization, the United Daughters of the Confederacy. As early as 1890, a ladies' auxiliary for a Missouri soldiers' home had chosen the name "Daughters of the Confederacy" in honor of President Jefferson Davis's youngest child, Varina Anne. Four years earlier, John Gordon, as commander of the United Confederate Veterans, had dubbed the same "Winnie" Davis—born in the White House of the Confederacy during the war—the "Daughter of the Confederacy." By 1894, then, it came as no surprise when a number of ladies' auxiliaries gathered in Nashville, Tennessee, and adopted the same phrase within the name of its new federation: the National Association of the United Daughters of the Confederacy. The UDC's purposes were to be "social, literary, historical, monumental, benevolent and honorable in every degree, without any political signification whatever." More specifically, the UDC was "to instruct and instill into the descendants of the people of the south a proper respect for and pride in the glorious war history, with a veneration and love for the deeds of their forefathers, which have created such a monument of military renown and to perpetuate a truthful record of the noble and chivalric achievements of their ancestors."[13]

The UDC grew rapidly in numbers and in influence. By 1900, the organization included 412 chapters and nearly seventeen thousand members in twenty states and territories. Much of the UDC's work was predictably memorial. Chapters spearheaded fund-raising drives for monuments to Jefferson Davis in Richmond, Virginia, and in Fairview, Kentucky. They gathered funds for a Confederate monument for the Shiloh battlefield, and even the "faithful slave" monument at Harpers Ferry, West Virginia. They also awarded distinguished service medals to Confederate veterans. Tens of thousands of UDC dollars went to endow scholarships for female and male descendants of Confederate veterans at colleges and universities throughout the country. The UDC also initiated an annual cash prize awarded to the author of an essay on a Confederate subject. The contest created a furor in 1909 when the prize was given to a woman whose essay on Robert E. Lee conflicted with the orthodox interpretation of the South's motives in the war.[14]

As early as 1894, within its first year, the United Daughters of the Confederacy had endorsed a pro-southern textbook as a corrective to the allegedly pro-northern texts then dominating the market. Five years later, in 1899, the UDC began the movement to make the term "War between the States" the official name for the 1861-1865 conflict. Kate Mason Rowland, the woman most closely associated with that fight, was also an active member and early officer of the Confederate Memorial Literary Society.[15]

So quickly did the UDC grow, and so powerful was its reach, that it overwhelmed the much older and more local monument associations. Under the leadership of Katie Walker Behan, of New Orleans, the other associations decided in 1900 to join together as the Confederated Southern Memorial Association. Formed six years after the UDC, the organization continued to meet into the 1930s but never enjoyed its counterpart's influence or public profile.[16]

It was within the context of this heightened Confederate memorial activity that the Hollywood Memorial Association enjoyed a renaissance in 1886 and four years later decided to rescue the former Confederate White House. After the reinterment of the Gettysburg dead, the association had entered a decade of almost complete inactivity. Despite the organization's many accomplishments, noted the recording secretary in 1895, the "death and removal from the city of so many of the most energetic members" had "so thinned the ranks of the Association that it languished, and with difficulty kept up with its work." Reviving public interest in the annual Memorial Day celebration became the association's primary objective. In particular, it wished to answer the R. E. Lee Camp's call for measures "to strengthen, in those now growing

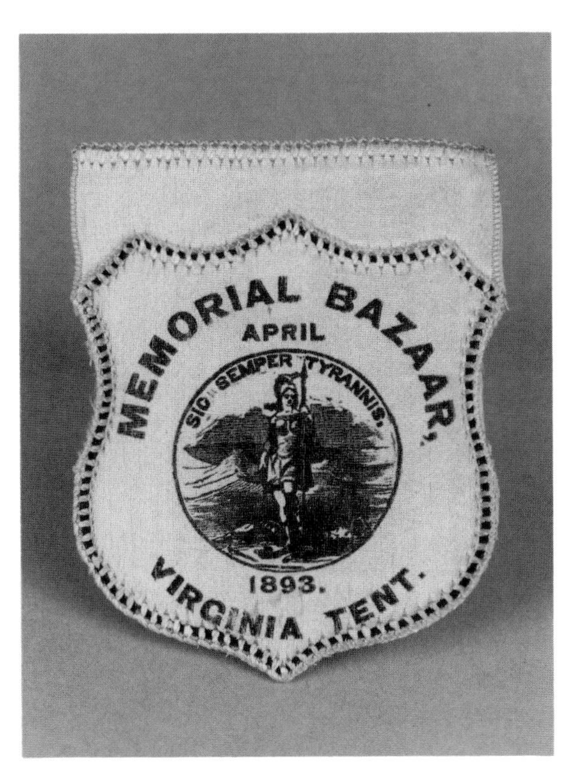

Virginia Tent badge, Memorial Bazaar, Richmond, Virginia. *A bazaar held in April 1893 constituted the Confederate Memorial Literary Society's first major fund-raising effort for the Davis Mansion restoration. In booths organized by state, members sold commemorative items including objects picked up from nearby battlefields. (White satinet badge, 1893.)* The Museum of the Confederacy

up around us, the virtues so strikingly illustrated in the lives of our noble dead, and to perpetuate the memories connected with their graves." While a few of the members of the rejuvenated association had been part of the original organization, most had been children or young adults during the war and were only in the 1880s first becoming involved in patriotic, memorial, and social organizations. They were, wrote Recording Secretary Mary Crenshaw, part of the Hollywood Memorial Association's "younger generation imbued with the spirit of its founders."[17]

The initiative for rescuing the Confederate White House and transforming it into a Confederate Museum came from just such a member of that generation, from a woman, in fact, who had no previous involvement with the Hollywood Memorial Association. The daughter of a Scottish-born merchant, and the wife of businessman and newspaper publisher Joseph Bryan, Isobel Lamont Stewart Bryan belonged to one of the wealthiest and most influential families in Richmond. That wealth and influence, along with her leadership in the newly established Association for the Preservation of Virginia Antiquities, led to her unanimous election in February 1890 as president of the twenty-four-year-old Confederate memorial organization. When "Belle" Bryan assumed the gavel on 4 March 1890, her first point of business was to state her desire "that the Davis Mansion . . . should belong to this Association and be made the repository of Confederate relics—should, in a word, become a Museum for the preservation of records or relics of any kind of the Confederacy."[18]

Rescuing the Davis mansion was a primary concern for Belle and Joseph Bryan and was probably the reason for her direct involvement with the Hollywood Memorial Association. Built in 1818 and considerably remodeled in the 1850s, the house had been home to a succession of wealthy Richmonders before the war. The last of its antebellum owners sold the structure to the city in 1861 expressly for use as the executive mansion. Four years as the Confederate White House had earned for the building a distinct identity, but little sanctity. Following a five-year occupation by federal troops during Reconstruction, the house reverted to a financially desperate city government. Richmond had little choice but to press the house into public service, using its rooms and outbuildings as quarters for its Central School. By 1889 there were still so few resources that the city government, despite being dominated by Confederate veterans, made the purely practical decision to raze the aging structure and replace it with a new public school building. One of the strongest protests came from the editorial pen of Joseph Bryan.[19]

And when Joseph Bryan's wife mobilized an organization of elite women to protest the proposed destruction of the Davis mansion, city officials went to great lengths to cooperate. On 14 March officers of the Hollywood Memorial Association petitioned the city

Officers of the Confederate Memorial Literary Society.

council to deed the mansion to the organization as a "Memorial Hall and Museum of Confederate relics." A committee met with Mayor (and Confederate veteran) James Taylor Ellyson four days later and reported that he was in favor of the proposal. An unfortunate technicality arose when the city attorney declared that Richmond could not deed property to a memorial organization. It could, however, transfer property to a society dedicated to educational, or literary, pursuits. The Hollywood Memorial Association therefore voted to create an "adjunct" organization initially called the Southern Memorial Literary Society. The new organization's members—essentially the same women who constituted the parent association's membership—met, changed the name to the more specific Confederate Memorial Literary Society, and on 31 May 1890 signed the charter. In due time, on 5 January 1891, the city council voted formally to deed the Davis mansion to the society as soon as the new Central School was complete. The transfer occurred on 3 June 1894

Officers of the Confederate Memorial Literary Society. *At the urging of Belle Bryan, a wealthy and active Richmonder and new president of the Hollywood Memorial Association, the CMLS was created in 1890 to save the Davis Mansion, recreating it as a "repository of Confederate relics . . . a Museum for the preservation of records or relics of any kind of the Confederacy." Bryan served as president of the CMLS from 1890 until her death in 1910. (Illustration from reunion program, United Confederate Veterans, 1896.)*
Eleanor S. Brockenbrough Library, The Museum of the Confederacy

—the eighty-sixth anniversary of Jefferson Davis's birth.[20]

The organization that assumed control of the Davis mansion was a mirror of Richmond's elite white power structure. The society's leaders were the daughters and wives of high-ranking officers in several local veterans' organizations. And although women composed the society's entire active membership, men influenced its governance through formal and informal channels. Typical of most women's patriotic and historical organizations of the era (except, notably, the United Daughters of the Confederacy), the CMLS, as it became more familiarly known, created a men's advisory board populated primarily by the husbands and fathers of its leaders. The original body also included three men whose positions—as city engineer, mayor, and chairman of the city council's school committee—had been instrumental in acquiring the Davis mansion. The school committee chairman was the father of one of the society's officers; the mayor was the husband of another. The other board members were influential politicians or businessmen and virtually all were Confederate veterans and relatives of CMLS leaders. While the society's charter did not specify the duties of the advisory board, in practice the women consulted the men about financial, property, and legal matters.[21]

Whatever the role of the male advisers, it was nevertheless a strong article of faith among the society's founders that the Confederate Museum "emanated from the brains of a band of women, and has been carried on by women ever since."[22] This was a significant point of pride. And, more important, it was true. Because ritualistic mourning had traditionally been regarded as a woman's role, southern women had been delegated as the leaders of the postwar memorial associations. That role, in turn, had by the 1890s evolved so that the preservation of historic structures and regional tradition had also become defined as an appropriate role for women.[23] The work of creating and maintaining a Confederate Museum combined these two distinct, but interrelated, memorial and educational roles for southern women.

The museum in the 1890s was thus simply another manifestation of the same devotion to the Confederate soldier and the Confederate cause that had been expressed in the late 1860s in tending soldiers' graves and erecting monuments. The task of that "band of loyal women," CMLS president Sally Archer Anderson explained to the UDC in 1916, was "to perpetuate the memory of a people overcome, but not conquered, and also to give the world the true history of that period, despite the garbled or erroneous statements often found in text-books." Discharging this duty, as a later officer described it, made the museum "a memorial to the work of Southern women."[24]

In expressing those sentiments the founders were not merely paying homage to their foremothers; they were commemorating their own lives. Most of the museum's founders were too young to have been involved in the wartime soldiers' aid societies or in other aspects of the war effort, or in the immediate postwar memorial associations. But almost all were children of the Confederacy whose personal experiences—or, at least, personal memories—emphasized loyalty to the Confederate cause.

Before she married Joseph Bryan, Isobel Stewart was a "special pet" of General Robert E. Lee; her home outside Richmond, Brook Hill, had been the scene of several wartime skirmishes. The museum's first house regent, Isabel Maury, was a cousin of famed Confederate naval officer Matthew Fontaine Maury and during the war had lived in the house where Maury conducted his experiments with underwater fuses. Her home was a block away from the Davis family, and Maury—among the oldest of the museum's founders—had sometimes visited the Confederate White House. Two of Matthew Fontaine Maury's daughters, Mary and Lucy, were also among the museum's founders and served as long-time committee chairwomen.

While their father lived in Richmond during the war, they had endured the Federal occupation of Fredericksburg, Virginia. Mary Maury had joined her father in England when the Confederate government transferred him overseas on special service.

Lora Hotchkiss Ellyson was a niece of Jedediah Hotchkiss, the school teacher who won Confederate immortality as "Stonewall Jackson's map maker." She had lived in the upper Shenandoah Valley during the war and recalled concerts held "to raise funds to send wagons of supplies to troops and the sewing and knitting parties, and the convalescent whom we nursed to health in our home on the farm." In her Richmond childhood, longtime corresponding secretary and yearbook chairwoman Virginia Morgan Robinson had wrapped bandages for the wounded and decorated the graves of Confederate soldiers. Katherine Clay Stiles, one of the few non-Virginians among the early leaders, spent her young adulthood in Georgia and regaled her CMLS colleagues with eyewitness stories of General William T. Sherman's campaign of destruction.[25]

The founder who recorded her wartime memories in the greatest detail was Janet Weaver Randolph.[26] Steeped in Confederate tradition, Randolph was the founder and guiding spirit of the UDC's Richmond chapter as well as one of the Confederate Memorial Literary Society's most active and influential leaders. Her recollections of the war years constitute a kind of prologue for her subsequent memorial work. Born near Warrenton, Virginia, in 1848, Janet Weaver spent the entire war in the Warrenton area, forty miles southwest of Washington, D.C. Although they owned a 179-acre farm and at least three slaves, her parents had been unionists before the war and maintained close ties with family members in the North. After Virginia seceded, however, the family became strong supporters of the Confederacy. Janet Weaver's thirty-eight-year-old father, "a lawyer and gentleman farmer," enlisted as a private in an infantry regiment in April 1861 but soon died of typhoid.

Janet, her mother, and her sister endured the trials of war without the assistance of men, save a "faithful" slave. That experience had an obvious influence in shaping Janet Randolph's character as a strong, independent woman. She particularly remembered when in 1863 her mother traveled to Philadelphia to seek material assistance from relatives. Arrested in Alexandria and jailed as a spy, the elder Janet Weaver received a parole and finally arrived in Philadelphia. She was, however, detained for four months because she refused to take an oath of allegiance to the United States government. "Think of it! four months without hearing from her two little girls," Janet Randolph wrote a half-century later. "If she had taken the oath of allegiance to the United States she would have been allowed to come home, but no, she would not do this and swear not to help the cause she held so dear."

The family's loyalty to the Confederacy was tested severely, as Warrenton, on the southern border of "Mosby's Confederacy," was behind Federal lines for much of the war. The Weavers boarded, befriended, and cared for a succession of sick and wounded men, Confederate and Union. Janet Randolph nurtured memories of life under military occupation: of pleading unsuccessfully with a Federal general to allow a wounded Confederate soldier to continue his convalescence in the Weaver home; of the kindness of another Federal officer who responded generously to her request to purchase sugar, coffee, and tea as a present for her teacher; and of her own proud spurning of an invitation to a ball held by a Federal cavalry regiment.

"How my mind goes back, and the thoughts come thick and fast of the trials of those years," Randolph wrote in 1913, "but misery loves company, and that was the reason we were not miserable, for we had so much company." Without livestock to farm the land, she remembered (erroneously) that the Weaver women sold off acre after acre

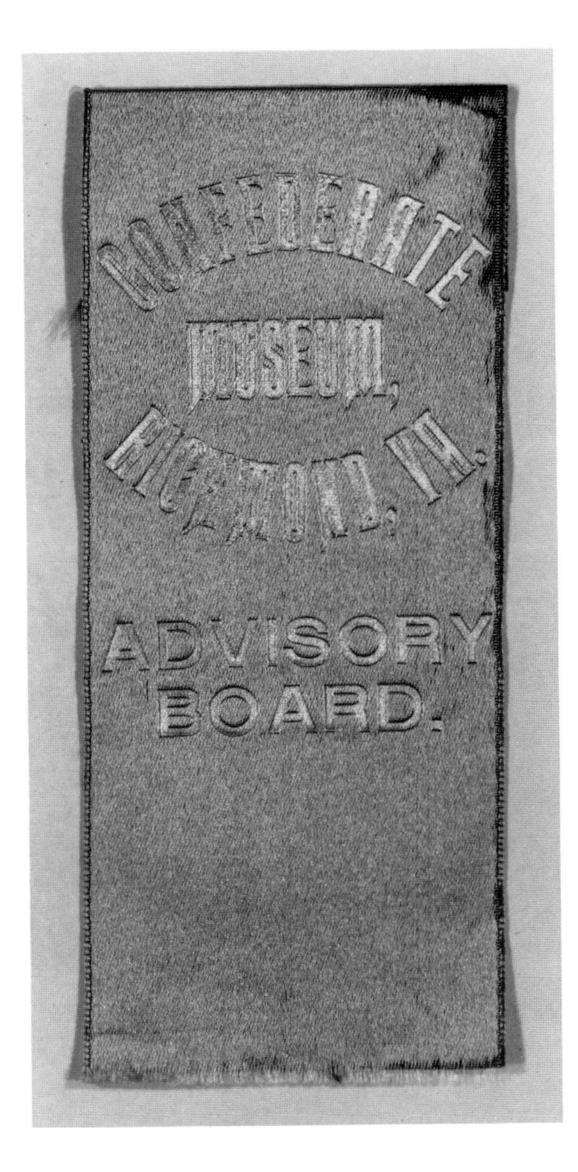

Confederate Museum, Advisory Board badge. *The Confederate Memorial Literary Society opened the Confederate Museum in the Davis Mansion on 22 February 1896. This badge was worn at a reception for Varina Howell Davis and her daughter Margaret held on 30 June 1896 in conjunction with the sixth reunion of United Confederate Veterans. Donations from Mrs. Davis formed an important component of the museum's early collections. (Blue satinet badge with gold letters, ca. 1896.)*
The Museum of the Confederacy

until only the house was left. A neighbor gave them a cow and the women sewed and knitted to earn their living, "so we managed to exist." During and immediately after the war, the women relied on the assistance of their former slaves: "We would have starved to death if the Negroes had not shared with us the rations given them by the United States government."

The feelings that seventeen-year-old Janet Weaver expressed at the end of the war presaged her subsequent work with Confederate memorial organizations. In July 1865 she wrote to a female friend:

> Oh! the thought is sickening that after all the hardships, and suffering our noble men have endured, and the many precious lives, that have been sacrificed to gain our independence, that at last we should have to submit to the hated yankees, the very thought makes my blood run cold. But it cannot be that their lives have been given up for nothing, and a day of reckoning must come although it may be far distant.[27]

She later recalled that her involvement in memorial work began before the end of the war. "Sunday after Sunday," the women of Warrenton "carried their offerings of love to place on these unkept, unknown graves . . . only to have their work destroyed by the invaders of their Home."[28]

For Janet Weaver and for many of her CMLS colleagues, their marriage to a Confederate veteran reinforced this determination not to forget the sacrifices of the South's soldiers. Although she had been engaged immediately after the war to a young veteran of Colonel John S. Mosby's Partisan Rangers, Weaver did not marry until 1880. Her husband, Norman V. Randolph, had also served with Mosby's rangers and after the war earned the rank of major in a militia company. Active in the Lee Camp of Confederate veterans, Randolph served as a member of the board of trustees of the Lee Camp soldiers' home and as its president from 1891 until his death in 1903. Typical of such couples, Janet Randolph became head of the Lee Camp ladies' auxiliary and spent fifteen years collecting and disbursing money for the benefit of the soldiers' home.[29]

Like Janet Weaver Randolph, raised in loyal Confederate households and married to men who became increasingly involved in veterans' activities, the founders of the Confederate Museum perceived their work as a sacred trust to be discharged in the memory of Confederate soldiers. Urging her CMLS colleagues to meet the challenges of the future, Belle Bryan in 1899 spoke of their "high calling as custodians of so much that is dear to our hearts, & necessary to the education of the generations to come."[30] As society members proudly remembered in subsequent decades, establishing the museum and ensuring its survival fulfilled their trust as custodians of a heritage.

From 1890 to 1896, the women of the Hollywood Memorial Association and the Confederate Memorial Literary Society laid the groundwork for transforming the Davis mansion into the Confederate Museum. The building had become dilapidated after a quarter-century as a school and required repairs and fireproofing before it could be considered a safe repository for artifacts. To raise money for this new undertaking, the women once again sponsored a bazaar. Held at a local armory in April and May 1893, the Memorial Bazaar raised over $30,000, a remarkable sum that was divided evenly between the museum and a campaign to complete a Richmond monument to Confederate soldiers and sailors.[31]

The organizational structure, ideology, and attitude of the Confederate Museum had begun to take shape long before its official opening on 22 February 1896. The operating framework of the CMLS, even the distribution of space within the museum itself, closely followed Belle Bryan's original concept. In addition to the customary organizational officers (president, vice presidents, recording secretary, corresponding secretary, and treasurer) and the usual committees, the CMLS created a series of regents and vice regents representing the states that had joined or supported the Confederacy. Appointed primarily to win prestige and influence for the museum throughout the South, the regents were prominent women within their respective states, often women highly placed in state divisions of the UDC or related to prominent Confederate veterans. Among the first regents, for example, were the widow and daughter of Jefferson Davis, one of the daughters of Robert E. Lee, the sister of Kentucky general John Hunt Morgan, and the daughter of Confederate cavalryman and South Carolina governor Wade Hampton. The vice regents were Richmond women who, ideally, had some personal connection to the state they represented. Their function, however, was more practical than the regents': to oversee the collections and exhibits created within the rooms named for each of the southern and several of the border states in the new museum. It was in these positions that the most active CMLS leaders such as Lora Ellyson, in behalf of the Virginia Room, and Janet Randolph, for the Tennessee Room, served.[32]

Collections of artifacts and mementos for the "State Rooms" began filling the homes of CMLS members four years before the museum opened. What the society first acquired, and how it did so, reflected the new institution's purpose and ideology. According to its charter, the society's purpose was to collect "all books and other literary productions pertaining to the late war between the States, and of those engaged therein; all works of art or science, all battle-flags, relics, and other emblems of that struggle; and to preserve and keep the same for the use of said Society and the public."[33] An appeal for donations distributed throughout the South in early 1892 detailed the plans for the "Permanent Museum for Confederate Relics":

> The clothes, the arms, the money, the belongings of the Confederate soldier, and of the women whose loyal enthusiasm kept him in the field, are properly objects of historical interest.
>
> The glory, the hardships, the heroism of the war are a noble heritage for our children. To keep green such memories and to commemorate such virtues, it is our purpose to gather together and preserve in the Executive Mansion of the Confederacy the sacred relics of those glorious days.[34]

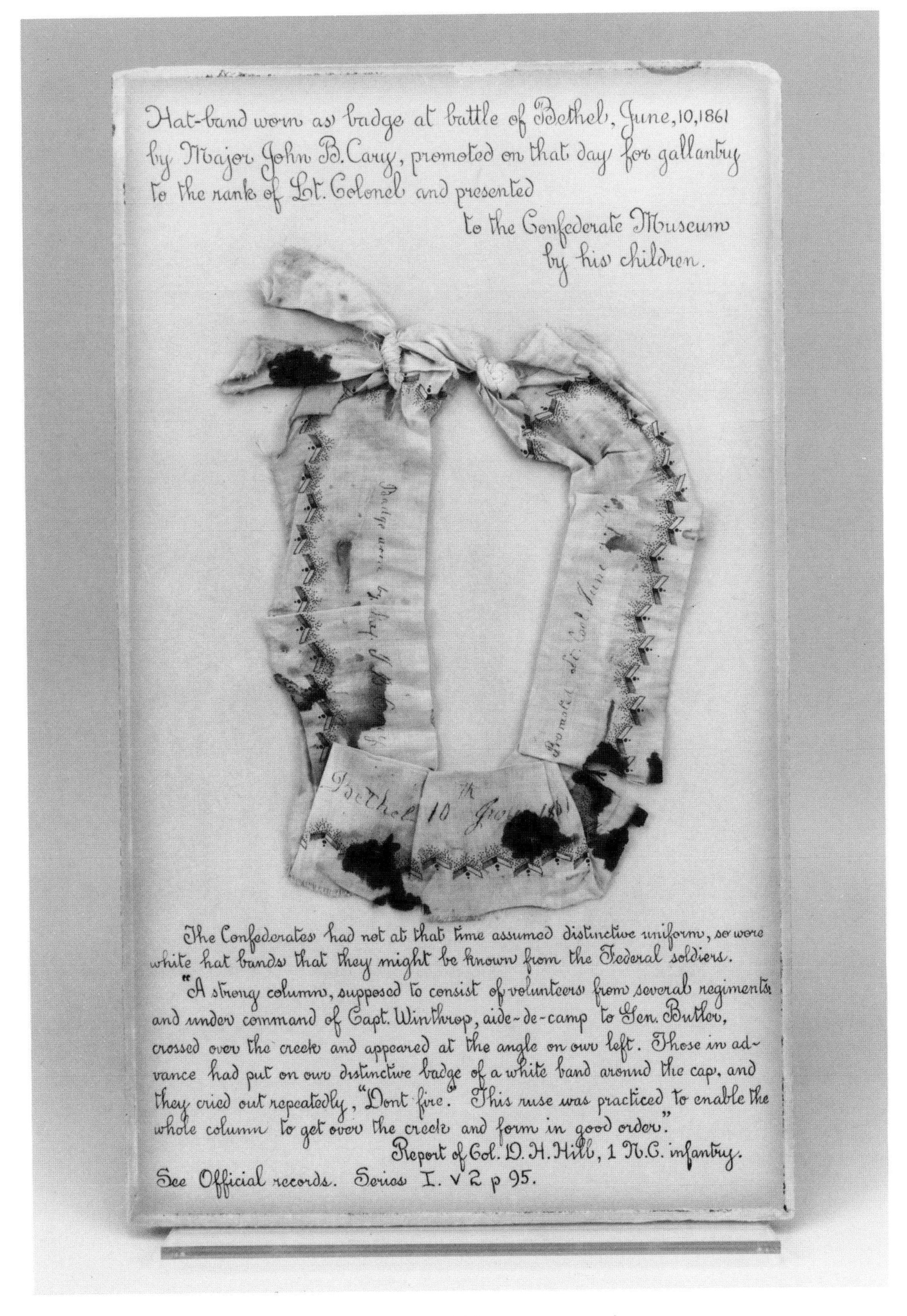

Hatband worn by Major John B. Cary at the battle of Bethel Church, Virginia, 10 June 1861. *The Confederate Museum's regents and vice regents lavished great attention on the careful documentation of items accepted into the collection. Artifacts, like the 1861 hatband, were often accompanied by written labels outlining their individual significance to Confederate history. The item, presented to the museum by the former officer's children, had served a useful purpose: since the opposing armies that early in the war had not yet adopted a "distinctive uniform," Cary and his fellow soldiers "wore white hat bands that they might be known from the Federal soldiers." Cary later served as a member of the Confederate Museum's Advisory Board. (Copperplate-printed cotton, with ink, 1861.)* The Museum of the Confederacy

"Relic" was an accurate and revealing term to describe the objects sought and received. Along with the uniforms and possessions of famous Confederate heroes came curiosities and oddities valued because of their sometimes close and sometimes tangential associations with those same heroes: a brick from the home where J. E. B. Stuart died, a brooch made from the hoof of Turner Ashby's horse, locks of hair belonging to Thomas J. "Stonewall" Jackson and Robert E. Lee, a bit of mane from Lee's horse, Traveller, and pieces of the ropes used in 1890 to pull the equestrian statue of R. E. Lee through the streets of Richmond to its place on Monument Avenue.[35]

To the members of the CMLS and other southerners, the assembled relics offered dramatic testimony to the virtues of the Confederate leaders and soldiers and to the hardships they suffered in their noble, but ultimately hopeless, fight. The ideology was apparent in notes made by CMLS Relics Committee member Mary Maury Werth on the

Board of Lady Managers, Jefferson Davis Monument Association, Richmond, Virginia. *In 1899 Richmond's all-male Jefferson Davis Monument Association turned to the United Daughters of the Confederacy to help raise the funds needed to complete the Davis monument planned for the city. Assuming full responsibility for the fund-raising, the women secured the remaining $70,000 over the next eight years. (Photograph, by George Cook, 1902.)* Mildred Rutherford Scrapbooks, Vol. 7, Eleanor S. Brockenbrough Library, The Museum of the Confederacy

first donations—donations that she collected from members of her own distinguished family. Many of the first objects were associated with the Confederate commerce raider *Shenandoah*, the vessel that continued to prey on Union shipping for months after the surrender at Appomattox until the crew at last learned of the Confederacy's collapse. Werth donated photographs of the ship's captain, James I. Waddell, who turned the *Shenandoah* over to the British rather than surrender the vessel to U.S. authorities, and of Lieutenant Dabney Minor Scales, "whose hands," Werth wrote, "hauled down the flag that never surrendered." She also donated items related to the war service of her husband, James Werth, of the Fourth Virginia Cavalry, including the last ration of coffee issued to his mess before the surrender at Appomattox. "This table-spoon full," she noted, "a ration for 12 men!"[36]

Similar kinds of objects testified to the spirit and patriotism of women on the Confederate home front. Establishing the link between home front and battlefield were several silk flags made by women—sometimes out of their own dresses—for local military units. There were also many samples of plantation-made homespun cloth—presented as the South's answer to the North's attempts at economic strangulation. More engaging were the examples of Confederate home-front ersatz, or substitutes: a shoe made of raccoon skin, a sleeve pattern made of newspaper, pants fashioned from cow hair, and buttons made of persimmon seeds. Other objects provided material evidence of how Confederate women resisted and undermined "Yankee" dominance: a pair of socks that Mrs. Hugh Lee, of Winchester, Virginia, knitted with fabric she unravelled from a Union army tent and a wad of surgical lint made by two sisters working secretly at night in the attic of their Unionist family's Washington, D.C., home and smuggled to Confederate hospitals.[37]

Such relics and testimonials were hardly unique to the CMLS and, in fact, the Richmond museum was not the first of its kind. A year before the society's formation, the Louisiana Historical Society received its charter and, in 1891, dedicated its own Confederate Memorial Hall in New Orleans. Within a decade, the hall included more than fifteen thousand artifacts, requiring the construction of an annex onto the original building. Unlike the CMLS, administered by women, the Louisiana museum was the idea of local Confederate veterans' organizations, and much of its collections came from those same groups.[38]

What most distinguished the Richmond institution from its potential rivals was its claim to being the paramount Confederate museum. It was an ambitious goal, particularly since the museum had been founded at a time of intense competition among southern cities and states for the monuments, institutions, and any other tangible associations with the Confederacy. Even the body of Jefferson Davis, moved from New Orleans to Richmond in 1893, had created a spirited rivalry over which city should have the honor of caring for the remains of the Confederate president.[39] The Confederate Museum's system of State Rooms, combined with its regional appeals for donations of funds and artifacts, suggested just how determined the institution was. Though located in Richmond, it was not to be a merely local entity. Supporting a museum located in the former Confederate executive mansion was, the Confederate Memorial Literary Society insisted, the patriotic duty of all southerners.[40]

The leaders of the CMLS saw an opportunity to strengthen their claim to primacy when a wealthy Confederate veteran proposed the creation of a "Battle Abbey" of the South. "The mementos of the struggle of the South for civil liberty and the evidences of her glorious prowess in the field are scattered . . . over the country," observed Charles Broadway Rouss. And "should they not," he asked, "be collected and provision made for their preservation as a rich inheritance for our children and a patriotic lesson for generations to come?" Both points were familiar ones to the Confederate Museum's far-reaching Relic Committee. Rouss, though, went further: he estimated that a memorial hall could be built for $200,000 and hinted that he might provide half the amount if Confederate veterans could raise the other half.[41]

Mary Maury Werth saw Rouss's offer as "fulfilling & perpetuating the very objects for which the Confederate Memorial Literary Society was established" and recommended action "to secure the valuable cooperation & assistance of so zealous a Confederate as Mr. Rouss." Several husbands of the society's members—particularly Lee Camp soldiers' home president Norman Randolph—thus appealed to Rouss to locate the proposed memorial hall on the grounds of the museum and entrust its management to the society. While Rouss pledged publicly not to create an institution that "threatened or endangered the memorial fabric which our noble women have erected, with so much loving devotion and unremitting toil," he avoided promising his Battle Abbey to the CMLS. He confided to a number of veterans' organizations that he wanted his project to be "national in character," and implied that the Confederate Museum, despite its pretensions, was still a distinctly Richmond institution. Nevertheless, the society's officers and advisers remained so confident that Rouss would present his memorial hall to the museum that they agreed in 1896 to raze the outbuildings surrounding the White House of the Confederacy in order to create a "little park" in anticipation of an adjacent Battle Abbey. It was no accident that Bradley T. Johnson in his 22 February 1896 keynote address had referred to the museum as a "Battle Abbey."[42]

The existence of the museum did play an important role in 1898 when Richmond veterans succeeded in securing their city as the site for a memorial hall, formally called the Confederate Memorial Institute and administered by a newly formed Confederate Memorial Association. J. Taylor Ellyson represented Richmond's case before a veterans' committee and cited the Confederate Museum, its building, grounds, and collections in his bid. In subsequent years, Richmond's representatives to the Confederate Memorial Association—many of them members of the Confederate Museum's advisory board—consulted with the leaders of the Confederate Memorial Literary Society to decide the best location and exact nature of the still-unconstructed Battle Abbey. On several occasions in the ensuing decade, Ellyson assured the society that the institute would not threaten the museum. In fact, he said "there was a unanimous wish on the part of the C.M.A. to place the Abbey under the management of the ladies, as it would be impolitic to have two such organizations in one city."[43]

Ellyson's assurances to the Confederate Memorial Literary Society's leaders were indicative of the gender relationships within the southern memorial movement. In its first public statement, the Confederate Memorial Association's executive committee left little doubt that while the Battle Abbey was a creature of the veterans, it was to be placed in the hands of Confederate women.

> For, in whose hands could this sacred trust more properly be placed, and with more certainty of success, than into those of the gentle women of the South, who have never faltered or failed in the performance of any duty, either in war or in peace, imposed upon them for the Southern cause? To the ladies, who did everything for the Southern cause, during the "sixties" except fight its battles, and who encouraged Confederate soldiers by their smiles, their cheers, their matchless patriotism, fortitute [*sic*] and self-sacrifices, we appeal for aid, with the assurances that every assistance will be rendered them to accomplish any work they may undertake, which we further

Monument to "Our Confederate Dead," Hollywood Cemetery, Richmond, Virginia. *One of the earliest Confederate memorials, the stone pyramid at Hollywood Cemetery was dedicated on 6 November 1869. The distinctive landmark—built of large stones carefully fit together without mortar—was intended as a "Memorial Granite Pile—pyramidal in form . . . clad with vines and roses." Its construction, however, dictated that the cemetery periodically remove any growth, for fear thickening vines might in time topple the monument. The pyramid served as the logogram for the cemetery itself and for the Hollywood Memorial Association. (Stereograph, by David H. Anderson, Richmond, Virginia.)* Eleanor S. Brockenbrough Library, The Museum of the Confederacy

> assure them shall be done under their own organizations in such manner and at such times as they shall prescribe, in their respective states.[44]

Behind this inflated rhetoric lay a realistic assessment of the interrelationships within Confederate memorial organizations. By 1900, leaders of Confederate veteran and other male associations had come to depend on, and enjoy, the work of their female counterparts. Some of this dependence was symbolic and promoted the traditional view of southern women as objects to be protected and venerated. For example, as part of the evolving ritual of United Confederate Veterans' reunions, the former soldiers increasingly surrounded themselves with female sponsors, usually women of their own generation, and with adoring younger women as maids of honor, usually their daughters and granddaughters. Both age groups were clearly there for reasons beyond simple gratitude for wartime sacrifices. Women became so much a part of veterans' gatherings that the United Daughters of the Confederacy at its 1898 annual convention passed a resolution (introduced by Janet Randolph) asking that the United Confederate Veterans limit the number of women included in its formal activities "because the Confederate Reunions have been of late years an entertainment for the Sponsors and Maids of Honor instead of for the Veterans."[45]

In response to this resolution, the United Confederate Veterans' adjutant general composed a three-page paean to southern womanhood that was excessive even by the standards of the day. The veterans, he confessed, were guilty of idolizing southern women, but they were militantly unrepentant: "Never was devotion more intensely sincere and idolatrous, never was worship more richly deserved." The adjutant agreed to forward the UDC resolution to the various camps, but declined to endorse it. "Even if it were possible for the Reunions to become an entertainment for the Sponsors and Maids of Honor instead of for the Veterans, as the resolution recites, it would be but doing simple justice to the descendants of the noble Women of the Confederacy" for their memorial work. "In honoring them we but honor ourselves," he concluded in an inversion of the usual relationship between Confederate veterans

and southern women.[46]

Confederate veterans in several instances decided to express their gratitude to southern women by erecting monuments to them rather than to the usual military and political figures—even as southern women at the same time erected monuments to prominent Confederate veterans. Debate raged within several organizations about the design of a prototype monument. After much arguing back and forth, the veterans finally settled on a female figure representing "Fame" gingerly cradling a wounded soldier in one arm and placing a wreath upon the head of a southern woman with the other hand. Janet Randolph was among the numerous women who opposed the idea of any monument to the southern female. If the veterans wished to honor the South's women, she replied, they should donate money to the Confederate Museum's endowment fund. At Randolph's suggestion, both the Confederate Memorial Literary Society and the Virginia Division of the United Daughters of the Confederacy passed resolutions urging that very alternative.[47]

Randolph and many other women in both

R. E. Lee Camp No. 1, United Confederate Veterans, Richmond, Virginia. *Close working relationships with influential members of Richmond's R. E. Lee Camp proved to be both a blessing and a curse for the Confederate Museum's women founders. While the veterans' financial, legal, and political connections sometimes proved invaluable, the men's own organizational objectives occasionally clashed with those of the museum. The veterans' wish to locate a Battle Abbey near the Lee Camp soldiers' home proved to be an especially contentious issue. The men also limited the women's individual freedom in the public arena. Lieutenant Governor J. Taylor Ellyson* (center), *a member of the museum's Advisory Board, chastised his wife, Lora Hotchkiss Ellyson, for appearing before a committee of the Virginia General Assembly in 1903 and demanded she never do it again.*
Eleanor S. Brockenbrough Library, The Museum of the Confederacy

organizations prided themselves on their more substantive work on behalf of Confederate veterans and the Confederate cause. Indeed, Confederate veterans were often woefully dependent on women for assistance in funding monuments and other ventures. For example, the society's highly successful 1893 bazaar had also benefited a memorial effort begun years earlier by an eager local committee of veterans. Two men instrumental in that effort subsequently became members of the museum's advisory board, Richmond mayor J. Taylor Ellyson and city engineer Wilfred E. Cutshaw, had appealed to the women of both the Hollywood Memorial Association and the Confederate Memorial Literary Society for help in raising money for the half-completed monument to Confederate soldiers and sailors. The 1893 bazaar exceeded all expectations and, as Belle Bryan hoped, was "a Grand Victory" for the civic-minded women of Richmond.[48]

The construction of a monument to Jefferson Davis in Richmond posed an even more difficult challenge. In the early 1890s, veterans had grandly announced plans for an elaborate $250,000 memorial. By 1899, however, J. Taylor Ellyson as president of the Jefferson Davis Monument Association had little choice but to confess to the United Daughters of the Confederacy that the veterans "found they had promised more than they could accomplish." He then asked the women to assume the task of completing the monument. The UDC agreed to do so. While veterans remained as officers of the association, most of the fund-raising labors fell to a central committee chaired by Janet Randolph. By the spring of 1903, the women had almost reached their revised target of $70,000. That May the monument association and the CMLS cosponsored a bazaar patterned after the 1893 effort, with the proceeds to be divided between the Davis monument project and the museum endowment fund. The event succeeded, Randolph reported, "far beyond what we even dared hope for." It was Randolph who convinced her CMLS colleagues to contribute an additional percentage of the proceeds and thereby complete the fund-raising for the monument. On 3 June 1907, Davis's ninety-ninth birthday, the largest crowd ever gathered for a Confederate memorial dedication watched as dignitaries unveiled the Davis monument.[49]

The completion of the Davis monument was a milestone in the history of women's memorial associations. Women and men had worked together before to honor Confederate heroes, but often with considerable uneasiness. It was, after all, only after nearly two decades of bitterness between rival men's and women's organizations that Richmond had at last been able in 1890 to unveil a monument to Robert E. Lee.[50] The Davis monument represented the ascendancy of southern women as fund-raisers and organizers.

The accomplishments of the Confederate Museum itself further solidified the reputation and confidence of postwar "Confederate women." The museum, for example, received several large and important manuscript collections, including the original Southern Historical Society Papers, and purchased significant sets of paintings and watercolors by Conrad Wise Chapman and William Ludwell Sheppard, both Confederate veterans. The collections grew so quickly that in 1898 the museum published a catalog of more than two hundred pages describing the contents of the various State Rooms. Museum officer Lizzie Cary Daniel noted in the widely read *Confederate Veteran* magazine, published in Nashville, that a new museum building or annex was "fast becoming a necessity." A second catalog published in 1905 required an additional sixty-five pages. The collection received a prestigious endorsement in 1905 and 1906 when the United States War Department entrusted to the museum 250 battle flags captured from Confederate military units during the war.[51]

The Confederate Museum exhibited its

FACING PAGE:
Confederate Museum house regent Isabel Maury (1842–1934). *On 3 April 1865, Isabel Maury had watched United States Colored Troops march into Richmond, down Clay Street, past her house, and on to the Confederate Executive Mansion a block away. "I felt how mean—how ignominious to try thus to humiliate us," she later remarked. On New Year's Day 1866, she appealed to her cousin (and future museum colleague), Mary Maury, living in exile in Britain: "do you know a* nice *fellow there who wants a* nice *wife? then tell him if he will deliver her from yankee rule here she is!" Maury never found someone to deliver her from "yankee rule," but serving as the Confederate Museum's first house regent delivered her from troubling memories. She expressed gratitude to a visitor from the North who claimed that the Federal army marched African-American troops into Richmond not to humiliate the occupants but because the soldiers "had been more accustomed to submission, and could more easily be controlled than white men." Maury lectured visitors to the museum on the folly of the "yankee rule" she remembered so vividly. When she died in 1934, she was buried in Hollywood Cemetery, where she had tended soldiers' graves since 1866. (Photograph, probably by Faris-Dementi Studios, Richmond, Virginia, ca. 1925.)*
Eleanor S. Brockenbrough Library, The Museum of the Confederacy

growing collection of artifacts in rapidly crowded wood-and-glass display cases scattered throughout the fifteen State Rooms. Each room's vice regent identified the objects with small labels, often written on the reverse of her husband's business cards. Typically, the only information offered about the objects was quoted or paraphrased from the correspondence that accompanied the donation. Consistent with museum practices of the era, there was no effort to interpret the objects or to put them within any historical context. Nor did the exhibits belabor the ideology of the Confederate cause. The exhibits instead emphasized the courage of the South's soldiers and people and the hardships they endured. "Every room echoes the bravery of our soldiers, the sacrifice of our women, and the strong loyalty of the whole South," explained the society's president to the UDC in 1915.[52]

Museum officials considered the objects "authenticated data" of the Confederate cause and appreciated the superior educational impact of three-dimensional objects over the written word. "The aim of the Confederate Museum is to preserve the true history of the War Between the States in written form and in object lessons that often mean more to some seeking knowledge than do books," explained Sally Archer Anderson, president of the society from 1912 to 1952. "Why is it unique?" she asked. "Because it is a Monument to the loyal devotion of a people to a Cause they know to be right, and because here are to be found most valuable treasures alongside of the pathetic evidences of the straits our people were put to for [their] very existence, all carefully preserved."[53]

The Confederate view of slavery and race relations was similarly presented without elaboration. The museum acquired a sizable collection of slave-related artifacts, especially samples of cloth and other homemade products. All were presented as evidence of the slaves' efforts in support of the integrated southern household. The intended message to be communicated by the "relics" was clear from the catalog entries: "Basket, made during the war by a faithful colored mammy, and sent in her memory"; "Wooden Shoe-soles, donated by the widow of Dr. Ben Randolph, of Albemarle county, Va. Made on his farm by his slaves during the war of the Confederacy"; or "Homespun, made in 1863 by a slave belonging to Miss Mary Pilgram, Woodruff, S.C."[54] Isabel Maury, who as house regent greeted and conversed with museum visitors from 1896 to 1912, made her views on slavery and race relations unequivocally clear. "That there were cruel masters, as there are sometimes cruel fathers & husbands I do not doubt: but they were never tolerated," she wrote in an unpublished 1899 essay. "And I do believe that there never existed a laboring class that as a rule were so well cared for and happy as were the negro slaves in the South." She contrasted the conditions of life and labor for slaves with those for laborers in industrial nations, finding the slaves' lot to be a far better one. "There were churches for them on the plantations, so they had moral training, And were gradually evolving from their native, savage condition. These are the masses of them on the large plantations, but, in the home where employed as house servants, etc. they were refined and improved by their personal contact & training."[55] Any charge that the Confederacy fought the war to preserve slavery was met with an equally fervent response, for that was a heresy that the society's founders, like most postwar southerners, worked hard to refute.

The acquisition and display of "relics" was not all the museum did to preserve and interpret the history of the Confederacy. From its inception, the institution had sought a broader mission in education and historic preservation. In 1898, for instance, the museum's Memorial Committee began compiling a partial roster of Confederate soldiers. The resulting "Roll of Honor" eventually grew to 346 volumes with some fifty thousand skeletal biographical entries. It was always clear that

the project's sole purpose was to glorify the Confederacy's soldiers, not record their collective experience for posterity. When the local Chesterfield Chapter of the United Daughters of the Confederacy submitted a form listing a soldier as a deserter, the society rejected it as "unsuitable for our records."[56] The society encouraged other projects as well. The CMLS asked railroad companies to place markers on battlefields along their routes. The organization also assisted in preserving a site on the Fredericksburg battlefield. Under the energetic leadership of Mary Maury Werth (and with financial assistance from other Confederate organizations), the society's Sites Committee placed over a dozen tablets in the Richmond area marking the locations of Confederate offices, residences, hospitals, and prisons.[57]

The Confederate Memorial Literary Society's name itself suggested that publications were also central to its work. "We must publish the information we have," wrote First Vice President Mary Maury Werth in the 1907 inaugural issue of the museum's *Year Book*. "How else," she asked, "can the truth be known? . . . We are making it possible to have historical facts placed where future historians can study from original papers the truth of events, leading up to and during the war and the following period of Reconstruction." Another publication, the *Calendar of Confederate State Papers*, published in 1908 and edited by the young historian Douglas Southall Freeman, reflected the museum's responsibility as a major repository of documents, while two short tracts—*The Treatment of Prisoners-of-War 1861–1865* and *Explainings of Objection to "Rebel"*—met the institution's role as propagandist for the Confederate point of view.[58]

Perhaps the Confederate Museum's most successful educational venture was the publication of the *Memorial Day Annual, 1912: The Causes and Outbreak of the War Between the States, 1861–1865*. The project was the brainchild of Kate Pleasants Minor, one of the few founders working in a paid, professional position. The widow of a prominent Richmond judge and Confederate veteran, Minor began work after her husband's death as a serials librarian at the Virginia State Library. After securing an agreement from the State Superintendent of Public Instruction to publish and distribute an educational booklet, she solicited brief essays on secession, slavery, and government in wartime Virginia from the state librarian and state archivist and from Douglas Freeman. She contributed her own article on the origin and meaning of Memorial

Day. The booklet, she told her CMLS colleagues, "is a practical way of educating our children" and of "rous[ing] public sentiment so that we may insure an official history for southern teachers." She urged her colleagues to create a committee, solicit the assistance of the United Daughters of the Confederacy, and encourage all the "seceding states" to publish their own version of the collection. The state of Virginia distributed at least sixteen thousand copies of the booklet to public school teachers. Minor had hoped to make the booklet an annual school supplement, but the initial text proved to be the only one published.[59]

The day-to-day administration of the museum and its programs demanded considerable time and energy, most of it provided by the Confederate Memorial Literary Society's membership. The museum's only compensated employees were House Regent Isabel Maury, Assistant Regent Susan B. Harrison (hired in 1907 and Maury's successor in 1912), two aged Confederate veterans who served as doormen and guides, and one African-American janitor. Those remained the only paid positions for more than a half-century. It fell, then, to the vice regents, alternates, and their volunteer committees (with the assistance of the salaried house regent) to accept, document, and place objects, and to "freshen" the display cases and State Rooms. It was therefore obvious to everyone that nearly every facet of the institution's operation had to be assumed by unpaid, volunteer members. The regents in their respective states, for example, made appeals for donations from state divisions and local chapters of the United Daughters of the Confederacy and from state legislatures. The corresponding secretary handled the institution's voluminous external communications. The treasurer maintained financial records of daily receipts and expenditures for the museum, while also overseeing the general endowment and fifteen separate endowments for the State Rooms. The work of several committee chairwomen, especially Sites Committee chair Mary Maury Werth, entailed not only internal paperwork and external interaction with printers and other businessmen but also sensitive negotiations with other organizations and public figures. Werth, for instance, found financial sponsors for most of the memorial tablets her committee proposed and negotiated successfully with several property owners—including the federal government—to place the tablets on the walls of historic buildings long since given over to other uses.[60]

The women of the CMLS were understandably proud of the importance and quality of their work. No doubt others shared the frustration that Solid South Room vice regent Minnie Baughman expressed when she wrote Douglas Freeman in 1907 that "the Museum is crowded every day & visitors are so interested the entire time—home duties detain us when we should like to be at our work at the Museum."[61]

Society members' sense of their worth is especially evident in their relationship with the far larger United Daughters of the Confederacy. Most of the early CMLS leaders and members were also members of the UDC. A few, such as Janet Randolph and Virginia Morgan Robinson, were as prominent in the United Daughters of the Confederacy as in the Confederate Memorial Literary Society. Robinson was the UDC's first historian general. It is not surprising, then, that the museum consciously and systematically exploited the UDC's extensive geographic network and growing membership to solicit donations of objects and money. Beginning with the UDC's November 1899 general convention held in Richmond, the society also made a concerted effort to convince the organization that the museum was part of its ongoing work and responsibility. Georgia Room regent Emily Hendree Park, also an officer of the UDC's Georgia Division, issued a plea that every state division form a committee to support the museum and lobby the state legislature for regular contributions. In spirit and in substance, this appeal became a touchstone for the museum's future relations with the United

The Story of the City on the Hill, ***by Mother Richmond [Janet Henderson Weaver Randolph (1848–1927)].*** *Serving as "Mother Richmond," the personification of the city's 1925 Community Fund, was yet another instance of Janet Weaver Randolph's advocacy of the needy. Randolph, for example, established within the United Daughters of the Confederacy several national and statewide relief funds for needy women, then goaded members to contribute to them. In 1920, she lectured the UDC's Virginia Division: "Do not write me, 'We have a very desperate case in our little town, a Confederate Woman, old and blind and helpless. Our chapter has lost interest in our work, they are busy with present day things. . . .' What is the matter—lost interest—and a Confederate Woman in your midst, poor, blind and helpless! Go out in your community and get assistance!" At a time when memorial organizations discussed building a monument to "faithful slaves," Randolph published a pointed Christmas-time appeal: "Send your missionaries to Africa if you will, but the African is at our door, and every cent you give here goes toward the betterment not only in individual, but religious training. . . . No monument to them, if you please, until we have attended to their earthly wants. . . . Don't forget them!" (Brochure, by the Richmond Community Fund, 1925.)*
Eleanor S. Brockenbrough Library, The Museum of the Confederacy

Daughters of the Confederacy. And while its support never met the most optimistic expectations, the UDC was for decades the museum's most important contributor.[62]

The effusive rhetoric about common purpose aside, museum officials were wary of conceding too much control to the UDC and occasionally betrayed contempt for what they believed to be its excessive sentimentalism. In the wake of the 1899 UDC convention, Lora Ellyson believed it "advisable" to place power for selecting State Room regents in the hands of the United Daughters of the Confederacy. The majority of the society's members present opposed the suggestion. Janet Randolph, seeking a compromise that would solidify the relationship with its logical partner, moved that the vice regents in Richmond continue to select the regents, but with the consultation of the presidents of the UDC's state divisions. According to the society's minutes, this "provoked so much discussion that the motion was withdrawn."[63]

Board members of the CMLS—even those who were officials in the larger group—viewed the UDC as an organization given to politics and sentimentalism, both of which they wished to avoid. UDC members themselves confirmed these fears. Tennessee Room regent Judith Winston Pilcher, who a year later resigned to become president of the UDC's Tennessee Division, complained about these very problems to her vice regent, Janet Randolph. "In U.D.C. work—no matter how straight we walk—and how altruistic [it] really is—friction will creep in—the result of envy & jealousy. I don't like to admit it, but I cannot account for some things in any other way. I do think if any organization should eschew politics—& work in harmony, it ought to be the U.D.C." Similarly, Texas Room regent Eleanor Darch Dibrell confided to CMLS president Lizzie Cary Daniel in 1911 that "like you I believe the U.D.C. must take active interest" in the museum. "But," she added, she would "always advise the Regents retaining their old charter and serving with powers to elect their own Regents to fill vacancies. We must not let state U.D.C. politics invade the Museum."[64]

The most scathing assessment came from Virginia Robinson, the UDC's first historian general. She was the Confederate Memorial Literary Society's delegate to the 1907 general convention and was charged with delivering the strongest appeal for UDC support of the museum since 1899. "What is the relation of the United Daughters of the Confederacy to the Confederate Museum in Richmond, Va.?" she asked the convention. The relation had been established, she answered, through Winnie Davis, the "Daughter of the Confederacy," born in the Confederate executive mansion, born in what became the Confederate Museum. She read aloud the UDC's 1899 resolution in support of the museum, then asked whether the United Daughters of

FACING PAGE:
Confederate Museum house regent Susan B. Harrison (1877–1939) and Confederate Memorial Literary Society president Sally Archer Anderson (1862–1954).
"The question of how this Museum is to be kept up in the future when those of us personally interested cease to be active in the work is one that concerns us," observed Sally Archer Anderson (right) *in 1926. "We must pray that when this loyal band of women pass away others will rise up to carry on the trust." The daughter of a Confederate staff officer and granddaughter of the owner of the famed Tredegar Iron Works, Anderson carried on the museum's work for forty years. Serving as the house regent for much of Anderson's presidency was Susan B. Harrison* (left), *daughter of a Confederate surgeon. As the museum's only paid professional staff member, Harrison was the subject of a 1927 newspaper article on "Richmond's Women Outside the Home." She told the reporter that she considered "her job one of the most interesting open to women" anywhere in the city. (Photograph,* Richmond News Leader, *20 February 1936.)*
Eleanor S. Brockenbrough Library, The Museum of the Confederacy

the Confederacy had come through with the promised support. Armed with detailed figures from the CMLS treasurer, she noted that while divisions and chapters had contributed $368 to the various museum rooms in 1906, virtually no money had been given to the general endowment. "Do such meagre results show a love for the tie that comes through our title? With just $5,000 in the endowment, are we proving ourselves worthy of this heritage, worthy of our wonderful history?" Once back in Richmond, Robinson expressed relief that the UDC convention had not followed what she perceived as business as usual. She noted that "the personnel was above the average," that the tenor was "businesslike," and that "there was no time-killing sentiment in the reports,—and few uselessly prolonged discussions." She was also gratified over the prolonged (half-hour) discussion about the museum's report and the interest the convention delegates had shown in the details of the museum's work. After the session, she had an hour-long private discussion with UDC officials: "That one hour is an epoch in the history of this Museum. Not one present expressed a word of sentiment,—not a reference was made to a monument, or a Confederate living, or dead, no device was used to kill time."[65]

It was not that the women of the Confederate Memorial Literary Society lacked sentiment for the Confederacy. They did, though, pride themselves on the importance—and the seriousness—of their work. In the same vein, the society scrupulously avoided anything that smacked of self-congratulation. While they welcomed "relics" that testified to hardships of the wartime home front, the founders did not want the museum to become a shrine to the society itself, or its members. By deliberate policy, the State Rooms did not contain portraits of women. Belle Bryan stirred a hornet's nest in 1909 when she suggested an amendment to the society's constitution that would allow the museum to acquire portraits of "women active in the Confederate Service from 1861-1865." Citing unspecified "difficulties and embarrassments threatening serious danger to the Society" that such an idea posed, Lizzie Cary Daniel moved that the motion be tabled. So rigid was this policy that in 1910 an offer of a portrait of Varina Davis from the United Daughters of the Confederacy provoked a heated debate. Because Varina Davis was the wife of the only Confederate president, the society agreed to break its rule, "provided, however, that this action shall not be taken as a precedent to admit a portrait of any other woman."[66]

The issue constituted yet another difference between the society and the UDC. In 1905, the UDC offered portraits of a former president-general and an unnamed woman to two of the museum's State Rooms. Janet Randolph answered for the Tennessee Room with an "emphatic refusal" and argued that accepting pictures of women at that point of its history violated the "whole sense" of the museum. Her colleagues agreed and with only one dissenting voice (Mary Maury Werth) passed a resolution that it was "not advisable" to accept portraits of women for the Confederate Museum. The UDC subsequently offered a portrait of one of its founders, Caroline Meriwether Goodlett. At the 1914 UDC convention and in the years following, Janet Randolph, vice regent of the room for which the Goodlett portrait had been offered, repeatedly had to defend the museum's policy against bitter attack. She cited this experience a few years later when she insisted that the society not honor one of its own with a tablet to be placed in the Georgia Room.[67]

Having proven their seriousness as well as their devotion to the cause, and having proven their abilities as caretakers of a multifaceted institution, the society's founders believed that they had earned for the museum a position as the best of the Confederate memorials. They could only feel betrayed when Charles Broadway Rouss's Battle Abbey, instead of being a capstone to their work, became a rival institution. Between 1898, when Richmond received word it would

be the site for the Battle Abbey, and 1921, when it finally opened, the veterans charged with organizing the institution acted in ways calculated to wound the pride and raise the gender consciousness of the society's leaders.

Just as the Richmond contingent of the Confederate Memorial Association had used the museum in 1898 to secure the Battle Abbey for the city, those same men used the institution in 1909 to retain it. During the intervening decade, fund-raising problems as well as legal and financial troubles had crippled every effort to complete Rouss's project. The Confederate Memorial Association knew, too, that if it failed to secure a specific site by the time of the 1909 United Confederate Veterans' reunion, Richmond might lose its claim. As he had on several earlier occasions, J. Taylor Ellyson (by then lieutenant governor of Virginia) went before a women's memorial organization to beg assistance. Upon his request, the Confederate Memorial Literary Society formally offered the plot of land adjacent to the museum as the site of the proposed Battle Abbey. Ellyson, in turn, reiterated his hope and belief that the ladies would someday control the new memorial. The preparations begun fifteen years earlier seemed finally to be coming to fruition.[68]

As some of the women soon realized, however, Ellyson and the Confederate Memorial Association were not committed to seeing the Battle Abbey incorporated physically and organizationally into the museum. The association continued to look for a better site and, by the time of the veterans' reunion in June 1909, it was public knowledge that the organization had settled on another site in the city's west end. The women of the CMLS, conscious that their site was probably too steeply sloped to be of much practical value anyway, were not surprised. Nevertheless, they felt ill used.[69]

"From the beginning I have considered the Battle Abbey scheme a factor in our city politics," wrote Virginia Robinson in a private letter. "Therefore I do not think that anything

Virginia governor Harry F. Byrd with* (left to right) *Janet Randolph, Sally Archer Anderson, and Lora Hotchkiss Ellyson. *The female officers of the Confederate Museum sought and benefited from the influence of prominent men. The Confederate Memorial Literary Society customarily hosted a reception for the governor and members of the General Assembly during the legislature's wintertime session. Photographed at the 1926 reception were Governor Byrd* (second from left) *and Delegate Henry T. Wickham* (far right). *A Richmond-area legislator and museum Advisory Board member, Wickham secured an annual state appropriation for the museum. (Photograph, by Faris-Dementi Studios, Richmond, Virginia, 1926.)* Eleanor S. Brockenbrough Library, The Museum of the Confederacy

that I say will have the slightest weight with these gentlemen. The women's organizations were not thought of until the Abbey became a 'white elephant' too big for storage. Then they flew to the Museum in order to affect public opinion." Janet Randolph voiced her complaints directly to Ellyson. The lieutenant governor had noted in a published interview that the Confederate Memorial Association would consider "expressions of opinion" from other Confederate bodies in Richmond, so she weighed in with her own. Reminding him that the association had promised cooperation and coordination with the Confederate Museum, she asked how this would be possible if the Battle Abbey were located in a different section of the city. "The women of the Confederate Memorial Literary Society, without appropriation from State or City have done their grand & glorious work," she reminded Ellyson. If Ellyson's association expected any further assistance from the society and the UDC, it ought to fulfill its promises to the museum. In contrast, Belle Bryan must have been relieved at the rift. From the beginning, she and her husband had been wary of the Battle Abbey scheme and repeatedly warned her colleagues against taking any action that would risk the museum's independence. Upon hearing rumors that the museum's collections were somehow destined to be turned over to the Battle Abbey, the society took Bryan's advice to heart. In 1910, the CMLS passed a pointed resolution: "That the

Confederate Museum is the work of women and a monument to the women of the South and can never pass from the care of the Confederate Memorial Literary Society as chartered in May 1890, and that members of the society contradict all rumors to the contrary."[70]

Wariness mixed with resentment characterized the society's attitude when the women again found themselves at odds with the veterans' group in 1919. Contrary to Ellyson's assurances, the still-unfinished Battle Abbey did constitute a threat to the museum's collecting ambitions. The association's efforts to define the Battle Abbey's mission—as a library and a memorial hall—trespassed on the Confederate Memorial Literary Society's understandable self-image as a major library and archive. The association trespassed further when it laid claim to the valuable portrait gallery amassed by the Lee Camp veterans. Although this claim was obvious and predictable, it challenged the museum's effort since 1894 to obtain the portrait gallery and any wartime artifacts belonging to the camp.

Transferring their holdings to the museum would have been an opportunity for the veterans to repay a considerable emotional and financial debt. In stating this case before the society, Janet Randolph systematically recited the occasions on which the veterans had sought and received assistance from Confederate women: the 1883 bazaar that raised $23,000 for the soldiers' home, the 1893 bazaar that completed the soldiers' and sailors' monument, and the 1903 bazaar that raised the final funds to complete the Jefferson Davis monument. "Therefore," she concluded, "if Lee Camp possessions revert to anyone it should be to the women who did so much."[71]

The following day, CMLS president Sally Archer Anderson formally invited the Lee Camp to construct a fireproof portrait gallery on the museum's property. Her request included an information sheet detailing the museum's demonstrated successes as a repository for relics, the advantages of its location, and the organization's fidelity to Confederate traditions. "It seems to us a fitting climax to the great work . . . Confederate Women and Men have done, that the fruits of their work should be found on the same ground, and virtually under the same roof," she wrote.[72]

Ultimately, it was not under the museum's roof, but under the Battle Abbey's, that the portrait gallery was to reside. This was not surprising, since the leaders of the Confederate Memorial Association were also influential members of the Lee Camp. Those men—some of whom were also long-time advisors to the CMLS—offered what appeared to be an olive branch. They promised that the Battle Abbey and its annex would soon pass into the society's control. Still reeling from the earlier blow, the society's leaders viewed this promise with marked skepticism and noted that the Sons of Confederate Veterans seemed to be the legal heirs of any Battle Abbey complex.[73]

The final showdown came in the spring of 1919. George L. Christian, a former compatriot of J. Taylor Ellyson in the wartime Richmond Howitzers artillery, succeeded to the Confederate Memorial Association presidency upon Ellyson's death in March 1919. Although he was one of the original members of the society's Advisory Board, his primary loyalty was to the Battle Abbey. Sensing the society's long-standing and understandable distrust, Christian decided to strike a preemptive blow, detailing a long list of grievances against the women he accused of failing to support the Battle Abbey project. "The trend of his lengthy remarks," wrote the society's recording secretary at a showdown meeting, "was to establish before our committee that our Confederate Memorial Literary Society was unreliable, unstable, and unfaithful to it's [*sic*] obligations." That meeting brought the long-repressed friction between the women's and men's organizations into the open. It also ended any remaining optimism that the CMLS would someday inherit control of the Battle Abbey and its collections.[74]

U.S. servicemen at the Confederate Museum, 14 July 1942.
The two world wars provided "Confederate Women" with the chance to demonstrate that their loyalty to the Confederate past did not exclude patriotism to the reunited nation. During both wars, the museum cooperated in promoting bond drives and organized special Sunday openings for uniformed servicemen and their families. "I feel that men in the service from all over the country meeting in this historic Museum is doing a great deal to make all feel it is one country now and one common cause," wrote Sally Archer Anderson in January 1943. Parke Chamberlayne Bagby Bolling, vice regent of the museum's Virginia Room and later president-general of the United Daughters of the Confederacy, hosted the 14 July 1942 tour of visiting servicemen. The world wars also gave new urgency to the museum's work: in 1920 the vice regent of the North Carolina Room pleaded that the endowment campaign be completed soon "as younger women will be more interested in building memorials to the soldiers of the World War." (Photograph, by A. J. Cahn, Richmond, Virginia, 1942.) Eleanor S. Brockenbrough Library, The Museum of the Confederacy

George Christian, J. Taylor Ellyson, John B. Cary, and other influential former Confederates in Richmond had for years assumed that they could count on the active support of their wives, daughters, and sisters for their veterans' activities. "Confederate women," after all, were recognized as the soldiers of the Confederate memorial movement. Motivated by a desire to honor the soldiers who fought and died for the Confederate cause, they rarely—if ever—failed to respond to requests from veterans' organizations. The veterans, in turn, honored the women—with profuse thanks, with grand gestures, even with monuments—and then reminded the women that it was for them and their honor that the Confederate soldier had fought.

As the founders of the Confederate Museum died, the men who had been their partners in memorial work praised them as women who had accomplished great things while still playing the parts of proper southern ladies. "Her admirers have said ten thousand times that if she had been born a man she would have been a great jurist or a great advocate or a great politician," Douglas Southall Freeman wrote of Janet Randolph. "For our part, we have always felt that her service had a peculiar value, because, with all its force and all its keen judgment, it was essentially the service of a woman." The *Richmond Times-Dispatch* declared her "the universal mother, mother of men and of women, of little children, of the very old, of the ill, of the forsaken, of the destitute, and of the downtrodden." Belle Bryan, according to George Christian, "fully recognized the limitations imposed on her sex, both by Providence and by custom, and she never chafed or fretted because of these, but within these limitations, and I believe because of these, Oh, what a power for good she was in the community." She was, the *Richmond Virginian* concluded, "the living answer to the complaint of the woman for work to do; she found her work and did it, in all sweetness and modesty, somewhat better, somewhat more graciously, than any man could have performed it."[75]

The founders of the Confederate Museum did not dissent from such views. But their work in behalf of the museum and the full range of their public activities reveal that they defined their roles within a broader context. As administrators of the Confederate Museum, they were not passive or submissive, but assertive. The vital work of commemorating a cause and the men that fought for it required them to be so. In turn, they believed that the successful discharge of their heart-felt obligation to the Confederate soldier earned them not only gratitude, but also certain rights, including the right to continue and expand their work and to prove their devotion and abilities anew.

The dynamics involved in Confederate memorial work at the turn of the century had immense implications for the museum's founders. Through their effort, they achieved a degree of freedom sufficient enough to cultivate their interests and talents and to make genuine contributions to the community around them. When they perceived that the men in their lives did not condone such independence, the founders chafed under the interference and even protested.

Though the focus of their cause was fixed in the historic past, the women of the Confederate Memorial Literary Society were receptive to new developments in women's roles. They were also interested in more than sectional causes. Few saw their affiliation with Confederate organizations as incompatible with allegiance to national patriotic and ancestral organizations, especially the Daughters of the American Revolution and the National Society of the Colonial Dames in America. Many founders coupled their devotion to history with an active interest in Virginia organizations preserving the legacies and structures of earlier periods, most notably the Virginia Historical Society and the Association for the Preservation of Virginia Antiquities. Two of the Confederate Memorial Literary Society's officers—Belle Bryan and Lora Ellyson—served as presidents of the APVA from 1890 to 1935. The earliest members of the CMLS were also active in cultural, educational, and social organizations. At least twenty were also members of the Woman's Club of Richmond, formed in 1894 and dedicated to cultural and intellectual pursuits. Virginia Morgan Robinson, one of the most dedicated of the museum's founders, was a driving force within the club.[76]

Each of the founders favored at least one social cause, typically an auxiliary for a local hospital or charity organization. Belle Bryan assumed the presidency of the Richmond branch of the Young Woman's Christian Association months before the establishment of the CMLS. She was credited with giving the YMCA its direction and, using her own funds, starting the day nursery for the children of working mothers. Kate Pleasants Minor was a vocal champion of reforming the state's juvenile justice system. Through her husband, she lobbied successfully for a juvenile court and detention home and for the creation of a state board of charities and corrections.[77]

Janet Randolph made the care of the destitute her life's work. Within the United Daughters of the Confederacy, for example, she championed the creation of "relief" funds for Confederate widows and then proceeded to hound Confederate organizations to contribute. As a well-known champion of the poor in Richmond, she was in 1925 named "Mother Richmond"—the figurehead of the annual community-fund drive. After destructive floods ravaged several black communities on the banks of the James River in 1923, she organized relief efforts and agitated successfully for improvements and flood prevention measures. At her death, Richmond's black churches mourned her passing.[78]

Consistent as all this was with her image as "the universal mother," Janet Randolph was not content to live within traditional gender roles. She was a member of the central committee of the Co-ordinate College League, an organization determined to create a college for women at the University of Virginia. At Randolph's request, both the Richmond Chapter and Virginia Division of the United Daughters of the Confederacy adopted resolutions asking the Virginia General Assembly to create a coordinate college. Depending on her audience, she sometimes cast the issue in sectional terms: why should Virginia's young women have to go north for higher education? In most instances, she emphasized how unjust it was of the state to require a female teacher to earn a baccalaureate degree to teach high school but not provide the requisite educational opportunities to do so. She also revealed an intense frustration with her own lack of opportunity. "I am an uneducated woman—growing up during the war," she wrote plaintively in a letter to the *Warrenton Fauquier Democrat* in 1916. "I had no opportunity to learn from College Teachers—there were no graded schools, grammar schools, Normal Schools, or College Degrees for women." With decided belligerence, she then went on to list the (unequal) opportunities that did exist for women at the University of Virginia, concluding that, in the end, "the women who spend their all to get the advantage of even a few months at the University are not accorded the degrees that will rank them with the men. Do you call this chivalry to women? Is it placing them on that lofty pedestal our opponents so delight to talk of?" She closed her letter with a scarcely veiled threat: "I am not a suffragist, but it is such injustice that will cause the women of Virginia to become suffragists."[79]

Several of Randolph's colleagues within the Confederate Memorial Literary Society were already suffragists and had no apparent difficulty reconciling their stance with Confederate memorial work. Kate Langley Bosher, a public speaker for the Equal Suffrage League of Virginia, was a life member of the society, though not among its leaders. May Gray Hodges, daughter of a North Carolina governor and long-time vice regent of the North Carolina Room, belonged to the suffrage league. The society's first corresponding secretary, Ellie Withers Putney, was an active member of the league. Kate Pleasants Minor, the society's indefatigable essayist and a librarian, was not only an officer in the Equal Suffrage League but also lived long enough to take advantage of the Nineteenth Amendment. She served as a delegate to both the state and national Democratic conventions of 1924.[80]

The members of the Confederate Memorial Literary Society had little difficulty combining their memorial work with other community, and even political, causes. First, the society was only one among many turn-of-the-century women's organizations in Richmond. Moreover, the society cooperated with those other organizations. The Confederate Museum and the city's Associated Charities, for example, were the beneficiaries of the 1913 Kirmess festival, sponsored by all the women's organizations of Richmond. These and other efforts provided Richmond women with direct experience in organizing and working in the public sphere.[81]

For its founders, then, the Confederate Museum served several purposes. It was a genuine and passionate expression of their continuing loyalty to the Confederate cause. It was a memorial to their fathers, brothers, and husbands. And it was a fulfillment of their individual and collective promises to remember and vindicate the Confederacy. It was also a means by which ambitious and energetic white southern women found personal satisfaction and public involvement while working within prescribed, but evolving, gender roles.

FORREST VETERAN

CHAPTER SIX

DIVIDED LEGACY

The Civil War, Tradition, and "the Woman Question," 1870-1920

MARJORIE SPRUILL WHEELER

Nina Pinckard at the Nashville headquarters of the Southern Women's League for Rejection of the Susan B. Anthony Amendment.
(Detail from photograph, August 1920.)
Tennessee State Library

That the Civil War had a profound impact on southern women is well known. Less well known is that this great conflict continued to affect the public debate over the role of women long after the shooting stopped. As the South confronted the so-called "woman question" in the late-nineteenth and early-twentieth centuries, the most bitterly contested issue was woman suffrage. Partisans on both sides of the debate made extensive use of Civil War rhetoric and references in their efforts to influence public opinion and policy. White southerners, whether for or against expanding the role of women, frequently referred to "the War" and "the Lost Cause."[1] Suffragists and antisuffragists alike spoke reverently of the Confederacy and of Confederate heroes and heroines, and both sides claimed that their positions were in harmony with traditional southern values.

The southern women who participated in the organized suffrage movement, a minority among southern white women, insisted that they sought the vote in part to fulfill their traditional obligations as "Southern Ladies" within a society that had changed in the aftermath of the war. Drawn from the ranks of elite and middle-class whites, they shared many of the values and assumptions of other southerners of their race and class and insisted that their movement was in fact a boon to "Southern Civilization."

Most white southerners, however, favored the position of the opponents of woman suffrage: that while the traditional role of the Southern Lady precluded her direct participation in politics, her indirect, inspirational role was indispensable—a source of pride and distinction for the South. In response, the suffragists at first attempted to convince the southern states that each one should chivalrously enfranchise "their own women." When that failed and it appeared that southern suffragists could win the vote only through an amendment to the federal constitution, the situation became even more difficult. Antisuffragists proclaimed that such an amendment was a dire threat to white supremacy and a direct assault on the fundamental principle for which Confederates had fought and died—states' rights. Any "true" son or daughter of the South, they insisted, would recognize that fact.

Although the suffragists convinced many of the validity of their cause, their opponents prevailed. Prior to the ratification of the Nineteenth Amendment in 1920, women gained full enfranchisement in no southern state and partial suffrage in only four. Moreover, of the ten states that failed to ratify the Nineteenth Amendment, nine were south of the Mason-Dixon line. Understandably, long before the suffrage battle ended, the southern suffragists who had invoked the Civil War and traditional southern values to

Mrs. W. W. Wadkins decorating the tombstone of Brigadier General Barnard E. Bee, Pendleton, South Carolina. *The Ladies' Memorial Association, of Columbus, Georgia, in March 1896 published an appeal to remember the Confederate dead: "we cannot raise monumental shafts and inscribe thereon their many deeds of heroism, but we can keep alive the memory of the debt we owe them by dedicating, at least one day in each year, to embellishing their humble graves with flowers. Therefore we beg the assistance of the press and the ladies throughout the South to aid us in the effort to set apart a certain day to be observed, from the Potomac to the Rio Grande, and be handed down through time as a religious custom of the South, to wreathe the graves of our martyred dead with flowers.... Let every city, town and village join in the pleasant duty. Let all alike be remembered, from the heroes of Manassas to those who expired amid the death throes of our hallowed cause." The women of Pendleton, South Carolina, answered the call, decorating the grave of one of the Confederacy's first martyrs, Barnard Bee, who died at the battle of First Manassas in July 1861.* Eleanor S. Brockenbrough Library, The Museum of the Confederacy

support their cause became increasingly disillusioned with tradition itself. The South, they concluded, was wallowing in the past and smothered by its memories. Only when the South was willing to shed the stranglehold of tradition, they concluded, would women be able to occupy a full and equal role in southern society.

With the end of the Civil War, women's rights advocates in the Northeast had renewed their activism and by 1869 had founded two vigorous suffrage associations, both focusing on gaining female enfranchisement and a wide variety of improvements in women's status.[2] In the South, a few women participated in this renewed women's movement, notably Anna Whitehead Bodeker in Virginia and the Rollin sisters in South Carolina. But the response in the South was generally quite hostile. Indeed, the fact that alleged "carpetbaggers" in Virginia and the wives of black politicians in South Carolina were supporting advocates of women's rights reinforced resistance in the South.[3]

In the postwar South, white conservatives were increasingly fearful of change. Deeply resentful of the social and political innovations imposed by Reconstruction and concerned about the potential impact of industrialization and urbanization, many feared these changes threatened what they believed was still, despite military defeat, a superior Southern Civilization. From Reconstruction well into the twentieth century, most white southerners spoke of the war as a contest between a paternalistic, harmonious, homogeneous, and God-fearing South and a materialistic, competitive, heterogeneous, and atheistic North. And as they struggled to cope with an increasingly competitive and dynamic society, they repeatedly recalled the Civil War as the height of southern virtue, a golden age in which southerners made undreamed-of sacrifices in defense of a just and stable society. Fearing that, as one Georgia minister put it, "the victory over southern Arms is to be followed by a victory over Southern opinions," the region's leaders urged their constituents to consecrate themselves anew to preserving the values of the Lost Cause. Southerners responded to this call with such devotion and intensity that historian Charles Reagan Wilson has described this "postwar attitude" as "a Southern civil religion."[4]

Unfortunately for advocates of women's rights, the commitment to preserving the traditional role of southern womanhood was an integral part of this intense, quasi-religious drive to protect the South against the "ravages" of northern culture. Conscious that the war had disrupted the traditional division of labor and responsibility and had forced many women out of the domestic sphere—even to work for *wages*—southern conservatives were eager to restore women to their traditional, protected, and privileged domestic sphere. They watched uneasily as growing numbers of women sought higher education, in many cases so that they could support themselves by teaching. And the growth of women's voluntary organizations such as the Woman's Christian Temperance Union, through which women became increasingly active in public affairs, spurred many southern conservatives to worry that women would neglect or even abandon their traditional domestic sphere—even, perhaps, seek the vote.[5]

This was a particularly frightening idea. After all, a crucial aspect of the Southern Civilization that devoted southerners wished to preserve was a dual conception of the natures and responsibilities of the sexes: a notion that precluded the direct participation of women in politics but assigned them an extremely useful role in southern culture and politics nonetheless. Just as the ideal southern woman, the Southern Lady, supremely compassionate and virtuous, had been useful as part of the pro-slavery defense, she continued to be useful in a society bent upon preserving its hierarchical, paternalistic, and white-controlled social structure.[6]

As postwar southerners described her, the plantation mistress of the Old South had ministered to the moral as well as physical needs of her extended household, including its African-American members, and had inspired morality and benevolent paternalism on the part of the planters who dominated southern society. Supposedly the most privileged creature in the universe, the Southern Lady willingly accepted a subordinate role, recognizing as she did the crucial differences in men and women, differences that made women ideally suited for their divinely appointed roles. Conscious of her own weaknesses in dealing with matters beyond the domestic sphere, the Southern Lady was grateful for the guidance and protection of southern men, who shouldered the harsh burdens of politics for the family and society as a whole. It was of the utmost importance in a society that insisted upon the right of its most eminent men to govern for the rest, that the most privileged members of that society—the elite white women—accept that subordinate role and that paternalistic system. To the outside world her acceptance signalled that southern society was just, tranquil, and morally sound. Within the region, the Southern Lady's traditional role was of vital importance in transmitting conservative political values to the next generation.

Thus, while northern advocates of women's rights stepped up their activities in the 1870s, southern conservatives insisted that southern white women continue to play this traditional role deemed so essential to the South's superior civilization. Indeed, in the postwar South, adherence to this originally elite ideal was increasingly expected of all southern white women who wished to be considered "respectable." Southern conservatives boasted of the traditional values and exemplary conduct of southern women in comparison to those of the North.

In 1871 one of the most influential clergymen of the Lost Cause, Albert Bledsoe, proclaimed in his oft-quoted sermon, "Mission of Woman," that southern women "still so live and so act in their own hallowed sphere that they are sacred in our eyes and an inspiration in our hearts." Speaking with fear of the growing number of northern women who, he said, despised the word of God and ignored the laws of nature while they denied their true mission, Bledsoe urged southern women to shun the fruit offered by northern feminists and remember the true source of woman's glory:

> Be this your glory, then O ye blessed and beautiful women of the South!—not that you can vote, or beat a negro for Congress, but that you can point to your sons as *your* jewels. . . . Be this your glory, not that you can equal man in the might and the majesty of his intellectual dominion, but that you can surpass him in the sublime mission of mercy to a fallen world. Be this your glory, not that you can harangue a mob, or thunder in the Senate, but that you can wear "the ornament of a meek and quiet spirit, which, in the sight of God, is of great price. . . ." Be this your glory, in short, not that you can imitate a Washington, or a Lee, or a Jackson, but that you can rear, and train, and educate, and mould the future Washingtons, and Lees, and Jacksons, of the South, to protect and preserve the sacred rights of woman as well as of man.[7]

In the late-nineteenth and early-twentieth century, the period in which an organized woman suffrage movement first appeared in the South, white southerners were redoubling their efforts to keep alive memories of Confederate martyrdom and to protect the South against an erosion of values, especially through the creation of Lost Cause rituals and institutions. New organizations created in the 1890s, including the United Confederate

Veterans and the United Daughters of the Confederacy, celebrated the wartime "Women of the Sixties" who had repeatedly demonstrated loyalty and a willingness to sacrifice and presented them as role models for a new generation of southern women.[8]

As historian Gaines M. Foster has noted, former Confederates gratefully accepted the support of white southern women for their men during both the war and its grim aftermath, and their subsequent "failure to challenge the patriarchy" despite southern men's failure on the field of battle. At their annual reunions, the United Confederate Veterans quite literally placed women on pedestals and eulogized the women of the South, who—long after the battles ended—remained as loyal and obedient and willing to sacrifice as ever, and who trusted their men to protect them. As one of the UCV organizers remarked, "Southern sentiment, Southern ideas and Southern manners are strengthened anew by these gatherings. Above all, the reunions tend to preserve in the South that respectful devotion to its splendid womanhood that the Southern manhood inherited from their chivalric ancestors." Young women seemed to be getting the message; one of them, observing the 1908 rituals, wrote, "Confederate Reunions are the finest of schools for us who didn't arrive in time to be part of the original excitement."[9]

Along with the countless statues of Confederate leaders and soldiers erected between 1890 and 1915 were monuments to the women of the Confederacy, monuments that, according to historian Elise L. Smith, depicted southern women as loyal, devoted, self-sacrificing, and unconscious of fame. And while the South lionized women's achievements as military suppliers, spies, nurses, and even soldiers, these were not the figures chosen for the statues on capitol lawns for future generations to see and emulate. These were not the ideal. It was instead, Smith noted, woman's "capacity for spiritual inspiration, for nurturing and sustaining the moral strength of the South, that was seen as their paramount contribution." The major purpose of these statues, after all, was to "sustain the traditions of the 'glorious Old South,' a patriarchal system based on 'frail, tender' women and their chivalric knights."[10]

There was an immediate rather than merely long-range utility in continuing to put white women on pedestals and keeping them out of politics. White supremacy was a crucial part of this Southern Civilization that late-nineteenth and early-twentieth-century white southerners were determined to preserve. The southern white woman in her traditional role had a vital part to play in the effort. Since the war ended, white men had resorted to fraud, violence, and bribery in order to restore white supremacy. Particularly after the Populist insurgency of the 1890s—with its unusual degree of interracial cooperation among disaffected southerners—elite white men had mounted a major drive to reassert both white supremacy and their own hegemony by "legally" disfranchising black men, an effort they described as "cleaning up" politics by reducing the need for fraud and violence.[11] And again, the Southern Lady had a significant, though indirect, role to play. White men justified their white supremacy campaign by suggesting that white women were threatened by black men—black men emboldened by their enhanced status and protected by black office-holders.

In North Carolina, for example, conservative Democratic leaders, seeking the support of the masses of white voters for a literacy test and a grandfather clause, manipulated voters by juxtaposing images of white womanhood with those of black men who allegedly endangered them. Charles Brantley Aycock, a leader of the white supremacy campaign of 1898, campaigned successfully for governor in 1900 by eulogizing the pure Anglo-Saxon heritage of his constituents, by describing blacks as rapacious "human fiends," and by appealing

OVERLEAF: ***A Georgia meeting of the United Daughters of the Confederacy.*** *"It is the women of the South who will preserve the legends of the war," declared Ella Clanton Thomas, of Georgia, in 1878. The United Daughters of the Confederacy, formed in 1894, vindicated her prediction, becoming a powerful memorial movement in the early-twentieth-century South. The UDC, for example, endorsed Confederate-oriented textbooks and even circulated its own* Catechism for Children. *The catechism was a blend of the uncontroversial (such as significant dates and names, for example), the controversial (such as how many men served in the Confederate armies), statements about the righteousness of the Confederate cause, and various interpretations of the war. The catechism concluded with a statement of the UDC members' mission: "To teach their children from generation to generation that there was no stain upon the action of their forefathers in the war between the States, and the women of the South who nobly sustained them in that struggle, and will ever feel that their deathless deeds of valor are a precious heritage to be treasured for all time to come."* Eleanor S. Brockenbrough Library, The Museum of the Confederacy

KENTUCKY

Monument to the women of the Confederacy, Columbia, South Carolina. *As did many of Confederate veterans' groups throughout the South, the South Carolina Division of the United Confederate Veterans in 1897 resolved to build a monument to their women compatriots in the war. The division convinced the state legislature to appropriate $7,500 for "a monument to the heroism, fidelity, and fortitude of the women of South Carolina during the War between the Confederate States and the United States." The* Confederate Veteran *magazine in May 1912 published an account of the fund-raising campaign, a photograph of the statue sculpted by F. W. Ruckstuhl, and the text by William E. Gonzales for the monument inscription. (Tinted postcard, undated.)*
Eleanor S. Brockenbrough Library, The Museum of the Confederacy

To the
South Carolina Women
of the
Confederacy
1861–65

Reared by the Men of the State
1909–11

In This Monument
Generations Unborn Shall Hear the Voice
of a Grateful People
Testifying to the Sublime Devotion
of the Women of South Carolina
in Their Country's Need.
Their Unconquered Spirit
Strengthened the Thin Lines of Gray.
Their Tender Care Was Solace to the Stricken.
Reverence for God
and Unfaltering Faith in a Righteous Cause
Inspired Heroism That Survived
the Immolation of Sons
and Courage That Bore the Agony of Suspense
and the Shock of Disaster.
The Tragedy of the Confederacy May Be Forgotten
But the Fruits of the Noble Service
of the Daughters of the South
Are Our Perpetual Heritage.

When Reverses Followed Victories
When Want Displaced Plenty
When Mourning for the Flower of Southern Manhood
Darkened Countless Homes
When Government Tottered and Chaos Threatened
the Women Were Steadfast and Unafraid.
They Were
Unchanged in Their Devotion
Unshaken in Their Patriotism
Unwearied in Their Ministrations
Uncomplaining in Sacrifices.
Splendid in Fortitude
They Strove While They Wept.
In the Rebuilding After the Desolation
Their Virtues Stood
as the Supreme Citadel
With Strong Towers of Faith and Hope
Around Which Civilization Rallied
and Triumphed.

At Clouded Dawn of Peace
They Faced the Future
Undismayed by Problems
and Fearless of Trials
in Loving Effort to Heal
Their Country's Wounds
and with Conviction
That from the Ashes of Ruin
Would Come the Resurrection
of Truth
with Glorious Vindication.

S. Glass to f1B 5/5/00 ESH C Sowe Research

...ck disfranchisement in the name of the ... Goddess of Democracy—the White ...hood of the State." According to one ...porary newspaper:

> ...own after town, Aycock was met by ...essions with bands, floats of pretty ... dressed in white to symbolize the ...y of white women. . . . At ...oro, he appeared on a float sur...ded by a bevy of Person County's ... beautiful daughters, inscribed in ... letters on each side of the float ... the words, "Protect Us."[12]

... after disfranchisement had been ... and white political supremacy ...stored, leading southern politicians determined to preserve this accomplishment saw the woman's movement as a threat to white supremacy in several ways. Many believed that more black women than black men would be able to pass literacy tests. And, all too aware of the fact that the women's rights movement was an offshoot of the antislavery movement, these same politicians feared (inaccurately) that white northern women would insist on their African-American sisters in the South being allowed to vote—and would bring about federal challenges to the new disfranchisement clauses in state constitutions. Particularly in the last decade of the suffrage movement, when national suffrage leaders began to focus increasingly on woman suffrage by federal amendment, white southern conservatives portrayed the movement as an assault on Southern Civilization.

Concerned about the growing numbers of southern women who supported woman suffrage, antisuffragists portrayed southern suffragists as dupes of the northern women, naively endangering their own culture as they tried to move from pedestal to politics. As one antisuffrage editor from Georgia wrote in a widely circulated antisuffrage pamphlet,

> May our Southern women remain on the pedestal, forever preserve that distinctive deference which is theirs so long as they remain as they are—our highest ideals of the true, the beautiful, and the good. . . . Deference to its womankind has always been a distinguished characteristic of the Southern people. Southern men would perpetuate it. But foreign forces have invaded us, established branches over the South of a huge National Woman's Association whose ideals are not our ideals; whose women are not like our Southern women. They are women of a different clay, and are of a different mould. Should these foreign crusaders succeed, pervert the tastes of our women, persuade them to abandon their old ideals and descend into the arena of politics . . . woe is the day for Southern civilization.[13]

In sum, from the end of the Civil War through 1920, the year the Nineteenth Amendment won ratification, the South was a most inhospitable climate for the growth and development of the woman suffrage movement. The traditional role of the Southern Lady was considered to be a key element of a culture that white southerners were determined to preserve. Furthermore, the most influential group of white southerners was not only sentimentally attached to this cherished image, a legacy of the Old South, but also found it politically useful in efforts to sustain a paternalistic, white-dominated society. Most white southerners were contemptuous of the women's rights movement as yet one more unfortunate product of an inferior northern culture, an offshoot with the same "naive" and dangerous belief in the equality of the sexes and disregard for vital social distinctions that characterized the abolitionists.

...*"No needy Confederate soldier, be his station in life what it may, ever passes our door empty handed. We care for him in life, and in death lay him tenderly away, marking his grave with a modest stone, bearing his name, date of his birth and death, adding that long ago in the past he shouldered his musket and went forth, not as a rebel against his country, but to defend his* State's rights *and* his home." Eleanor S. Brockenbrough Library, The Museum of the Confederacy.

Between the Civil War and the 1890s, a handful of "respectable," white, southern women began speaking out publicly for woman suffrage. By the late 1880s, there were enough southern suffragists that they began forming suffrage clubs, affiliated with national suffrage organizations. In the 1890s, under the direction of Laura Clay, of Kentucky, a crucial intermediary between northern and southern suffragists, a coordinated and vigorous—though not large—suffrage movement was underway in the South. The movement experienced a second period of activism between 1910 and 1920, a decade in which there were far more suffragists, more clubs, and more male supporters.

The vast majority of these white suffragists—and all of the leaders—were elite or middle-class southern women and for the most part shared the values of other southerners of their race and class. Proud to be southerners, and devoted to their states and to their region, most of them accepted the prevailing views about the Civil War, Reconstruction, and white supremacy and were admirers—though not totally uncritical admirers—of Southern Civilization.

Most had ties to the Confederacy and many had impressive Confederate or conservative southern credentials. For example, one of the first southern women to declare for woman suffrage, Elizabeth Avery Meriwether, of Memphis, Tennessee, the wife of a former Confederate officer, had been banished from Memphis by General William T. Sherman for aiding the Confederacy. After the war her husband helped form the Ku Klux Klan—by legend, in her parlor. She later published several books extolling the Lost Cause and romanticizing antebellum plantation culture, including *Facts and Falsehoods Concerning the War on the South, 1861–1865* (1904), written for school children to "offset the falsity of the Republican histories of the War." Virginia Clay-Clopton, pioneering suffragist in Alabama in the 1890s, was during the Civil War the wife of Clement Clay who served in the Confederate Senate. The Clays were part of the Confederate elite in Richmond during the war, and Clement Clay had been imprisoned with Jefferson Davis at Fort Monroe, Virginia. Rebecca Latimer Felton, a refugee in Georgia's Piney Woods during Sherman's invasion, was active in a ladies' society to aid Confederate widows and orphans and later in the United Daughters of the Confederacy. She was also for many years a close friend of Confederate vice president Alexander Stephens.[14]

Nellie Nugent Somerville, born during the war while her father was serving in the Confederate army, took pride in the fact that her father was one of the leaders in restoring "home rule" to Mississippi in the 1870s. Belle Kearney, whose father left the Mississippi legislature to serve in the Confederate army, eventually as a lieutenant colonel, proudly dubbed her 1900 autobiography *A Slaveholder's Daughter.* In it she described the "heroic" suffering of white southerners during the war and Reconstruction and praised southern politicians for their "pioneering statecraft" in restoring white supremacy in the 1890s. Among the second generation of southern suffragists, Mary Johnston was a relative of General Joseph E. Johnston. Her own father had been an artillery officer at Vicksburg. Among her twenty-three novels were several glorifying the Confederate cause (insisting that the war was fought gallantly and solely in defense of noble ideals rather than for the preservation of slavery), books that Margaret Mitchell later admired extravagantly. In 1905, Johnston wrote to a friend that "Virginia (and incidentally the entire South) is my country, and not the stars and stripes but the stars and bars is my flag."[15]

Far from accepting their opponents' premise that their movement was a threat to Southern Civilization or white supremacy, these women began their movement by promoting female enfranchisement as a means of restoring white dominance in politics. Though white southern women, like women elsewhere in the nation, wanted the vote in order to improve woman's condition and to promote reform, they recognized that politicians were likely to enfranchise them only if they saw some political advantage in it. As early as 1867, for example, Elizabeth Avery Meriwether suggested to her husband and his associates that white southerners could regain political control of the South by enfranchising "respectable" white women. In the 1890s, Laura Clay in Kentucky, Belle Kearney in Mississippi, Virginia Durant Young in South Carolina, Frances Griffen in Alabama, and Kate and Jean Gordon in Louisiana all advocated woman suffrage as a way of restoring white supremacy.[16]

These southern women were certainly not dupes of northern suffragists trying to enforce racial equality on the South. True, the strategy they pursued was suggested to them by former antislavery leader Henry Blackwell, of Massachusetts. But this "southern strategy" of the 1890s called for enfranchising women with restrictions that would ensure that mostly white, not black, women would qualify. By adding to the white electorate, the strategy also promised to solve the South's "negro problem" by restoring white supremacy to the South without the risks of disfranchising black men. Together with national suffrage leaders who came to the South to promote this strategy between 1890 and 1903, southern suffragists indignantly rebuked southern white men for allowing (as if they had any choice) black men to vote ahead of white women. Dr. Anna Howard Shaw, then vice president of the National American Woman Suffrage Association, scathingly rebuked a New Orleans audience for this, saying: "Never before in the history of the world have men made former slaves the political masters of their former mistresses!"

Southern politicians considered the suffragists' suggestion at the many state constitutional conventions of the era, but ultimately rejected it, agreeing with the Mississippi legislator who said that he refused "to cower behind petticoats and use lovely women as breast-protectors in the future political battles of the state." In the end, after most southern states had succeeded in disfranchising nearly all African-American men, southern suffragists no longer sought to exploit the race issue. Instead—placed on the defensive by antisuffragists—they insisted that woman suffrage would not affect white supremacy, as the same qualifications that governed the voting of black men would apply to black women.[17]

On no front, however, would these southern suffragists have ever conceded that their movement was a threat to Southern Civilization. They were proud to be southerners, indeed to be Southern Ladies, and they rejected the premise that adherence to their traditional role meant that they must remain entirely within the domestic sphere, submissive to men. Yet their own respect for tradition, as well as their keen understanding of its hold upon the mind of the South, led them to marshal southern history and tradition in support of their cause.

In their public statements promoting woman suffrage, they insisted that the expansion of woman's role—even into politics—was a natural extension of woman's sphere made necessary by changing times. Defending women's new public activism as a positive development, they nevertheless insisted that the changes resulted from new conditions directly traceable to the Civil War. Belle Kearney, for example, observed in 1900 that the expansion in the activities of southern white women, from working for wages to seeking political equality, were all the result of social and economic changes initiated in 1861:

> The women of the South have not sought work because they loved it; they have not gone before the public because it was desirable for themselves; they have not arrived at the wish for political equality with men simply by a process of reasoning; all this has been thrust upon them by a

changed social and economic environment. It is the result of the evolution of events which was set in motion by the bombardment of Fort Sumter.[18]

Kearney was no doubt aware that, in insisting that change had been *forced* upon women, she invoked a certain protection before a public eager to accuse women activists of "unwomanly" ambition, and of abandoning woman's domestic and subordinate role.

Nellie Nugent Somerville likewise insisted that the new public activism of southern women stemmed from the conditions created by the war, when women of leisure were compelled to abandon their pampered existence, suffered the loss of loved ones, had to earn a living, and learned to pay more attention to the political developments that had produced these disasters. In a newspaper article published in the early 1900s, she wrote, "We must go back fifty years to get at the genesis of the change in ideals of the Southern or Mississippi woman," when southern women were forced by disastrous events to recognize "that public policies and private conditions are interdependent and can not be separated." She added that during the 1860s,

> There came the shock of civil war. Southern women saw homes burned, estates pass to strangers, fathers and husbands dead upon the battlefield, and many a Southern grand dame was thrust from a routine of brilliant pleasure or indolency to the cook stove and the wash tub. The awakening came. Was not the war caused by politics? Was not the horror of reconstruction a game of politics? So Southern women pondered as they were forced to take the places of their own slaves.

In addition, wrote Somerville, "the need to work for wages" was "the next great forerunner of the suffrage movement." "The old time idea that a lady must not earn her livelihood," she insisted, "had to go down before stern need."

Thus, Somerville concluded, "by the hand of providence were Southern women forced out of their seclusion and into public affairs. . . ." She insisted, however, that the change was for the best, and was irreversible:

> The civic conscience has been awakened in the Southern woman and they are not going to dwindle and shrivel into a selfish, ease-loving way of living. The positively religious woman has had her conscience touched for temperance, child labor or other moral reform; the educated woman, whether religious or not, is impelled to help educational movements. The woman who takes absolutely no interest in any public question is no longer the typical or the ideal Southern woman.[19]

Change may have been forced upon southern women, the suffragists concluded, but considering the other changes—unfortunate changes—that had taken place in southern society, women's newly acquired interest in public affairs was a distinct advantage for Southern Civilization. Again invoking southern tradition, the suffragists insisted that in the unsavory political climate of the New South, woman's celebrated moral influence was badly needed. Indeed, they insisted, southern politics had deteriorated to the point that women's indirect influence was not enough: a *direct* infusion of feminine influence was required.

Though southern suffragists often had friends or relatives in public office, they believed that southern politics had degenerated to the point that too few honest and intelligent men were willing to serve. In her speeches of the 1890s, Somerville spoke nostalgically of the character and quality of leaders of bygone days, from the founding fathers to Robert E. Lee, and spoke of the "boys" of the Confederacy who "gave up prospects of material advancement to fight for principle." And she contrasted them with the politicians of the present who, she said, spoke of the rampant chaos and corruption in government as "practical politics"—deplorable, they might admit, but inevitable. Furthermore, she insisted that if "good men" continued to say "no man can go into politics and maintain his integrity . . . and therefore hold themselves aloof and do not even vote," the hope for the restoration of traditional morality to southern politics must rest with the women.[20]

In the 1890s in particular, the Woman's Christian Temperance Union was very popular in the South, and many a southern woman became a supporter of woman suffrage when politicians paid far more attention to the direct influence of the "Liquor Interests" than the indirect influence of wives and mothers. When Rebecca Latimer Felton attracted criticism for meddling in politics, she replied that the failure of men to give "sober homes to women and children" made it all the more necessary for women to become involved.[21]

The Gordon sisters, Kate and Jean, of New Orleans, deplored the crudeness as well as the corruption of Louisiana legislators, who spat streams of tobacco juice upon the carpets of the statehouse even as they denied the "dignified requests" of the women. Jean Gordon concluded that "in an ideal world," all legislators would be over thirty years old, sober, and possessed of "a certain dignity which comes only from an innate gentility and good breeding." Like Somerville, Jean Gordon was appalled that politicians seemed to accept graft and corruption as a routine part of their world—and yet had the gall to use this as an excuse for keeping women out of it.[22]

In the 1890s, some suffragists insisted that the "best" southern men could be counted upon to support their cause—but only if they could be assured that woman suffrage would not endanger white supremacy. Quite possibly their statements were strategic ploys reflecting the suffragists' hopes rather than their true assessment of the situation, but Laura Clay and Belle Kearney insisted that, in Clay's words, the South "had less real prejudice against woman suffrage than any other section." Clay—while in South Carolina to promote a proposal for woman suffrage, one with a property qualification that would have prevented the registration of most black women—told the state's constitutional convention that the South was "the strategic point and . . . our most hopeful field after the West." She received considerable support from South Carolina men described in the press as "of the highest social standing, educated and refined." Belle Kearney observed (too optimistically) in 1900 that

> Southern men, as a rule, are stronger advocates for the enfranchisement of women than men in any other section of the United States except in certain portions of the West. The old-time element of chivalry, which constituted so largely the make-up of the Southern gentleman, has been handed down through the generations and now begins to crystalize in the direction of equality before the law for men and women.

And, she predicted, these particular men would *insist* upon giving women the vote just as soon as most southern white women indicated that they wanted it. The opponents, she declared, were those men who would fight any progressive measure, including "the liquor dealers, the wily politicians of the lower stamp, the ultra-conservative ecclesiastics, the superfine 'swells' and men who have risen from the humbler walks of life deprived of early advantages of education and the refinements of elevated home environments."[23]

Indeed, the suffragists warned that men who lacked an understanding of or a commitment to southern traditions, particularly the traditions associated with *noblesse oblige,*

Virginia Tunstall Clay-Clopton. *Best known for her 1904 memoir,* A Belle of the Fifties, *Virginia Clay-Clopton (1822–1915) was the wife of an Alabama congressman and a fixture in the highest social circles of antebellum Washington, D.C., and wartime Richmond. After the death of Clement Clay and of her second husband, a judge, she became a prominent figure in disparate activist groups in Alabama. She was honorary life president of the Alabama Division, United Daughters of the Confederacy, and for many years belonged to a Huntsville chapter of the UDC later named for her. At the same time, she served twenty years as president of the Equal Suffrage League of Alabama and addressed that group as late as 1914, when she was ninety-two years old. (Photograph, by Collins, Huntsville, Alabama, ca. 1900.)*
Eleanor S. Brockenbrough Library, The Museum of the Confederacy

were gaining influence in southern politics, and that this deplorable situation required that the best women of the South have the political power to protect their traditional constituents, the "unprivileged" of the South, particularly women and children. Suffragists often expressed fear that the health, education, and welfare of the people were far less important to those shaping the welfare of the New South than the growth of the region's economy. Most of the suffragists favored the paternalistic model of government that the men of their race and class were attempting to restore, but they pointed out that paternalistic government was reciprocal in nature: that those who expected to lead had an obligation to protect the interests of the masses in return for their deference—in other words, to adhere to a tradition of *noblesse oblige*.

Suffrage leaders were particularly scornful of the cotton textile industry, successful against northern competition partly because southern legislatures refused to adopt—or at least adequately enforce—child-labor legislation. Madeline McDowell Breckinridge, a leading Progressive and suffragist from Kentucky, warned against trading "ideals of the past" for material prosperity:

> The South after the years of war and destruction and the succeeding years of despair and struggle is on its feet and she is on fire with the goal of material development. The dream of commercial advance is filling her brain and a new activity is in the land. [But] more than ever it needs to be reminded . . . that this very commercial advancement must rest upon the foundation of an educated and not an illiterate people.

Breckinridge expressed disgust at attempts to attract northern manufacturers by advertising "that we have not only the cotton and the fuel . . . but the cheap child labor as well." And she insisted that the men who proclaimed themselves chivalrous were failing to protect women or children, and that perhaps they needed women's insight in politics.[24]

Southern suffragists thus insisted that Southern Ladies needed the vote in order to fulfill traditional duties: to protect their own families and children as well as the region's poor. As Nellie Nugent Somerville explained, "When a child contracts scarlet fever or diphtheria at a public school the mother knows that the school board and board of health are closely connected with her family life. The ante-bellum mother with children under a governess or in a small private school knew nothing of the school boards and boards of health." Indeed, as the Progressive movement spread even into the South, southern suffragists joined suffragists elsewhere in the nation in pointing out that, as Lila Meade Valentine observed, "there is a whole group of interests which belong peculiarly to women and which with the expanding functions of government have become political questions." Valentine, president of the Equal Suffrage League of Virginia and a well-known advocate of improved public health measures, saw the two causes as closely related: "Questions concerning food, water, sanitation, education, light, heat, plumbing, treatment of diseases, child labor, hours of labor for women and children . . . all these questions nearly concern the home and the child."[25]

Again knowing that they had only a measure of indirect influence with which to gain direct influence, and that they were treading on slippery ground when suggesting that southern men inadequately protected women and children, southern suffragists proceeded with care. They pleaded for equal partnership in government with the men of their class by cleverly emphasizing the differences in interests and responsibilities of the sexes—a tactful way of saying that the interests of women and children would never be adequately protected so long as women were relying on men to protect them.

Anne Dallas Dudley, a Nashville socialite and suffrage leader, used this theme in a 1911 speech entitled "The Southern Temperament as Related to Woman Suffrage." Particularly adept in the use of "honey-tongued charm" (a tactic that often shocked northern suffragists), Dudley remarked that

> As long as it was a question of woman's rights; as long as the fight had any appearance of being against man; as long as there seemed to be a vestige of sex antagonism, the Southern woman stood with her back turned squarely toward the cause. She wouldn't even turn around to look at it. She would have none of it at all. But when she awoke slowly to a social consciousness, when eyes and brain were at last free after a terrible reconstruction period, to look out upon the world as a whole; when she found particularly among the more fortunate classes that her leisure had come to mean laziness, when she realized that through the changed conditions of modern life so much of her work had been taken out of the home, leaving her to choose between following it into the world or remaining idle; when with a clearer vision she saw that man needed her help in governmental affairs, particularly where they touched her own interests, she said, "Oh, that is so different!"

To the southern man, Dudley continued, the southern woman said:

> In the past you have not shown yourself averse to accepting my help in very serious matters; my courage and fortitude and wisdom you have continually praised. Now that there is a closer connection between the government and the home than ever before in the history of the world, will you not let me help you?[26]

The equally diplomatic Mary Johnston likewise called upon southern men, who perhaps surpassed all others in adulation of "their" women, to grant women the compliment of trusting them to assist in government. In a speech of 1910 or 1911 entitled "The Woman Movement in the South," Johnston remarked:

> To a very large extent I think that the Southern woman in the fight for the franchise may count upon the active help of the Southern man. The man of the South has a very true regard for the woman of the South. He has seen her tried in many a contingency, and he has seen her come out well. At the moment there is much confusion of ideas, much dragging into the question of irrelevant matters, some bewilderment, some terror for fear the roof will

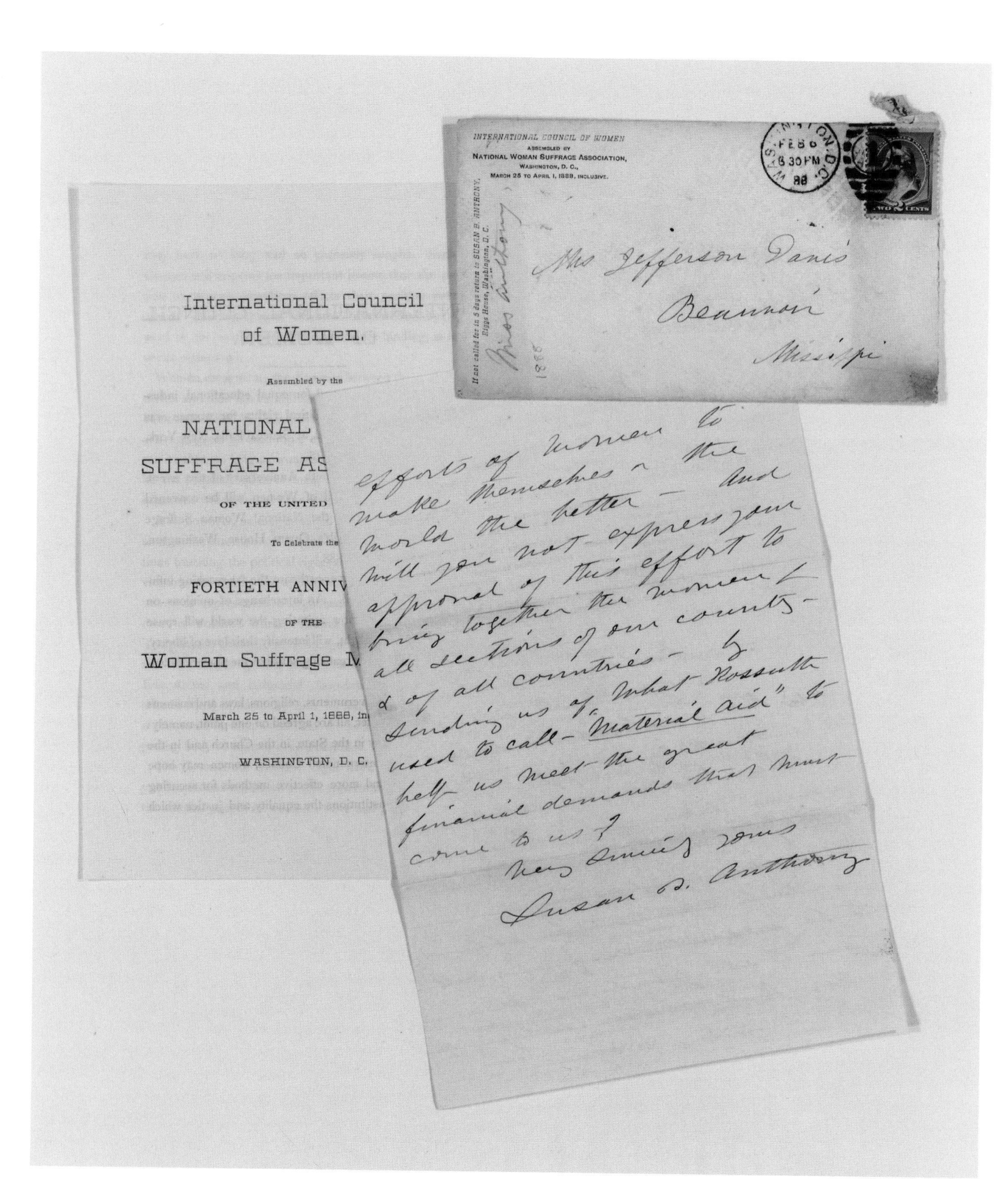

International Council of Women.

Assembled by the

NATIONAL

SUFFRAGE AS

OF THE UNITED

To Celebrate the

FORTIETH ANNIV

OF THE

Woman Suffrage M

March 25 to April 1, 1888, in

WASHINGTON, D. C.

INTERNATIONAL COUNCIL OF WOMEN
ASSEMBLED BY
NATIONAL WOMAN SUFFRAGE ASSOCIATION,
WASHINGTON, D. C.,
MARCH 25 TO APRIL 1, 1888, INCLUSIVE.

If not called for in 5 days return to SUSAN B. ANTHONY,
Riggs House, Washington, D. C.

Miss Anthony

1888

WASHINGTON D.C. FEB 6 6 30 PM 88

Mrs Jefferson Davis
Beauvoir
Missippi

efforts of women to
make themselves & the
world the better — And
will you not express your
approval of this effort to
bring together the women of
all sections of our country —
& of all countries — by
sending us of, what Kossuth
used to call — "material aid" to
help us meet the great
financial demands that must
come to us?

Very Sincerely yours
Susan B. Anthony

***Susan B. Anthony letter to Varina Howell Davis.** On behalf of the National Woman Suffrage Association, Anthony in 1888 invited Davis to join with "representative women from all classes" in the "reforms which women are now conducting." (Manuscript, 6 February 1888.)*
Jefferson Davis Collection, Eleanor S. Brockenbrough Library, The Museum of the Confederacy

> fall. Time and events will assuage these fears. The men of the South will come to see that the woman struggling for her political independence is just the pioneer woman, the Revolutionary woman, the woman, unselfish and brave, of the War between the States—just the Southern woman working out her destiny now as then. He honoured her under the earlier aspects; he will honour her under this, for he will come to see that it is the same woman. Justice, fair-play, self government, development, realization—these have been his ideals, and he will come to recognize their value in his sister and his mate. The best of the Southern men may, I think, be depended upon to give their voice for the enfranchisement of the women of the South.[27]

Southern white men, Johnston implied, must either chivalrously enfranchise these sterling southern women they had so honored in the past and trust them to continue to work for good within southern society—or be exposed as hypocrites. Some southern politicians, and countless newspaper editors across the region, accepted this assessment of woman suffrage. But most, however, continued to see woman suffrage as a direct contradiction to southern tradition.

The suffragists may have had to stretch a point occasionally. After all, they were invoking tradition in support of change. The opponents of woman suffrage had no such problem. Southern tradition was very clear about woman's relation to politics. Her role was to inspire, to suggest—not to influence politics directly. Women were applauded who understood their weaknesses as well as their strengths, trusted men to protect them—and appreciated that protection.

By the turn of the century, southerners had at least become somewhat accustomed to seeing women exercising a public role as lobbyists. Though women's clubs had been suspect initially, the influence of organized womanhood in public affairs was by then widely accepted—as long as they avoided controversy. The postwar period had produced, as George Rable has observed, "change without change," "modest reform and the survival of conservative attitudes," "a crazy-quilt pattern of modest and limited improvements in an atmosphere of ideological reaction."[28] Women's clubs received the least resistance, of course, when there was a clear connection between their projects and goals and woman's traditional role. When women engaged in charitable work, or lobbied for better schools, libraries, and public health programs, for example, the work was regarded as the logical extension of woman's role.[29]

The United Daughters of the Confederacy was a prime example of a woman's organization that bent rather than broke tradition. The UDC was much appreciated for its role in honoring the Confederate dead, erecting statues, and aiding aging and impoverished Confederate veterans and widows. And despite the fact that the UDC's impressive fund-raising and lobbying efforts clearly involved women in non-traditional, non-domestic activities, "the Daughters" were applauded for their educational programs in which they acted to ensure that the "true" history of the "War between the States" was taught to future generations of southerners. Certainly this work was consistent with the true "mission" of southern women, "to rear and train and educate, and mould the future Washingtons, and Lees, and Jacksons of the South." And they took care to pursue these activities while offering no direct challenge to male authority.[30]

Women's clubs encountered the most opposition, however, when they sought clear leadership roles for women. For example, efforts to enable women to serve on school boards, on boards of trustees of public institutions, or as factory inspectors met strong resistance. Organized women also encountered opposition when trying to change inheritance, guardianship, property, or divorce laws; to raise the age of consent; or to win the admission of women to exclusively male educational institutions. But even in these areas, advocates of change gradually made some headway.

None of these reforms, however, constituted the direct threat to the very notion of female subordination and separation of spheres represented by woman suffrage. And though the suffragists rose from the ranks of the clubwomen, many southern clubwomen disdained to support suffrage either as the result of personal antipathy or the very real fear of antagonizing the men upon whom they relied for support. The closing years of the suffrage campaign saw endorsements of woman suffrage by many and varied women's organizations—and even some *individual* UDC members became suffragists. But in doing so the women took a calculated risk: they might diminish rather than enhance their influence, at least in the short run.[31] One thing was certain. No matter how much the suffragists tried to conceal it, the demand for suffrage constituted a rejection of male authority and an implicit accusation of male failure to represent the interests of women—an accusation that southern conservatives understood and did not appreciate. Woman suffrage, many opponents insisted, was a direct contradiction to southern tradition.

Antisuffragists of both sexes were highly effective in exploiting the southern prejudices against, and fears of, woman suffrage. They presented woman suffrage as a threat to southern womanhood and the home and to white supremacy—indeed, as antithetical to southern values. They depicted southern suffragists as misguided and ungrateful. Female antisuffragists claimed that *they*, not the suffragists, were the true representatives of the wishes of southern white women, and stressed their devotion to their traditional sphere. Antisuffrage women in Alabama once declined to take the podium at an open hearing before the legislature. Instead, they asked a senator to read their statement proclaiming that they had no desire to "mix in politics" and begging legislators not to force them "from the quietude of our homes into the contaminating atmosphere of political struggle."[32]

Suffrage opponents attacked suffragists as traitors to their region who would betray their birthright, the Lost Cause. In 1914, UDC historian-general Mildred Rutherford, speaking for the Georgia chapter of the National Association Opposed to Woman Suffrage, told the state legislature:

> The women who are working for this measure are striking at the principles for which their fathers fought during the Civil War. Woman's suffrage comes from the North and West and from women who do not believe in states' rights and who wish to see negro women using the ballot. I do not believe the state of Georgia has sunk so low that her good men can not legislate for the women. If this time ever comes then it will be in time for women to claim the ballot.[33]

Alabama state senator J. B. Evans, in a widely circulated 1917 pamphlet, *Politics and Patriotism*, conceded that "most of the members of the Alabama Suffrage Association are daughters and granddaughters of Confederate Veterans," but charged that they had "allowed themselves to be misled by bold women who are the product of the peculiar social conditions of our Northern cities into advocating a political innovation the realization of which would be the undoing of the South." "These misguided daughters of the South," he said, "are endorsing the principles for which Thad Stevens, Fred Douglass, Susan B. Anthony and other bitter enemies of the South contended, and if they succeed then indeed was the blood of their fathers shed in vain."[34]

Antisuffragists repeatedly insisted that woman suffrage threatened white supremacy by questioning its underlying principles or by tampering with election laws that had successfully reestablished white dominance in politics. Without explaining why the laws of Virginia that disqualified black men would not apply to black women, the *Richmond Times-Dispatch* warned that woman suffrage "would double the number of uncertain and dangerous voters and put the balance of political power in the hands of 165,000 colored women, only to gratify the whims of a small group of women who don't really know what they are about."[35]

A 1915 editorial from the *Richmond Evening Journal,* reprinted as a pamphlet, *Virginia Warns Her People Against Woman Suffrage,* attacked southern suffragists as spoiled and illogical creatures who failed to comprehend the stern realities of politics and were ungrateful to the men who had assumed this burdensome task for their sakes. "Probably the ladies engaged in the suffrage movement," the newspaper declared,

> are not very practical or very logical or very well informed or disposed to bother their heads with the actual facts of politics. . . . But men are compelled and accustomed to face and deal with hard facts when considering important affairs in business or in politics. . . . We do not suppose, or imagine, that the suffrage ladies would suggest . . . counting out the colored people of their own sex or to stuffing the ballot boxes or padding registration lists. We wicked and inefficient and tyrannical men who are supposed to have made such a mess of government in Virginia, became ashamed of such methods and alarmed by them and contrived to remove the necessity for them. Surely we are not to be incited to return to the slimepit from which we dug ourselves.[36]

As support grew in the West and North for woman suffrage, and the suffrage movement began to focus increasingly on the adoption of a federal woman suffrage amendment, the suffrage struggle did indeed take on the appearance of a renewed regional struggle. Although a storm of criticism from his colleagues from the North and West caused him to have it stricken, South Carolina's Senator Benjamin "Pitchfork Ben" Tillman had Albert Bledsoe's 1871 "Mission of Woman"—replete with its vicious attack on northern women—introduced into the *Congressional Record* in 1913. Tillman accused suffrage supporters in Congress of being cowards for failing to stand up against woman suffragists and appealed to them to resist the "craze" that, if successful, would "usher in another thousand years of moral blight, sexual depravity and degradation."[37] Southern Democrats constituted a formidable block and long delayed congressional approval of the amendment, insisting that the federal government *still* did not have the right to dictate suffrage qualifications and policies within the states.

When President Woodrow Wilson, born in Virginia and claimed as their own by southerners, endorsed the federal woman suffrage amendment despite earlier objections based on states' rights, southern Democrats were both astonished and furious. Wilson was promptly denounced by the Alabama Association Opposed to Woman Suffrage, which then insisted Wilson could not possibly understand the traditions they cherished since he had only one "native-born" (meaning southern) ancestor.[38] Wilson tried valiantly to persuade Democrats in Congress to support an amendment for which success, he insisted, was only a matter of time. In contrast, Senator John Sharp Williams, of Mississippi, voiced the sentiments of southern conservatives who believed that their constituents expected them to resist to the end rather than submit to the inevitable: "If they make me a party to it it is not my fault, but if I become a party to it of my own accord, it ceases to be rape and becomes fornication."[39]

After Congress approved the amendment and sent it to the states on 4 June 1919, the suffrage struggle entered its last, and perhaps nastiest, phase. Antisuffragists continued to oppose woman suffrage as irreligious and as a threat to southern womanhood, but they now concentrated increasingly on the *method* of enfranchisement—the federal amendment—which, they insisted, was the greatest threat to white supremacy since the Fifteenth Amendment. Just six days after Congress submitted the amendment to the states, Senator Lee Overman, of North Carolina, issued a statement that national suffrage leader Carrie Chapman Catt called the "keynote of the opposition," reiterating the idea that suffrage advocates were unwittingly supporting a grave threat to their society. "In my opinion," Senator Overman declared,

> the Woman Suffrage Amendment just adopted by Congress is a reaffirmation of the Fifteenth Amendment. I wonder if this is appreciated throughout the South? This latter amendment simply goes a step further than the Fifteenth Amendment. In addition to saying that the right of suffrage shall not be

> abridged by reason of race, color or previous condition of servitude the new amendment adds the word "sex." The language is not identical, but it is evident that the Woman Suffrage resolution is a postscript to the former amendment, which we have always opposed in the South. . . . Congress reserves the right of "appropriate legislation" to enforce this mandate, regardless of the State. That is the condition in a nutshell. I wonder if woman suffrage advocates in the South have taken into consideration all the embarrassing features possible under such legislation.

Overman and other suffrage opponents turned the ratification fight into a full-scale battle over the survival of state sovereignty and the South's ability to preserve "the Southern Way of Life."[40] In the ensuing struggle over ratification, those in opposition made it clear that they regarded a southerner's position on the suffrage amendment as *the* crucial test of loyalty to the South and its values.

Virginia novelist Thomas Nelson Page, who contributed his considerable prestige to the antisuffrage cause, insisted in an antisuffrage pamphlet that whatever the merits or demerits of woman suffrage, he could not imagine "how any one, man or woman, who is in the least familiar with the history of suffrage in Virginia and in other States or the South, could think for a moment of advocating placing the suffrage under the control of the National Government." Page went even further:

> During more than a generation the South lay in the throes of a great struggle to preserve its local self-government and everything on which its civilization rested from destruction, and it has only been in the last few years, since the new constitutions of the several States were adopted and were held to be constitutional by the highest courts in the land, that the people of Virginia and the other Southern States have been able to breathe freely. To reopen this question now by an attempt to bring about a new amendment to the Constitution of the United States, dealing with suffrage, would in my judgement, be an immeasurable injury to the South and indeed the whole Nation.

The fundamental question underlying the federal suffrage amendment, Page insisted, "is that which the South fought against during the entire generation following our war, the question not only of equality of the sexes, but the equality of the races."[41]

Eager to remind southerners of the historic connection between woman suffrage and abolitionism, antisuffragists always spoke of the federal suffrage amendment derisively as "the Susan B. Anthony Amendment" and attacked national leaders of the movement as advocates of racial equality and enemies of the South. They described Anthony as "a rabid hater of the Southern people to the day of her death, and an absolute worshiper of the negro." They vilified suffragist Anna Howard Shaw as the "bosom friend" of Anthony and "thoroughly imbued with all of her South-hating, negro-loving propensities." Many antisuffrage brochures emphasized the friendship between suffragists and Frederick Douglass and other blacks. Other opponents pointed out that in the *History of Woman Suffrage* Elizabeth Cady Stanton spoke of her pride and pleasure in walking "arm in arm" with Douglass and "revealed" that Susan B. Anthony privately "approved" of Douglass's marriage to a white woman. One antisuffrage brochure, entitled *Character of Robert E. Lee Defamed*, accused Anthony and Elizabeth Cady Stanton of using "calumny and falsehood" in claiming that Lee had banished his daughter Annie from his home for her Unionist sympathies. The suffragists, many southerners claimed, sought to "stab the name

Nina Pinckard* (left), *Josephine Pearson* (right), *and an unidentified Confederate veteran at the Nashville headquarters of the Southern Women's League for Rejection of the Susan B. Anthony Amendment.
The grandniece of John C. Calhoun, Nina Pinckard served as president-general of the antisuffrage organization. She captioned the photograph "Truth crushed to the Earth will rise again." (Photograph, August 1920.)
Tennessee State Library

and fame of General Lee" and thereby "commit so many southern women to their creed—a creed that means wreck and ruin of our southern ideals."[42]

In true Lost Cause fashion, southern opponents of ratification were determined to prevent this "immeasurable injury to American society" and portrayed the mission of the South as saving the nation from itself. One prominent southern antisuffragist, James Callaway, of Georgia, wrote a pamphlet entitled *Will the States Consent to Blot the Stars from Old Glory, Leaving Only a Meaningless Square of Blue?* and subtitled *A Message from the Old South to an United Nation of To-Day.* Its central message was that the nation must not *once again* pass a constitutional amendment "in war times when the public mind is out of joint and not in a normal condition."[43]

Southern opponents plotted to kill the amendment by securing "rejection resolutions" from at least thirteen southern states and then asking for a "Proclamation of Defeat." Although they failed in this specific effort, most southern states—except Texas, Arkansas, and Kentucky—refused to ratify the amendment. For those that might waver, southern antisuffragists kept up a constant pressure, even as the amendment steadily gained endorsements from northern and

Mildred Lewis Rutherford (1850–1928). *Mildred Rutherford, as historian-general of the United Daughters of the Confederacy from 1911 to 1916, was the UDC's most prolific and energetic defender of the Confederate faith. Bedecked in historical costumes, she often lectured on such topics as "Wrongs of History Righted" and "Historical Sins of Omission and Commission." An avowed defender of tradition and a stubborn enemy of the concept of a "New South," she declared in 1912 that "the South of today is the South of yesterday, remade to fit the new order of things. And the men and women of today are readjusting themselves to the Old South remade." "If we must yield our states rights, whether for National prohibition or for National Woman Suffrage or for any other cause," she told a Dallas, Texas, audience in 1916, "while our negro population is so great, yes greater in Georgia today than in all of the New England States and the Northern states combined, we will have a Reconstruction Period worse than that which followed the War Between the States." (Photograph portrait, from* Four Addresses by Miss Mildred Lewis Rutherford, *1912.)*
Eleanor S. Brockenbrough Library, The Museum of the Confederacy

western states. When at last thirty-five of the thirty-six states needed for approval had ratified the amendment, and at President Wilson's urging the governors of North Carolina and Tennessee had called special legislative sessions to consider the issue, antisuffragists dug in for a final battle.[44] The North Carolina antisuffrage newspaper, the *State's Defense*, asked:

> Can a State which boasts of being "Last at Appomattox" run up the white flag and say, "It is coming, we surrender"? God grant that North Carolina has enough men with the spirit of the Old South left in them to go down with their backs to the wall fighting to preserve the last vestige of what their forefathers fought during four years of civil strife to preserve—the sovereignty of the State.

The North Carolina legislature, in fact, defeated the ratification resolution and urged Tennessee to "fight to the last ditch, and then some."[45]

Tennessee antisuffragists took up the challenge and in a no-holds-barred struggle, pledged themselves to "Save the South." Antisuffrage men and women from all over the United States descended upon Tennessee, but the fight still had a distinctly southern flavor. The leader of the Tennessee chapter of the Southern Women's League for Rejection of the Susan B. Anthony Amendment, Josephine Pearson, spoke of the antisuffrage fight as a "Holy War" against the suffragists and their leader, Carrie Chapman Catt, who would "level" the standards of southern women to those of men. Pearson considered the suffrage movement to be a "plebeian" movement beneath the dignity of southern women "to the manner born." The fight against ratification, she said, was nothing less than a "crucial test of Southern rights and honor." It was a bitter struggle. Tennessee ratified the Nineteenth Amendment by the narrowest of margins and only after a twenty-four-year-old legislator, expected to oppose ratification, voted for the proposal at the request of his aged mother.[46]

This final battle over ideology and influence clearly demonstrated the continued strength of tradition and its power over white southerners. Nowhere was this more clearly demonstrated than in the *opposition* to the federal amendment by several southern *suffragists* who had devoted several decades of their lives to fighting for women's right to vote. Even Laura Clay, ironically the daughter of a Union officer and abolitionist, was so committed to states' rights that she opposed the federal woman suffrage amendment as a threat to state sovereignty. Her close associates, Kate and Jean Gordon, of New Orleans, who had worked for suffrage since the 1890s, did likewise. All three women actually went to Nashville to oppose ratification, though they hated being associated with the despised antisuffragists. To the dismay of Mississippi suffragists, Kate Gordon spoke publicly against ratification in Jackson, where she urged Mississippians not to "vindicate Thaddeus Stevens and in the same breath repudiate that long dead company of her distinguished and patriotic sons" who had fought for Southern Civilization and Mississippi.[47]

Most southern suffragists, however, even the oldest ones, did not share this point of view. Loyalty to their states meant that they had *preferred* to be enfranchised by state legislation, action that would have indicated acceptance of women's equality and signalled to the world that the states and region they loved had progressed. Still, most supported the federal amendment when their efforts to gain state amendments had been rebuffed. They were bitterly disappointed, however, when, in all but four southern states, women gained the right to vote only over the figurative dead bodies of their legislators.

Long before the suffrage struggle ended, many women had become disillusioned with southern tradition. They were sick to death of hearing about southern chivalry and about women being too good to vote. In a 1910 speech to women college graduates, Mary Johnston said, "Last year at the Capitol I heard more talk in one day about chivalry from the lawyer in the pay of the knitting mills who were under indictment from overworking women and children than you could perhaps have heard from . . . [English poet] Sir Phillip Sidney in a year."[48] Nellie Nugent Somerville revealed her exasperation over men's claims that women were too good to be exposed to politics in a 1914 newspaper article:

> It is quite common for men to say . . . that women should not vote because they are too good and must not be degraded to the level of men. . . . Now the facts in the case are that there is not a word of truth in this proposition. It is exasperating because it is short-sighted, unreasonably and historically false. . . . Exclusion from the right to vote is a degradation—always has been, always will be, never was intended as anything else, can not be sugarcoated into anything else.[49]

In her flowery prose, Mary Johnston insisted that the South was so busy looking to the past that it could not advance into the future. "The Southern mind," she wrote, "is still hypnotized by its own success into forgetfulness that the age for which it theorized is passed. It stares fixedly at the shell, and does not see that the life within it was transformed and is now elsewhere. It has a tendency to become rigid with the weight of the past." Southern men and women, she said, must "let the dead past bury its dead." But instead, so many of them "elect to stay by the corpse rather than to accompany the escaped spirit in its swift, onward flight." They have "placed their ideal in the past rather than in the future." Southern suffragists ("the awakened women"), on the other hand, she said, "also keep green the memory of what has been. But they do not stand like Lot's wife and look back. Their star shines before them, shines above a fairer, happier, higher, nobler world."[50]

The constant evocation of the Civil War and the Lost Cause eventually disgusted even Rebecca Latimer Felton, a member of the United Daughters of the Confederacy, who wrote in 1919:

> The children of the Southern States are being unwisely taught by Southern agitators, women as well as men, that the political issues of the Civil War are still germane and worthy of adoration. They are instructed to call the Lost Cause a glorious cause. They resent any change in public opinion, because the change would mean their own retirancy to back seats in politics and from public attention. They are barnacles on the ship of state, and they have inoculated hatred to "D__n Yankees" as a creed to be eulogized and fostered.[51]

The suffragists grew weary of hearing about white supremacy, states' rights, and regional animosity—constantly and successfully invoked to defeat them. Repeatedly the suffragists insisted that race was a non-issue, trumped up by their opponents. "If it wasn't the negro woman (Poor soul!) it would be something else," wrote Mary Johnston to Lila Valentine in 1913. "Anything or everything—far fetchedness wouldn't matter."[52]

Furious when southern Democrats expected southern suffragists to "understand" that they could not support the federal suffrage amendment because of states' rights, Tennessee suffragist Sue Shelton White retorted, "Moss-backed traditions of political parties will no longer be accepted as an excuse for withholding democracy from women. There are suffragists born Democrats who have hoped to live and die in the political faith of their fathers who can no longer accept such an excuse."[53]

Indeed, having worked so hard to gain

enfranchisement through the "chivalrous" action of the men of their home states, nothing infuriated the suffragists so much as politicians' ratification-era claims that they were now willing to enfranchise women but could not do so out of respect for states' rights. As Pattie Ruffner Jacobs, of Alabama, said:

> If these men who invoke the doctrine of states rights when it suits their purposes and who are still dominated by those old, unhappy, far-off memories of fifty years ago were sincere, we who live in the present might more easily forgive them. If they really wished the ballot to come to the Southern women by the state route, we would have had more referenda. The test of their sincerity has been in repeatedly declining even that medium of relief to the voteless women. They are opposed to justice, not merely its method of attainment.[54]

For years, it had been a bitter experience for these loyal daughters of the South to have each defeat of the Nineteenth Amendment celebrated in state after southern state as a "Keeping of the Faith," a "Triumph for Southern Civilization," and a display of "loyalty to tradition." Pattie Jacobs described her own feelings (and those of southern suffragists whose states refused to ratify) in a remarkable address at the 1920 National American Woman Suffrage Association—a speech she entitled "Tradition Vs. Justice."

Speaking to a largely northern and western audience, Jacobs explained that southern suffragists respected their heritage but were convinced that the South was severely limited by this "tyranny of tradition," which was "difficult to explain" and to whose dominance southern men seemed "particularly susceptible." And she insisted that "while many of the traditions of the old South were gracious and kindly, beautiful and honorable, if their product is injustice they are no longer admirable."

Somewhat defensive before her non-southern audience, Jacobs refused to fault the South for its hierarchical, tightly controlled, "aristocratic" society. But she said the South had now "moved beyond the period in which the practices of repression created by the exigencies of a by-gone day can longer be justified." It was natural, she said, that democracy had evolved more slowly in the region as it had "further to go." And she acknowledged that southerners, herself included, were still "nursing our respect for the past," including "the old heritage of guardianship toward the unprivileged." Jacobs insisted, however, that a state could not base present policy on "outlived conditions," and while the "unprivileged" might still be in need of the protection of "guardianship," such paternalism was, she believed, completely inappropriate for southern women like herself. Indeed, Jacobs and other proud white southern suffragists considered the failure of southern men to enfranchise them as degrading, "for we of all people understand the symbolism of the ballot, especially in states where its use is restricted and professedly based upon virtue and intelligence."

Southern suffragists, she insisted, wanted the power to help bring about justice as they saw it. Indeed, said Jacobs, for southern women, administering "justice had become our tradition. Justice to all women, children, to the illiterates in our midst, justice to the women in industry still working unlimited hours, justice to all the hitherto unprivileged." Yet through the successful invocation of southern tradition, Jacobs explained, the women of the region were being denied the opportunity to dispense justice by assisting in the governance of their society. Participation in the suffrage movement had given Jacobs and the southern leaders a bitter education about the strength of tradition in southern society and the need to free themselves from its restraining power. "We know we have background and an honorable past," she said, "but we wish to occasionally be allowed to forget it, and to live in the present and build for the future."[55]

NOTES

FOREWORD
SUZANNE LEBSOCK

[1] Anne Firor Scott, *The Southern Lady: From Pedestal to Politics, 1830–1930* (Charlottesville, Va., 1995), 79.

[2] These works include, in order of their publication, Suzanne Lebsock, *The Free Women of Petersburg: Status and Culture in a Southern Town, 1784–1860* (New York, 1984); Jean E. Friedman, *The Enclosed Garden: Women and Community in the Evangelical South, 1830–1900* (Chapel Hill, N.C., 1985); George C. Rable, *Civil Wars: Women and the Crisis of Southern Nationalism* (Urbana, Ill., 1989); and Drew Gilpin Faust, *Mothers of Invention: Women of the Slaveholding South in the American Civil War* (Chapel Hill, N.C., 1996). Joan E. Cashin, "Women at War," *Reviews in American History* 18 (1990): 343–48, provides a very useful analysis of this debate to 1990. Peter W. Bardaglio, *Reconstructing the Household: Families, Sex, and the Law in the Nineteenth-Century South* (Chapel Hill, N.C., 1995), redirects the conversation by pointing to significant changes in family law after the Civil War.

A WOMAN'S WAR: Southern Women in the Civil War
DREW GILPIN FAUST, THAVOLIA GLYMPH, AND GEORGE C. RABLE

[1] On white women in slaveholding families see Drew Gilpin Faust, *Mothers of Invention: Women of the Slaveholding South in the American Civil War* (Chapel Hill, N.C., 1996); George C. Rable, *Civil Wars: Women and the Crisis of Southern Nationalism* (Urbana, Ill., 1989); Catherine Clinton, *Tara Revisited: Women, War and the Plantation Legend* (New York, 1995); and Francis Butler Simkins and James Welch Patton, *The Women of the Confederacy* (Richmond, 1936).

[2] "A Planter's Wife" to Governor John J. Pettus, 1 May 1862, John J. Pettus Papers, Mississippi Department of Archives and History, Jackson; Amanda Walker to Confederate Secretary of War George Wythe Randolph, 31 October 1862, Letters Received, Confederate Secretary of War (LR-CSW), Record Group 109, reel 79, W1106, National Archives, Washington, D.C. (NA); Ellen Moore to Samuel Moore, 23 March 1862, Samuel J. C. Moore Papers, Southern Historical Collection, University of North Carolina, Chapel Hill (SHC-UNC); Ira Berlin, Barbara J. Fields, Steven F. Miller, Joseph P. Reidy, and Leslie S. Rowland, eds., *Free at Last: A Documentary History of Slavery, Freedom, and the Civil War* (New York, 1992), 108.

[3] Lucy Watkins to Confederate Secretary of War George Wythe Randolph, 13 October 1862, LR-CSW, Record Group 109, reel 79, M1091; Harriet Pipkin to Confederate Adjutant General Samuel Cooper, Letters Received, Confederate Adjutant General, ser. 12, box 18, H2636, NA; Mary Watts to Confederate Secretary of War James H. Seddon, 15 May 1863, LR-CSW, Record Group 109, reel 116, W315.

[4] Leila Callaway to Morgan Callaway, 22 January 1863, Morgan Callaway Papers, Emory University, Atlanta, Ga.; Joan E. Cashin, "'Since the War Broke Out': The Marriage of Kate and William McClure," in *Divided Houses: Gender and the Civil War*, ed. Catherine Clinton and Nina Silber (New York, 1992), 200–212; Beth G. Crabtree and James W. Patton, eds., *"Journal of a Secesh Lady": The Diary of Catherine Ann Devereux Edmondston, 1860–1866* (Raleigh, N.C., 1979), 293.

[5] Lizzie Neblett to Will Neblett, 18 August 1863, Lizzie Neblett Papers, Center for American History, University of Texas, Austin (CAH-UT); Bell Irvin Wiley, *Southern Negroes, 1861–1865* (New Haven, 1938), 76; Sarah Kennedy Diary, 19 August 1863, Tennessee State Library and Archives, Nashville.

[6] Faust, *Mothers of Invention*, 78.

[7] Charles East, ed., *The Civil War Diary of Sarah Morgan* (Athens, Ga., 1991), 77; Kate Cumming, *Kate: The Journal of a Confederate Nurse*, ed. Richard Barksdale Harwell (Baton Rouge, La., 1959), 38–39.

[8] Lucy Wood to Waddy Butler, 2 May 1861, Lucy Wood Butler Papers, University of Virginia Library, Charlottesville; Rable, *Civil Wars*, 138–44.

[9] See Phoebe Yates Pember, *A Southern Woman's Story: Life in Confederate Richmond. Including Unpublished Letters Written from the Chimborazo Hospital*, ed. Bell Irvin Wiley (1959; reprint, Saint Simons Island, Ga., 1974); Cumming, *Kate: The Journal*; J. Fraise Richard, *The Florence Nightingale of the Southern Army: Experiences of Mrs. Ella K. Newsom, Confederate Nurse in the Great War of 1861–1865* (New York, 1914); Mrs. Fielding Lewis Taylor, "Capt. Sallie Tompkins," *Confederate Veteran* 24 (November 1916): 521, 524; Lucille Griffith, "Mrs. Juliet Opie Hopkins and Alabama Military Hospitals," *Alabama Review* 6 (1953): 99–120.

[10] Emma Crutcher to Will Crutcher, 20 March 1862, Crutcher-Shannon Papers, CAH-UT; Cumming, *Kate: The Journal*, 135.

[11] Pember, *A Southern Woman's Story*, 105, 114.

[12] W. Buck Yearns and John G. Barrett, eds., *North Carolina Civil War Documentary* (Chapel Hill, N.C., 1980), 231, 237; Thomas Woody, *A History of Women's Education in the United States* (New York, 1929), 1:498.

[13] Rable, *Civil Wars*, 131.

[14] Faust, *Mothers of Invention*, 88–92.

[15] Inspection Report, Richmond, 26 August 1864, Confederate Quartermaster Department Inspection Reports, Record Group 109, reel 7, M935, NA; *Richmond Inquirer*, 4 November 1862, 17 March 1863; Memorandum, John Whitford Papers, North Carolina Division of Archives and History, Raleigh (NC-DAH).

[16] Frontis W. Johnston, ed., *The Papers of Zebulon Baird Vance* (Raleigh, N.C., 1963), 1:308.

[17] Michael Chesson, "Harlots or Heroines? A New Look at the Richmond Bread Riot," *Virginia Magazine of History and Biography*

92 (1984): 131–75; Victoria E. Bynum, "'War Within a War': Women's Participation in the Revolt of the North Carolina Piedmont," *Frontiers* 9 (1987): 43–49; Paul D. Escott, *Many Excellent People: Power and Privilege in North Carolina, 1850–1900* (Chapel Hill, N.C., 1986), 67.

[18] Mary Elizabeth Massey, *Refugee Life in the Confederacy* (Baton Rouge, La., 1964); George Rable, *Civil Wars*, 181–220; Faust, *Mothers of Invention*, 40-45.

[19] Diary of Mary Greenhow Lee, 14 March 1865, Winchester–Frederick County Historical Society, Handley Library, Winchester, Va.

[20] Mrs. M. P. Caudle to Governor Zebulon Vance, 7 October 1863, Zebulon Vance Papers, NC-DAH.

[21] Berlin et al., eds., *Free at Last*, 150.

[22] Mrs. A. P. Acors to Jefferson Davis, 23 March 1862, LR-CSW, Record Group 94, reel 29, 437.

[23] Yearns and Barrett, eds., *North Carolina Civil War Documentary*, 22, 97.

[24] *Montgomery Daily Advertiser*, 16 July 1864; Constance Cary Harrison, *Recollections Grave and Gay* (New York, 1911), 83.

[25] Diary of L. Virginia French, 26 March 1863, Tennessee State Library, Nashville; Mary Greenhow Lee diary, 21 May 1865; Annie Upshur to Jefferson Davis, 3 January 1865, LR-CSW, Record Group 109, reel 114, U2.

[26] John Marszalek, ed., *Diary of Miss Emma Holmes, 1861–1866* (Baton Rouge, La., 1979), 26.

[27] J. Michael Welton, ed., *"My Heart Is So* Rebellious*": The Caldwell Letters, 1861–1865* (Warrenton, Va., 1991), 241, 255; Alice Ready Diary, 24 March 1862, SHC-UNC; Grace Elmore Diary, 10 May 1865, South Caroliniana Library, University of South Carolina, Columbia.

[28] Margaret Mitchell, *Gone With the Wind* (New York, 1936), 428.

[29] Ira Berlin, Barbara J. Fields, Thavolia Glymph, Joseph P. Reidy, and Leslie S. Rowland, eds., *The Destruction of Slavery*, ser. 1, vol. 1, of *Freedom: A Documentary History of Emancipation, 1861–1867* (Cambridge, 1985), 71, 78–83; U.S. Naval War Records Office, *Official Records of the Union and Confederate Navies in the War of the Rebellion* (Washington, D.C., 1894–1922), ser. 1, 5:40–43.

[30] U.S. War Department, *War of the Rebellion: A Compilation of the Official Records of the Union and Confederate Armies* (Washington, D.C., 1880–1901), ser. 1, 6:78–81.

[31] Berlin et al., eds., *The Destruction of Slavery*, 89; Edwin S. Redkey, ed., *A Grand Army of Black Men: Letters from African-American Soldiers in the Union Army, 1861–1865* (Cambridge, 1992), 23; Barbara Jeanne Fields, *Slavery and Freedom on the Middle Ground: Maryland during the Nineteenth Century* (New Haven, 1985), 119.

[32] Berlin et al., eds., *The Destruction of Slavery*, 89; Fields, *Slavery and Freedom*, 119–21.

[33] Berlin et al., eds., *The Destruction of Slavery*, 150–51; Noralee Frankel, *Break Those Chains at Last: African Americans 1860–1880* (New York, 1995), 21; see also Frankel, "The Southern Side of Glory: Mississippi African-American Women During the Civil War," in *"We Specialize in the Wholly Impossible": A Reader in Black Women's History*, ed. Darlene Clark Hine, Wilma King, and Linda Reed (New York, 1995), 335–41.

[34] Ira Berlin, Joseph P. Reidy, and Leslie S. Rowland, eds., *The Black Military Experience*, ser. 2 of *Freedom: A Documentary History of Emancipation, 1861–1867* (Cambridge, 1982), 29–30, 268, 269, 656–61, 686 (Valentine), 687–88 (Hubbard); Berlin et al., eds., *Free at Last*, 400 (Leach).

[35] Ira Berlin, Thavolia Glymph, Steven F. Miller, Joseph P. Reidy, Leslie S. Rowland, and Julie Saville, eds., *The Wartime Genesis of Free Labor: The Lower South*, ser. 1, vol. 3, of *Freedom: A Documentary History of Emancipation, 1861–1867* (Cambridge, 1990), 244–49, 248 (quote).

[36] Redkey, ed., *A Grand Army of Black Men*, 124; Berlin et al., eds., *The Destruction of Slavery*, 150–54.

[37] James M. McPherson, *Battle Cry of Freedom: The Civil War Era* (New York, 1988), 497.

[38] Berlin, et al., eds., *The Wartime Genesis of Labor: The Lower South*, 226–34 (Smith), 314–16 (Mercherson).

[39] Susie King Taylor, *A Black Woman's Civil War Memoirs: Reminiscences of My Life in Camp With the 33rd U.S. Colored Troops, Late 1st South Carolina Volunteers*, ed. Patricia W. Romero (New York, 1988), 91; see also James H. Gooding, *On the Altar of Freedom: A Black Soldier's Civil War Letters from the Front*, ed. Virginia M. Adams (Amherst, Mass., 1991), 27, 111; Ira Berlin, Steven F. Miller, Joseph P. Reidy, and Leslie S. Rowland, eds., *The Wartime Genesis of Free Labor: The Upper South*, ser. 1, vol. 2, of *Freedom: A Documentary History of Emancipation, 1861–1867* (Cambridge, 1993), 1–82.

[40] Berlin et al., eds., *The Black Military Experience*, 715–18.

[41] Redkey, ed., *A Grand Army of Black Men*, 124; Berlin et al., eds., *The Destruction of Slavery*, 150–51.

[42] Elizabeth Hyde Botume, *First Days Amongst the Contrabands* (1893; reprint, New York, 1968), 150, 154; Redkey, ed., *A Grand Army of Black Men*, 167, 176–77.

[43] Berlin, et al., eds., *The Destruction of Slavery*, 686–87.

[44] George P. Rawick, Jan Hillegas, and Ken Lawrence, eds., *The American Slave: A Composite Autobiography, Supplement, Series 1* (Westport, Conn., 1977), Miss., 8: pt. 3, 837.

INTO THE TRACKLESS WILDERNESS: The Refugee Experience in the Civil War

JOAN E. CASHIN

The author is grateful to Jean Baker, Robert Kenzer, and Steven Mintz for their helpful criticisms of this article.

[1] Filia [Sarah Anne Dorsey], *Lucia Dare, A Novel* (New York, 1867), 106–8; Bertram Wyatt-Brown, *The House of Percy: Honor, Melancholy, and Imagination in a Southern Family* (New York, 1994), 131–32.

[2] J. A. Simpson and E. S. C. Weiner, prep., *The Oxford English Dictionary*, 2d ed. (Oxford, 1989), 13:493; Lucia Ann McSpadden and Helene Moussa, "I Have a Name: The Gender Dynamics in Asylum and in Resettlement of Ethiopian and Eritrean Refugees in North America," *Journal of Refugee Studies* 6 (1993): 203–25; Ron Redmond, ed., *Focus: Refugee Women* (Geneva, 1995); George C. Rable, *Civil Wars: Women and the Crisis of Southern Nationalism* (Urbana, Ill., 1989), 181–92; Michael Fellman, *Inside War: The Guerilla Conflict in Missouri during the American Civil War* (New York, 1989), 75; Clarence L. Mohr, *On the Threshold of Freedom: Masters and Slaves in Civil War Georgia* (Athens, Ga., 1986), 99–119; Jean E. Friedman, *The Enclosed Garden: Women and Community in the Evangelical South, 1830–1900* (Chapel Hill, N.C., 1985), 92–98. See also Mary Elizabeth Massey, *Refugee Life in the Confederacy* (Baton Rouge, La., 1964). Massey's well-researched, valuable book argues that most refugees were poor whites and does not concentrate on slave owners, nor does it focus on women.

[3] This essay does not treat the mass evacuations of women from particular locations, which raise different issues, nor does it discuss Appalachian women, who typically stayed home while their male kinfolk became refugees. See Michael D. Hitt, *Charged with Treason: Ordeal of Four Hundred Mill Workers During Military Operations in Roswell, Georgia, 1864–1865* (Monroe, N.Y., 1992); Gordon B. McKinney, "Women's Role in Civil War Western North Carolina," *North*

Carolina Historical Review 69 (1992): 53–54. For general works on women, see Catherine Clinton and Nina Silber, eds., *Divided Houses: Gender and the Civil War* (New York, 1992); Bell Irvin Wiley, *Confederate Women* (Westport, Conn., 1975).

[4] Clarence Mondale, "Place-on-the-Move: Space and Place for the Migrant," in *Mapping American Culture*, ed. Wayne Franklin and Michael Steiner (Iowa City, 1992), 7; Eliza Frances Andrews, *The War-Time Journal of a Georgia Girl, 1864–1865* (New York, 1908), 21; Joan E. Cashin, *A Family Venture: Men and Women on the Southern Frontier* (New York, 1991), 15–16, 81–83; Patricia Cline Cohen, "Safety and Danger: Women on American Public Transport, 1750–1850," in *Gendered Domains: Rethinking Public and Private in Women's History*, ed. Dorothy O. Helly and Susan M. Reverby (Ithaca, N.Y., 1992), 109–22; Michael O'Brien, ed., *An Evening When Alone: Four Journals of Single Women in the South, 1827–67* (Charlottesville, Va., 1993), 110, 153, 166, 174; "Recollections of Letitia Dabney Miller," 14–15, 18, Mrs. Cade Drew Gillespie Papers, Special Collections, University of Mississippi (UMISS); Memoir of Gay Robertson Blackford, 1, Division of Manuscripts and Archives, Virginia Historical Society, Richmond (VHS). See also Steven M. Stowe, "City, Country, and the Feminine Voice," in *Intellectual Life in Antebellum Charleston*, ed. Michael O'Brien and David Moltke-Hansen (Knoxville, Tenn., 1986), 295–301.

[5] Eliza Ripley, *Social Life in Old New Orleans: Being Recollections of My Girlhood* (New York, 1912), 16–17, 40–41; Daniel E. Sutherland, "The Rise and Fall of Esther B. Cheesborough: The Battles of a Literary Lady," *South Carolina Historical Magazine* 84 (1983): 24; "Recollections of Letitia Dabney Miller," 5, 19, Gillespie Papers; Theodore Rosengarten, *Tombee: Portrait of a Cotton Planter* (New York, 1986), 697; Catherine Clinton, *Tara Revisited: Women, War and the Plantation Legend* (New York, 1995), 62. On women's absence from most urban places in the antebellum era, see Mary P. Ryan, *Women in Public: Between Banners and Ballots, 1825–1880* (Baltimore, 1990), 4–41.

[6] Victoria E. Bynum, *Unruly Women: The Politics of Social and Sexual Control in the Old South* (Chapel Hill, N.C., 1992), 1–110; "A Plain Old Farmer" and "The Farmer's Proverbs," *Farmer's Register* 3 (December 1835): 495, VHS; Charles C. Bolton, *Poor Whites of the Antebellum South: Tenants and Laborers in Central North Carolina and Northeast Mississippi* (Durham, N.C., 1994), 62–65, 71.

[7] Diary of Kate S. Carney, 17 August 1859, Southern Historical Collection, University of North Carolina, Chapel Hill (SHC-UNC).

[8] Diary of Ann Webster (Gordon) Christian, 25 January 1860, VHS; Margaret Ripley Wolfe, *Daughters of Canaan: A Saga of Southern Women* (Lexington, Ky., 1995), 64.

[9] Gustavus W. Dyer and John Trotwood Moore, comp., *The Tennessee Civil War Veterans Questionnaires* (Easley, S.C., 1985), 1:250, 2:465; Fred B. Kniffen, "Folk Housing: Key to Diffusion," in *Common Places: Readings in American Vernacular Architecture*, ed. Dell Upton and John Michael Vlach (Athens, Ga., 1986), 3–26; Joan E. Cashin, *Our Common Affairs: Texts from Women in the Old South* (Baltimore, 1996); Orville Vernon Burton, *In My Father's House Are Many Mansions: Family and Community in Edgefield, South Carolina* (Chapel Hill, N.C., 1985), 123–24; Deborah Gray White, *Ar'n't I a Woman? Female Slaves in the Antebellum South* (New York, 1985), 51–53; Suzanne Lebsock, *The Free Women of Petersburg: Status and Culture in a Southern Town, 1784–1860* (New York, 1984), 148–64; "Recollections of Letitia Dabney Miller," 2, Gillespie Papers.

[10] Lily Logan Morrill, ed., *My Confederate Girlhood: The Memoirs of Kate Virginia Cox Logan* (Richmond, 1932), 13–15; Judith W. McGuire, *Diary of a Southern Refugee during the War, by a Lady of Virginia* (1867; reprint, Lincoln, Nebr., 1995), 66. On the emotional significance of home and family, see Witold Rybczynski, *Home: A Short History of An Idea* (New York, 1986); Steven Mintz, *A Prison of Expectations: The Family in Victorian Culture* (New York, 1983). Some scholars have found that the average white southern

woman married at age twenty, one to two years earlier than white northerners, and typically had more children than her northern counterpart (Burton, *In My Father's House,* 118).

[11] Christian diary, 2 March 1860; Cary O'Neale, "Memoir of John O'Neale," 101, John O'Neale Papers, Duke University, Durham, N.C.; Emma Tyler Blalock, "War Memoirs," *Athens (Georgia) Ledger*, n.d. [1891], in scrapbook collection "Historical Records of the United Daughters of the Confederacy," comp. Mildred Lewis Rutherford, 40:234, Eleanor S. Brockenbrough Library, Museum of the Confederacy, Richmond, Va. (MOC); Robert C. Kenzer, *Kinship and Neighborhood in a Southern Community: Orange County, North Carolina, 1849–1881* (Knoxville, Tenn., 1987), 6–28; Paul D. Escott, *Many Excellent People: Power and Privilege in North Carolina, 1850–1900* (Chapel Hill, N.C., 1985), 3–4; Jane Turner Censer, *North Carolina Planters and Their Children, 1800–1860* (Baton Rouge, La., 1984), 7–8.

[12] Jean V. Berlin, ed., *A Confederate Nurse: The Diary of Ada W. Bacot, 1860–1863* (Columbia, S.C., 1994), 60–63; Diary of Fannie Page Hume Braxton, 15 August 1862, VHS; Charles East, ed., *The Civil War Diary of Sarah Morgan* (Athens, Ga., 1991), 101, 312; C. Vann Woodward, ed., *Mary Chesnut's Civil War* (New Haven, 1981), 424; Elizabeth Mayo (Thom) Ross to her son, 16 July [1863 or 1864], Thom Family Papers, VHS; Diary of Maria Mason Tabb Hubard, 23 July 1862, VHS.

[13] Braxton diary, 17 March 1862, 30 July 1862; George S. Savage to Governor [Oliver Hazard Perry Throck] Morton, 23 April 1862, Confederate Prisoners of War Correspondence, Civil War Miscellany, File 107–69, Indiana State Archives, Indianapolis; John Rozier, ed., *The Granite Farm Letters: The Civil War Correspondence of Edgeworth and Sallie Bird* (Athens, Ga., 1988), 69.

[14] Julia G. Tyler to her mother, 1 April 1863, and W. H. Clopton to Julia G. Tyler, 18 October 1863, Tyler Family Papers, Earl Gregg Swem Library, College of William and Mary, Williamsburg, Va.; William Faber to Georgia Knox, 24 December 1864, Archives and Special Collections, University of Arkansas-Little Rock (UA-LR); Diary of Harriet Palmer, 2 March 1865, Palmer Family Papers, South Caroliniana Library, University of South Carolina, Columbia (SCL-USC); Cornelia A. Calmes Black, "The New Orleans Refugees," *Calmes Notes* 2 (July 1993): 1–2; Parthenia Antoinette Hague, *A Blockaded Family: Life in Southern Alabama during the Civil War* (Boston, 1888), 147. Women and children have constituted approximately 80 percent of refugees in the twentieth century, and it seems likely that they constituted the majority of refugees in the American Civil War (Susan Forbes Martin, prep., *Refugee Women* [London, 1992], 5). Between 1861 and 1865, at least a quarter of a million people became refugees, approximately 5 percent of the five million whites who lived in the South in 1860 (Rable, *Civil Wars*, 183).

[15] Mrs. Roger A. Pryor [Sara Agnes Rice Pryor], *Reminiscences of Peace and War* (New York, 1904), 221–22; Arthur Asa Berger, *Reading Matter: Multidisciplinary Perspectives on Material Culture* (New Brunswick, N.J., 1992), 8; Diary of Elvira Ascenith Weir Scott, 18 September 1863, Western Historical Manuscript Collection, University of Missouri-Columbia (WHMC-UMC); McGuire, *Diary of a Southern Refugee*, 54–55.

[16] Mary H. Lancaster and Dallas M. Lancaster, eds., *The Civil War Diary of Anne S. Frobel of Wilton Hill in Virginia* (Birmingham, Ala., 1986), 1; Thomas Felix Hickerson, *Echoes of Happy Valley: Letters and Diaries, Family Life in the South, Civil War History* (Chapel Hill, N.C., 1962), 66; Eliza Ripley, *From Flag to Flag: A Woman's Adventures and Experiences in the South during the War, in Mexico, and in Cuba* (New York, 1889), 36.

[17] Diary of Sally Armstrong, 12 May 1863, VHS; Margaret McCalla to Richard McCalla, 20 September 1863, McCalla Civil War Letters, University Archives, Auburn University, Ala.; Memoir of Elizabeth Lea Neely, 11, Smith/Buckingham Papers, University of Memphis, Tenn.; Henry C. Lay to his wife, 8 March 1863, Henry C. Lay Collection, UA-LR.

[18] Lucy Johnson to "My Dear Sister," 22 February 1863, Jacob-Johnson Family Papers, Filson Club Historical Society, Louisville, Ky.

(FCHS); Diary of Frances Woolfolk Wallace, 7 April 1864, SHC-UNC; East, ed., *Civil War Diary of Sarah Morgan*, 477. For the participation of some white women in pro-Confederate public ceremonies during the war, see Ryan, *Women in Public*, 141.

[19] East, ed., *Civil War Diary of Sarah Morgan*, xxi; Scott diary, 23 November 1862; John A. Meroney to Governor Morton, 10 April 1862, Confederate Prisoners of War Correspondence, Civil War Miscellany.

[20] Louise Babcock Clack, "My Experience of the Civil War of 1861–1865 by a New Orleans Woman," 5–8, Robert Livingston Papers, Manuscripts Division, Library of Congress, Washington, D.C.; Kate Mason Rowland and Mrs. Morris L. Croxall [Agnes E. (Browne) Croxall], eds., *The Journal of Julia Le Grand: New Orleans, 1862–1863* (Richmond, 1911), 30–32; Mrs. Charles Smith [Maria McGregor Campbell Smith], "Narrative of My Blockade Running," 14, VHS; Diary of Frances Woolfolk Wallace, 18 August 1864, SHC-UNC; Ripley, *From Flag to Flag*, 66–124; Charlotte R. Holmes, ed., *The Burckmyer Letters: March, 1863–June, 1865* (Columbia, S.C., 1926).

[21] Friedman, *The Enclosed Garden*, 95–98; McCalla to McCalla, 20 September 1863, McCalla Civil War Letters; Braxton diary, 13 August 1862; Alexander Hunter, *The Women of the Debatable Land* (Washington, D.C., 1912), 247–48; Diary of Josephine Hooke, 26 November 1863, 31 December 1863, Special Collections, University Libraries, University of Tennessee, Knoxville. For the tensions that could develop while refugees lived with kinfolk, see Rable, *Civil Wars*, 190, 346–47.

[22] Wallace diary, 13 May 1864; Eugenia Kelly Bitting to Carrie D. Gillespie, n.d. 1928, Gillespie Papers. See also Mrs. D. Giraud Wright [Louise Wigfall Wright], *A Southern Girl in '61: The War-Time Memories of a Confederate Senator's Daughter* (New York, 1905), 245.

[23] Smith, "Narrative of My Blockade Running," 3, 11; Bitting to Gillespie, n.d. 1928, Gillespie Papers; Hubard diary, 4 August 1862; Hooke diary, 31 August 1863; Braxton diary, 13 March 1862.

[24] McGuire, *Diary of a Southern Refugee*, 65, 32; Braxton diary, 20 August 1862; Hubard diary, 25 July 1862; John Q. Anderson, ed., *Brokenburn: The Journal of Kate Stone, 1861–1868* (Baton Rouge, La., 1955), 204, 300, 318, 320, 312; East, ed., *Civil War Diary of Sarah Morgan*, 270; Andrews, *War-Time Journal*, 61–62.

[25] Virginia Clay-Clopton, *A Belle of the Fifties: Memoirs of Mrs. Clay, of Alabama, Covering Social and Political Life in Washington and the South, 1853–1866*, ed. Ada Sterling (New York, 1904), 20, 185, 192, 194, 207, 224, 225–27, 258–68; Ruth Ketring Nuermberger, *The Clays of Alabama: A Planter-Lawyer-Politician Family* (Lexington, Ky., 1958), 183–266.

[26] Kate Cumming, *A Journal of Hospital Life in the Confederate Army of Tennessee from the Battle of Shiloh to the End of the War* (Louisville, 1866), 59; East, ed., *Civil War Diary of Sarah Morgan*, 449; M. P. Stringer to Varina Howell Davis, 1 June 1863, box 3–5–4, Jefferson Davis Collection, MOC; Anderson, ed., *Brokenburn*, 293.

[27] Stringer to Davis, 1 June 1863, Davis Collection; John E. Talmadge, *Rebecca Latimer Felton: Nine Stormy Decades* (Athens, Ga., 1960), 21–23; Sutherland, "Esther Cheesborough," 31; George P. Rawick, ed., *The American Slave: A Composite Autobiography* (Westport, Conn., 1972), Ga., 13: pt. 3, 187.

[28] McGuire, *Diary of a Southern Refugee*, 79 (quotes).

[29] East, ed., *Civil War Diary of Sarah Morgan*, 265, 274; Mary D. Robertson, ed., *A Confederate Lady Comes of Age: The Journal of Pauline DeCaradeuc Heyward, 1863–1888* (Columbia, S.C., 1992), 36–37; Woodward, ed., *Mary Chesnut's Civil War*, 765; Anderson, ed., *Brokenburn*, 271, 774.

[30] East, ed., *Civil War Diary of Sarah Morgan*, 453–54; Hickerson, *Echoes of Happy Valley*, 67; Memoir of Catherine Cochran, 1:25, 2:7, VHS; Woodward, ed., *Mary Chesnut's Civil War*, 763.

[31] Frances F. [Moore] G. Kabrick to A. J. Adair, 1 March 1897, Beauford James George, Jr., Collection, WHMC-UMC; Robert Manson Myers, ed., *The Children of Pride: A True Story of Georgia and the Civil War* (New Haven, 1972), 1174, 1191, 1258; Wallace diary, 17 May 1864; Reminiscences of Margaret Stanly Beckwith, 2:29, VHS; McGuire, *Diary of a Southern Refugee*, 200–201; Woodward, ed., *Mary Chesnut's Civil War*, 717; "Recollections of Letitia Dabney Miller," 12, Gillespie Papers; Pryor, *Reminiscences*, 217–18; Lucy Johnson to "My Dear Brother," 11 January 1864, Jacob-Johnson Family Papers, FCHS; Hooke diary, 9 September 1863, "List of goods bought since living in Decatur"; Woodward, ed., *Mary Chesnut's Civil War*, 777; McGuire, *Diary of a Southern Refugee*, 87, 243.

[32] Berger, *Reading Matter*; Anderson, ed., *Brokenburn*, 203; Fanny W. Tinsley, "Mrs. S. G. Tinsley's War Experience," 7, VHS; Myers, ed., *Children of Pride*, 1225; Beckwith reminiscences, 2:28; Stringer to Davis, 1 June 1863, Davis Collection; Anderson, ed., *Brokenburn*, 191; Scott diary, 30–31 August 1863; East, ed., *Civil War Diary of Sarah Morgan*, 95–96; Pryor, *Reminiscences*, 301. On the piano's cultural significance, see Scott Sandage, "Deadbeats, Drunkards, and Dreamers: A Cultural History of Failure in America, 1819–1893" (Ph.D. diss., Rutgers University, 1995).

[33] J. B. Jones, *A Rebel War Clerk's Diary at the Confederate States Capital* (Philadelphia, 1866), 1:165; Myers, ed., *Children of Pride*, 1119, 1258–59; Cumming, *Journal of Hospital Life*, 121; Anderson, ed., *Brokenburn*, 202–3; Bitting to Kelly, n.d. 1928, Gillespie Papers; "Recollections of Letitia Dabney Miller," 11, Gillespie Papers; Clack, "My Experience," 8, Livingston Papers; "Recollections of Elizabeth Gordon Rennolds," 4, VHS; Tinsley, "Tinsley's War Experience," 12.

[34] Memoir of Elizabeth Churchill Jones Lacy, 6, Oscar H. Darter Collection, VHS; Anderson, ed., *Brokenburn*, 211, 258, 338; C. M. Stacy to James Hamner, 19 April 1863, Hamner-Stacy Correspondence, West Tennessee Historical Society, University of Memphis, Tenn. (WTHS); Woodward, ed., *Mary Chesnut's Civil War*, 721, 733.

[35] Cumming, *Journal of Hospital Life*, 172; McGuire, *Diary of a Southern Refugee*, 172–73; Sutherland, "Esther Cheesborough," 31; "Recollections of Letitia Dabney Miller," 10, 12, Gillespie Papers; Kabrick to Adair, 1 March 1897, George Collection; "S. C." to "Maria," 1 April 1865, Occasional Book of Lizzie Rowland, Kate Mason Rowland Papers, MOC; Sallie A. Brock [Putnam], *Richmond During the War: Four Years of Personal Observation* (1867; reprint, Alexandria, Va., 1983), 253; Woodward, ed., *Mary Chesnut's Civil War*, 749; Elisabeth Muhlenfeld, *Mary Boykin Chesnut: A Biography* (Baton Rouge, La., 1981), 126–27; Ripley, *From Flag to Flag*, 99; McGuire, *Diary of a Southern Refugee*, 327.

[36] McGuire, *Diary of a Southern Refugee*, 257, 325; Hooke diary, 23, 28 September, 1863; Woodward, ed., *Mary Chesnut's Civil War*, 737, 748, 751, 760; Smith, "Narrative of My Blockade Running," 10; East, ed., *Civil War Diary of Sarah Morgan*, 460; McGuire, *Diary of a Southern Refugee*, 324; Woodward, ed., *Mary Chesnut's Civil War*, 723–24.

[37] Mary Elizabeth Massey, *Ersatz in the Confederacy* (Columbia, S.C., 1952), 81–85; Bitting to Gillespie, n.d. 1928, Gillespie Papers; Smith, "Narrative of My Blockade Running," 14; Clack, "My Experience," 5, Livingston Papers; Hooke diary, 25 October 1863; East, ed., *Civil War Diary of Sarah Morgan*, 92; Kabrick to Adair, 1 March 1897, George Collection; Elizabeth Meriwether to Lee Meriwether, 25 December 1880, Meriwether Family Papers, WTHS; Woodward, ed., *Mary Chesnut's Civil War*, 751; McGuire, *Diary of a Southern Refugee*, 240, 327; Ripley, *From Flag to Flag*, 99.

[38] Hubard diary, 25 July 1862; Kabrick to Adair, 1 March 1897, George Collection; Brock, *Richmond During the War*, 129; Myers, ed., *Children of Pride*, 1157; Pryor, *Reminiscences*, 252; Ripley, *From Flag to Flag*, 114, 118; Andrews, *War-Time Journal*, 42–43; Robert L. Kerby, *Kirby Smith's Confederacy: The Trans-Mississippi South, 1863–1865* (New York, 1972), 87; Diary of Harriet Palmer, 13 August 1863, Palmer Family Papers, SCL-USC; James I. Robertson, Jr., ed., *The Diary of Dolly*

Lunt Burge (Athens, Ga., 1962), 92; "Reminiscences of Grace P. J. Beard," 1, SHC-UNC; Clack, "My Experience," 8, Livingston Papers; Andrews, *War-Time Journal*, 48; Bitting to Gillespie, n.d. 1928, Gillespie Papers.

[39] Sally G. McMillen, *Motherhood in the Old South: Pregnancy, Childbirth, and Infant Rearing* (Baton Rouge, La., 1990), 79–110, 192; Diary of Jacob S. McCullough, 22 June 1863, 6 January 1864, Indiana State Library, Indianapolis (ISL); Charlotte E. McKay, *Stories of Hospital and Camp* (Philadelphia, 1876), 151; Tinsley, "Tinsley's War Experience," 13; Meriwether to Meriwether, 25 December 1880, Meriwether Family Papers; Neely memoir, 4, Smith/Buckingham Papers.

[40] K. David Patterson, "Disease Environments of the Antebellum South," in *Science and Medicine in the Old South*, ed. Ronald L. Numbers and Todd L. Savitt (Baton Rouge, La., 1989), 152–65; James H. Cassedy, *Medicine in America: A Short History* (Baltimore, 1991), 46; Talmadge, *Rebecca Latimer Felton*, 22; Kate Shaifer Sholars, "Our People," 17, David Todd Collection, Special Collections, UMISS; Brock, *Richmond During the War*, 207–8; Andrews, *War-Time Journal*, 167; unsigned [Mrs. Ethel E. Porter] to Jessie Porter, 24 March 1863, Porter-Rice Papers, UMISS; Diary of Walter Carpenter, 19 January 1864, Ohio Historical Society, Columbus (OHS); C. M. Stacy to James Hamner, 15 February 1863, Hamner-Stacy Correspondence, UMISS; Anderson, ed., *Brokenburn*, 239, 254, 309; Ripley, *From Flag to Flag*, 38; McGuire, *Diary of a Southern Refugee*, 97, 236; Smith, "Narrative of My Blockade Running," 8; Tinsley, "Tinsley's War Experience," 11, 13.

[41] Ripley, *From Flag to Flag*, 76; Dyer and Moore, comp., *Tennessee Civil War Veterans Questionnaires*, 2:467; Bitting to Gillespie, 1928, Gillespie Papers; Myers, ed., *Children of Pride*, 1184; Anna Maria Cook, *The Journal of a Milledgeville Girl, 1861–1867*, ed. James C. Bonner (Athens, Ga., 1964), 71–72; Asbury P. Gatch to Etta Gatch, 11 March 1864, Asbury P. Gatch Papers, OHS.

[42] James Briggs to Mary Briggs, 14 March 1862, Letters of James Briggs, ISL; Jones, *Rebel War Clerk's Diary*, 1:195.

[43] Anderson, ed., *Brokenburn*, 221; McGuire, *Diary of a Southern Refugee*, 276; C. M. Stacy to James Hamner, 2 August 1863, Hamner-Stacy Correspondence; Ripley, *From Flag to Flag*, 36; William C. Davis, ed., *Diary of a Confederate Soldier: John S. Jackman of the Orphan Brigade* (Columbia, S.C., 1990), 146; Beckwith reminiscences, 2:34.

[44] Sara Ruddick, *Maternal Thinking: Toward a Politics of Peace* (Boston, 1989), 143–45; Christian G. Appy, *Working-Class War: American Combat Soldiers and Vietnam* (Chapel Hill, N.C., 1993), 101, 250–97; Katharine M. Jones, ed., *Heroines of Dixie: Confederate Women Tell Their Story of the War* (Indianapolis, 1955), 206; Anderson, ed., *Brokenburn*, 196, 297; "Mitt" to her mother, 2 September 1863, Priscilla "Mittie" Munnikuysen Bond Papers, Louisiana and Lower Mississippi Valley Collections, Hill Memorial Library, Louisiana State University, Baton Rouge; C. M. Stacy to James Hamner, 19 April 1863, Hamner-Stacy Correspondence; "Reminiscenes of Grace P. J. Beard," 6; "Recollections of Letitia Dabney Miller," 9, Gillespie Papers.

[45] Hickerson, *Echoes of Happy Valley*, 68, 69; Black, "New Orleans Refugees," 8; Anderson, ed., *Brokenburn*, 294. See also Martha Hodes, "Wartime Dialogues on Illicit Sex: White Women and Black Men," in *Divided Houses*, ed. Clinton and Silber, 239; Rable, *Civil Wars*, 160–61.

[46] Robert I. Alotta, *Civil War Justice: Union Army Executions under Lincoln* (Shippensburg, Pa., 1989), 30–32; United Nations High Commissioner for Refugees, *Sexual Violence Against Refugees: Guidelines on Prevention and Response* (Geneva, 1995), 1, 8–9; Bynum, *Unruly Women*, 118–19. On rape during the war, see Reid Mitchell, *The Vacant Chair: The Northern Soldier Leaves Home* (New York, 1993), 102–10; Fellman, *Inside War*, 207; Rable, *Civil Wars*, 161.

[47] Cook, *Journal of a Milledgeville Girl*, 63; Rozier, ed., *Granite Farm Letters*, 223–24; Lee Kennett, *Marching through Georgia: The Story of Soldiers and Civilians during Sherman's Campaign* (New York, 1995), 306; Myers, ed., *Children of Pride*, 1228; Hunter, *Women of the Debatable Land*, 31–32.

[48] Rowland and Croxall, eds., *Journal of Julia LeGrand*, 247; Clack, "My Experience," 6, Livingston Papers; Flora C. Bryne to Eliza Mayer, 17 March [1864], Mayer Papers, Maryland Historical Society, Baltimore.

[49] Gatch to Gatch, 11 March 1864, Gatch Papers; Myers, ed., *Children of Pride*, 1151–52. On the significance of class distinctions in the antebellum years, see Elizabeth Fox-Genovese, *Within the Plantation Household: Black and White Women of the Old South* (Chapel Hill, N.C., 1988).

[50] McGuire, *Diary of a Southern Refugee*, 88–89, 301–2; Wallace diary, 17 May 1864; Woodward, ed., *Mary Chesnut's Civil War*, 768.

[51] Anderson, ed., *Brokenburn*, 238, 321; Clack, "My Experience," 3–7, Livingston Papers; Pryor, *Reminiscences*, 238–39, 293. See also Escott, *Many Excellent People*, 67.

[52] Cochran memoir, 2:15; Brock, *Richmond During the War*, 105, 203, 272; Bitting to Gillespie, n.d. 1928, Gillespie Papers; Bertram Wallace Korn, *American Jewry and the Civil War* (Philadelphia, 1951); Eli N. Evans, *Judah P. Benjamin: The Jewish Confederate* (New York, 1988); David A. Gerber, ed., *Anti-Semitism in American History* (Urbana, Ill., 1986), 3–54.

[53] Sholars, "Our People," 16–17, Todd Collection; Kabrick to Adair, 1 March 1897, George Collection; Anderson, ed., *Brokenburn*, 209.

[54] Rebecca Latimer Felton, *Country Life in Georgia in the Days of My Youth* (Atlanta, 1919), 100; Myers, ed., *Children of Pride*, 1230, 1233; Neely memoir, 14–15, Smith/Buckingham Papers. On wartime rapes of black Southern women, see Mitchell, *Vacant Chair*, 106–9; Fellman, *Inside War*, 210–13. On antebellum miscegenation, see Melton A. McLaurin, *Celia, A Slave* (Athens, Ga., 1991); White, *Arn't' I a Woman*, 34–44.

[55] Joan E. Cashin, "'Decidedly Opposed to *the Union*': Women's Culture, Marriage, and Secession in Antebellum South Carolina," *Georgia Historical Quarterly* 78 (1994): 735–59; Smith, "Narrative of My Blockade Running," 5, 11; Blalock, "War Memoirs," 6, 11; Pryor, *Reminiscences*, 219, 231, 251.

[56] Ripley, *Flag to Flag*, 38–39, 72, 104–5, 120–21; Meriwether to Meriwether, 25 December 1880, Meriwether Family Papers.

[57] Myers, ed., *Children of Pride*, 1172; Pryor, *Reminiscences*, 297; Beckwith reminiscences, 2:32–33.

[58] Myers, ed., *Children of Pride*, 1220–21; Neely memoir, 11, Smith/Buckingham Papers; Wallace diary, 19 April 1864.

[59] East, ed., *Civil War Diary of Sarah Morgan*, 89–90; "Recollections of Letitia Dabney Miller," 9–10, Gillespie Papers; Hague, *A Blockaded Family*, 159; Mohr, *Threshold of Freedom*, 118–19. See also Wayne K. Durrill, *War of Another Kind: A Southern Community in the Great Rebellion* (New York, 1990), 145–65.

[60] Clay-Clopton, *Belle of the Fifties*, 244; Smith, "Narrative of My Blockade Running," 2; Cochran memoir, 2:20; McKay, *Stories of Hospital and Camp*, 131–32; Andrews, *War-Time Journal*, 38; "Recollections of Elizabeth Gordon Rennolds," 2; Beckwith reminiscences, 2:22, 26; Charles W. Ramsdell, *Behind the Lines in the Southern Confederacy*, ed. Wendell H. Stephenson (Baton Rouge, La., 1969), 25–26, 62–66; Glenna R. Schroeder-Lein, *Confederate Hospitals on the Move: Samuel H. Stout and the Army of Tennessee* (Columbia, S.C., 1994), 149; Frank E. Vandiver, ed., *The Civil War Diary of General Josiah Gorgas* (University, Ala., 1947), 184; McSpadden and Moussa, "'I Have a Name,'" 205.

[61] Christian diary, 31 December 1865; Bitting to Gillespie, n.d. 1928, Gillespie Papers; Anderson, ed., *Brokenburn*, 364; "Recollections of Elizabeth Gordon Rennolds," 3; Woodward, ed., *Mary Chesnut's Civil War*, 802–3; Pryor, *Reminiscences*, 383; Tinsley, "Tinsley's War Experience," 13.

[62] Michael R. Marrus, *The Unwanted: European Refugees in the Twentieth Century* (New York, 1985), 4–26; Omer Bartov, *Hitler's*

Army: Soldiers, Nazis, and War in the Third Reich (New York, 1991), 61–94; U. S. Grant to Edwin M. Stanton, 20 June 1865, in *The Papers of Ulysses S. Grant*, ed. John Y. Simon, vol. 15, *May 1–December 31, 1865* (Carbondale, Ill., 1988), 187; Escott, *Many Excellent People*, 52. The author thanks Robert Zalimas for bringing the Grant letter with its reference to Benjamin Butler to her attention.

[63] Margaret Randolph Higonnet et al., eds., *Behind the Lines: Gender and the Two World Wars* (New Haven, 1987), 1–17; James L. Roark, *Masters Without Slaves: Southern Planters in the Civil War and Reconstruction* (New York, 1977); Anne Firor Scott, *The Southern Lady: From Pedestal to Politics, 1830–1930* (Chicago, 1970), 92–96. For a description of the increasing freedom that women enjoyed in public places (most of them in the North) in the late-nineteenth century, see Ryan, *Women in Public*, 58–63, 76–82.

"THIS SPECIES OF PROPERTY": Female Slave Contrabands in the Civil War

THAVOLIA GLYMPH

[1] Ira Berlin, Thavolia Glymph, Steven F. Miller, Joseph P. Reidy, Leslie S. Rowland, and Julie Saville, eds., *The Wartime Genesis of Free Labor: The Lower South*, ser. 1, vol. 3, of *Freedom: A Documentary History of Emancipation, 1861–1867* (Cambridge, 1990), 715.

[2] James M. McPherson, *The Negro's Civil War: How American Negroes Felt and Acted During the War for the Union* (New York, 1965), 61.

[3] Allan Nevins, *The War for the Union: The Organized War, 1863–1864*, vol. 7 of *Ordeal of the Union* (New York, 1971), 31, 418. For one of the earliest, detailed narratives on fugitive slaves, and one that takes women into account, see W. E. B. Du Bois, *Black Reconstruction in America: An Essay Toward a History of the Part Which Black Folk Played in the Attempt to Reconstruct Democracy in America, 1860–1880* (1935; reprint, New York, 1973), 55–83.

[4] McPherson, *The Negro's Civil War*, 17–18; Barbara Jeanne Fields, *Slavery and Freedom on the Middle Ground: Maryland during the Nineteenth Century* (New Haven, 1985), 100.

[5] The narrow concept of the term "contrabands of war" has until recent years been due in part to a traditional omission of questions of gender and race in historical scholarship. A still small but growing body of research is reversing this trend and demonstrates how the issues of gender and race lead to a fuller understanding of the Civil War. The wartime experience of African-American women—slave and free—though greatly remarked upon by contemporaries, remains the least studied. Recent works that document the experience of Southern women in the war include the four volumes published thus far by the Freedmen and Southern Society Project under the series title *Freedom: A Documentary History of Emancipation, 1861–1867.* Other works include Joseph P. Reidy, *From Slavery to Agrarian Capitalism in the Cotton South: Central Georgia, 1800–1880* (Chapel Hill, N.C., 1992); George C. Rable, *Civil Wars: Women and the Crisis of Southern Nationalism* (Urbana, Ill., 1989); Drew Gilpin Faust, *Mothers of Invention: Women of the Slaveholding South in the American Civil War* (Chapel Hill, N.C., 1996); Catherine Clinton and Nina Silber, eds., *Divided Houses: Gender and the Civil War* (New York, 1992); Patricia Morton, ed., *Discovering the Women in Slavery: Emancipating Perspectives on the American Past* (Athens, Ga., 1996); Jacqueline Jones, *Labor of Love, Labor of Sorrow: Black Women, Work, and the Family from Slavery to the Present* (New York, 1985); Clarence L. Mohr, *On the Threshold of Freedom: Masters and Slaves in Civil War Georgia* (Athens, Ga., 1986); Wayne K. Durrill, *War of Another Kind: A Southern Community in the Great Rebellion* (New York, 1990); and Ervin L. Jordan, Jr., *Black Confederates and Afro-Yankees in Civil War Virginia* (Charlottesville, Va., 1995).

[6] Jones, *Labor of Love, Labor of Sorrow*, 49.

[7] U.S. War Department, *War of the Rebellion: The Official Records of the Union and Confederate Armies* (Washington, D.C., 1880–1901), ser. 1, 9:353; Fields, *Slavery and Freedom on the Middle Ground*, 101.

[8] *Official Records*, ser. 1, 2:648–51; Ira Berlin, Barbara J. Fields, Thavolia Glymph, Joseph P. Reidy, and Leslie S. Rowland, eds., *The Destruction of Slavery*, ser. 1, vol. 1, of *Freedom: A Documentary History of Emancipation, 1861–1867* (Cambridge, 1985), 15–16.

[9] Berlin et al., eds., *The Destruction of Slavery*, 71.

[10] Ira Berlin, Joseph P. Reidy, and Leslie S. Rowland, eds., *The Black Military Experience*, ser. 2 of *Freedom: A Documentary History of Emancipation, 1861–1867* (Cambridge, 1982), 728.

[11] *Official Records*, ser. 1, 9:199; see also Jordan, *Black Confederates and Afro-Yankees*, 69–90; Joseph P. Reidy, "Coming from the Shadow of the Past: The Transition from Slavery to Freedom at Freedmen's Village, 1863–1900," *Virginia Magazine of History and Biography* 95 (1987): 403–28.

[12] Ira Berlin, Barbara J. Fields, Steven F. Miller, Joseph P. Reidy, and Leslie S. Rowland, eds., *Free at Last: A Documentary History of Slavery, Freedom, and the Civil War* (New York, 1992), 99.

[13] Jordan, *Black Confederates and Afro-Yankees*, 85.

[14] For a discussion of these measures and other Federal policies regarding slavery and emancipation, see Berlin et al., eds., *The Destruction of Slavery*, 1–56; Barbara J. Fields, "Who Freed the Slaves?" in Geoffrey C. Ward, *The Civil War: An Illustrated History* (New York, 1990), 178–81.

[15] For an excellent discussion of the notion of republican motherhood within the context of the Civl War see Reid Mitchell, *The Vacant Chair: The Northern Soldier Leaves Home* (New York, 1993).

[16] Used in Confederate military hospitals from the beginning of the war, black women eventually made up as much as half the hospital nursing staffs (James M. McPherson, *Ordeal by Fire: The Civil War and Reconstruction* [New York, 1982], 191, 266).

[17] For a discussion of the "education" of slave men to manhood, see Mitchell, *The Vacant Chair*, 55–69; Thomas Wentworth Higginson, *Army Life in a Black Regiment* (1869; reprint, New York, 1984); Luis F. Emilio, *A Brave Black Regiment: The History of the 54th Massachusetts, 1863–1865* (1870; reprint, New York, 1995); Jim Cullen, "'I's a Man Now': Gender and African American Men," in *Divided Houses*, ed. Clinton and Silber, 76–91.

[18] Francis Butler Simkins and Charles Pierce Roland, *A History of the South*, 4th ed. (New York, 1972), 229; see also Elizabeth D. Leonard, *Yankee Women: Gender Battles in the Civil War* (New York, 1994); Faust, *Mothers of Invention*.

[19] Slaves who remained behind chipped away at the institution of slavery from within and often played critically important roles assisting others to escape by providing encouragement, food, and sanctuary to fugitive slaves (see for example Emory M. Thomas, *The Confederate Nation, 1861–1865* [New York, 1979], 238).

[20] For a discussion of slave-initiated flight in wartime Georgia see Mohr, *On the Threshold of Freedom*, 70–75.

[21] Ibid.

[22] Susie King Taylor, *A Black Woman's Civil War Memoirs: Reminiscences of My Life in Camp with the 33rd U.S. Colored Troops, Late 1st South Carolina Volunteers*, ed. Patricia W. Romero (New York, 1988), 33, 42, 62; Edward A. Miller, Jr., *Gullah Statesman: Robert Smalls from Slavery to Congress, 1839–1915* (Columbia, S.C., 1995), 12; see also Jordan, *Black Confederates and Afro-Yankees*, 69–90.

[23] Charles Joyner, *Down by the Riverside: A South Carolina Slave Community* (Urbana, Ill., 1984), 55.

[24] Berlin, et al., eds., *Wartime Genesis of Free Labor: The Lower South*, 655–57, 657–58n.

[25] *Official Records*, ser. 1, 9:400. Within a week of Stanly's protest, Congress passed the

Second Confiscation Act, which declared slaves owned by masters disloyal to the Union to be "forever free"; the act also made it unlawful for commanders and soldiers to surrender slaves to any masters.

[26] *Official Records*, ser. 1, 6:79

[27] Berlin, et al., eds., *Wartime Genesis of Free Labor: The Lower South*, 209–10.

[28] Colonel Henry Moore to Captain Louis H. Pelouze, March 1862, Records of the U.S. Army Continental Commands, Record Group 393, C-1642, National Archives, Washington, D.C.

[29] Henry L. Swint, ed., *Dear Ones at Home: Letters from Contraband Camps* (Nashville, Tenn., 1966), 11–73; Robert Francis Engs, *Freedom's First Generation: Black Hampton, Virginia, 1861–1890* (Philadelphia, 1979), 25–43.

[30] Berlin, et al., eds., *Wartime Genesis of Free Labor: The Lower South*, 97.

[31] Swint, ed., *Dear Ones at Home*, 89–91, 100–110, 134.

[32] Ibid., 90.

[33] Ibid., 73, 134.

[34] Edwin S. Redkey, ed., *A Grand Army of Black Men: Letters from African-American Soldiers in the Union Army, 1861–1865* (Cambridge, 1992), 46–47.

[35] Ibid., 82.

[36] Swint, ed., *Dear Ones at Home*, 66–67.

[37] Berlin, et al., eds., *Wartime Genesis of Free Labor: The Lower South*, 843–44.

[38] Ibid., 845-46.

[39] Berlin, et al., eds., *The Black Military Experience*, 709.

[40] Redkey, ed., *A Grand Army of Black Men*, 150.

[41] Berlin, et al., eds., *The Black Military Experience*, 713–14.

[42] Ibid., 715–18. Within days, the secretary of war countermanded the order, and the families returned.

[43] Ibid., 719–20.

[44] Ibid., 694–95.

[45] Henry Steele Commager, *The Blue and the Gray: The Story of the Civil War as Told by Participants* (1950; reprint, New York, 1982), 724.

[46] See for example Berlin, et al., eds., *Wartime Genesis of Free Labor: The Lower South*, 824–26; Nevins, *War for the Union*, 417, 441.

[47] Berlin, et al., eds., *Wartime Genesis of Free Labor: The Lower South*, 712–13, 714n.

[48] Ibid., 824.

[49] See for example Berlin, et al., eds., *The Black Military Experience*, 721–23.

[50] Elizabeth Hyde Botume, *First Days Amongst the Contrabands* (1893; reprint, New York, 1968), 152.

[51] McPherson, *Ordeal by Fire*, 462.

[52] Taylor, *A Black Woman's Civil War Memoirs*, 141–42.

VOICES FROM THE TEMPEST: Southern Women's Wartime Experiences
KYM S. RICE AND EDWARD D. C. CAMPBELL, JR.

[1] Sarah Rousseau Espey Diary, 1859–1868, SPR2, 23–27, Alabama Department of Archives and History, Montgomery.

[2] Clarence Phillips Denman, *The Secession Movement in Alabama* (Montgomery, Ala., 1933), 121–22.

[3] Grady McWhiney and Perry D. Jamieson,

Attack and Die: Confederate Military Tactics and the Southern Heritage (University, Ala., 1982), 8.

[4] "A Lady of Louisiana" to P. G. T. Beauregard, 23 April [1862], and P. G. T. Beauregard reply, 28 April 1862, both Manuscript Division, Chicago Historical Society, Ill.

[5] Lettie Kennedy to Confederate Secretary of War George Wythe Randolph, 15 September 1862, Letters Received, Confederate Secretary of War (LR-CSW), Record Group 109, reel 56, K148, National Archives, Washington, D.C. (NA).

[6] Winthorp D. Jordan, *Tumult and Silence at Second Creek: An Inquiry into a Civil War Slave Conspiracy* (Baton Rouge, La., 1993), 14n.

[7] Herbert Aptheker, *American Negro Slave Revolts* (1943; reprint, New York, 1974), 363.

[8] Fannie Christian to Confederate Secretary of War George Wythe Randolph, 22 June 1862, LR-CSW, Record Group 109, reel 39, C622.

[9] William Kaufman Scarborough, *The Overseer: Plantation Management in the Old South* (Baton Rouge, La., 1966), 140; Ervin L. Jordan, Jr., and Herbert A. Thomas, Jr., *19th Virginia Infantry* (Lynchburg, Va., 1987), 62.

[10] Mary E. Bullock to Confederate Secretary of War George Wythe Randolph, 21 September 1862, LR-CSW, Record Group 109, reel 35, 1093.

[11] Edward H. Phillips, *The Lower Shenandoah Valley in the Civil War: The Impact of War Upon the Civilian Population and Upon Civil Institutions* (Lynchburg, Va., 1993), 61

[12] Laura Lee, "A History of Our Captivity," 11 March 1862–5 April 1865, Special Collections, Earl Gregg Swem Library, College of William and Mary, Williamsburg, Va.

[13] Roger U. Delauter, Jr., *Winchester in the Civil War* (Lynchburg, Va., 1992), 110–18.

[14] E. Merton Coulter, *The South During Reconstruction, 1865–1877* (Baton Rouge, La., 1947), 6–7.

[15] Petition of Delila Day, 21 June 1871, Records of the U.S. Court of Claims, Southern Claims Commission (SCC), Record Group 123, Claim 2858 (disallowed), fiche 317C, NA.

[16] Testimony of Clarise Randall regarding claim of Marcia Carnahan, 26 August 1874, SCC, Record Group 123, Claim 18512 (disallowed), fiche 2415.

[17] Susan M. Robinson to Jefferson Davis, 19 October 1864, LR-CSW, Record Group 109, reel 137, N183.

[18] C. Vann Woodward, ed., *Mary Chesnut's Civil War* (New Haven, 1981), 199.

[19] Robert Ardry to his father, 3 June 1864, Private Collection, transcript provided by Kathleen Dietrich.

[20] Annie Samuels et al. to Confederate Secretary of War James A. Seddon, 2 December 1864, LR-CSW, Record Group 109, reel 122, B692.

[21] Fitzgerald Ross, *Cities and Camps of the Confederate States*, ed. Richard Barksdale Harwell (Urbana, Ill., 1958), 116; Arthur J. L. Fremantle, *Three Months in the Southern States* (1863; reprint, Alexandria, Va., 1984), 174.

[22] *Lynchburg Virginian*, 6 October 1864.

[23] Richard Hall, *Patriots in Disguise: Women Warriors of the Civil War* (New York, 1993), 200, 203–4.

[24] Ann Rozier to her husband, 31 March 1865, Soldiers' Letters, M-Z, Solid South Collection (SL-SSC), Eleanor S. Brockenbrough Library, Museum of the Confederacy, Richmond, Va.

[25] Unknown to J. A. Walters, 2 April 186?, SL-SSC.

[26] Avery O. Craven, *The Growth of Southern Nationalism, 1848–1861* (Baton Rouge, La., 1953), 170; Frank Lawrence Owsley, *Plain Folk of the Old South* (Baton Rouge, La., 1949), 146–47.

[27] Fannie A. Beers, *Memories: A Record of Personal Experience and Adventure during Four Years of War* (1888; reprint, Alexandria, Va., 1985), 138–50.

[28] Richard N. Current, ed., *Encyclopedia of the Confederacy* (New York, 1993), 1:152–53.

[29] H. H. Cunningham, *Doctors in Gray: The Confederate Medical Service* (Baton Rouge, La., 1958), 74–78.

[30] Petition of Amelia Kimball, 28 June 1873, SCC, Record Group 123, Claim 16270 (disallowed), fiche 1624.

[31] Paul D. Escott, *Slavery Remembered: A Record of Twentieth-Century Slave Narratives* (Chapel Hill, N.C., 1979), 122–28.

[32] Petition of Jane Holmes, 6 February 1873, SCC, Record Group 123, Claim 19717 (disallowed), fiche 1876.

[33] Lee Kennett, *Marching through Georgia: The Story of Soldiers and Civilians during Sherman's Campaign* (New York, 1995), 288–89. 293.

[34] See for example Frederick H. Dyer, *A Compendium of the War of the Rebellion* (New York, 1959), 1:138, 145, 230, 238.

[35] Statement of Mary Smith, December 1863, Letters Received (misc.) 1861–1867, U.S. Army Department of the Missouri, Record Group 393, box 12, NA.

A MONUMENT TO SOUTHERN WOMANHOOD: The Founding Generation of the Confederate Museum
JOHN M. COSKI AND AMY R. FEELY

[1] "The South's Museum," *Southern Historical Society Papers* 12 (1896): 354–58; Virginia Armistead Garber, *In Memorium Sempiternam* (Richmond, Va., 1896), 36–37, 54–60.

[2] Garber, *In Memorium Sempiternam*, 53.

[3] Ibid, 39–41. See also Minor T. Weisiger, "Charles T. O'Ferrall: 'Gray Eagle' from the Valley," in *The Governors of Virginia 1860–1978*, ed. Edward Younger and James Tice Moore (Charlottesville, Va., 1982), 136–46.

[4] Karen Cox, "Gender, Race, and the Lost Cause, 1890–1930" (paper presented at the annual meeting of the Southern Historical Association, New Orleans, La., November 1995); Sarah Gardner, "'We Are No Accidental Thing': The United Daughters of the Confederacy and the Imperative of Historical Inquiry, 1895–1915" (paper presented at the annual meeting of the Organization of American Historians, Washington, D.C., March 1995); Angie Parrott, "'Love Makes Memory Eternal': The United Daughters of the Confederacy in Richmond, Virginia, 1897–1920," in *The Edge of the South: Life in Nineteenth-Century Virginia*, ed. Edward Ayers and John Willis (Charlottesville, Va., 1991), 219–38; Nancy A. Parrott, "'Love Makes Memory Eternal': The United Daughters of the Confederacy in Richmond, Virginia, 1897–1920" (master's thesis, University of Virginia, 1989); Fred Arthur Bailey, "The Textbooks of the 'Lost Cause': Censorship and the Creation of Southern State Histories," *Georgia Historical Quarterly* 75 (1991): 507–33; Fred Arthur Bailey, "Free Speech and the Lost Cause in the Old Dominion," *Virginia Magazine of History and Biography* 103 (1995): 237–66.

[5] See for example Charles Reagan Wilson, *Baptized in Blood: The Religion of the Lost Cause, 1865–1920* (Athens, Ga., 1980); Thomas L. Connelly and Barbara L. Bellows, *God and General Longstreet: The Lost Cause and the Southern Mind* (Baton Rouge, La., 1982). On the Confederate Museum see Gaines M. Foster, *Ghosts of the Confederacy: Defeat, the Lost Cause, and the Emergence of the New South, 1865 to 1913* (New York, 1987), 116; Michael Kammen, *Mystic Chords of Memory: The Transformation of Tradition in American Culture* (New York, 1991), 381;

and especially Amy R. Feely, "Southern Lady Meets New Woman: Women of the Confederate Memorial Literary Society and the Lost Cause in Richmond, Virginia" (master's thesis, University of Virginia, 1995); Michael Shoop, "A History of The Museum of the Confederacy, Richmond, Virginia, and Its Library, 1896–1946" (master's thesis, University of North Carolina, 1983); Emory M. Thomas, "Of Health and Medicine: The Museum of the Confederacy," (Centennial Scholar Lecture presented at the University of Richmond, Richmond, Va., May 1996); Nancy Bowman, "The Confederate Memorial Literary Society: Southern Women and the Creation of Identity and Place" (paper presented at the annual meeting of the Southern Association for Women Historians, Houston, Tex., June 1994); Tucker H. Hill, *Victory In Defeat: Jefferson Davis and the Lost Cause* (Richmond, 1986); Malinda W. Collier, John M. Coski, Richard C. Cote, Tucker H. Hill, and Guy R. Swanson, *White House of the Confederacy: An Illustrated History* (Richmond, 1993); John M. Coski, "A Century of Collecting: The History of The Museum of the Confederacy," *Museum of the Confederacy Journal*, no. 74 (1996): 2–24.

[6] Hollywood Memorial Association minutes (HMA minutes), 3, 7, 14, 15, 21, 23, and 28 May 1866, Hollywood Memorial Association Papers (HMA Papers), Eleanor S. Brockenbrough Library, Museum of the Confederacy, Richmond, Va. (MOC); Mary G. Crenshaw, "Ladies Memorial Association, Richmond, Virginia," in *History of the Confederated Memorial Associations of the South*, comp. Confederated Southern Memorial Association (New Orleans, 1904), 300; Ladies' Hollywood Memorial Association, *Our Confederate Dead* (Richmond, 1896); Kate Pleasants Minor, "The Origin and Meaning of Memorial Day," in *Memorial Day Annual, 1912* (Richmond, 1912), 88; Mary H. Mitchell, *Hollywood Cemetery: The History of a Southern Shrine* (Richmond, 1985), 64–92. For a discussion of the elite origins of the Hollywood Memorial Association see Susan Barber, "White Women's Organizations in Civil War and Reconstruction Richmond," (draft chapter, Ph.D. diss., University of Maryland, 1995), 29.

[7] "The Confederate Dead," *Richmond Daily Dispatch*, 1 June 1866; "Hollywood Day," *Richmond Dispatch*, 1 June 1886; "Graves of Our Confederate Dead," *Richmond Dispatch*, 31 May 1890; see also Amy E. Murrell, "Two Armies: Women's Activism in Civil War Richmond" (undergraduate honor's thesis, Department of History, Duke University, 1993), 93–104; William A. Blair, "The Political Implications of Civic Ceremonies in Post-Emancipation Virginia" (paper presented at the annual meeting of the Organization of American Historians, Washington, D.C., March 1995).

[8] "Hollywood Memorial Association Tableaux at Virginia Hall," *Richmond Daily Dispatch*, 2 June 1866; Treasurer's Report, 22 October 1867, HMA Papers; Barber, "White Women's Organizations," 27–39; Mitchell, *Hollywood Cemetery*, 83–92.

[9] Mrs. Stephen Beveridge, "Oakwood Memorial Association, Richmond, Virginia," in *History of the Confederated Memorial Associations*, 304–7; Oakwood Memorial Association Minutes, MOC; Lizzie Rutherford Chapter, United Daughters of the Confederacy (UDC), *A History of the Origin of Memorial Day* (Columbus, Ga., 1898), 24–25, in "Origins of the Ladies' Memorial Associations," vol. 2 of scrapbook collection "Historical Records of the United Daughters of the Confederacy," comp. Mildred Lewis Rutherford, MOC.

[10] Patricia R. Loughridge and Edward D.C. Campbell, Jr., *Women in Mourning* (Richmond, 1985); "Ladies Confederate Memorial Association, Winchester, Virginia," in *History of the Confederated Memorial Assocations*, 314–18; Mrs. John T. Goolrick, "Ladies' Memorial Association of Fredericksburg, Va.," 12 April 1916, in "Origins of the Ladies' Memorial Associations."

[11] Foster, *Ghosts of the Confederacy*; Mrs. B. A. C. Emerson, comp., *Historic Southern Monuments* (New York, 1911); Ralph W. Widener, Jr., *Confederate Monuments: Enduring Symbols of the South and the War Between the States* (Washington, D.C., 1982).

[12] "The Soldiers Home, Richmond, Virginia," *Southern Historical Society Papers* 20 (1892): 315–24; Emily J. Williams, "'A Home . . . for the old boys': The Robert E. Lee Camp Confederate Soldiers' Home," *Virginia Cavalcade* 29 (1979): 40–47; R. B. Rosenburg, *Living Monuments: Confederate Soldiers' Homes in the New South* (Chapel Hill, N.C., 1993).

[13] Mrs. Roy Weeks McKinney, "Origins," in *The History of the United Daughters of the Confederacy*, ed. Mary B. Poppenheim, et al. (Raleigh, N.C., 1956), 1:2–10; *Minutes of the First Annual Convention of the United Daughters of the Confederacy, Nashville, 10 September 1894* (Nashville, Tenn., 1896), 1–2 (quotes); *Minutes of the Called Meeting of the United Daughters of the Confederacy, Nashville, 30 March 1895* (Nashville, Tenn., 1896), 7.

[14] Margaret Nell Price, "The Development of Leadership by Southern Women Through Clubs and Organizations" (Ph.D. diss., University of North Carolina, 1945), 180; for an overview of the work of the UDC see Poppenheim et al., eds., *History of the United Daughters of the Confederacy*.

[15] Bailey, "Textbooks of the 'Lost Cause'"; E. Merton Coulter, "A Name for the American War of 1861–1865," *Georgia Historical Quarterly* 26 (1952): 120–22; *Minutes of the Sixth Annual Meeting of the United Daughters of the Confederacy, 1899* (Nashville, Tenn., 1900), 72–74; see also Kate Mason Rowland Papers, MOC.

[16] See Confederated Southern Memorial Association constitution and by-laws, as amended 1910, in *Minutes of the Twelfth Annual Convention of the Confederated Southern Memorial Association, 1911* (New Orleans, 1912), 37. In an effort to delineate the roles of the two organization, Kate Behan concluded that "the Memorial women honor the memory of the Dead—the Daughters honor the living" (Mrs. W. J. Behan, "The Origin of Memorial Day," in "Origins of the Ladies' Memorial Associations").

[17] Mary G. Crenshaw, Annual Report of the Ladies' Hollywood Memorial Association, 3 May 1895; and R. E. Lee Camp No. 1, United Confederate Veterans, "To the Memorial Societies of the South," 8 April 1887, both HMA Papers.

[18] HMA minutes, 17, 25 February, 4 March 1890 (quote), HMA Papers.

[19] Collier, et al., *White House of the Confederacy*; [Joseph Bryan], "Preservation of Our Historical Landmarks," *Richmond Daily Times*, 28 November 1889.

[20] Petition, "To the Honorable Members of the City Council of the City of Richmond," 14 March 1890; and HMA minutes, 18 March, 15 May 1890, both HMA Papers. See also Confederate Memorial Literary Society minutes (CMLS minutes), 26 May 1890, MOC; Garber, *In Memorium Sempiternam*, 16.

[21] Confederate Memorial Literary Society, *Charter, Constitution, and By-Laws of CMLS* (Richmond, 1906), 12; biographical entry for John B. Cary, "The Roll of Honor," 8:150, 86:19, MOC; "James Taylor Ellyson" in *Men of Mark in Virginia*, ed. Lyon G. Tyler (Washington, D.C., 1906), 1:183–85; Ellyson Scrapbooks, E1–E11, MOC; Belle Gayle Ellyson, *The Story of the Ellyson Family* (privately printed, 1976), 23–34; Robert K. Krick, "Wilfred E. Cutshaw," in *Lee's Colonels: A Biographical Register of the Field Officers of the Army of Northern Virginia* (Dayton, Ohio, 1979), 98–99.

[22] Sally Archer Anderson, Annual Report of the CMLS President, January 1927, in *Year Book 1926* (Richmond, 1927), 7.

[23] See for example James M. Lindgren, *Preserving the Old Dominion: Historic Preservation and Virginia Traditionalism* (Charlottesville, Va., 1993).

[24] Report to the United Daughters of the Confederacy, 23 October 1916, CMLS minutes, 25 October 1916; Parke Bagby Bolling, Annual Report of the CMLS Finance Committee, 1 January 1916, in *Year Book, 1914–1915* (Richmond, 1916), 19.

[25] W. Gordon McCabe, "Proceedings of the Virginia Historical Society at its Annual Meeting, 29 December 1910," *Virginia Magazine*

of History and Biography 19 (1911): xix; John Stewart Bryan, *Joseph Bryan: His Times, His Family, His Friends* (Richmond, 1935), 168–74; [Douglas Southall Freeman], "Miss Belle," *Richmond News Leader*, 3 July 1934, Confederate Memorial Literary Society scrapbook (CMLS scrapbook), C10:15, MOC; Isabel Maury, notes on her mother, ca. 1910, HMA Papers; Mary Maury Werth, notes on Confederate torpedoes, MOC; Mary Maury Werth obituary, *Richmond Times-Dispatch*, 28 November 1928, CMLS scrapbook, C8:123; *Confederate Veteran*, 37 (1929): 5; Anne Fontaine Maury, *Intimate Virginiana: A Century of Maury Travels by Land and Sea* (Richmond, 1941); "Mrs. J. Taylor Ellyson," *Richmond Times-Dispatch*, 23 March 1935, CMLS scrapbook, C10:74; Peter W. Roper, *Jedediah Hotchkiss: Rebel Mapmaker and Virginia Businessman* (Shippensburg, Pa., 1992); Archie McDonald, ed., *Make Me a Map of the Valley: The Civil War Journal of Stonewall Jackson's Topographer* (Dallas, 1973), xviii–xxii; Virginia Morgan Robinson obituary, *Richmond Times-Dispatch*, 28 May 1920, CMLS scrapbook, C7:228; Virginia Morgan Robinson, UDC membership application, United Daughters of the Confederacy Business Office, Richmond, Va.; [Douglas Southall Freeman], "Bespeaking a Generation," *Richmond News-Leader*, 21 February 1921, CMLS scrapbook, C7:102.

[26] Janet Weaver Randolph, "Recollections of My Mother," Richmond Chapter Papers (bound volume), United Daughters of the Confederacy Collection, MOC; Richard A. Weaver to Janet C. Weaver, April 1862; and Janet Weaver Randolph note, 15 May 1909, both MOC; Lee A. Wallace, Jr., *17th Virginia Infantry* (Lynchburg, Va., 1990), 143; Janet H. Randolph, "A Confederate Christmas," *Confederate Veteran* 13 (December 1905): 572; Nell R. Lee Murphy, "Looking Backward One-Half Century: An Interview with Mrs. N. V. Randolph," *Richmond Magazine* 1 (April 1915): 18; Mrs. N. V. Randolph biographical sketch, MOC; John A. C. Keith, "The Home Front," in *The Years of Anguish: Fauquier County, Virginia, 1861–1865*, ed. Emily G. Raney et al. (Warrenton, Va., 1965), 55; dance card, 1864, MOC; Real Property Tax Records, Fauquier County: 1861–1870; and Personal Property Tax Records, Fauquier County: 1860–1870, both Archives Collection, Library of Virginia, Richmond (LVA); United States Census, 1860: Virginia, National Archives microfilm series M593, reel 109:100; United States Census, 1870: Virginia, National Archives microfilm series M593, reel 1645:443.

[27] Janet H. Weaver to Miss Jenkins, 12 July 1865, MOC.

[28] Mrs. N. V. Randolph biographical sketch.

[29] Hugh C. Keen and Horace Mewborn, *43rd Battalion Virginia Cavalry: Mosby's Command* (Lynchburg, Va., 1993), 359; Evelyn D. Ward, *The Children of Bladensfield* (New York, 1978), 100–1; "Maj. Norman V. Randolph," *Confederate Veteran* 11 (1903): 177–78; R. E. Lee Camp No. 1, United Confederate Veterans, Soldiers' Home Minute Book, LVA; Janet Weaver Randolph to R. E. Lee Camp No. 1 commander and veterans, n.d., R. E. Lee Camp No. 1, United Confederate Veterans, Papers (Lee Camp Papers), Division of Manuscripts and Archives, Virginia Historical Society, Richmond (VHS).

[30] CMLS minutes, 6 November 1899.

[31] Isobel Bryan to HMA members, 26 October [1891]; and HMA minutes, 13 November 1891; 2 February, 3 May 1892, both HMA Papers; "Opening the Bazaar," *Richmond Times*, 12 April 1893; *Southern Historical Society Papers* 22 (1894): 336-90; see also Soldiers' and Sailors' Monument Papers, MOC.

[32] Lists of officers, regents, and vice regents, CMLS Annual Reports, MOC.

[33] Garber, *In Memorium Sempiternam*, 24.

[34] HMA Relics Committee circular, 5 January 1892, HMA Papers.

[35] *Catalogue of the Confederate Museum, Richmond, Va., 1898* (Richmond, 1898); *Catalogue of the Confederate Museum of the Confederate Memorial Literary Society* (Richmond, 1905); Accession Records, Office of the Registrar, Museum of the Confederacy, Richmond, Va.

[36] See for example Mary Maury Werth to Lora H. Ellyson, 24 May 1892, CMLS Relics Committee record book, MOC.

[37] Accession Records, Office of the Registrar.

[38] "Memorial Hall, New Orleans," *Confederate Veteran* 6 (December 1898): 547–48; "Louisiana Historical Association, Memorial Hall, New Orleans, Louisiana," in *History of the Confederated Memorial Associations*, 198–201. After visiting the Memorial Hall in 1901, Isobel Bryan assured her CMLS colleagues that their museum was far superior: "Do not allow yourself to envy what anybody else owns" (CMLS minutes, 6 December 1901).

[39] The Confederate Memorial Association (CMA) intensely felt the competition for funds among Confederate memorial organizations. See CMA Minute Book: 1902–1921, 13–15, 63–67, Confederate Memorial Association Papers (CMA Papers), VHS. The competition for Jefferson Davis's gravesite is documented in the Ellyson Scrapbooks, E2, E5.

[40] [Clara Reese], "White House of the Confederacy," *Confederate Veteran* 1 (1893): 22–23; "Confederate Museum," *Confederate Veteran* 6 (1898): 356–58; "Confederate Museum, Richmond," *Confederate Veteran* 15 (1907): 105.

[41] "Preserving Records," *Richmond Dispatch*, 11 November 1894, in CMLS Museum Committee Minute Book, MOC. For the origins of the CMA, see George L. Christian, *Sketch of the Origin and Erection of the Confederate Memorial Institute at Richmond, Virginia* (Richmond, [1919?]). The Confederate Memorial Institute ("Battle Abbey") foundered, then closed in 1946; the building subsequently became the headquarters for the Virginia Historical Society.

[42] Clippings, CMLS Museum Committee Minute Book; *Southern Historical Society Papers* 22 (1894): 388; *Minutes of the Fifth Annual Meeting and Reunion of the United Confederate Veterans, 1895* (New Orleans, 1896), 57–58; CMLS minutes, 4 February 1896; Garber, *In Memorium Sempiternam*, 52–53.

[43] CMA minutes, 19 July 1898, CMA Papers; CMLS minutes, 17 June 1902, 8 January 1909 (quotes).

[44] "To the Public," 17 December 1896, CMA minutes, CMA Papers.

[45] Foster, *Ghosts of the Confederacy*, 98–100; *Minutes of the Fifth Annual Meeting of the United Daughters of the Confedederacy, 1898* (Nashville, Tenn., 1899), 85.

[46] [George Moorman], Circular Letter No. 103, Adjutant General's Office, United Confederate Veterans, 9 March 1899, Ellyson Family Papers (Acc. #4130), University of Virginia Library, Charlottesville.

[47] Foster, *Ghosts of the Confederacy*, 175–78; Richmond Chapter UDC minutes, 14 September 1904, MOC; *Minutes of the Tenth Annual Meeting of the Virginia Division, United Daughters of the Confederacy, 1904* (Richmond, 1904), 20; CMLS minutes, 28 September 1904.

[48] Isobel Bryan to HMA members, 26 October [1891], HMA Papers; Louise Gurkin Adamson, "Cast Memories: Richmond's Confederate Soldiers' and Sailors' Monument," *Virginia Cavalcade* 44 (1994): 14–27.

[49] *Minutes of the Fifth Annual Meeting of the United Daughters of the Confederacy*, 65–66 (quote); Janet Randolph to J. Taylor Ellyson, 15, 23 July 1899, Ellyson Family Papers; *Minutes of the Meetings of the Board of Directors of the Jefferson Davis Monument Association* (Richmond, 1904); CMLS minutes, 10 June 1903; Poppenheim, et al., *History of the United Daughters of the Confederacy*, 49–50. At the United Confederate Veterans' convention that formally requested assistance from the UDC in completing the Davis monument, General William L. Cabell observed "that when the Daughters were gotten to work something would be done, and that all the good that it seemed was being done these days was through women's work anyway" (*Minutes of the Ninth Annual Meeting and Reunion of the United Confederate Veterans, 1899* [New Orleans, 1900], 134–35).

[50] For background on the Lee monument

controversy see Thomas L. Connelly, *The Marble Man: Robert E. Lee and His Image in American Society* (New York, 1977), 41–63; Kathy Edwards, Esme Howard, and Toni Prawl, *Monument Avenue: History and Architecture* (Washington, D.C., 1992), 12–16; see also *The Three Competitions for a Design for a Monument to Gen. Robert E. Lee, 1877–1887: A Protest and a Review* (Richmond, 1887).

[51] Accession Records, Office of the Registrar; *The Returned Battle Flags: The Flags of the Confederate Armies* (Washington, D.C., 1905).

[52] Report of CMLS president to UDC, in *Minutes of the Twenty-Second Annual Meeting of the United Daughters of the Confederacy, 1915* (Charlotte, N.C., 1916), 138.

[53] Annual Report of President Sally Archer Anderson, January 1920, CMLS Officer and Committee Reports, MOC.

[54] Accession Records, Office of the Registrar

[55] Isabel Maury, "Some Incidents Illustrated of the Relationship between Master and Slave that I remember!," June 1899, MOC; Isabel Maury notes, CMLS scrapbook, C3:51; CMLS scrapbook, B7:4, 9, 11, 14; "Concerning Miss Maury," *Richmond News Leader*, 28 November 1912, CMLS scrapbook, C6:21; Isabel Maury, "An Account of the Confederate Museum. What the Confederate Memorial Literary Society has accomplished," n.d. [ca. 1908], MOC.

[56] CMLS minutes, 30 March 1921. The work of collecting information for the "Roll of Honor" is documented in the Annual Reports of the Memorial Committee, CMLS Officer and Committee Reports.

[57] The committee's work is documented in the Annual Reports of the Sites Committee, CMLS Officer and Committee Reports. The period of Mary Werth's greatest activity is further documented in CMLS minutes, 30 March 1910; 29 March 1911; 29 October 1913; 24 February, 28 April 1915; 28 May 1924; CMLS, *Year Book, 1911–1912* (Richmond, 1912), 22–28; CMLS, *Year Book, 1911–1912* (Richmond, 1913), 23–28.

[58] CMLS, *Year Book, 1907* (Richmond, 1908), 11–12; Douglas Southall Freeman, ed., *A Calendar of Confederate Papers* (Richmond, 1908); Samuel E. Lewis, *The Treatment of Prisoners-of-War, 1861–1865* (Richmond, 1910); Rev. S. A. Steel, *Explainings of Objection to "Rebel"* (Richmond, 1913).

[59] CMLS minutes, 20 May 1910, 24 September 1912; Kate Pleasants Minor, ed., *Memorial Day Annual, 1912* (Richmond, 1912).

[60] For detailed information on the Confederate Museum's work, staff, and the division of labor among officers and regents see the museum's *Year Book* series, published (with few interruptions) between 1907 and 1928.

[61] Minnie A. Baughman to Douglas Southall Freeman, 17 October 1907, Douglas Southall Freeman Papers, Manuscripts Division, Library of Congress, Washington, D.C.

[62] *Minutes of the Sixth Annual Meeting of the United Daughters of the Confederacy, 1899* (Nashville, Tenn., 1900), 3–5; CMLS minutes, 27 September, 17 October, 6 December 1899; 28 June 1905; *In Memoriam: Emily Hendree Park* (Athens, Ga., 1911).

[63] CMLS minutes, 16 January 1900.

[64] Judith Winston (Mrs. M. B.) Pilcher to Mrs. Randolph, 6 April 1907, Regents and Vice Regents Papers, MOC; Mrs. M. B. Pilcher to CMLS, 14 January 1908, CMLS Letterbook, 1:251, MOC; Ella Darcy Dibrell to Lizzie Cary Daniel, ca. August 1911, Lizzie Cary Daniel Papers, MOC.

[65] *Minutes of the Fourteenth Annual Meeting of the United Daughters of the Confederacy, 1907* (Opelika, Ala., 1908), 225–28; Mrs. J. Enders Robinson, Report on 1907 UDC convention, CMLS minutes, 29 January 1908; Mrs. J. Enders Robinson, Report on 1908 UDC Convention, CMLS minutes, 11 November 1908.

[66] CMLS minutes, 26 April, 31 May 1905; 28 April 1909; 11 September, 26 October 1910.

[67] *Minutes of the Twenty-First Annual Meeting of the United Daughters of the Confederacy, 1914* (Raleigh, N.C., 1915), 70–71; CMLS minutes, 6 November 1911; 31 October, 29 November 1917; 27 March 1918.

[68] CMLS minutes, 8 January 1909.

[69] J. Taylor Ellyson, Report to United Confederate Veterans, CMA minutes, 7 June 1909, CMA Papers; *Minutes of the Nineteenth Annual Meeting and Reunion of the United Confederate Veterans, 1909* (New Orleans, 1910), 53–54; CMLS minutes, 30 December 1908, 8 January 1909.

[70] Virginia Robinson to Janet Randolph, 20 January 1909, MOC; Janet Randolph to J. Taylor Ellyson, 20 July 1909, President's Correspondence, CMA Papers; CMLS minutes, 6 February 1909, 30 November 1910; Joseph Bryan to Lizzie Cary Daniel, 9 September 1898, Joseph Bryan Letterbook, VHS. See also Robinson's similar letter distinguishing between men's and women's organizations, Virginia Robinson to DeWitt Webb, 11 April 1910, CMLS Letterbook, 2:712.

[71] CMLS minutes, 29 June 1898, 31 October 1906, 11 March 1919; mss. memorandum, n.d., Janet Randolph Memorandum Book, HMA Papers.

[72] Sally Archer Anderson to R. E. Lee Camp No. 1, 12 March 1919, Lee Camp Papers; "Information," CMLS minutes, 11 March 1919.

[73] Eppa Hunton, Jr., to Sally Archer Anderson, 1, 25 April 1919, Eppa Hunton Papers, VHS; James Power Smith to Sally Archer Anderson, n.d. [1919], Sally Archer Anderson Papers, MOC; George L. Christian to Sally Archer Anderson, President's Correspondence, CMA Papers; Sally Archer Anderson to George L. Christian, 1 May 1919, Sally Archer Anderson Papers.

[74] George L. Christian to Douglas Southall Freeman, 21 April 1922, President's Correspondence, CMA Papers; CMLS minutes, 30 April 1919.

[75] "Mother Richmond Asked Editorial Be Her Obituary," *Richmond News Leader*, 18 October 1927, CMLS scrapbook, C8:76; "Dedicate Gates As Memorial to Mrs. Joseph Bryan," *Richmond Times-Dispatch*, 15 April 1913, CMLS scrapbook, C6:53; *Richmond Virginian*, 13 September 1910.

[76] Mrs. J. Taylor Ellyson, "President's Report," in *1911–12 Year Booke of the APVA* (Richmond, 1912), 14; Virginia Morgan Robinson biographical sketch, Every Monday Club Papers, VHS; Virginia Morgan Robinson autobiographical sketch, ca. 1917, in "Historical Work of the United Daughters of the Confederacy," vol 4 of scrapbook collection "Historical Records of the United Daughters of the Confederacy," comp. Mildred Lewis Rutherford; Sandra Gioia Treadway, *Women of Mark: A History of the Woman's Club of Richmond, Virginia, 1894–1994* (Richmond, 1995), 6–8; Adele Clark, "Women in Virginia Have Many Groups," *Richmond News Leader*, 28 May 1929, CMLS scrapbook C8:179.

[77] Elizabeth Stevens Brinson, "Helping Others to Help Themselves: Social Advocacy and Wage-Earning Women in Richmond, Virginia, 1910–1932" (Ph.D. diss., Union for Experimenting Colleges and Universities, 1984), 85–86; CMLS minutes, 24 September 1912; "Young Women's Christian Association Tribute to Isobel Bryan," *Richmond Times-Dispatch*, ca. September 1910, CMLS scrapbook, C4:131; Elizabeth Stevens Brinson, "Isobel Lamont Stewart Bryan," in *The Dictionary of Virginia Biography*, ed. Sandra Gioia Treadway, Brent Tarter, and John T. Kneebone (Richmond, forthcoming), draft copy courtesy of the Library of Virginia; "Mrs. Minor Dies in Her Home," *Richmond News Leader*, 31 December 1925.

[78] Poppenheim, et al., *History of the United Daughters of the Confederacy*, 199, 348; *Minutes of the Fifteenth Annual Meeting of the Virginia Division, United Daughters of the Confederacy, 1910* (Suffolk, Va., 1910), 22–23; CMLS minutes, 30 November 1908; Mrs. N. V. Randolph, "Our Colored People's Christmas," *Richmond Times-Dispatch*, 17 December 1913, CMLS scrapbook, C6:126; Mother

Richmond, "The Story of the City on a Hill," Community Fund pamphlet, 1925, UDC Collection, MOC; clipping "Negroes Honor White Friends," 2 January 1928, CMLS scrapbook, C8:77.

[79] Richmond Chapter UDC minutes, 11 January 1911, 10 January 1912; *Minutes of the Eighteenth Annual Convention of the Virginia Division, United Daughters of the Confederacy, 1913* (Richmond, 1914), 23–24; "Women Explain Why They Support Bill," *Richmond Times-Dispatch*, Clippings Book: Richmond Dailies, 1910–1913; and J. H. R. to *Warrenton Fauquier Democrat*, 8 August 1916, Clippings Book: Non-Richmond, both Mary Branch Munford Papers, LVA.

[80] Equal Suffrage League Rosters, Equal Suffrage League Papers, LVA; May Gray Hodges obituary, *Richmond Times-Dispatch*, 9 August 1936, CMLS scrapbook, C10:174; Ellie Putney obituary, *Richmond Times-Dispatch*, 28 March 1918, CMLS scrapbook, C7:35; "Mrs. Minor Dies In Her Home"; and [Douglas Southall Freeman], "Mrs. Minor and the Library," both *Richmond News Leader*, 31 December 1925.

[81] *Kirmess Bulletin*, 12 April 1911, CMLS scrapbook, C4:6. On the role of Confederate memorial associations and other women's patriotic groups as training grounds for social and political activism see Price, "The Development of Leadership by Southern Women"; Anne Firor Scott, *Natural Allies: Women's Associations in American History* (Urbana, Ill., 1991); Anne Firor Scott, *The Southern Lady: From Pedestal to Politics* (Chicago, 1970), 155, 180; John Carl Rouff, "Southern Womanhood, 1865–1920: An Intellectual and Cultural Study" (Ph.D. diss., University of Illinois, 1976).

DIVIDED LEGACY:
The Civil War, Tradition, and "the Woman Question," 1870–1920
MARJORIE SPRUILL WHEELER

[1] Much of the essay is drawn from Marjorie Spruill Wheeler, *New Women of the New South: The Leaders of the Woman Suffrage Movement in the Southern States, 1890–1920* (New York, 1993). On the "Lost Cause," see Charles Reagan Wilson, *Baptized in Blood: The Religion of the Lost Cause, 1865–1920* (Athens, Ga., 1980); Gaines M. Foster, *Ghosts of the Confederacy: Defeat, the Lost Cause, and the Emergence of the New South, 1865 to 1913* (New York, 1987); Angie Parrott, "'Love Makes Memory Eternal': The United Daughters of the Confederacy in Richmond, Virginia, 1897–1920," in *The Edge of the South: Life in Nineteenth-Century Virginia*, ed. Edward L. Ayers and John C. Willis (Charlottesville, Va., 1991), 219–38; and Karen L. Cox, "Women of the Lost Cause: The United Daughters of the Confederacy and the Transmission of Confederate Culture, 1894–1920" (Ph.D. diss., University of Southern Mississippi, forthcoming).

[2] See Marjorie Spruill Wheeler, ed., *One Woman, One Vote: Rediscovering the Woman Suffrage Movement* (Troutdale, Ore., 1995).

[3] Anna Whitehead Bodeker, who had moved to Virginia from New Jersey in 1837 at age ten, was as an adult still regarded as an outsider by conservative Virginians, particularly after her husband won election to the General Assembly in 1869 and she became a suffragist in 1870. A Richmond newspaper reported that Bodeker and the other suffragists were not native Virginians and that, though "ladies of great respectability," they were "not our people, and their advanced ideas are no indication of a 'progressive spirit' in the South" (Sandra Gioia Treadway, "'A Most Brilliant Woman': Anna Whitehead Bodeker and the First Woman Suffrage Association in Virginia," *Virginia Cavalcade* 43 [1994]: 166–77). See also Charlotte Jean Sheldon, "Woman Suffrage and Virginia Politics, 1909–1920" (master's thesis, University of Virginia, 1969), 5–9; Rosalyn Terborg-Penn, "African American Women and the Woman Suffrage Movement," in Wheeler, ed., *One Woman, One Vote*, 140–41; Barbara Bellows (then Ulmer), "Virginia Durant Young: New South Suffragist" (master's thesis, University of South Carolina, 1979), 51–52.

[4] See Foster, *Ghosts of the Confederacy*; Wilson, *Baptized in Blood*, 7 (quote).

[5] Anne Firor Scott, *The Southern Lady: From Pedestal to Politics, 1830–1930*, rev. and enl. (Charlottesville, Va., 1995).

[6] Dorothy Ann Gay, "The Tangled Skein of Romanticism and Violence in the Old South: The Southern Response to Abolitionism and Feminism, 1830–1861" (Ph.D. diss., University of North Carolina, 1975).

[7] Wheeler, "The Southern Lady: Hostage to 'the Lost Cause,'" in *New Women of the New South*, 3–37, 7–8 (quotes).

[8] See John M. Coski and Amy R. Feely, "A Monument to Southern Womanhood: The Founding Generation of the Confederate Museum," in *A Woman's War: Southern Women, Civil War, and the Confederate Legacy*, ed. Edward D. C. Campbell, Jr., and Kym S. Rice (Charlottesville, Va., 1996), 131–63; LeeAnn Whites, *The Civil War as a Crisis in Gender: Augusta, Georgia, 1860–1890* (Athens, Ga., 1995).

[9] Foster, *Ghosts of the Confederacy*, 26–33, 124–25, 135 (quote), 135–39.

[10] Elise L. Smith, "Belle Kinney and the Confederate Women's Monument," *Southern Quarterly* 32, no. 4 (1994): 7–31, 26–27 (quotes).

[11] On fraud and violence accompanying the end of Reconstruction, see Eric Foner, *Reconstruction: America's Unfinished Revolution, 1863–1877* (New York, 1988); on Populism, see Lawrence Goodwyn, *Democratic Promise: The Populist Moment in America* (New York, 1976); Robert C. McMath, Jr., *American Populism: A Social History, 1877–1898* (New York, 1993); on disfranchisement, see J. Morgan Kousser, *The Shaping of Southern Politics: Suffrage Restriction and the Establishment of the One-Party South, 1880–1910* (New Haven, 1974).

[12] Wheeler, *New Women of the New South*, 13–20; on Aycock, see Oliver Orr, *Charles Brantley Aycock* (Chapel Hill, N.C., 1961), 118, 119, 174 (quote); see also Anastatia Sims, *The Power of Femininity in the New South: Women in Politics in North Carolina, 1883–1930* (Columbia, S.C., forthcoming).

[13] James Callaway, antisuffrage pamphlet, 1919, in antisuffrage literature sent to Laura Clay by Martin Lee Calhoun, of Alabama, Laura Clay Papers, Special Collections and Archives, University of Kentucky Library, Lexington.

[14] Kathleen Christine Berkeley, "Elizabeth Avery Meriwether, 'An Advocate for Her Sex': Feminism and Conservatism in the Post–Civil War South," *Tennessee Historical Quarterly* 63 (1984): 390–407; Ruth Ketring Nuermberger, "Virginia Carolina Tunstall Clay-Clopton," in *Notable American Women, 1607–1950: A Biographical Dictionary*, ed. Edward T. James (Cambridge, Mass., 1971), 1:348–49; John E. Talmadge, *Rebecca Latimer Felton: Nine Stormy Decades* (Athens, Ga., 1960).

[15] Anne Firor Scott, "Nellie Nugent Somerville," in *Notable American Women, The Modern Period: A Biographical Dictionary*, ed. Barbara Sicherman and Carol Hurd Green (Cambridge, Mass., 1980), 654–56; clippings, Somerville-Howorth Family Papers, Schlesinger Library, Radcliffe College, Cambridge, Mass. (SL-RC); Belle Kearney, *A Slaveholder's Daughter* (1900; reprint, New York, 1969); Marjorie Spruill Wheeler, introduction to Mary Johnston, *Hagar* (1913; reprint, Charlottesville, Va., 1994); Anne Goodwyn Jones, *Tomorrow Is Another Day: The Woman Writer in the South, 1859–1936* (Baton Rouge, La., 1981), 186 (quote).

[16] See Wheeler, "Southern Suffragists and 'the Negro Problem,'" in *New Women of the New South*, 100–32; Berkeley, "Elizabeth Avery Meriwether," 396–97; Bellows, "Virginia Durant Young"; on Frances Griffin, see Lee Norcross Allen, "The Woman Suffrage Movement in Alabama" (master's thesis, Alabama Polytechnic Institute [Auburn University], 1949).

[17] Anna Howard Shaw with Elizabeth Garver Jordan, *Story of a Pioneer* (New York, 1915), 310–11; Wheeler, "Southern Suffragists," 117 (quote). Suzanne Lebsock emphasizes the moderate racial views of the suffragists compared to the antisuffragists in Virginia after 1909 (Lebsock, "Woman Suffrage and White Supremacy: A Virginia Case Study," in *Visible Women: New Essays on American Activism*,

ed. Nancy A. Hewitt and Suzanne Lebsock [Urbana, Ill., 1993], 62–100).

[18] Kearney, *A Slaveholder's Daughter*, 112.

[19] Nellie Nugent Somerville, clipping "Mississippi Women Desert Boudoir For Work On Hustings," n.d., Somerville-Howorth Family Papers.

[20] Nellie Nugent Somerville, "Christian Citizenship," 1898, Somerville-Howorth Family Papers, 1–2 (quote).

[21] Rebecca Latimer Felton, "The Subjugation of Women and the Enfranchisement of Women," No. 2, Rebecca Latimer Felton Papers, Special Collections, Hargrett Rare Book and Manuscript Library, University of Georgia, Athens; LeeAnn Whites, "Rebecca Latimer Felton and the Problem of 'Protection' in the New South," in Hewitt and Lebsock, eds., *Visible Women*, 41–61.

[22] Carmen Meriwether Lindig, "The Woman's Movement in Louisiana, 1879–1920" (Ph.D. diss., North Texas State University, 1983), 164, 165.

[23] Paul E. Fuller, *Laura Clay and the Woman's Rights Movement* (Lexington, Ky., 1975), 62–72, 70 (second quote), 71 (first quote); Kearney, *A Slaveholder's Daughter*, 118–20.

[24] Sophonisba Breckinridge, *Madeline McDowell Breckinridge: A Leader in the New South* (Chicago, 1921), 34–42, 41–42 (quote).

[25] Somerville, "Mississippi Women Desert Boudoir"; Lloyd C. Taylor, Jr., "Lila Meade Valentine: FFV as Reformer," *Virginia Magazine of History and Biography* 70 (1962): 471–87, 481 (quote).

[26] On Dudley, see Marjorie Spruill Wheeler, ed., *Votes for Women! The Woman Suffrage Movement in Tennessee, the South, and the Nation* (Knoxville, Tenn., 1995), 162–68; on how the use of "honey-tongued charm" shocked northern suffragists, see Scott, *The Southern Lady*, 183–84.

[27] Mary Johnston, "The Woman Movement in the South," Suffrage Speeches, 1910–1911, Mary Johnston Papers, Alderman Library, University of Virginia, Charlottesville.

[28] George C. Rable, *Civil Wars: Women and the Crisis of Southern Nationalism* (Urbana, Ill., 1989), 288.

[29] This theme is developed in Sims, *The Power of Femininity*.

[30] According to Angie Parrott, "In towns and states throughout the South, UDC members could later be found actively campaigning for woman suffrage. Even so, neither the national nor any state organizations ever came out in open support of the measure. Moreover, a substantial number of UDC members, many of them high-ranking officers, continued to oppose suffrage" (Parrott, "'Love Makes Memory Eternal,'" 231).

[31] Sims, *The Power of Femininity*.

[32] Antisuffrage literature, Clay Papers; Allen, "Woman Suffrage Movement in Alabama," 145–46.

[33] A. Elizabeth Taylor, "The Last Phase of the Woman Suffrage Movement in Georgia," *Georgia Historical Quarterly* 43 (1959): 11–28, 18 (quote).

[34] Antisuffrage literature, Clay Papers.

[35] Sheldon, "Woman Suffrage and Virginia Politics," 20.

[36] Pamphlet, reprinted from *Richmond Evening Journal*, 4 May 1915, antisuffrage literature, Clay Papers.

[37] Benjamin Tillman speech, National American Woman Suffrage Association Papers, Manuscripts Division, Library of Congress, Washington, D.C.

[38] *Richmond Times-Dispatch*, 31 August 1919.

[39] David Morgan, *Suffragists and Democrats: The Politics of Woman Suffrage in America* (East Lansing, Mich., 1972), 131 (quote).

[40] Carrie Chapman Catt and Nettie Rogers Shuler, *Woman Suffrage and Politics: The Inner Story of the Suffrage Movement* (1923; reprint, Seattle, 1970), 463, 464.

[41] Antisuffrage leaflet, "Thomas Nelson Page, Late Ambassador to Italy and Distinguished Virginia Novelist Warns Against Legislative Ratification of the Woman Suffrage Amendment," 2 December 1919, NAWSA Papers.

[42] See antisuffrage pamphlets, especially "Some Facts About Suffrage Leaders," "The 'Three Immediate Women Friends' of the Anthony Family," and "Dr. Anna Howard Shaw and Frederick Douglass," Clay Papers; see also antisuffrage literature, NAWSA Papers.

[43] Antisuffrage literature, Clay Papers.

[44] See Wheeler, ed., *Votes for Women!*; Anastatia Sims, "Armageddon in Tennessee: The Final Battle Over the Nineteenth Amendment," in Wheeler, ed., *One Woman, One Vote.*

[45] See Elna C. Green, "Those Opposed: The Antisuffragists in North Carolina, 1900–1912," *North Carolina Historical Review* 67 (1990): 316–333, 327–28 (quote); *Raleigh News and Observer*, 12, 14 August 1920.

[46] See especially Josephine Pearson, "President's Message: Retiring from Antisuffrage Leadership of Tennessee, September 30, 1920" and "My Story: Of How and Why I Became an Antisuffrage Leader," in Wheeler, ed., *Votes for Women*, 214–23, 218 (quote), 224–242.

[47] Laura Clay to Kate Gordon, 31 July 1920, Clay Papers; Fuller, *Laura Clay*, 60; on Gordon in Mississippi, see clipping, *Jackson Clarion-Ledger*, n.d., Clay Papers.

[48] Mary Johnston, "Speech: Woman's College Alumnae, May 31," Suffrage Speeches, 1910–1911, Johnston Papers.

[49] Nellie Nugent Somerville, clipping "Are Women Too Good to Vote," ca. 1914, Somerville-Howorth Family Papers.

[50] Mary Johnston, "The Woman Movement in the South," Suffrage Speeches, 1910–1911, Johnston Papers.

[51] Rebecca Latimer Felton, *Country Life in Georgia in the Days of My Youth* (Atlanta, 1919), 93; see also, White, "Rebecca Latimer Felton," 54, 55.

[52] Mary Johnston to Lila Meade Valentine, 5 January 1912, Lila Hardaway Meade Valentine Papers, Division of Manuscripts and Archives, Virginia Historical Society, Richmond.

[53] Clipping "Democratic Party May Lose Support," n.d., Sue Shelton White Papers, SL-RC.

[54] Pattie Ruffner Jacobs, speech "Tradition Vs. Justice," NAWSA "Jubilee Convention," Chicago, 1920, Clay Papers.

[55] Ibid.

Lucy A. Cox. Co. A. 30. Va Reg.
Knipe
45 WEST KING ST
LANCASTER, PA.

SUGGESTIONS FOR FURTHER READING

Lucy Ann Cox. *(Carte-de-visite, postwar.)* Eleanor S. Brockenbrough Library, The Museum of the Confederacy

Lucy Cox's needle and thimble. *Although reportedly not disguised as a soldier, Lucy Ann Cox spent part of the war with her husband's unit, Company A, Thirteenth Virginia Regiment. (Steel needle and thimble, ca. 1861–1865.)* The Museum of the Confederacy

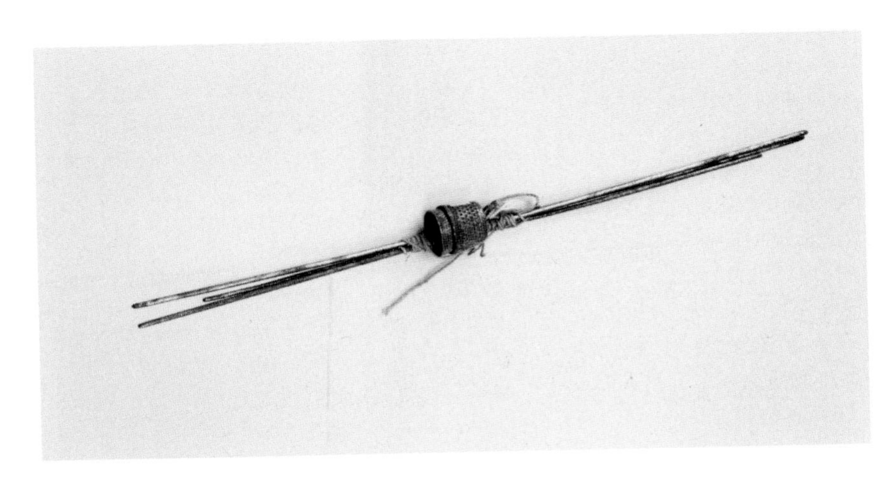

Alexander, Adele Logan. *Ambiguous Lives: Free Women of Color in Rural Georgia, 1789–1879.* Fayetteville: University of Arkansas Press, 1991.

Allan, Elizabeth Randolph, ed. *The Life and Letters of Margaret Junkin Preston.* Boston: Houghton Mifflin, 1903.

Amos, Harriet E. "'All-Absorbing Topics': Food and Clothing in Confederate Mobile." *Atlanta Historical Journal* 22 (fall-winter 1978): 17–28.

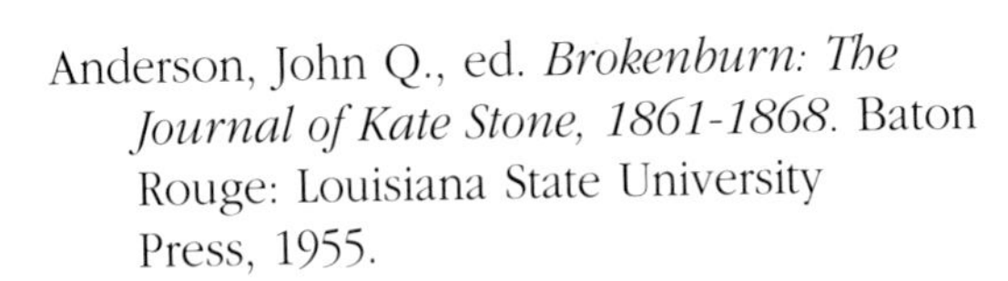

Anderson, John Q., ed. *Brokenburn: The Journal of Kate Stone, 1861-1868.* Baton Rouge: Louisiana State University Press, 1955.

Anderson, Lucy Worth, ed. *North Carolina Women of the Confederacy.* Fayetteville, N.C.: Cumberland Printing, 1926.

Andreae, Christine, ed. "Kate Sperry's Diary, 1861–1866." *Virginia Country's Civil War* 1 (1983): 45-75.

Andrews, Eliza Frances. *The War-Time Journal of a Georgia Girl, 1864–1865.* Edited by Spencer Bidwell King, Jr. Macon, Ga.: Ardivan Press, 1960.

Ash, Stephen V. *Middle Tennessee Society Transformed, 1860–1870: War and Peace in the Upper South.* Baton Rouge: Louisiana State University Press, 1988.

———. *When the Yankees Came: Conflict and Chaos in the Occupied South, 1861–1865.* Chapel Hill: University of North Carolina Press, 1995.

Ashcraft, Allan C., ed. "Mrs. Russell and the Battle of Raymond, Mississippi." *Journal of Mississippi History* 25 (1963): 38–40.

Ashkenazi, Elliott, ed. *The Civil War Diary of Clara Solomon: Growing Up in New Orleans, 1861–1862.* Baton Rouge: Louisiana State University Press, 1995.

Avary, Myrta Lockett. *A Virginia Girl in the Civil War, 1861–1865: Being a Record of the Actual Experiences of the Wife of a Confederate Officer*. New York: Appleton, 1903.

———. *Dixie After the War: An Exposition of Social Conditions Existing in the South, During the Twelve Years Succeeding the Fall of Richmond*. With an introduction by Clement A. Evans. 1906. Reprint, Boston: Houghton Mifflin, 1937.

Baird, Nancy Chappelear, ed. *Journals of Amanda Virginia Edmonds, Lass of the Mosby Confederacy, 1859–1867*. Stephens City, Va.: Commercial Press, 1984.

Bartlett, Catherine Thom, ed. *"My Dear Brother": A Confederate Chronicle*. Richmond: Dietz Press, 1952.

Beale, Jane Howison. *The Journal of Jane Howison Beale of Fredericksburg, Virginia, 1850–1862*. Fredericksburg: Historic Fredericksburg Foundation, 1979.

Beers, Fannie A. *Memories: A Record of Personal Experience and Adventure during Four Years of War*. 1888. Reprint, Alexandria, Va.: Time-Life Books, 1985.

Bell, Malcolm, Jr. *Major Butler's Legacy: Five Generations of a Slaveholding Family*. Athens: University of Georgia Press, 1987.

Bellows, Barbara L. *Benevolence Among Slaveholders: Assisting the Poor in Charleston, 1670–1860*. Baton Rouge: Louisiana State University Press, 1993.

Berkeley, Kathleen Christine. "Elizabeth Avery Meriwether, 'An Advocate for Her Sex': Feminism and Conservatism in the Post–Civil War South." *Tennessee Historical Quarterly* 43 (1984): 390–407.

Berlin, Ira, Barbara J. Fields, Thavolia Glymph, Joseph P. Reidy, and Leslie S. Rowland, eds. *The Destruction of Slavery*. Ser. 1, vol. 1, of *Freedom: A Documentary History of Emancipation, 1861–1867*. New York: Cambridge University Press, 1985.

Berlin, Jean V., ed. *A Confederate Nurse: The Diary of Ada W. Bacot, 1860–1863*. Columbia: University of South Carolina Press, 1994.

Bernhard, Virginia, Betty Brandon, Elizabeth Fox-Genovese, Theda Perdue, and Elizabeth Hayes Turner, eds. *Hidden Histories of Women in the New South*. Columbia: University of Missouri Press, 1994.

Billington, Ray Allen, ed. *The Journal of Charlotte L. Forten*. New York: Dryden Press, 1953.

Blackiston, Henry C., ed. *Refugees in Richmond: Civil War Letters of a Virginia Family*. Princeton: Princeton University Press, 1989.

Blanton, DeAnne. "Women Soldiers of the Civil War." *Prologue* (spring 1993): 27–33.

Bleser, Carol, ed. *The Hammonds of Redcliffe*. New York: Oxford University Press, 1981.

———, ed. *In Joy and in Sorrow: Women, Family, and Marriage in the Victorian South, 1830–1900*. New York: Oxford University Press, 1991.

———, ed. *Tokens of Affection: The Letters of a Planter's Daughter in the Old South*. Athens: University of Georgia Press, 1996.

Bleser, Carol K., and Frederick M. Heath. "The Impact of the Civil War on a Southern Marriage: Clement and Virginia Tunstall Clay of Alabama." *Civil War History* 30 (1984): 197–220.

Bolton, Charles C. *Poor Whites of the Antebellum South: Tenants and Laborers in Central North Carolina and Northeast Mississippi*. Durham, N.C.: Duke University Press, 1994.

Botume, Elizabeth Hyde. *First Days Amongst the Contrabands*. 1893. Reprint, New York: Arno Press, 1968.

Brock, Sallie A. *Richmond during the War: Four Years of Personal Observation, by a*

Richmond Lady. 1867. Reprint, Alexandria, Va.: Time-Life Books, 1983.

Brockman, Charles L., Jr. "Life in Confederate Athens, Georgia." *Georgia Review* 21 (1967): 107–25.

Brown, Louis A., ed. "The Correspondence of David Olando McRaven and Amanda Nantz McRaven, 1864-1865." *North Carolina Historical Review* 26 (1949): 41–98.

Bryan, Janet Allan, ed. *A March Past: Reminiscences of Elizabeth Randolph Preston Allan*. Richmond: Dietz Press, 1938.

Bryan, T. Conn, ed. "A Georgia Woman's Civil War Diary: The Journal of Minerva Leah Rowles McClatchey, 1864–65." *Georgia Historical Quarterly* 51 (1967): 197–216.

Buck, William Pettus, ed. *Sad Earth, Sweet Heaven: The Diary of Lucy Rebecca Buck during the War Between the States, Front Royal, Virginia, December 25, 1861–April 15, 1865*. Birmingham, Ala.: Cornerstone, 1973.

Burge, Dolly Sumner. *A Woman's Wartime Journal: An Account of the Passage Over a Georgia Plantation of Sherman's Army on the March to the Sea*. Macon, Ga.: J. W. Burke, 1927.

Burger, Nash K. *Confederate Spy: Rose O'Neal Greenhow*. New York: Franklin Watts, 1967.

Burr, Virginia Ingraham, ed. *The Secret Eye: The Journal of Ella Gertrude Clanton Thomas, 1848–1889*. Chapel Hill: University of North Carolina Press, 1990.

Burton, Orville Vernon. *In My Father's House Are Many Mansions: Family and Community in Edgefield, South Carolina*. Chapel Hill: University of North Carolina Press, 1985.

Burwell, Letitia M. *A Girl's Life in Virginia Before the War*. New York: Frederick A. Stokes, 1895.

Bynum, Hartwell T. "Sherman's Expulsion of the Roswell Women in 1864." *Georgia Historical Quarterly* 54 (1970): 169–82.

Bynum, Victoria E. *Unruly Women: The Politics of Social and Sexual Control in the Old South*. Chapel Hill: University of North Carolina Press, 1992.

_______. "'War Within a War': Women's Participation in the Revolt of the North Carolina Piedmont." *Frontiers* 9 (1987): 43–49.

Campbell, Edward D. C., Jr., ed. "'Strangers and Pilgrims': The Diary of Margaret Nourse, 4 April-11 November 1862." *Virginia Magazine of History and Biography* 91 (1983): 440–508.

Campbell, Randolph B., and Donald K. Pickens. "'My Dear Husband': A Texas Slave's Love Letters, 1862." *Journal of Negro History* 65 (1980): 361–64.

Cashin, Joan E. "'Decidedly Opposed to *the Union*': Women's Culture, Marriage, and Secession in Antebellum South Carolina." *Georgia Historical Quarterly* 78 (1994): 735–59.

_______. *A Family Venture: Men and Women on the Southern Frontier*. New York: Oxford University Press, 1991.

_______. "Varina Howell Davis (1826–1906)." In *Portraits of American Women: From Settlement to the Present*, edited by G. J. Barker-Benfield and Catherine Clinton, 259–77. New York: St. Martin's Press, 1991.

Censer, Jane Turner. *North Carolina Planters and Their Children, 1800-1860*. Baton Rouge: Louisiana State University Press, 1984.

Chancellor, Sue M. "Personal Recollections of the Battle of Chancellorsville." *Register of the Kentucky Historical Society* 66 (1968): 137–46.

Chesson, Michael. "Harlots or Heroines? A New Look at the Richmond Bread Riot." *Virginia Magazine of History and Biography* 92 (1984): 131–75.

Revival of the Old Slave Laws of Louisiana—A Scene in New Orleans—Arrest of Contrabands on the Night of January 30.
In January 1863, the Federal provost marshall in New Orleans arrested all African Americans out after nine o'clock in the evening without passes. (Engraving, Frank Leslie's Illustrated Newspaper, *7 March 1863.)*
Historic New Orleans Collection

Clay-Clopton, Virginia. *A Belle of the Fifties: Memoirs of Mrs. Clay, of Alabama, Covering Social and Political Life in Washington and the South, 1853-1866.* Edited by Ada Sterling. New York: Doubleday, Page, 1904.

Clift, G. Glenn, ed. *The Private War of Lizzie Hardin: A Kentucky Confederate Girl's Diary of the Civil War in Kentucky, Virginia, Tennessee, Alabama, and Georgia.* Frankfort: Kentucky Historical Society, 1963.

Clinton, Catherine. "Bloody Terrain: Freedwomen, Sexuality, and Violence During Reconstruction." *Georgia Historical Quarterly* 76 (1992): 313-32.

_______, ed. *Half Sisters: Southern Women and the American Past.* Durham, N.C.: Duke University Press, 1994.

_______. "In Search of Southern Women's History: The Current State of Academic Publishing." *Georgia Historical Quarterly* 76 (1992): 420-27.

_______. *The Plantation Mistress: Woman's World in the Old South.* New York: Pantheon, 1982.

_______. *Tara Revisited: Women, War and the Plantation Legend.* New York: Abbeville Press, 1995.

Clinton, Catherine, and Nina Silber, eds. *Divided Houses: Gender and the Civil War.* New York: Oxford University Press, 1992.

Coleman, Kenneth, ed. "Ladies Volunteer Aid Association of Sandersville, Washington County, Georgia, 1861-1862." *Georgia Historical Quarterly* 52 (1968): 78-95.

_______. "Mary Ann Cobb in Confederate Athens." *Georgia Review* 22 (1968): 360-69.

Collier, Malinda W., John M. Coski, Richard C. Cote, Tucker H. Hill, and Guy R. Swanson. *White House of the Confederacy: An Illustrated History.* Richmond: Cadmus Marketing, 1993.

Coulter, E. Merton, ed. *Confederate Receipt Book: A Compilation of Over One Hundred Receipts Adapted to the Times.* Athens: University of Georgia Press, 1960.

Confederated Southern Memorial Association, comp. *History of the Confederated Memorial Associations of the South.* New Orleans: Graham Press, 1904.

Connor, Seymour V., ed. *Dear America: Some Letters of Orange Cicero and Mary America (Aikin) Connor.* Austin, Tex.: Jenkins Publishing Company, 1971.

Cook, Anna Maria. *The Journal of a Milledgeville Girl, 1861–1867.* Edited by James C. Bonner. Athens: University of Georgia Press, 1964.

Coski, John. "A Century of Collecting: The History of the Museum of the Confederacy." *The Museum of the Confederacy Journal*, no. 74 (1996): 2–24.

Coulling, Mary Price. *The Lee Girls.* Winston-Salem, N.C.: John F. Blair, 1987.

_______. *Margaret Junkin Preston: A Biography.* Winston-Salem, N.C.: John F. Blair, 1993.

Crabtree, Beth G., and James W. Patton, eds. *"Journal of a Secesh Lady": The Diary of Catherine Ann Devereux Edmondston, 1860-1866.* Raleigh: Division of Archives and History, Department of Cultural Resources, 1979.

Cross, Eleanor P., and Charles B. Cross, Jr., eds. *Glencoe Diary: The War–Time Journal of Elizabeth Curtis Wallace.* Chesapeake,Va.: Norfolk County Historical Society of Chesapeake, Virginia, 1968.

_______, eds. *Child of Glencoe: Civil War Journal of Katie Darling Wallace.* Chesapeake, Va.: Norfolk County Historical Society of Chesapeake, Virginia, 1983.

Crossley, Martha Jane. "A Patriotic Confederate Woman's War Diary, 1862–1863." Edited by H. E. Sterkx. *Alabama Historical Quarterly* 20 (1958): 611–17.

Culpepper, Marilyn Mayer. *Trials and Triumphs: Women of the American Civil War*. East Lansing: Michigan State University Press, 1991.

Cumming, Kate. *Kate: The Journal of a Confederate Nurse*. Edited by Richard Barksdale Harwell. Baton Rouge: Louisiana State University Press, 1959.

———. *Gleanings from Southland: Sketches of Life and Manners of the People of the South Before, During and After the War of Secession*. Birmingham, Ala.: Roberts and Son, 1895.

Currey, Mary Eliza. "'What An Awful and Grand Spectacle It Is': Fear in the Heart of North Carolina." Edited by Ted Yeatman. *Civil War Times Illustrated* 22 (January 1984): 41–43.

Currie-McDaniel, Ruth. "Northern Women in the South, 1860-1880." *Georgia Historical Quarterly* 76 (1992): 284–312.

Cuttino, George Peddy, ed. *Saddle Bag and Spinning Wheel: Being the Civil War Letters of George W. Peddy, M.D., Surgeon, 56th Georgia Volunteer Regiment, C.S.A., and His Wife Kate Featherston Peddy*. Macon, Ga.: Mercer University Press, 1981.

Dannett, Sylvia G. L., and Katherine M. Jones. *Our Women of the Sixties*. Washington, D.C.: U.S. Civil War Centennial Commission, 1963.

Darst, W. Maury, ed. "Six Weeks to Texas." *Texana* 6 (Summer 1968): 140–52; also published in *American History Illustrated*, 14 (June 1979): 30–37.

———, ed. "The Vicksburg Diary of Mrs. Alfred Ingraham (May 2-June 13, 1863)." *Journal of Mississippi History* 44 (1982): 148–79.

Davis, Curtis Carroll, ed. *Belle Boyd in Camp and Prison, Written by Herself*. South Brunswick, N.J.: Thomas Yoseloff, 1968.

Dawson, Francis W., ed. *"Our Women in the War": The Lives They Lived, The Deaths They Died*. Charleston, S.C.: News and Courier Book Press, 1885.

Dawson, Sarah Morgan. *A Confederate Girl's Diary*. Edited by James I. Robertson, Jr. Bloomington: Indiana University Press, 1960.

Deen, Jeannie Marie, ed. *Annie Harper's Journal: A Southern Mother's Legacy*. Denton, Miss.: Flower Mound Writing, 1983.

DeLeon, T. C. *Belles, Beaux, and Brains of the 60's*. New York: G. W. Dillingham, 1909.

Deloach, Olivia. "Journey of a Confederate Mother, June 7-September 12, 1864." Edited by John A. Holden. *West Tennessee Historical Society Papers* 19 (1965): 36–37.

Dunbar, Mary Conway. *My Mother Used to Say: A Natchez Belle of the Sixties by Elizabeth Dunbar Murray*. Boston: Christopher Publishing House, 1959.

Durrill, Wayne K. *War of Another Kind: A Southern Community in the Great Rebellion*. New York: Oxford University Press, 1990.

East, Charles, ed. *The Civil War Diary of Sarah Morgan*. Athens: University of Georgia Press, 1991.

Eno, Clara B. "Activities of the Women of Arkansas during the War between the States." *Arkansas Historical Quarterly* 3 (1944): 5–27.

Erwin, John Seymour, ed. *Like Some Green Laurel: Letters of Margaret Johnson Erwin, 1821–1863*. Baton Rouge: Louisiana State University Press, 1981.

Escott, Paul D. "'The Cry of the Sufferers': The Problem of Welfare in the Confederacy." *Civil War History* 23 (1977): 228–40.

Farnham, Christie Anne. *The Education of the Southern Belle: Higher Education and Student Socialization in the Antebellum South*. New York: New York University Press, 1994.

Faust, Drew Gilpin. "Altars of Sacrifice: Confederate Women and the Narratives of War." *Journal of American History* 76 (1989–90): 1200–1228.

_______. *The Creation of Confederate Nationalism: Ideology and Identity in the Civil War South*. Baton Rouge: Louisiana State University Press, 1988.

_______. "In Search of the Real Mary Chesnut." *Reviews in American History* 10 (1982): 54–59.

_______. *Mothers of Invention: Women of the Slaveholding South in the American Civil War*. Chapel Hill: University of North Carolina Press, 1996.

_______. "Race, Gender, and Confederate Nationalism: William D. Washington's *Burial of Latané*." *Southern Review* 25 (1989): 297–307.

_______. "'Trying to Do a Man's Business': Gender, Violence, and Slave Management in Civil War Texas." *Gender and History* 4 (1993): 197–214.

Fearn, Frances, ed. *Diary of a Refugee*. New York: Moffat, Yard, 1910.

Feely, Amy R. "Southern Lady Meets New Woman: Women of the Confederate Memorial Literary Society and the Lost Cause in Richmond, Virginia." Master's thesis, University of Virginia, 1995.

Finley, Linda, ed. "Notes from the Diary of Susan E. Foreman." *Chronicles of Oklahoma* 47 (1969–70): 388–97.

Fischer, LeRoy H., ed. "A Civil War Experience of Some Arkansas Women in Indian Territory." *Chronicles of Oklahoma* 57 (1979): 137–63.

Foster, Gaines M. *Ghosts of the Confederacy: Defeat, the Lost Cause, and the Emergence of the New South, 1865 to 1913*. New York: Oxford University Press, 1987.

Fox-Genovese, Elizabeth. *Within the Plantation Household: Black and White Women of the Old South*. Chapel Hill: University of North Carolina Press, 1988.

Friedman, Jean E. *The Enclosed Garden: Women and Community in the Evangelical South, 1830–1900*. Chapel Hill: University of North Carolina Press, 1985.

Fulknier, Virginia. *Dear Annie: A Collection of Letters, 1860–1886*. Parsons, W.Va.: McClain Printing, 1969.

Galbraith, William, and Loretta Galbraith, eds. *A Lost Heroine of the Confederacy: The Diaries and Letters of Belle Edmondson*. Jackson: University Press of Mississippi, 1990.

Gay, Mary Ann Harris. *Life in Dixie During the War*. Atlanta: Constitution Job Office, 1892; Atlanta: C. P. Byrd, 1897.

Gemmill, Chalmers L., ed. "Midway Hospital, 1861–1863: The Diary of Miss Clarke of South Carolina." *Magazine of Albemarle County History* 22 (1963-64): 161–90.

Ginzberg, Lori D. *Women and the Work of Benevolence: Morality, Politics, and Class in the Nineteenth-Century United States*. New Haven: Yale University Press, 1990.

Gorgas, Amelia. "As I Saw It." Edited by Sarah Woolfolk Wiggins. *Civil War Times Illustrated* 25 (May 1986): 40–43.

Gould, Virginia Meacham. "'In Full Enjoyment of Their Liberty': The Free Women of Color of the Gulf Ports of New Orleans, Mobile, and Pensacola, 1769–1860." Ph.D. diss., Emory University, 1991.

Griffith, Lucille. "Mrs. Juliet Opie Hopkins and Alabama Military Hospitals." *Alabama Review* 6 (1953): 99–120.

Gutman, Herbert G. *The Black Family in Slavery and Freedom, 1750–1925*. New York: Pantheon, 1976.

Gwin, Minrose C. *Black and White Women of the Old South: The Peculiar Sisterhood in American Literature*. Knoxville: University of Tennessee Press, 1985.

Haggard, P. H. "A Sketch of My Early Life." Edited by James R. Jones. *Civil War Times Illustrated* 20 (August 1981): 34–43.

Hague, Parthenia Antoinette. *A Blockaded Family: Life in Southern Alabama during the Civil War*. 1888. Reprint, Lincoln: University of Nebraska Press, 1991.

Hall, Jacquelyn Dowd. *Revolt Against Chivalry: Jessie Daniel Ames and the Women's Campaign against Lynching*. New York: Columbia University Press, 1979.

Hall, James O., ed. "'An Army of Devils': The Diary of Ella Washington." *Civil War Times Illustrated* 16 (February 1978): 18–25.

Hall, Richard. *Patriots in Disguise: Women Warriors of the Civil War*. New York: Paragon House, 1993.

Harding, Elizabeth McGavock. "Letters from Nashville, 1862: A Portrait of Belle Meade." Edited by Ridley Wills. *Tennessee Historical Quarterly* 33 (1974): 70–84.

Harrison, Constance Cary. "A Virginia Girl in the First Year of the War." *Century Magazine* 30 (1885): 606–14.

———. *Recollections Grave and Gay*. New York: Scribners, 1911.

Harwell, Richard Barksdale, ed. "Louisiana Burge: The Diary of a Confederate College Girl." *Georgia Historical Quarterly* 36 (1952): 144–63.

Helmreich, Jonathan E. "A Prayer for the Spirit of Acceptance: The Journal of Martha Wayles Robertson, 1860-66." *Historical Magazine of the Protestant Episcopal Church* 46 (1977): 397–408.

Herd, Elmer Don, Jr., ed. "Sue Sparks Keitt to a Northern Friend, March 4, 1861." *South Carolina Historical Magazine* 62 (1961): 82–87.

Hickerson, Thomas Felix. *Echoes of Happy Valley: Letters and Diaries, Family Life in the South, Civil War History*. Chapel Hill, N.C.: Bull's Head Bookshop, 1962.

Holmes, Charlotte R., ed. *The Burckmyer Letters: March, 1863–June, 1865*. Columbia, S.C.: State Company, 1926.

Holt, Thad, Jr., ed. *Miss Waring's Journal: 1863 and 1865, Being the Diary of Miss Mary Waring of Mobile, During the Final Days of the War Between the States*. Chicago: Wyvern Press, 1964.

Hoobler, James, ed. "The Diary of Louisa Brown Pearl." *Tennessee Historical Quarterly* 38 (1979): 308–21.

Huckaby, Elizabeth Paisley, and Ethel C. Simpson, eds. *Tulip Evermore: Emma Butler and William Paisley, Their Lives in Letters, 1857–1887*. Fayetteville: University of Arkansas Press, 1985.

Hudson, Larry E., Jr. *To Have and To Hold: Slave Work and Family Life in Antebellum South Carolina*. Athens: University of Georgia Press, 1997.

Huff, Mary Ann. "The Role of Women in Confederate Georgia." Master's thesis, Emory University, 1967.

Hunt, Frances Caldern de la Barca. "The Last Days of Richmond." *Civil War Times Illustrated* 12 (February 1974): 20–22.

Inscoe, John. "Coping in Confederate Appalachia: A Portrait of a Mountain Woman and Her Community at War." *North Carolina Historical Review* 69 (1992): 388–413.

Jervey, Susan R., and Charlotte St. J. Ravenel. *Two Diaries from Middle St. John's, Berkeley, South Carolina, February–May 1865: Journals Kept by Susan R. Jervey and Miss Charlotte St. J. Ravenel*. Pinopolis, S.C.: St. John's Hunting Club, 1921.

Johnson, Whittington. "Free African-American Women in Savannah, 1800–1860: Autonomy and Affluence Amid

Adversity." *Georgia Historical Quarterly* 76 (1992): 260–83.

Jones, Anne Goodwyn. *Tomorrow Is Another Day: The Woman Writer in the South, 1859–1936*. Baton Rouge: Louisiana State University Press, 1981.

Jones, J. B. *A Rebel War Clerk's Diary at the Confederate States Capital*. 1866. Reprint, Alexandria, Va.: Time-Life Books, 1982.

Jones, Jacqueline. "Encounters, Likely and Unlikely, Between Black and Poor White Women in the Rural South, 1865–1940." *Georgia Historical Quarterly* 76 (1992): 333–53.

_______. *Labor of Love, Labor of Sorrow: Black Women, Work, and the Family from Slavery to the Present*. New York: Basic Books, 1985.

_______. *Soldiers of Light and Love: Northern Teachers and Georgia Blacks, 1865–1873*. Chapel Hill: University of North Carolina Press, 1980; Athens: University of Georgia Press, 1992.

Jones, Katharine M., ed. *Heroines of Dixie: Confederate Women Tell Their Story of the War*. Indianapolis: Bobbs-Merrill, 1955.

_______. *Heroines of Dixie: Winter of Desperation*. 2 vols. 1955. Reprint, Saint Simons Island, Ga.: Mockingbird Books, 1975.

_______. *Ladies of Richmond, Confederate Capital*. Indianapolis: Bobbs-Merrill, 1962.

_______. *When Sherman Came: Southern Women and the "Great March."* Indianapolis: Bobbs-Merrill, 1964.

Jones, Mary Sharpe, and Mary Jones Mallard. *Yankees A'Coming: One Month's Experience During the Invasion of Liberty County, Georgia, 1864–1865*. Edited by Haskell Monroe. Tuscaloosa, Ala.: Confederate Publishing, 1959.

Jones, Virginia K., ed. "The Journal of Sarah G. Follansbee." *Alabama Historical Quarterly* 27 (1965): 213–58.

Juncker, Clara. "Behind Confederate Lines: Sarah Morgan Dawson." *Southern Quarterly* 30 (fall 1991): 7–18.

Kaufman, Janet E. "Treasury Girls." *Civil War Times Illustrated* 25 (May 1986): 32–38.

_______. "'Under the Petticoat Flag': Women Soldiers in the Confederate Army." *Southern Studies* 23 (1984): 363–75.

Kennett, Lee. *Marching through Georgia: The Story of Soldiers and Civilians during Sherman's Campaign*. New York: HarperCollins, 1995.

Kenzer, Robert C. *Kinship and Neighborhood in a Southern Community: Orange County, North Carolina, 1849–1881*. Knoxville: University of Tennessee Press, 1987.

Kimball, William J. "The Bread Riot in Richmond." *Civil War History* 7 (1961): 149–54.

_______. *Starve or Fall: Richmond and Its People, 1861–1865*. Ann Arbor, Mich.: University Microfilms International, 1976.

Kinchen, Oscar A. *Women Who Spied for the Blue and the Gray*. Philadelphia: Dorrance, 1972.

King, C. Richard, ed. *Victorian Lady on the Texas Frontier: The Journal of Ann Raney Coleman*. Norman: University of Oklahoma Press, 1971.

King, Spencer Bidwell, Jr., ed. "A Poor Widow Asks for Food: 1865." *Georgia Historical Quarterly* 52 (1968): 449–50.

_______, ed. *Ebb Tide: As Seen Through the Diary of Josephine Clay Habersham, 1863*. Athens: University of Georgia Press, 1958.

King, Wilma, ed. *A Northern Woman in the Plantation South: Letters of Tryphena*

Blanche Holder Fox, 1856–1876. Columbia: University of South Carolina Press, 1993.

Kremenak, Ben, ed. "Escape from Atlanta: The Huntington Memoir." *Civil War History* 11 (1965): 160–77.

Krug, Donna Rebecca Dondes. "The Folks Back Home: The Confederate Home Front during the Civil War." Ph.D. diss., University of California, Irvine, 1990.

Laas, Virginia Jeans, ed. *Wartime Washington: The Civil War Letters of Elizabeth Blair Lee.* Urbana: University of Illinois Press, 1991.

Lancaster, Mary H., and Dallas M. Lancaster, eds. *The Civil War Diary of Anne S. Frobel of Wilton Hill in Virginia.* Birmingham, Ala.: Birmingham Printing and Publishing, 1986.

Lander, Ernest M., Jr., ed. "A Confederate Girl Visits Pennsylvania, July–September 1863." *Western Pennsylvania Historical Magazine* 59 (1966): 111–26, 197–211.

_______, ed. "Mrs. John C. Calhoun and the Coming of the Civil War." *Civil War History* 22 (1976): 308–17.

Lebsock, Suzanne. *The Free Women of Petersburg: Status and Culture in a Southern Town, 1784–1860.* New York: W. W. Norton, 1984.

_______. "Radical Reconstruction and the Property Rights of Southern Women." *Journal of Southern History* 43 (1977): 195–216.

Lee, Mary Charlton. "An Abstract from the Journal of Mrs. Hugh H. Lee of Winchester, Va., May 23–31, 1862." *Maryland Historical Magazine* 53 (1958): 380–93.

Lee, Mary Custis. "They Surrendered Honorably." Edited by Edith Snowden and Philip Gibson. *Civil War Times Illustrated* 20 (November 1981): 17–18.

Le Guin, Charles A., ed. *A Home-Concealed Woman: The Diaries of Magnolia Wynn Le Guin, 1901–1913.* Athens: University of Georgia Press, 1990.

Leslie, Kent Anderson. *Woman of Color, Daughter of Privilege: Amanda America Dickson, 1849–1893.* Athens: University of Georgia Press, 1995.

Litwack, Leon F. *Been in the Storm So Long: The Aftermath of Slavery.* New York: Alfred A. Knopf, 1979.

Lohrenz, Mary. "Two Lives Intertwined on a Tennessee Plantation: Textile Production as Recorded in the Diary of Narcissa L. Erwin Black." *Southern Quarterly* 27 (fall 1988): 73–93.

Lohrenz, Mary Edna, and Anita Miller Stamper. *Mississippi Homespun: Nineteenth-Century Textiles and the Women Who Made Them.* Jackson: Mississippi Department of Archives and History, 1989.

Loughridge, Patricia R., and Edward D. C. Campbell, Jr. *Women in Mourning.* Richmond: Museum of the Confederacy, 1986.

Macon, Emma Cassandra, and Reuben Conway Macon. *Reminiscences of the Civil War.* Cedar Rapids, Iowa: [Torch Press], 1911.

Malone, Ann Patton. *Sweet Chariot: Slave Family and Household Structure in Nineteenth-Century Louisiana.* Chapel Hill: University of North Carolina Press, 1992.

Marszalek, John, ed. *The Diary of Miss Emma Holmes, 1861–1866.* Baton Rouge: Louisiana State University Press, 1979.

Martin, Florence Ashmore Cowles Hamlett, ed. *Courageous Journey: The Civil War Journal of Laetitia LaFon Ashmore Nutt.* Miami, Fla.: E. A. Seemann Publishing, 1975.

Mason, Emily. "Memories of a Hospital Matron." *Atlantic Monthly* 90 (1902): 305–18, 475–85.

Massey, Mary Elizabeth. *Bonnet Brigades: American Women and the Civil War.* New York: Alfred A. Knopf, 1966. Reprinted as *Women in the Civil War.* Lincoln: University of Nebraska Press, 1994.

_______. "Confederate Refugees." *Civil War Times Illustrated* 10 (November 1971): 14–24.

_______. "The Confederate Refugees in North Carolina." *North Carolina Historical Review* 40 (1963): 158–82.

_______. *Ersatz in the Confederacy.* Columbia: University of South Carolina Press, 1952.

_______. *Refugee Life in the Confederacy.* Baton Rouge: Louisiana State University Press, 1964.

May, Robert. "Southern Elite Women, Sectional Extremism, and the Male Political Sphere: The Case of John A. Quitman's Wife and Female Descendants, 1847–1931." *Journal of Mississippi History* 50 (1988): 251–86.

McCants, Dorothea, trans. and ed. *They Came to Louisiana: Letters of a Catholic Mission, 1854–1882.* Baton Rouge: Louisiana State University Press, 1970.

McCurry, Stephanie. *Masters of Small Worlds: Yeoman Households, Gender Relations, and Political Culture in the Antebellum South Carolina Low Country.* New York: Oxford University Press, 1995.

_______. "The Two Faces of Republicanism: Gender and Proslavery Politics in Antebellum South Carolina." *Journal of American History* 78 (1992): 1245–64.

McDonald, Cornelia Peake. *A Diary with Reminiscences of the War and Refugee Life in the Shenandoah Valley, 1860–1865.* Nashville: Cullom and Ghertner, 1935.

_______. *A Woman's Civil War: A Diary, with Reminiscences of the War, from March 1862.* Edited by Minrose C. Gwin. Madison: University of Wisconsin Press, 1992.

McGee, Charles M., Jr., and Ernest M. Lander, Jr., eds. *A Rebel Came Home: The Diary of Floride Clemson Tells of her Wartime Adventures in Yankeeland, 1863–1865, Her Trip Home to South Carolina, and Life in the South During the Last Few Months for the Civil War and the Year Following.* Columbia: University of South Carolina Press, 1961.

McGuire, Judith. *Diary of a Southern Refugee during the War, by a Lady of Virginia.* 1867. Reprint, Lincoln: University of Nebraska Press, 1995.

McKinney, Gordon B. "Women's Role in Civil War Western North Carolina." *North Carolina Historical Review* 69 (1992): 37–56.

McLaurin, Melton A. *Celia: A Slave.* Athens: University of Georgia Press, 1991.

McMillen, Sally G. *Motherhood in the Old South: Pregnancy, Childbirth, and Infant Rearing.* Baton Rouge: Louisiana State University Press, 1990.

_______. *Southern Women: Black and White in the Old South.* Arlington Heights, Ill.: Harlan Davidson, 1992.

Mendenhall, Marjorie Stratford. "Southern Women of a 'Lost Generation.'" *South Atlantic Quarterly* 33 (1934): 334–53.

Merrick, Caroline E. *Old Times in Dixie Land: A Southern Matron's Memoirs.* New York: Grafton Press, 1901.

Middleton, Sarah Matilda, and Harriet Middleton. "Middleton Correspondence, 1861-1865." Edited by Isabella Middleton Leland. *South Carolina Historical Magazine* 64 (1963): 28–38, 95–104, 158–68, 212–19; 65 (1964): 33–44.

Miers, Earl Schenck, ed. *When the World Ended: The Diary of Emma LeConte.* New York: Oxford University Press, 1957.

Miller, Randall. "Letters from Nashville, 1862: 'Dear Master.'" *Tennessee Historical Quarterly* 33 (1974): 85–92.

Mitchell, Patricia B. *Cooking for the Cause: Confederate Recipes, Documented Quotations, Commemorative Recipes.* Chatham, Va.: Sims-Mitchell House, 1988.

Mohr, Clarence. *On the Threshold of Freedom: Masters and Slaves in Civil War Georgia.* Athens: University of Georgia Press, 1986.

Moneyhon, Carl H., ed. "Life in Confederate Arkansas: The Diary of Virginia Davis Gray, 1863–1865." *Arkansas Historical Quarterly* 42 (1983): 47-85, 134–69.

Monroe, Haskell, ed. *"Yankees a'comming": One Month's Experience During the Invasion of Liberty County Georgia, 1864–1865.* Tuscaloosa, Ala.: Confederate Publishing, 1959.

Moore, John Hammond, ed. *A Plantation Mistress on the Eve of the Civil War: The Diary of Keziah Goodwyn Hopkins Brevard, 1860–1861.* Columbia: University of South Carolina Press, 1993.

Morgan, Julia. *How It Was: Four Years among the Rebels.* Nashville, Tenn.: Publishing House of the Methodist Episcopal Church, 1892.

Morrill, Lily Logan, ed. *My Confederate Girlhood: The Memoirs of Kate Virginia Cox Logan.* Richmond: Garrett and Massie, 1932.

Morton, Patricia, ed. *Discovering the Women in Slavery: Emancipating Perspectives on the American Past.* Athens: University of Georgia Press, 1996.

Moss, Elizabeth. *Domestic Novelists in the Old South: Defenders of Southern Culture.* Baton Rouge: Louisiana State University Press, 1992.

Muhlenfeld, Elisabeth. *Mary Boykin Chesnut: A Biography.* Baton Rouge: Louisiana State University, 1981.

Myers, Robert Manson, ed. *The Children of Pride: A True Story of Georgia and the Civil War.* New Haven: Yale University Press, 1972.

Neverdon-Morton, Cynthia. *Afro-American Women of the South and the Advancement of the Race, 1895–1925.* Knoxville: University of Tennessee Press, 1989.

O'Brien, Michael, ed. *An Evening When Alone: Four Journals of Single Women in the South, 1827–67.* Charlottesville: University Press of Virginia, 1993.

Owsley, Frank Lawrence. *Plain Folk of the Old South.* Baton Rouge: Louisiana State University Press, 1949.

Painter, Nell Irvin. "Of *Lily*, Linda Brent, and Freud: A Non-Exceptionalist Approach to Race, Class, and Gender in the Slaveholding South." *Georgia Historical Quarterly* 76 (1992): 241–59.

Parmalee, Alice Maury, ed. *The Confederate Diary of Betty Herndon Maury, 1861–1863.* Washington, D.C.: privately printed, 1938.

Parrott, Angie. "'Love Makes Memory Eternal': The United Daughters of the Confederacy in Richmond, Virginia, 1897–1920." In *The Edge of the South: Life in Nineteenth-Century Virginia,* edited by Edward Ayers and John Willis, 219–38. Charlottesville: University Press of Virginia, 1991.

Partin, Robert. "The Wartime Experiences of Margaret McCalla: Confederate Refugee from East Tennessee." *Tennessee Historical Quarterly* 24 (1965): 39–53.

Pearson, Alden B., Jr. "A Middle-Class, Border-State Family During the Civil War." *Civil War History* 22 (1976): 318–36.

Pease, Jane H., and William H. Pease. *Ladies, Women, and Wenches: Choice and Constraint in Antebellum Charleston and Boston.* Chapel Hill: University of North Carolina Press, 1990.

Pember, Phoebe Yates. *A Southern Woman's Story: Life in Confederate Richmond. Including Unpublished Letters Written from the Chimborazo Hospital.* Edited by Bell Irvin Wiley. Jackson, Tenn.: McCowat-Mercer Press, 1959; Saint Simons Island, Ga.: Mockingbird Books, 1974.

Phillips, Edward H. *The Lower Shenandoah Valley in the Civil War: The Impact of War Upon the Civilian Population and Upon Civil Institutions.* Edited by Loving H. Phillips. Lynchburg, Va.: H. E. Howard, 1993.

Pond, Cornelia Jones. *Life on a Liberty County Plantation.* Edited by Josephine Bacon Martin. Darien, Ga.: privately printed, 1974.

Poppenheim, Mary B., and others. *The History of the United Daughters of the Confederacy.* Richmond: Garrett and Massie, 1938; Richmond: United Daughters of the Confederacy, 1994.

Postel, Marie Monroe. "Sherman's Occupation of Savannah: Two Letters." *Georgia Historical Quarterly* 50 (1966): 109–15.

Pringle, Elizabeth Allston [Patience Pennington]. *A Woman Rice Planter.* 1913. Reprint, Columbia: University of South Carolina Press, 1992.

Proctor, Samuel, ed. "The Call to Arms: Secession from a Feminine Point of View." *Florida Historical Quarterly* 35 (1957): 266–70.

Pryor, Mrs. Roger A. [Sara Agnes Rice Pryor]. *My Day: Reminiscences of a Long Life.* New York: Macmillan, 1909.

_______. *Reminiscences of Peace and War.* 1904. Reprint, New York: Macmillan, 1924.

Quattlebaum, Isabel. "Twelve Women in the First Days of the Confederacy." *Civil War History* 7 (1961): 370–85.

Rable, George C. *Civil Wars: Women and the Crisis of Southern Nationalism.* Urbana: University of Illinois Press, 1989.

Racine, Philip N. "Emily Lyles Harris: A Piedmont Farmer During the Civil War." *South Atlantic Quarterly* 79 (1980): 386–97.

Rainwater, Percy L., ed. "The Civil War Letters of Cordelia Scales." *Journal of Mississippi History* 1 (1939): 169–81.

Ramsdell, Charles William. *Behind the Lines in the Southern Confederacy.* Baton Rouge: Louisiana State University Press, 1944.

Reilly, Wayne E., ed. *Sarah Jane Foster, Teacher of the Freedmen: A Diary and Letters.* Charlottesville: University Press of Virginia, 1990.

Richard, J. Fraise. *The Florence Nightingale of the Southern Army: Experiences of Mrs. Ella K. Newsom, Confederate Nurse in the Great War of 1861–1865.* New York: Broadway, 1914.

Ripley, Eliza. *From Flag to Flag: A Woman's Adventures and Experiences in the South during the War, in Mexico, and in Cuba.* New York: D. Appleton, 1889.

_______. *Social Life in Old New Orleans: Being Recollections of My Girlhood.* New York: D. Appleton, 1912.

Roark, James L. "Hidden Lives: Georgia's Free Women of Color." *Georgia Historical Quarterly* 76 (1992): 410–19.

Robertson, Mary D., ed. *A Confederate Lady Comes of Age: The Journal of Pauline DeCaradeuc Heyward, 1863–1888.* Columbia: University of South Carolina Press, 1992.

_______, ed. "The Dusky Wings of War: The Journal of Lucy G. Breckinridge, 1862–1864." *Civil War History* 23 (1977): 26–51.

_______, ed. *Lucy Breckinridge of Grove Hill: The Journal of a Virginia Girl, 1862–1864.* Kent, Ohio: Kent State University Press, 1979; Columbia: University of South Carolina Press, 1994.

Rosenburg, R. B. *Living Monuments: Confederate Soldiers' Homes in the New South*. Chapel Hill: University of North Carolina Press, 1993.

Ross, Ishbel. *First Lady of the South: The Life of Mrs. Jefferson Davis*. New York: Harper, 1958.

_______. *Rebel Rose: Life of Rose O'Neal Greenhow, Confederate Spy*. New York: Harper, 1954.

Rowland, Kate Mason, and Mrs. Morris L. Croxall [Agnes E. (Browne) Croxall], eds. *The Journal of Julia Le Grand, New Orleans, 1862-1863*. Richmond: Everett Waddey, 1911.

Rozier, John, ed. *The Granite Farm Letters: The Civil War Correspondence of Edgeworth and Sallie Bird*. Athens: University of Georgia Press, 1988.

Ryan, David O., ed. *A Yankee Spy in Richmond: The Civil War Diary of "Crazy Bet" Van Lew*. Mechanicsburg, Pa.: Stackpole Books, 1996.

Ryan, Mary. *Women in Public: Between Banners and Ballots, 1825–1880*. Baltimore: Johns Hopkins University Press, 1990.

Samuels, Kathleen Boone, and Green Berry Samuels. *A Civil War Marriage in Virginia: Reminiscences and Letters*. Compiled by Carrie Esther Spencer, Bernard Samuels, and Walter Berry Samuels. Boyce, Va.: Carr Publishing, 1956.

Saxon, Elizabeth. *A Southern Woman's War Time Reminiscences*. Memphis, Tenn.: Pilcher, 1905.

Scarborough, Ruth. *Belle Boyd: Siren of the South*. Macon, Ga.: Mercer University Press, 1983.

Schultz, Jane E. "The Inhospitable Hospital: Gender and Professionalism in Civil War Medicine." *Signs* 17 (1992): 363–92.

Schwartz, Gerald, ed. *A Woman Doctor's Civil War: Esther Hawks' Diary*. Columbia: University of South Carolina Press, 1984.

Scott, Anne Firor. *Natural Allies: Women's Associations in American History*. Urbana: University of Illinois Press, 1991.

_______. *The Southern Lady: From Pedestal to Politics, 1830–1930*. Chicago: University of Chicago Press, 1970; Charlottesville: University Press of Virginia, 1995.

_______, ed. *Unheard Voices: The First Historians of Southern Women*. Charlottesville: University Press of Virginia, 1993.

Scott, Margaret Phelan, and Rachel Wilson. "Hollins and the Civil War." *Hollins Alumnae Bulletin* (spring 1961): 16–18.

Seidel, Kathryn Lee. *The Southern Belle in the American Novel*. Tampa: University of South Florida Press, 1985.

Sigaud, Louis A. *Belle Boyd: Confederate Spy*. Richmond: Dietz Press, 1944.

Simkins, Francis Butler, and James Welch Patton. *Women of the Confederacy*. Richmond: Garrett and Massie, 1936.

Simkins, Francis Butler, and James Welch Patton. "The Work of Southern Women among the Sick and Wounded of the Confederate Armies." *Journal of Southern History* 1 (1935): 475–96.

Skarstedt, Vance R. "The Confederate Veteran Movement and National Reunification." Ph.D. diss., Florida State University, 1993.

Skinner, Arthur N., and James L. Skinner, eds. *The Death of a Confederate: Selections from the Letters of the Archibald Smith Family of Roswell, Georgia, 1864–1956*. Athens: University of Georgia Press, 1996.

Smedes, Susan Dabney. *Memorials of a Southern Planter*. Edited by Fletcher Green. New York: Alfred A. Knopf, 1965.

Stevenson, Mary, comp. *The Diary of Clarissa Adger Bowen, Ashtabula Plantation, 1865, with Excerpts from Other Family Diaries and Comments by Her Granddaughter, Clarissa Walton Taylor, and Many Other Accounts of the Pendleton Clemson Area, South Carolina, 1776–1889*. Pendleton, S.C.: Foundation for Historic Restoration in Pendleton Area, 1973.

Sterkx, H. E. *Partners in Rebellion: Alabama Women in the Civil War*. Rutherford, N.J.: Fairleigh Dickinson University Press, 1970.

Sterling, Dorothy, ed. *We Are Your Sisters: Black Women in the Nineteenth Century*. New York: W. W. Norton, 1984.

Stillman, Rachel Bryan. "Education in the Confederate States of America, 1861–1865." Ph.D. diss., University of Illinois, Champaign-Urbana, 1972.

Stock, Mary Wright, ed. *Shinplasters and Homespun: Diary of Laura Nisbet Boykin*. Rockville, Md.: Printex, 1975.

Stowe, Steven M. *Intimacy and Power in the Old South: Ritual in the Lives of the Planters*. Baltimore: Johns Hopkins University Press, 1987.

_______. "'The *Thing* Not Its Vision': A Woman's Courtship and Her Sphere in the Southern Planter Class." *Feminist Studies* 9 (1983): 113–30.

Straight, William M., ed. "The Pensacola Campaign Through a Nurse's Eye." *Florida Medical Association Journal* 56 (1969): 632–36.

Sullivan, Walter, ed. *The War the Women Lived: Female Voices from the Confederate South*. Nashville, Tenn.: J. S. Sanders, 1995.

Sutherland, Daniel. "Introduction to War: The Civilians of Culpeper County, Virginia." *Civil War History* 37 (1991): 120–37.

_______. "Looking for a Home: Louisiana Emigrants during the Civil War and Reconstruction." *Louisiana History* 21 (1980): 341–59.

_______. *Seasons of War: The Ordeal of a Confederate Community, 1861–1865*. New York: Free Press, 1995.

Swint, Henry L., ed. *Dear Ones at Home: Letters from Contraband Camps*. Nashville, Tenn.: Vanderbilt University Press, 1966.

Tatum, Georgia Lee. *Disloyalty in the Confederacy*. Chapel Hill: University of North Carolina Press, 1934.

Taylor, Mrs. Fielding Lewis. "Capt. Sallie Tompkins." *Confederate Veteran* 24 (November 1916): 521, 524.

Taylor, Susie King. *A Black Woman's Civil War Memoirs: Reminiscences of My Life in Camp with the 33rd U.S. Colored Troops, Late 1st South Carolina Volunteers*. Edited by Patricia W. Romero. New York: Markus Wiener Publishing, 1988.

Taylor, Mrs. Thomas, Mrs. A. T. Smythe, Mrs. August Kohn, Miss M. B. Poppenheim, and Miss Martha Washington, eds. *South Carolina Women in the Confederacy*. 2 vols. Columbia, S.C.: State Co., 1903–07.

Thomas, Charles E., ed. "The Diary of Anna Hasell Thomas." *South Carolina Historical Magazine* 74 (1973): 128–43.

Thomas, Cornelius M. Dickinson, ed. *Letters from the Colonel's Lady: Correspondence of Mrs. (Col.) William Lamb Written from Fort Fisher, N.C., C.S.A., to her Parents in Providence, R.I., U.S.A., December 1861 to January 1865*. Winnabow, N.C.: Charles Towne Preservation Trust, 1965.

Thomas, Emory M. "The Richmond Bread Riot of 1863." *Virginia Cavalcade* 18 (summer 1968): 41–47.

_______. "To Feed the Citizens: Welfare in Wartime Richmond." *Virginia Cavalcade* 22 (summer 1972): 22–29.

Tice, Douglas O. "'Bread or Blood': The Richmond Bread Riot." *Civil War Times Illustrated* 12 (February 1974): 12–19.

Tillett, Wilbur Fisk. "Southern Womanhood as Affected by the War." *Century Magazine* 43 (1891): 9–16.

Tompkins, Ellen Wilkins, ed. "The Colonel's Lady: Some Letters of Ellen Wilkins Tompkins, July-December 1861." *Virginia Magazine of History and Biography* 69 (1961): 387–419.

Treadway, Sandra Gioia. "'The Delightful Friction of Well Trained Minds': The Founding of the Woman's Club of Richmond, 1894–1900." *Virginia Cavalcade* 44 (1995): 174–91.

Turner, Charles W., ed. *Civil War Letters of Arabella Speairs and William Beverley Pettit of Fluvanna County, Virginia, March 1862-March 1865*. 2 vols. Roanoke: Virginia Lithography and Graphics, 1988–89.

_______, ed. "General David Hunter's Sack of Lexington, Virginia, June 10–14, 1864: An Account by Rose Page Pendleton." *Virginia Magazine of History and Biography* 83 (1975): 173–83.

Underwood, J. L. *The Women of the Confederacy*. N.p., 1906.

Varon, Elizabeth R. "'The Ladies Are Whigs': Lucy Barbour, Henry Clay, and Nineteenth-Century Virginia Politics." *Virginia Cavalcade* 42 (1992): 72–83.

_______. "Tippecanoe and the Ladies, Too: White Women and Party Politics in Antebellum Virginia." *Journal of American History* 82 (1995): 494–521.

Viener, Saul. "Rosena Hutzler Levy Recalls the Civil War." *American Jewish Historical Quarterly* 62 (1973): 306–13.

Walker, Georgiana Freeman. *Private Journal, 1862–1865, with Selections from the Post-War Years, 1865–1876*. Edited by Dwight Franklin Henderson. Tuscaloosa, Ala.: Confederate Publishing Co., 1963.

Ward, Evelyn Douglas. *The Children of Bladensfield*. With an essay by Peter Matthiessen. New York: Viking Press, 1978.

Wedell, Marsha. *Elite Women and the Reform Impulse in Memphis, 1875–1915*. Knoxville: University of Tennessee Press, 1991.

Weiner, Jonathan M. "Female Planters and Planters' Wives in Civil War and Reconstruction Alabama, 1850–1870." *Alabama Review* 30 (1977): 135–49.

Weiner, Marli Frances, ed. *A Heritage of Woe: The Civil War Diary of Grace Brown Elmore, 1861–1868*. Athens: University of Georgia Press, 1997.

_______. "Plantation Mistress and Female Slaves: Gender, Race, and South Carolina Women, 1830–1880." Ph.D. diss., University of Rochester, 1985.

Welton, J. Michael, ed. *"My Heart Is So Rebellious": The Caldwell Letters, 1861–1865*. Warrenton, Va.: Fauquier National Bank, 1991.

Wheeler, Marjorie Spruill. *New Women of the New South: The Leaders of the Woman Suffrage Movement in the Southern States, 1890–1920*. New York: Oxford University Press, 1993.

_______, ed. *One Woman, One Vote: Rediscovering the Woman Suffrage Movement*. Troutdale, Ore.: NewSage Press, 1995.

_______, ed. *Votes for Women! The Woman Suffrage Movement in Tennessee, the South, and the Nation*. Knoxville: University of Tennessee Press, 1995.

White, Deborah Gray. *Ar'n't I a Woman? Female Slaves in the Plantation South*. New York: W. W. Norton, 1985.

Whites, LeeAnn. "The Charitable and the Poor: The Emergence of Domestic

Politics in Augusta, Georgia, 1860–1880." *Journal of Social History* 17 (1984): 606–16.

_______. *The Civil War as a Crisis in Gender: Augusta, Georgia, 1860–1890.* Athens: University of Georgia Press, 1995.

Wiley, Bell Irvin. *Confederate Women.* Westport, Conn.: Greenwood Press, 1975.

_______. *The Plain People of the Confederacy.* Baton Rouge: Louisiana State University Press, 1944.

Williams, Emma Inman, ed. "Hettie Wisdom Tapp's Memoirs." *West Tennessee Historical Society Papers* 36 (1982): 117–23.

Williams, Ora G. "Muskets and Magnolias: Four Civil War Diaries by Louisiana Girls." *Louisiana Studies* 4 (1965): 187–99.

Williams, Robert W., and Ralph A. Wooster, eds. "Life in Civil War Central Texas: Letters from Mr. and Mrs. Thomas Affleck to Private Isaac Dunbar Affleck." *Texana* 7 (summer 1969): 146–62.

Wilson, Charles Reagan. *Baptized in Blood: The Religion of the Lost Cause, 1865–1920.* Athens: University of Georgia Press, 1980.

Windler, Penny Nichols. *Placid: A Collection of Authentic Tales Centering Around Placid Plantation, Person and Cranville Counties, North Carolina, During the Period 1861 Through 1865.* Warwick, Va.: High-Iron Publishers, 1961.

Winn, Sally Kiger, ed. *The Civil War Diary of Mrs. Henrietta Fitzhugh Barr (Barre), 1862–1863, Ravenswood, Virginia (West Virginia).* Marietta, Ohio: Marietta College Press, 1963.

Winter, Kari J. *Subjects of Slavery, Agents of Change: Women and Power in Gothic Novels and Slave Narratives, 1790–1865.* Athens: University of Georgia Press, 1992.

Wolfe, Margaret Ripley. *Daughters of Canaan: A Saga of Southern Women.* Lexington: University Press of Kentucky, 1995.

Wood, W. Kirk, ed. *A Northern Daughter and a Southern Wife: The Civil War Reminiscences and Letters of Katherine H. Cumming, 1860–1865.* Augusta, Ga.: Richmond County Historical Society, 1976.

Woodell, Harold, ed. *The Shattered Dream: A Southern Bride at the Turn of the Century, The Day Book of Margaret Sloan.* Columbia: University of South Carolina Press, 1990.

Woodward, C. Vann, ed. *Mary Chesnut's Civil War.* New Haven: Yale University Press, 1981.

Woodward, C. Vann, and Elizabeth Muhlenfeld, eds. *The Private Mary Chesnut: The Unpublished Civil War Diaries.* New York: Oxford University Press, 1984.

Wright, Mrs. D. Giraud [Louise Wigfall Wright]. *A Southern Girl in '61: The War-Time Memoirs of a Confederate Senator's Daughter.* New York: Doubleday, Page, 1905.

Beaufort S.C. Aug 12th/1867

Mr. Arthur Leary.

Dear Sir:

I have hitherto refrained from applying to your society for aid and I had hoped that necessity would never force me to it. Since the close of the war, in which I lost everything, I have been striving to maintain myself by the most strenuous exertions; but my health has utterly failed. I have been prostrated with illness for the past two months; my medical adviser says it will be utterly impossible for me to recover my health if I still persist in working as I have done hitherto.

Under these circumstances I apply to you for aid. I am only eighteen years of age and have a very delicate constitution. Six younger brothers and sisters are partly dependent on my exertions for their

SUGGESTIONS FOR FURTHER RESEARCH

JOHN J. AHLADAS, JOHN M. COSKI, AND ERIC D. M. JOHNSON

Application for Relief, Beaufort, South Carolina. *Beginning in late 1866, the New York Ladies' Southern Relief Association offered modest relief to southern women of genteel backgrounds in reduced circumstances. A Beaufort resident based her claim on a "very delicate constitution" and the need to support six younger brothers and sisters. (Manuscript, Susannah Perry to Arthur Leary, 12 August 1867.)* New York Ladies' Southern Relief Association Papers, Eleanor S. Brockenbrough Library, The Museum of the Confederacy

The Museum of the Confederacy's Eleanor S. Brockenbrough Library houses a significant amount of valuable material for researchers interested in women's history in the South during the Civil War and postwar "memorial" periods. Although the museum's founders considered their institution a memorial to Confederate soldiers and thus did not organize or catalogue its collections to highlight particular materials relating to women's history, those materials are now consolidated within the Southern Women's History Collection, with other relevant sources cross-referenced in a comprehensive finding aid.

These suggestions for research resources within the Brockenbrough Library are divided into categories that clarify the origin and nature of the library's materials, describe their contents, and assess their potential research value. More specific finding aids are available in the library. The Brockenbrough Library is open to the public by appointment only. Researchers may write The Museum of the Confederacy, 1201 East Clay Street, Richmond, Virginia 23219-1615.

I. CONFEDERATE IMPRINTS

Through early donations and a conscious acquisition policy, the museum has amassed a sizable collection of Confederate imprints. The designation Confederate imprint includes a broad range of official and unofficial items (including, for example, military regulations, novels, and broadsides) published in Confederate-controlled territory from secession until Federal occupation. Over the last half-century, bibliographers have devised several organizational and numbering schemes for Confederate imprints. The primary and most useful compilations include *Confederate Imprints: A Check List Based Principally on the Collection of the Boston Athenaeum* (Boston, 1955), by Marjorie Lyle Crandall; *More Confederate Imprints* (Richmond, 1957), by Richard Barksdale Harwell; and *Confederate Imprints: A Bibliography of Southern Publications from Secession to Surrender* (Austin, Tex.; Katonah, N.Y., 1987), by T. Michael Parrish and Robert M. Willingham, Jr. The museum library follows the most recent (Parrish and Willingham) system. Of the approximately 700 extant imprints bearing some relevance to Southern women, the museum collections include at least 130. The Parrish and Willingham bibliography includes a reliable list of the known repositories for every surviving imprint; the museum's holdings are listed with the symbol ViRC.

The Crandall, Harwell, and Parrish-Willingham systems distinguish between official and unofficial imprints. Official imprints are those published by any branch or level of the Confederate government or of the state governments. Most of the official imprints relating to women are legislative bills, acts, and resolutions providing relief to indigent women and children and to the families of soldiers. The museum's only official imprint relating to women is a copy of the Confederate Senate's January 1865 bill "to regulate the pay and allowances of certain female employees of the government."

Unofficial imprints within the museum's collections include a broad range of materials with specific subjects or attributions relating to women, such as broadsides, sheet music, schoolbooks, pamphlets, novels, and religious tracts. Only a few of these imprints relate directly to the war or to the public life of the Confederacy, notably a guide for civilians claiming deceased soldiers, a memorial from a group of Fredericksburg, Virginia, women to the Confederate government suggesting the adoption of a new national flag, and several broadsides announcing such events as a "GRAND CONCERT for the Benefit of the Wives and Children of the Maryland Volunt'rs" at a Richmond Presbyterian Church. Approximately half of the museum's imprints relating to Southern women are published pieces of sheet music composed by, for, or about women.

Of the remaining unofficial imprints, most are literary works or tracts by Southern women. One such tract, a religious pamphlet by Frances Blake Brockenbrough, *A Mother's Parting Words to Her Soldier Boy,* was initially published by the Evangelical Tract Society, of Petersburg, Virginia, and subsequently issued in at least two other editions. The tract consists of a letter from a mother to her young son in which she willingly gives him up to fight a war "forced upon us" while also stressing to him "the importance of enlisting under the banner of the Cross." That said, the young, prospective soldier is warned against the "temptations of the camp" and reminded that he would "not cease to a moral agent when you become a soldier."

Literary works within the library's Confederate imprint collection include novels such as *Macaria; or, Altars of Sacrifice* by Augusta Jane Evans, printed in Richmond in 1864 and in Columbia, South Carolina, in 1865; *Raids and Romances of Morgan and His Men* (Mobile, Ala., 1863) by Sally R. Ford; and *Aurora Floyd* (Richmond, 1863), *Eleanor's Victory* (Richmond, 1864), and *John Larchmont's Legacy* (Richmond, 1865), all by Mary E. Braddon. Books of verse include Margaret Junkin Preston's *Beechenbrook; A Rhyme of the War* (Richmond, 1865).

II. Personal and Government-Related Papers

The Eleanor S. Brockenbrough Library contains letters and numerous other documents written by and to Southern women. Originally scattered among the library's extensive alphabetical and military records files, the correspondence has been assembled together so as to offer details on daily life in the wartime South; on relationships between Southern women and their family members, friends, and other men in Confederate military service; and on women's changing responses to wartime conditions.

Personal Correspondence

The museum's manuscripts include several hundred personal letters from Southern women, white and black. Unique among them is a large and rich collection of letters among members of the Henderson, Abernathy, and Fite families of North Carolina, Texas, and Arkansas. Arranged chronologically in a scrapbook, the letters span the years from 1852 to 1886 and present an often intensely personal family saga.

The museum's personal letters collection also consists of a few letters each from scores of different women. Several of the correspondents later became museum founders, including Lora Hotchkiss, Abby Manly Gwathmey, and Mary Maury. Among the most interesting are a half-dozen letters from teenager Janet Weaver, of Warrenton, Virginia, to a female friend. Weaver later was closely involved with the museum's early years and served as a long-time leader of the United Daughters of the Confederacy.

The museum's largest group of manuscripts relating to women is a collection of approximately two hundred letters written by women to husbands, brothers, other relatives, and friends in the Confederate army. Many of these are arranged by the state of origin and then alphabetically by the name of the sender. Most, however, are from the museum's pre-1976 Solid South Room collection, which consists of letters donated from all the Southern states. They are arranged alphabetically by sender. The letters—most of which date from 1864 and 1865—provide details of life on the home front and often revealing glimpses into the emotional texture of Confederate family life. In one, a little girl named Cora asks her uncle to "excuse all mistakes . . . Ma says she will send me to school when the war gets over." In another, for example, a wife prays that her husband will survive "to raise your children right." And in yet another, a woman pleads, "you must come home . . . i want to see you so bad i do not no what to do"; in the same letter, as head of the family, she imparts news of other family members, especially how her brother "one year a go left hom to go to Va to his old [regiment] but he never reached his command & we have never have heard one word from him since."

Not surprisingly, the few letters from African-American correspondents represent the perspective of "faithful servants" and are dated immediately after the war. Most notably, Lizzie Hayden, a self-proclaimed "Rebel Nigger," wrote her former mistress, Nora Fontaine Davidson, from Baltimore in June 1866, declaring her hatred of "abominable Yankees" and her homesickness for "Dear Old Dixie Land." The museum's extensive Jefferson Davis Collection includes post-war letters written by (or for) former slaves and servants of the Davis family.

Government-Related Papers

Letters from Southern women to Confederate military officers and government officials—especially those to the secretary of war—have proven extremely valuable to historians and other researchers. The museum's collections contain several dozen letters of this nature. The majority of the correspondence (scattered among the Military Records Series) is from mothers asking that their sons be released from military service, usually because the soldiers were reputedly underage. Among the other government-related items is a petition signed by eighty-three women from DeKalb County, Georgia, asking President Jefferson Davis to detail a military doctor to the civilians within their district.

There are a number of documents, including many in the museum's accession files, that offer details on women's contributions to the Confederate war effort. There are, for example, histories of community-made flags and the details of their formal presentations to military units. There are also materials that speak directly to the roles women were expected to play. In August 1861, to cite one such document, officials in Coffee County, Alabama, issued an open letter to local women, urging them "to meet at some Conveniant place in their respective neighborhood for the purpose of forming suitable regulations for making such Clothing as will greatly releave the wants of our volunteer Soldiers that has gon and may go to fight for our Rights & liberty." Other materials speak to women's monetary support of the war effort. A Treasury Department book lists dozens of women who subscribed to the 19 August 1861 sale of government bonds.

Confederate government records and official papers occasionally reveal evidence of women's lives and their activities within the public sphere. For example, the Brockenbrough Library collection includes passes issued to women traveling within the

United Daughters of the Confederacy scrapbooks. *The Eleanor S. Brockenbrough Library's UDC collection includes sixty-one scrapbooks assembled by Mildred Rutherford, historian-general of the UDC between 1911 and 1916. The volumes contain typed reminiscences, newspaper clippings, and pamphlets related to the Lost Cause.* Mildred Rutherford Scrapbooks, Eleanor S. Brockenbrough Library, The Museum of the Confederacy

Confederacy or between the lines (some on forms with the printed title "Ladies Pass"). The provost marshal of Federal-occupied New Orleans in September 1862 issued a different kind of document to Margaret Simmons: once she identified herself as "an Enemy of the United States," she was compelled to leave her home.

The Brockenbrough Library also has an extensive collection of Confederate currency, signed by women known as "Treasury girls" and employed for their careful penmanship. Two wartime Southern currency designs bear representative portraits of Southern women. Julie Opie Hopkins, who administered the Alabama General Hospital in Richmond, and Lucy Pickens, wife of South Carolina governor Francis Pickens, served as models for images on an Alabama state note and a Confederate note, respectively.

Household Documents

Although the museum's object collections contain many items that suggest how women coped with wartime shortages, the Brockenbrough Library collections include only a few documents that offer glimpses of wartime household management. Especially interesting is a recipe book made in South Carolina out of "Confederate paper" bound with a homespun cloth cover. It contains such recipes as "Confederate cheese" (a meat substitute), "Confederate plum cake," and "Confederate Black Cake." There is also a recipe for lye soap.

Other records are sparse and fragmentary, such as an anonymous account book detailing household expenses for January 1864. Mrs. Rida Ruffin Archer, of northern Virginia, recorded her household expenses beginning 19 March 1863. Virginia Garland Sully, of Richmond, kept lists of household debits and credits (including fees for hiring slaves) for 1863 and for 1866. Several letters in the museum's collections offer details about the greatest wartime disruption of white households: the self-emancipation of slaves.

Scrapbooks

Among the museum's scrapbook volumes are more than a dozen kept by Southern women during the war. While a few of the books originated in Mississippi, Alabama, and Georgia, most belonged to women in Richmond and elsewhere in Virginia. Consisting mostly of newspaper clippings, copied verses, and occasional manuscripts, the scrapbooks document their compilers' interests and activities. Miss Sue Devereaux, of Petersburg, Virginia, for example, pasted into her scrapbook a membership certificate for the Bible Society of the Confederate States of America. The scrapbook of Lizzy Lane contains not only her own copied verse and personal notes but also small, elaborate sketches and landscape paintings lovingly inscribed to her by Confederate soldiers (several of whom completed their artwork while in Northern prison camps). Several dozen other women's scrapbooks date from the postwar Confederate-memorial period, but contain scattered wartime items.

Prisoner of War Letters

Anna Miller, of Washington, D.C., and Virginia Miller, of York, Pennsylvania, corresponded with and apparently channeled material relief to Confederate prisoners. Several hundred letters written to the women by grateful prisoners not only describe details of prison life but also suggest something about the roles of female Southern sympathizers living in the North. Mrs. George Gelston, of Fort Hamilton, New York, received similar letters from prisoners in New York's Fort Lafayette and included them in her wartime scrapbook.

Kate Mason Rowland Collection and Diary

A young woman during the war, Kate Mason Rowland worked in several Confederate hospitals and was in Richmond during the evacuation of 1865. Her three-volume diary (excerpted in such published works as Katharine M. Jones's *Ladies of Richmond, Confederate Capital* [Indianapolis, 1962]) is a valuable source of unflagging pro-Confederate opinion and information on hospital work. She was also the self-appointed chronicler of her family's wartime adventures. Her papers (five manuscript boxes) include correspondence with her brother (a young cavalry and staff officer) and a cousin (a naval midshipman). A few documents give cursory evidence of her sister's short stint as tutor of the children of Confederate president Jefferson Davis. Rowland also wrote a short biography of her mother, Catherine Rowland, and a narrative of the family's escape from Federal-occupied northern Virginia. Kate Mason Rowland lived until 1916, remained thoroughly "unreconstructed," and wrote extensively after the war.

Jefferson Davis Collection

The papers of President Jefferson Davis (1808–1889); his wife, Varina Howell Davis (1826–1906); and their family comprise one of the museum's most important and largest collections, measuring fifteen linear feet. The Davis Collection includes a few letters from women throughout the South to Davis during and after the war concerning the prosecution and memorialization of the conflict, but the collection is most valuable for studying the postwar memorial period. Varina Davis labored to protect and burnish her late husband's reputation and corresponded widely with friends in the South and the North (where she lived after his death) about the war. The museum possesses the manuscript copy of her two-volume 1890 work, *Jefferson Davis: A Memoir by His Wife,* as well as her correspondence with the publisher. Varina Davis and her two daughters, Margaret Davis Hayes (1855–1909) and Varina Anne Davis (1864–1898), were active in the establishment of the Confederate Museum and contributed to its collections. Voluminous correspondence between the three Davis women and museum officials details their concern with Jefferson Davis's legacy and reputation.

Perhaps as fascinating—and better documented—is the record of the overwhelming popularity of Varina Anne "Winnie" Davis, the "Daughter of the Confederacy" as she was affectionately known. The penultimate Confederate symbol of Southern womanhood, Winnie Davis lived her short life under the intense scrutiny of regional fame. The Davis Collection includes several letters from her, scores written to her, and over three hundred telegrams sent to her mother upon Winnie's death in 1898.

Postwar Reminiscences

As part of their historical work, the museum and the United Daughters of the Confederacy collected women's reminiscences about their lives during the war. Many of the contributors were museum officials, including Isabel Maury and Janet Weaver Randolph. Although nearly all the reminiscences are by elite or middle-class white women, the collection also includes an eight-page account by Sallie Young, identified as "a colored woman."

III. Wartime Organization Papers

Women's wartime employment in military hospitals and their active participation in voluntary associations resulted in a substantial volume of documentary material. Soldiers' aid and defense societies emulated peacetime benevolent and other community associations, especially in their attention to maintaining minutes and other records. Those that survived are among the most valuable items in the museum's collections.

Hospital Records

Records of Confederate army hospitals reveal much direct and indirect evidence about wartime Southern women. The records include lists of female employees (black and white) of Richmond's General Hospital No. 8

and Winder Hospital, rules governing matrons at Richmond's Jackson Hospital, and a list of supplies in charge of the chief matron of the general hospital in Danville, Virginia. The only diary of hospital service is that of Kate Mason Rowland, who was employed at the Winder Hospital, but the collections include the unpublished reminiscences of women who worked at Howard's Grove Hospital and the Ladies' Relief Hospital in Lynchburg, Virginia.

The collections also include the papers of two women who administered hospitals in Richmond. Maria Gaitskell Clopton founded and oversaw the Clopton Hospital. The museum owns the Clopton Hospital register, account book, and over forty of Maria Clopton's wartime letters. Sally Tompkins lives in Confederate legend as reputedly the only woman commissioned in the Confederate army. The museum has her captain's commission, along with several record books from the Robertson Hospital, which she administered throughout the war. A large file of correspondence contains letters written to her by former patients. Much postwar biographical information and tributes to her are in historical records amassed by the United Daughters of the Confederacy and by the museum's founders.

Soldiers' Aid Society Records

Not surprisingly, the museum's founders preserved evidence of women's organized efforts to support the Confederate war effort. The Black Oak Soldiers' Relief Association, of St. John's Berkeley Parish, Charleston County, South Carolina, collected and dispensed funds. The museum's collections include its book of minutes and proceedings from August 1861 through June 1864. The association recorded donations from "ladies" and "gentlemen" in separate columns. The Savannah Wayside Home was founded in February 1863 to provide room and board for furloughed and wounded soldiers. Though its major officers were clergymen, the organization consisted primarily of women. The museum has a book containing the organization's constitution, bylaws, and rules and regulations. Two small receipt books of the Ladies' Soldiers' Relief Society, of Macon, Georgia, detail the organization's every expenditure. A group of Richmond women in August 1861 founded the Ladies' Ridge [Church] Benevolent Society. The society used a small pocket-calendar as a minute book, complete with lists of members and the clothing items they agreed to make or provide to needy soldiers and their families. Pages of the same book contain entries of contributions for a postwar Confederate soldiers' home.

Ladies' Defense Associations Records

Perhaps the most valuable wartime organizational records are the papers and minutes of the Ladies' Defense Association of Richmond—an organization formed to assist in funding the war effort and hence colloquially known as the Ladies' Gunboat Society. Maria G. Clopton, organizer of the Clopton Hospital, was also president of the Defense Association. The museum has the organization's bound minute book and a collection of over twenty-five letters and sundry papers spanning the association's entire short life, 1862–1863. The collection provides more details on the patriotic efforts of the women than on the assistance given to the construction of the CSS *Virginia II*.

In addition to the papers of the Richmond society and its several Virginia branches, the museum collections include a small file of the correspondence of Mrs. J. W. Harris, leader of a similar society in Columbus, Mississippi.

New York Ladies' Southern Relief Association Papers

Although they date from a postwar organization, the papers of the New York Ladies' Southern Relief Association (NYLSRA) afford a vivid picture of conditions in the South in the immediate aftermath of the war. In late 1866, Mary Mildred Sullivan, a native Virginian living in New York City, decided to relieve the suffering of (white) women and children of the war-torn South. She founded and became corresponding secretary of the NYLSRA. The organization raised funds in the North, then entrusted the money to ministers and selected lay people in the South. These agents distributed the funds in small quantities (usually five to ten dollars) on a case-by-case basis, with the objective of staving off starvation or of providing clothes. The recipients—often the widows of Confederate soldiers—had little ready cash (sometimes holding only worthless Confederate currency) and little seed or labor to work their land.

Containing several hundred items, the NYLSRA papers were donated to the museum in the 1930s through Mrs. Sullivan's son. The Mary Mildred Sullivan Chapter, United Daughters of the Confederacy, published selections from the papers in 1926. Some of the correspondence describes the fund-raising process and other organizational matters. Most of the collection, however, consists of letters from applicants for aid or from the ministers distributing the aid money. The letters describe impoverished conditions and heroic efforts to cope with it. They make clear that most recipients of NYLSRA assistance were white southerners who had enjoyed "easy circumstances" before the war.

IV. Postwar Memorial Organization Papers

The museum is not only a repository of papers on wartime Southern women, but also is itself worthy of study as an example of postwar women's activities. The Museum of the Confederacy's Brockenbrough Library serves as the archive for the voluminous records of its parent organization, the Confederate Memorial Literary Society, and its antecedent organization, the Hollywood Memorial Association. The archive also includes records of the United Daughters of the Confederacy, whose chapters and divisions often deposited their records at the museum before the opening of a UDC national headquarters building in 1957.

Hollywood Memorial Association

The ancestral organization of The Museum of the Confederacy was founded on 3 May 1866 for the purpose of caring for Confederate soldiers' graves in Richmond's Hollywood Cemetery. The Hollywood Memorial Association (HMA) helped establish the tradition of Confederate Memorial Day, was responsible for the erection of one of the South's earliest Confederate monuments, and coordinated the transfer of Confederate dead from the Gettysburg battlefield to Richmond. Even after the creation of the Confederate Memorial Literary Society in 1890 and the opening of the Confederate Museum in 1896, the HMA remained active until 1934.

The museum library is the repository for all of the HMA's records, totaling seven linear feet. These include burial lists, chronologically arranged correspondence files, speeches, accounts, detailed financial records, complete minute books (1866–1934), clippings files, and the personal record book of long-time HMA president Janet Weaver Randolph, as well as papers relating to the transfer of the Gettysburg dead and a plat map of soldiers' graves. Similar, though less voluminous, records exist for the Junior Hollywood Memorial Association, founded in 1892.

Oakwood Memorial Association

Oakwood Cemetery in Richmond's east end is the final resting place for over fifteen thousand Confederate soldiers. A few weeks before the founding of the HMA, a similar group of ladies joined to tend and decorate the soldiers' graves in Oakwood. The museum library contains some of the association's records, most notably its constitution and bylaws, ledgers, minute books (1866–1950), and the minutes of the Junior Oakwood Memorial Association (1896–1909).

Monument Associations

Local memorial associations as well as elements of the United Daughters of the Confederacy and the United Confederate Veterans often formed new, single-purpose organizations to raise money for Confederate monuments. The Eleanor S. Brockenbrough Library has the papers of several of these organizations. Particularly useful are the minute books of the Jefferson Davis Monument Association, especially for the period after 1899 when women assumed the leading role in the effort to erect a Richmond monument to the former Confederate president. One of the UDC's most important early projects was the monument to Confederate soldiers on the Shiloh battlefield. The Shiloh Monument Committee's minute book for the period 1907–1917 is in the museum's collections. The significant role of women in fundraising is also reflected in the minutes and correspondence of the Soldiers and Sailors Monument Association, formed in Richmond by Confederate veterans but ultimately dependent on the assistance of several women's groups. Scores of local ladies' memorial and monument associations, many formed as early as 1866, became affiliated under the auspices of the New Orleans–based Confederated Southern Memorial Association (CSMA) in 1900. The museum has no official records of the CSMA but does own a complete set of the published proceedings of its annual meetings (1900–1936).

United Daughters of the Confederacy

Until 1957, the UDC had no headquarters building, so the records of the thousands of local chapters and state divisions are now scattered throughout public and private collections. Many Richmond-area records were donated to the museum, which in 1899 began systematically soliciting UDC contributions and support. The museum's UDC papers are extensive and include more than fourteen linear feet of manuscript material as well as hundreds of published volumes; there is a finding aid available for the manuscript collection.

Among the UDC records are minutes, membership rolls, and other working papers of various chapters. A scrapbook volume contains the charter, history, and other documents of the Camden (Arkansas) Chapter, 1907–1910. The most complete collection is of the Richmond Chapter, Virginia Division, 1896–1924; its founder and moving spirit, Janet Weaver Randolph, was also a founder of the Confederate Museum. Another museum founder, Virginia Morgan Robinson, was the UDC's first historian-general, and her official papers, 1908–1911, are included in the museum's collection. Boxes of thematically related correspondence compiled by Randolph and Robinson give details on issues that preoccupied the early UDC: the origin of Memorial Day; the expansion of the Lee Chapel in Lexington, Virginia; the resurrection of the Ku Klux Klan after 1915; and the correct size and shape of the Confederate battle flag. The records also document the UDC's patriotic work, notably its Cross of Honor awarded for military service and its Red Cross activities during World War I.

In addition to UDC manuscripts, the library has a complete collection of annual convention minutes and proceedings of the General Division and an extensive collection of annual-meeting minutes for the Alabama, Florida, North Carolina, Tennessee, Texas, and Virginia divisions as well as scattered issues of published minutes for the Arkansas, Mississippi, and New York divisions.

Other UDC records include reminiscences of life on the Confederate home front collected by the local chapters' historical committees. In form and content they closely resemble Francis W. Dawson's 1885 volume, *"Our Women in the War": The Lives They Lived, The Deaths They Died.* Most valuable are the 1913 scrapbook and the 1914–1915 bound manuscripts assembled by the Hanover (Virginia) Chapter.

UDC chapters, as did the museum,

assembled scrapbooks of clippings relating to their own activities and items relating to Confederate history. The museum collection includes scrapbooks from the Sophie Bibb Chapter, Montgomery, Alabama, and the Nashville, Tennessee, chapter. Most important, the museum is the repository for the extensive, sixty-one-volume set of scrapbooks assembled by the industrious and outspoken UDC historian-general Mildred Lewis Rutherford between 1911 and 1916. The Rutherford scrapbooks consist primarily of clippings from other sources (especially *Confederate Veteran* magazine and state historical publications) but also contain handwritten and typed reminiscences and observations. Most of the scrapbooks deal with constitutional issues, the causes of the war, the Confederate government and government leaders, battles and military leaders, etc. Eleven of the volumes are directly related to Southern women during the war and the history and activities of the UDC and of ladies' memorial associations.

Confederate Memorial Literary Society Records

The museum's own records and archives represent a nationally important collection for the study of a woman's voluntary association. As the essay in this book suggests, the museum's founders were conscious of their identity as women and of their work as a vindication of women's capabilities. The records reveal much about the inner workings of a southern woman's voluntary association and its relationships with other women's and men's organizations. Because of this, the CMLS records are also valuable for the study of the UDC, CSMA, and the several ladies' monument associations.

The most valuable CMLS records include the meeting minutes and the papers of the recording and corresponding secretaries. From 1890 to 1932, the handwritten minutes are complete and detailed and often include original copies of correspondence and reports. The minutes from 1932 to 1946 apparently did not survive, and the minutes after the 1970s offer few details. For the period 1907–1915, corresponding secretary Virginia Morgan Robinson assembled copies of all correspondence (both received and sent) into five large volumes. The society's other early correspondence is pasted in minute books, arranged in alphabetical subject files, or included in several diverse files kept by CMLS president Sally Archer Anderson and in letter boxes maintained by House Regent Susan B. Harrison. The details of the society's activities are well documented in annual reports submitted by State Room regents and vice regents, officers, and committee chairs. From 1907 to 1928 (except for 1918–1919), those reports were published in the museum *Yearbook*.

One of the house regent's official duties was to keep a scrapbook of clippings pertaining to the museum and to Confederate history. Consequently, the museum collection includes twenty-five CMLS scrapbooks covering the period from the 1890s to the late 1940s. Supplementing the society's eleven "official" scrapbooks—which include materials primarily from Richmond newspapers between 1902 and 1947—are a dozen others compiled by Isobel Stewart Bryan and other society officers. Though they are fragile, most of the scrapbooks include name and subject indexes and represent one of the most convenient sources of information on "Confederate" issues in the early- to mid-twentieth century. In addition, CMLS officers attended annual meetings of the UDC's Virginia Division and all General Convention yearly gatherings held in Virginia; in commemorating the events they compiled an extensive collection of clippings from the local newspapers. CMLS officers and advisors similarly preserved (and bound) an extensive collection of newspaper coverage of United Confederate Veterans' annual meetings and reunions.

Kate Mason Rowland Collection

A descendant of George Mason, of Gunston Hall, and a vocal member of the UDC, Rowland wrote extensively in defense of Southern constitutional principles and the righteousness of the Confederate cause. Widely credited with leading the effort within the South to make the term "war between the states" the accepted name for the conflict, Rowland was an important figure in the "Lost Cause" movement. She was a member of the CMLS and served briefly as chair of the short-lived Lecture Committee. Her postwar papers include drafts of articles (some unpublished); extensive correspondence with the iconoclastic biographer of Abraham Lincoln, Charles L. C. Minor; correspondence with and autographs of Confederate military and civilian leaders; and Lost Cause ephemera.

INDEX

References to captions are in italic.

Notes on Contributors

John J. Ahladas, a former high school history teacher, is a curator of collections at The Museum of the Confederacy. As an adjunct to his primary work with the museum's extensive collection of military artifacts and memorabilia, he has assisted in organizing the manuscript collections within the museum's Eleanor S. Brockenbrough Library.

Edward D. C. Campbell, Jr., is a former director of The Museum of the Confederacy and currently director of the Archival and Information Services Division of the Library of Virginia, Richmond. He is the author of *The Celluloid South: Hollywood and the Southern Myth* (1981), as well as numerous essays on southern popular and material culture, and the coeditor of *Before Freedom Came: African-American Life in the Antebellum South* (1991) and *The Hornbook of Virginia History: A Ready-Reference Guide to the Old Dominion's People, Places, and Past* (1994).

Joan E. Cashin is associate professor of history at Ohio State University and coeditor of the John Hopkins University Press series Gender Relations in the American Experience. She is the author of *A Family Venture: Men and Women on the Southern Frontier* (1991), as well as many articles on women's history, and the editor of *Our Common Affairs: Texts from Women in the Old South* (1996).

John M. Coski is historian for The Museum of the Confederacy, for which he has written "A Century of Collecting: The History of The Museum of the Confederacy" (1996) and, as coauthor, *White House of the Confederacy: An Illustrated History* (1993). His other publications include *The Army of the Potomac at Berkeley Plantation: The Harrison's Landing Occupation of 1862* (1989), *Four Centuries of the Southern Experience: Charles City County from the Earliest Settlement Through the Modern Civil Rights Era* (coeditor, 1989), and *Capital Navy: The Men, Ships, and Operations of the James River Squadron* (1996).

Drew Gilpin Faust is the Walter H. Annenberg Professor of History at the University of Pennsylvania. Her many publications include *A Sacred Circle: The Dilemma of the Intellectual in the Old South, 1840–1860* (1977), *The Ideology of Slavery: Proslavery Thought in the Antebellum South, 1830–1860* (1981), *James Henry Hammond and the Old South: A Design for Mastery* (1982), *The Creation of Confederate Nationalism: Ideology and Identity in the Civil War South* (1988), *Southern Stories: Slaveholders in Peace and War* (1992), *"A Riddle of Death": Mortality and Meaning in the American Civil War* (1995), and *Mothers of Invention: Women of the Slaveholding South in the American Civil War* (1996).

Amy R. Feely received her master's degree from the University of Virginia, where she is now a doctoral student in history. She is the author of "When Southern Lady Meets New

Woman: Women of the Confederate Memorial Literary Society and the Lost Cause in Richmond, Virginia" (master's thesis, 1995).

Thavolia Glymph is assistant professor of history at the Pennsylvania State University and the coeditor of *Essays on the Postbellum Southern Economy* (1985). As a member of the Freedmen and Southern Society Project, she served as coeditor of two volumes, *The Destruction of Slavery* (1985) and *The Wartime Genesis of Free Labor: The Lower South* (1990), in the award-winning series *Freedom: A Documentary History of Emancipation, 1861–1867.*

Eric D. M. Johnson is a library assistant in the Archives Research Services Branch of the Library of Virginia, Richmond, and a graduate intern at The Museum of the Confederacy. He is enrolled in the graduate history program at George Mason University, Fairfax, Virginia.

Suzanne Lebsock is professor of history at the University of Washington at Seattle. She is the author of *The Free Women of Petersburg: Status and Culture in a Southern Town, 1784–1860* (1984), winner of the Bancroft Prize of Columbia University and the Book Prize of the Berkshire Conference of Women Historians. She is also the author of *"A Share of Honour": Virginia Women, 1600–1945* (1984), published to accompany an exhibition of the same title coordinated by the Virginia Women's Cultural History Project. Her other publications include *Virginia Women: The First Two Hundred Years* (with Anne Firor Scott, 1988) and *Visible Women: New Essays on American Activism* (coeditor, 1993).

George C. Rable is professor of history at Anderson University in Anderson, Indiana. He is the author of numerous publications, including *But There Was No Peace: The Role of Violence in the Politics of Reconstruction* (1984), *Civil Wars: Women and the Crisis of Southern Nationalism* (1989), and *The Confederate Republic: A Revolution Against Politics* (1994).

Kym S. Rice is an assistant professor and assistant director of the Museum Studies program at the George Washington University, Washington, D.C. She has served as guest curator for The Museum of the Confederacy's exhibitions *Before Freedom Came: African-American Life in the Antebellum South* and *A Woman's War: Southern Women, Civil War, and the Confederate Legacy* and has organized exhibitions for the Library of Congress, the New York Public Library, and the Virginia Women's Cultural History Project.

Marjorie Spruill Wheeler is associate professor of history at the University of Southern Mississippi and the author of *New Women of the New South: The Leaders of the Woman Suffrage Movement in the Southern States, 1890–1920* (1993). She is also the editor of *One Woman, One Vote: Rediscovering the Woman Suffrage Movement* (1995) and *Votes for Women! The Woman Suffrage Movement in Tennessee, the South, and the Nation* (1995), as well as a reprint edition of Mary Johnston's classic 1913 novel, *Hagar* (1994).

ACKNOWLEDGMENTS

As so often happens, a project of this size incurs many debts. We deeply appreciate the help of our many colleagues—too numerous to name—in museums, historical organizations, and universities across the United States who have assisted us with our research.

We owe a special debt of gratitude to Drew Gilpin Faust, Annenberg Professor of History at the University of Pennsylvania. She graciously allowed us to translate a large portion of her research into an exhibition format and also provided access to primary materials at the National Archives that we might not have stumbled across on our own. We are very grateful as well to our other consultants for their assistance and support in nearly every aspect of the project—Joan E. Cashin, Ohio State University; Thavolia Glymph, Pennsylvania State University; Suzanne Lebsock, University of Washington; George C. Rable, Anderson University; and Marjorie Spruill Wheeler, University of Southern Mississippi. Their advice greatly enhanced the scope of *A Woman's War.*

Through planning and implementation, the entire project received support from the National Endowment for the Humanities. Special thanks to Clay Lewis, Nancy Rogers, Suzi Jones, and Nancy E. Davis. In a time when NEH's resources were severely limited, the museum is especially appreciative of their support.

This book has been the special province of Tucker H. Hill, The Museum of the Confederacy's Director of Interpretation, who served as the project director. Like all parts of the project, the publication greatly benefited from Tucker's careful fine tuning and thoughtful approach. In addition to coauthoring an essay, John M. Coski, the museum's Historian, assisted Hill with copyediting and production management. Without complaint, he quickly selected further photographs for the final two essays and wrote their captions. John spent many additional hours tirelessly answering the guest curator's questions and also fact checking, both of which she deeply appreciated. Thanks to Eric Johnson, a graduate student at George Mason University, for his survey of the museum's Eleanor S. Brockenbrough Library. William R. Melton, the museum's Communications Specialist, also helped with the book's proofreading, and Joanna Raczynska provided research assistance. We also benefited from the superb skills of Katherine Wetzel, who took most of the photographs for *A Woman's War.* The book's splendid appearance is due entirely to its designer, Douglas W. Price. We also thank the University Press of Virginia for its longtime interest in this project; we are especially appreciative of the support of press director Nancy Essig, assistant director Mary Kathryn Hassett, and Richard Holway, editor for history and social sciences.

At The Museum of the Confederacy, Robin Edward Reed, the Executive Director, strongly supported the project from the beginning and went to bat for it on numerous occasions.

Many other staff members served on the project team. Malinda W. Collier, the museum's Director of Collections, oversaw the exhibition's site preparation, installation, and the numerous details associated with this complicated process. She was masterfully assisted by her staff, Robert F. Hancock, Eva-Maria Ahladas, and Rebecca A. Rose. Through John Ahladas's efforts, many uncatalogued documents related to Southern women were made available from the Brockenbrough Library collections. Corrine P. Hudgins helped in the selections of images from the museum's photograph collection. Michael Steen and Patricia Dunn Balderson of the Education Program staff organized and managed the museum centennial's complementary public programming and adult education activities, including the week-long Summer Teachers Institute, and Lisa B. Middleton prepared the curriculum packet and other classroom materials that accompany the exhibition. Ashley Rawlings Bagby cheerfully oversaw the project's financial management, with James J. Spencer.

No project of this magnitude can be accomplished without the underpinning of a strong development, marketing, and retail effort, led by Douglas G. Knapp, Janene Charbeneau, and May Reed. Thank you also to Eric App, Ruth Ann Coski, Charity B. Coman, Carolyn Corbin, Brooke Fillmore, Melissa J. Jacobson, Bobbie Jarrett, Margaret Jones, Patsy McNamara, and Guy R. Swanson. John Crank and Wei-Ming Hsu, of the 1717 Design Group, Inc., ably designed the installation and supervised the fabrication of the exhibition, *A Woman's War*, at The Museum of the Confederacy.

KYM S. RICE
Guest Curator

EDWARD D. C. CAMPBELL, JR.
Editor

A Woman's War: Southern Women, Civil War, and the Confederate Legacy was designed and produced by Douglas W. Price, of Goochland, Virginia, using a Power Macintosh computer and Quarkxpress 3.32. Text was composed in Garamond roman and italic. Katherine Wetzel, of Richmond, Virginia, served as principal photographer and Tucker H. Hill, of The Museum of the Confederacy, as production manager. Printed on acid-free Centura dull-coated paper, 70-lb. text, by Carter Printing Company, of Richmond, Virginia.